Economic Organization

Economic Organization

Firms, Markets and Policy Control

Oliver E. Williamson

*Gordon B. Tweedy Professor of Economics of Law
and Organization, Yale University*

NEW YORK UNIVERSITY PRESS
Washington Square, New York
1986

First published in the USA in 1986 by
NEW YORK UNIVERSITY PRESS
Washington Square, New York, N.Y. 10003

Library of Congress Cataloging-in-Publication Data

Williamson, Oliver E.
  Economic organization.

  Includes index.
  1. Industrial organization.   2. Industrial management.
    I. Title.
  HD31.W5172   1985   658.4'02   85-15397
  ISBN 0-8147-9208-1

Typeset in Times Roman in 10 point by KEYTEC, Bridport,
Dorset, England

Printed in Great Britain

To Dolores, good friend, wife, and coventurer throughout

Contents

Preface

The Editor of Wheatsheaf Books Limited, Mr Romesh Vaitilingam, invited me to add a biographical statement. Although my first inclination was to decline, the statement that appears below nevertheless began to take shape. It does not correspond very closely to the 'sample' statement that Mr Vaitilingam sent to me; but biographies are, by definition, idiosyncratic.

The statement maintains a rather optimistic metre. This does not mean that there were no setbacks or no blood spilt along the way. But these are forgettable in the overall scheme of things—which is, I think, as I describe it.

An Autobiographical Sketch

I became an economist with interdisciplinary interests because, in the convoluted course of events, that was the natural thing to do. It is always gratifying to make easy choices. This was one of them.

I was born in Superior, Wisconsin in 1932. I was the second of three children born to Scott and Lucille Williamson. My parents met as teachers at the high school in the small rural community of Alma Center. My father was teaching physics, chemistry, and manual training and coached the baseball team. My mother taught Latin, French, and German and was the high school principal. My relatives used to rib my father about marrying the boss.

My mother had grown up in Superior. My parents were married in Superior and made their home there, where my father joined my grandfather (after whom I was named) in the real estate business. He remained a small businessman until retirement.

Superior was then, and is now, a town of about 30,000 population. It is a port community on the western end of Lake Superior. Employment is highly seasonal because shipping is closed during the long and cold winter. Even during the war years, when the shipyards were booming, there were a lot of families in Superior living on the fringes.

Strapped as Superior was for resources, the schools were not very strong—though I didn't know that until later. They had a compensating quality, however, that I have not experienced in equivalent degree since: it was a thoroughly democratic experience. A small parochial school system excepted, the public schools were the only game in town. Talents could take many forms and were everywhere assessed on merit. Virtually everyone worked in some kind of labouring capacity during the summer. I painted houses one summer (when I became fond of the rain), was a digger laying drainage pipes the next, then worked as a steamfitters' helper before getting a job in the lab of the local petroleum refinery.

My mother was the more intellectual of my parents. She was painfully shy, however, and needed to be drawn out. Her recall of languages— Latin, in particular, which I took in high school—was extraordinary. And she had a determined taste for excellence.

My father was more outgoing and had an unusual gift with children. His own children were devoted to him. He was friends with and was regularly consulted by other youngsters. He was Superior's Santa Claus—at the Kiwanis, the orphanage, for neighbourhood kids, his grandchildren, and on request—for about fifteen years. He was also active in civic affairs—the Chamber of Commerce, the hospital and was on the City Council for about twelve years, ten of them as its President. His generous spirit was combined with fiscal conservatism. His integrity was legendary.

Although I had originally thought of becoming a lawyer, I was attracted to maths and science in high school and began talking instead of becoming an engineer. My mother declared that MIT was the place to go. With the advice of the physics teacher in the local college, it was decided that I would reach MIT through the combined plan program that MIT offered with Ripon College.

My first semester at Ripon was something of a shock. Partly this was a matter of developing study habits. But I also had some catching up to do. I shudder to think of having gone to MIT directly. I soon got to know several students in the class ahead of me at Ripon who were also combined plan students. Rather than do the programme in accordance with the 3–2 sequence that had been approved, Dr Clifford Crump, my calculus teacher, encouraged me to reverse it, and I did it 2–3 instead.

MIT was an impressive place with a strong research atmosphere. To my surprise, I found it less demanding scholastically than Ripon. And it was a stark social experience. I nevertheless had a sense of full value, and an MIT degree served me well in my first regular job and thereafter.

My first job after graduation was as a project engineer for the U.S. Government. It was a marvellous group of people and a satisfying introduction to research and development. It gave me an opportunity to learn about both big government and big business—since I was regularly visiting the latter in my capacity as a project engineer. I was impressed by the quality of the people in both, especially the former. And I got a good idea of how bureaucracy functioned. The government flew me to Japan, Korea, and Taiwan the first spring I was there, and around the world the next.

I met my wife, Dolores Celeni, within days after arriving in Washington. The two of us had the good fortune of being processed through the same office. We were married two years later and she has been my steady companion and supporter and the mother of our five children ever since. Volunteer work—with the League of Women Voters, the local library, and the American Cancer Society—has since given way to a job at the local art gallery.

I arrived at Stanford in 1958 with the intention of getting a PhD in business administration. The field of specialization was a bit vague, but I was leaning towards marketing. All that was changed in the first quarter, when I had James Howell as my economics teacher and Paul Samuelson's principles text from which to learn. All of these fascinating problems on which engineering skills could be brought to bear! My programme underwent a vast transformation under Jim Howell's instruction, and I found myself in the classrooms of Kenneth Arrow, Herman Chernoff, Bernard Haley, Emanuel Parzen, Melvin Reder, and Hirofumi Uzawa.

Also, because of an office-crowding condition, I found myself sharing an office in my second year at Stanford with a freshly minted Carnegie-Tech graduate who had just joined the Stanford faculty, Charles Bonini. Chuck, after learning of my interests, urged that Carnegie was the natural place for me to go to complete my PhD. When the then Dean George Leland Bach responded to my queries with two page letters, I began to melt. I showed up at Carnegie in September 1960.

Carnegie was a perfectly incredible experience. The hum of research activity was evident upon walking through the doors. Students were deferential to faculty, but their junior status did not preclude active participation in research. Indeed, it was fully anticipated that most students would be writing publishable articles before they got their degrees. Herbert Simon's influence at Carnegie was massive. Everything was within his purview: economics, statistics, sociology, psychology, computer science, philosophy, organization theory, political science. He was publishing major articles in all. But other mere mortals were also critical to the Carnegie experience and made things run: Richard Cyert, James March, and Allan Meltzer were especially important to me. The atmosphere was infectious, and I came down with the disease.

My dissertation had its origins in Jim March's class on organizations when he uttered the phrase—which he denies—that managers of corporations 'maximise organizational slack'. I began, shortly thereafter, working on such a model. And I began to involve myself with other more conventional problems of industrial organization—of which barriers to entry was one. The paper that I wrote for Herbert Simon's course on mathematical social science found its way (with revisions) into pages of the February 1963 issue of *Quarterly Journal of Economics*. I received my PhD in May 1963, when Dick Cyert, who was then Dean of GSIA, boomed my name across the lawn—where my parents, Dolores, and our first three children were seated.

Andreas Papandreou was responsible for recruiting in economics at the University of California, Berkeley that year. Aaron Gordon was chairman and Henry Rosovsky was vice chairman of the Economics Department. I had decided to present myself as an industrial organization specialist. Joe Bain approved and an offer from Berkeley materialized. We were thrilled to go there—all the more so when we met the other assistant professors who had been recruited by Berkeley that same year: Peter Diamond, David Laidler, Daniel McFadden, and Sidney Winter.

I was gratified to learn in December 1963 that my dissertation was awarded the Ford Foundation Prize and thus would be published by Prentice-Hall. My article 'Managerial Discretion and Business Behavior' which is the first essay in this book, had already been accepted by the *American Economic Review* (actually, it had been turned down once, without the benefit of a referee's report; the new editor, with the benefit of a referee's report, liked the new version better). I could scarcely believe that people were prepared to pay me to teach and do research on what I liked best.

I spent the summer of 1964 at the RAND Corporation—where I got to know Armen Alchian, Anthony Downs, Roland McKean, and Almarin Phillips, and to renew relations with Richard Nelson, who had been a visitor and my teacher at Carnegie. I was concerned that Armen would dismiss my treatment of managerial discretion as unorthodox and uninformed. But Alchian and Simon had the same criterion for evaluating social science research: anything that deepens our understanding of complex phenomena is valued.

I received several offers to take appointments at other universities in the fall of 1964, but approached the new chairman at Berkeley, Tibor Scitovsky, only with one: an offer to go to the University of Pennsylvania as a non-tenured associate professor. Berkeley did not have a corresponding non-tenured associate professor position, so I asked that I be considered for tenure. What I thought was a good case was regarded as premature by others. We left for Penn the next year, but not before spending another summer in Los Angeles.

The summer of 1965 was spent at UCLA. Armen Alchian and Roland McKean had assembled a group of scholars interested in the Economics of Property Rights. This remarkable group included Gary Becker, Harold Demsetz, Sam Peltzman, William Meckling and Gordon Tullock. Jack Hirschleifer was nearby and frequently chimed in. Although I was working on peak load pricing and limits to firm size issues, I was becoming more intrigued with property rights formulations.

I arrived at Penn at a time when the Economics Department was witnessing substantial growth. Appointments that occurred at or about the time of mine included Jere Behrman, Edwin Burmeister, Edmund Phelps, Robert Pollak, Stephen Ross, Karl Shell, Paul Taubman and Michael Wachter. Thomas Sargent, who had been a research assistant of mine at Berkeley, was appointed shortly thereafter.

As at Berkeley, the main field at Penn with which I was identified was industrial organization. Almarin Phillips and I were the two people on the faculty with primary responsibility for the field. Neither of us had ever taken an industrial organization course. We shaped a curriculum that had somewhat non-standard features.

I received a telephone call from Carl Kaysen, whom I had never met, in the spring of 1966 inquiring if I would be interested in going to Washington to serve as the Special Economic Assistant to the head of the Antitrust Division, Donald Turner. I responded with interest and, with the enthusiastic approval of Irving Kravis, who chaired the Economics Department at Penn at the time, I went to Washington to discuss the appointment. I met with Turner and his First Assistant, Edwin Zimmerman, and we came to terms.

We moved to Washington in September 1966 and I became immediately engaged in a wide set of antitrust issues. Turner and Zimmerman had staffed the Evaluation Section with a wonderful group of young lawyers, recruited mainly from Stanford and Harvard. Those with whom I worked most closely were Donald Baker, Joel Davidow, Lionel Kestenbaum, Ronald Lewis, Robert Johnson and Jonathan Rose. Stephen Breyer was another of Turner's Special Assistants. He also worked closely with this group. Upstairs, moreover, in the Solicitor General's office was that wunderkind Richard Posner. His capacity for work and legal reasoning were even then legendary. It was a vibrant place.

Among the more interesting issues with which I became involved that year were the Schwinn case (where I advised Turner and Posner against proceeding with their line of argument, but my advice came too late to influence the brief), the Ford–Autolite merger (where vertical integration issues were posed), the newspaper cases (which is the context where I first set out the trade-off that became the basis for subsequent work on economies as an antitrust defence), the P&G–Clorox merger (where I attended oral argument before the Supreme Court), the Utah Pie case (where the government was asked, but declined, to intervene on the issue of predatory pricing), and the design of policy statements on merger guidelines and truth in insurance.

It was a wonderful year. But I was growing impatient to get back to the university and persuaded Turner and Zimmerman to allow me to quit a month earlier than had been originally agreed. It was thus easy to decline Caspar Weinberger's invitation in 1970, at a time when he was chairman of the Federal Trade Commission, to have my name presented to the Senate for confirmation as an FTC Commissioner. (I was naturally pleased, however, that my name should have come up in the connection. And I was especially pleased when Weinberger expressed ignorance of my political registration and held it to be irrelevant to the appointment).

Shortly after I returned to the University of Pennsylvania, where I resumed my teaching and research, the Directorship of the Fels Center of State and Local Government became vacant. I was asked to help fill it. I had met Julius Margolis when we were both on the faculty at Berkeley and urged his candidacy, which in fact succeeded. Julie has a grand sense of curriculum design and a great taste for academics. He put together a new PhD programme in public policy analysis and recruited Bruce Ackerman, Edward Banfield and Scott Boorman to join the faculty. As described in the introduction to Part II, Julie asked me to design a course in organization theory, which was centrally implicated in my shift in research from applied price theory to transaction cost economics.

The four key academic figures in my research—at this time and since—were Kenneth Arrow, Alfred D. Chandler, Jr., Ronald Coase, and Herbert Simon. Although I had only two (Arrow and Simon) in the classroom, I regard Chandler and Coase as my teachers nonetheless. Each has had a profound impact on my understanding of the economics of organization. From Arrow I learned about the importance of information and not to shoe-horn difficult problems into orthodox boxes. Chandler taught me that organizational innovation was an important and neglected phenomenon that had pervasive ramifications for understanding American industry. Coase taught me that transaction costs were central to the study of economic organization and that such studies should be performed in a comparative institutional manner. And Simon taught me that behavioural assumptions were important and not to be intimidated by disciplinary boundaries.`

Upon working through the vertical integration problem in transaction cost terms (see essay 4), it was clear to me that a large number of other problems would yield to this very same formulation. An outstanding graduate student named Jeffrey Harris was working with me. We began to work through the ramifications for labour organization. Jeff's wife was a lawyer and called his attention to links with the labour law literature. It was exciting to read and be able to offer a transaction cost interpretation for what Archibald Cox, Harry Shulman, and Clyde Summers had to say. *Markets and Hierarchies* began to take shape. It was published in 1975 by The Free Press after the Brookings Institution, which had rights of first refusal, declined.

I purchased my parents' summer place in northern Wisconsin after my father died in 1971. It had long been the fixed point in our experience as a family over the years and has been all the more since. Our children regularly reassemble there and my sister Sara flies in from California. I get an enormous amount of work done in Wisconsin, but manage to blend it with an enormous amount of play. My high school friend Ed Bankey, and I make our annual canoe trip down the Brule, where we normally catch close to our limit of trout. My boys and I have had less success fishing the Boundary Waters Canoe Area, but we have some great memories nonetheless.

My family and I spent the spring of 1973 in Europe. Dolores and I took the twins and our station wagon across the Atlantic on the *Leonardo*

DaVinci and met the three older children at the airport in Milan ten days later. A highlight of the journey, for nautical buffs, is that we sailed through an 11 point storm (on a 12 point scale).

We camped through Italy and France during the month of April. The weather was unbelievably good and, though we had no prior experience, the family took to camping like ducks to water. The twins celebrated their sixth birthday in Pisa.

We lived in a marvellous Georgian house in Leamington Spa during May and June. The children were all enrolled in English schools, the neighbours insisted that Dolores accompany them (or maybe the other way around) for trips to nearby towns and villages, and I taught economics at Warwick. Although there were grave reservations about transaction cost economics, John Cable, Keith Cowling, and Hywel Jones nevertheless gave me a sympathetic hearing. I naturally gave a number of seminars while in England. Much to my delight, my Cambridge talk was billed as a major lecture and there was a large student turnout. The faculty—which included Kenneth Arrow, who was visiting, Frank Hahn, and Nicholas Kaldor—seemed genuinely interested.

I discussed with Ken Arrow the merits of organizing a conference on the Economics of Internal Organization during my visit to Cambridge. Ken was enthusiastic and helped to identify a variety of other possible participants. The conference was held at the University of Pennsylvania in October 1974. Main papers were given by Ken Arrow, Scott Boorman, James Coleman, Leonid Hurwicz, Harvey Leibenstein, James Mirrlees, Roy Radner, Joseph Stiglitz, Robert Wilson and myself (with Jeffrey Harris and Michael Wachter as co-authors). Most of these papers were subsequently published in the *Bell Journal of Economics*, of which I had become the editor.

These conference papers helped to signal new directions in industrial organization and in *The Bell Journal*—which quickly moved up to take over eighth place among economics journals in terms of citations to articles published in 1975–1979. One of the real joys of this experience was working with the Editorial Board—which included, in various capacities, Jerry Hausman, Dale Jorgenson, Paul Joskow, Alvin Klevorick, Peter Linhart, Richard Nelson, Richard Quandt, Michael Spence, and Leigh Tripoli, to which Avinash Dixit and Sherwin Rosen were added later.

I spent the academic year 1977–78 at the Center for Advanced Study in the Behavioural Sciences. I was agonizing during much of this time over how to bring greater order into the study of contractual variety. I had been especially intrigued by the recent research on contract law by Ian Macneil and Victor Goldberg. Macneil's distinctions between classical, neoclassical and relational contract categories were especially instructive. My paper 'Transaction Cost Economics: The Governance of Contractual Relations' (Chapter 7) was the result.

It was clear by this time that transaction cost economics had enormous explanatory power. Vertical integration turned out to be a paradigm problem—which is evident from Chapters 6 to 12, below, and is developed more fully in my recent book, *The Economic Institutions of Capitalism: Firms, Markets, Relational Contracting*. Parts of this book were written in the spring of 1983 when Dolores, the twins, and I were in Kyoto. I was a visiting professor of economics at the Kyoto University at the time. We all enjoyed Japan enormously. And although I was unable to unpack many of the puzzles of Japanese economic organization, Banri Asanuma and Masahiko Aoki were very helpful in acquainting me with Japanese business practices and pointing out some of the pitfalls.

With many fond memories and even regrets, I left Penn in 1983 to accept an appointment at Yale. The chair to which I was appointed was expressly designated as one which the Law School and the School of Organization and Management were to fill jointly. The Economics Department at Yale thereafter expanded the appointment to include Economics as well. I am still in the process of working this appointment out. One of the interesting aspects of my move to Yale is that a new journal—the *Journal of Law, Economics and Organization*—has been created, of which Jerry Mashaw and I are co-editors. The intersection of law, economics, and organization is, I think, a fruitful one. The LEO Journal should help to encourage interdisciplinary research. The recent development of a new field of specialization in the 'Economics of Organization' at the Yale School of Organization and Management also has exciting prospects.

As I look back on the topics on which I have worked, I am impressed by the importance of first-hand contact: complex bureaucracies were something that I had been a part of and could relate to; managerial discretion was something that I had observed and participated in (R&D projects do not run themselves); the hazards of applying received theory too literally were evident from my experience with antitrust; that franchise bidding was a problematic solution for cable television was evident from the time I had spent working on these matters as part of Mayor Lindsay's CATV Task Force; that the organization of work was a fit subject for research was evident from the variety of jobs that I had held; that all forms of organization deserve only qualified respect was revealed by experience (including the Free Speech Movement at Berkeley) and by the insistent teachings of Arrow and Coase; that it was all right to remark about the emperor's clothes was encouraged by my father's forthrightness and my teachers at Carnegie.

Oliver E. Williamson

Part 1
THE ECONOMICS OF INTERNAL
ORGANIZATION

1. Introduction

Accidents play a role in the intellectual development of every scholar. Of the various accidents of my academic life, I count none more fortuitous than the events which led to my decision to attend Carnegie Tech (now Carnegie–Mellon) to complete work on a PhD in economics.

Carnegie was an infectious place. It fairly bubbled with research excitement, much of it of an interdisciplinary kind. Although orthodoxy was respected, heterodox insights and intuitions were given a serious hearing. Among other things, the Berle and Means' query 'have we any justification for assuming that those in control of the modern corporation will also choose to operate it in the interests of the shareholders?' (1932, p. 121) was regarded not as heresy but was accorded respect. Indeed, it could not be otherwise. In a world in which bounds on rationality and sub-goal pursuit are admitted, the Berle–Means query could be avoided only upon declaring that all matters relating to the emperor's attire should be suppressed. Thus Carnegie, in my experience and that of others of an early 1960s vintage, was important not least of all because it nurtured and refined heterodox insights and intuitions.

The first essay in this section is based on my dissertation and expressly deals with managerial discretion issues. The implicit organizational structure is that of the functional or unitary form corporation. Managers are assumed to maximize a utility function in which, subject to minimum performance constraints, the objectives of top management are prominently featured. Of the three models of managerial discretion that were advanced at this time—William Baumol's sales maximization hypothesis (1959), Robin Marris's growth maximization hypothesis (1964), and my utility maximization formulation (1964)—mine was closest to a property rights formulation and was happily incorporated in this literature. Armen Alchian's survey (1965) was instrumental in effecting this bridge.

The second essay is concerned with limits to firm size that arise because of limited spans of control, where span restrictions have their origins in bounded rationality and give rise to hierarchy. Again, the unitary form structure is assumed. Each transfer of information across successive levels in such an organization experiences 'control loss'. These losses are cumulative and arguably exponential in form, whence the radial expansion of such a hierarchical enterprise eventually

3

experience limitations to firm size.

I thought at the time when I wrote this paper that the puzzle posed by Ronald Coase—'Why is not all production carried on in one big firm?' (1952, p. 340)—had finally been solved. The query is important not merely to specialists in industrial organization, but even more to students of comparative economic systems. Any insight on this elusive matter was thus welcomed. I was pleased with the interest that this paper stimulated. It was not, however, until ten years later that I realized that I had not posed the issue in a genuinely comparative institutional way.

The comparative institutional formulation requires that at least two structures be examined simultaneously. One useful way to pose the question is this: Why can't a large firm do everything that a collection of small firms can, and more? My first effort to deal with this emphasized the incentive distortions that internal organization (unified ownership of assets in which disputes are settled administratively rather than through autonomous bargaining) experiences as compared with market procurement of the same goods and services (1975, Chapter 7). I have subsequently focused more closely on the incentive disabilities of internal organization by asking why firms are unable to manage assets by intervening selectively. If firms can both replicate markets in all relevant respects and, wherever net gains are in prospect, can do more, then internal organization will never do worse and will usually outperform the market. This assumes, however, that firms are able to preserve the high-powered incentives that market organization affords. A comparative institutional examination of the differences between firms and markets discloses that incentives in firms are unavoidably degraded (Williamson, 1985, Chapter 6).

The third essay (which was written jointly with Narrotam Bhargava) expressly makes provision for organization form differences among firms. It has its origins in my reading of Alfred D. Chandler, Jr's pathbreaking treatment of business history, *Strategy and Structure* (1962). I did not come upon this book until the late 1960s and was profoundly disturbed when I discovered it. As one who had taken managerial discretion seriously, I regarded competition in the product market and competition in the capital market as means by which to bring managerial discretion under control. Some product markets were effectively insulated from rivalry for long intervals, however, and the principal capital market device for displacing incumbent management, the proxy contest, was enormously cumbersome and ineffective. While others sought checks on managerial discretion through intensified regulation, I was sceptical of such proposals. But how, if at all, was managerial discretion to be more effectively attenuated?

Chandler's book suggested that we had been looking in the wrong place. External (market or regulatory) controls do not exhaust the possibilities. Internal (hierarchical) controls should also be considered. However paradoxical it seemed at the time, might managerial problems yield to managerial solutions?

Such a novel possibility was alien to the enormous literature that flowed from the Berle–Means tradition. If, however, Chandler's account of the reforms that were associated with the invention and diffusion of the multidivisional structure was substantially correct, then the conclusion that managerial discretion was being checked by internal organizational changes could not be avoided. The argument and, such as it was, the evidence that organization form was central to the unfolding story of the modern corporation seemed persuasive. Albeit cautiously and even reluctantly, I was thus induced to advance the M-form hypothesis—which, it should be noted, is expressed in comparative institutional terms—to wit: the organization and operation of the large enterprise along the lines of the M-form favours goal pursuit and least-cost behaviour more nearly associated with the neoclassical profit-maximization hypothesis than does the U-form organizational alternative. Even to entertain such a hypothesis had far-reaching ramifications for the manner in which the corporation was thereafter conceptualized.

REFERENCES

Alchian, Armen, 'The Basis of Some Recent Advances in the Theory of Management of the Firm', *Journal of Industrial Economics*, December 1965, 14, 30-41.

Baumol, William, *Business Behavior, Value, and Growth*. New York: Macmillan, 1959.

Berle, A.A. and Means, G.C., *The Modern Corporation and Private Property*. New York: Commerce Clearing House, 1932.

Chandler, Alfred D. Jr, *Strategy and Structure*. New York: Doubleday. Anchor Books edn, 1966.

Coase, Ronald H. 'The Nature of the Firm', *Economics N.S.* 1937, 4, 386-405, in G.J. Stigler and K.E. Boulding (eds), *Readings in Price Theory*. Homewood, Ill.: Richard D. Irwin, 1952.

Marris, Robin, *The Economic Theory of 'Managerial' Capitalism*. New York: The Free Press, 1964.

Williamson, Oliver E., *The Economics of Discretionary Behavior: Managerial Objectives in a Theory of the Firm*. Englewood Cliffs, N.J.: Prentice–Hall, 1964.

Williamson, Oliver E., *Markets and Hierarchies: Analysis and Antitrust Implications*. New York: The Free Press, 1975.

Williamson, Oliver E., *The Economic Institutions of Capitalism: Firms, Markets, Relational Contracting*. New York: The Free Press, 1985.

2. Managerial Discretion and Business Behaviour*

The importance of managerial discretion in the operations of the large corporation has been widely recognized. Carl Kaysen characterized the large corporation as one 'in which the constraints imposed by market forces are loose, and the scope for managerial choice is considerable' (Kaysen, 1960, p.90), and Gordon holds that the development of the large corporation has led 'to a greater emphasis on the non-profit goals of interest groups other than the stockholders. Almost certainly, the personal and group goals of . . . executives are a part of the total value system—the desires for security, power, prestige, advancement within the organization, and so on. . . . Profits are viewed as the basic constraint subject to which other goals can be followed' (Gordon, 1961, p.xii).

Although there is substantial support for these views, it is by no means universal,[1] and before general acceptance can be attained a number of questions need to be answered. Can operational significance be provided to these managerial goals? Can such a translation of managerial objectives be integrated into a theory of the firm from which meaningful theorems can be derived? What is the evidence that discretion has an important and systematic impact on business behaviour? Specifically, what influence does competition in the product market, managerial tastes and the diffusion of stockholder control have on the allocation of resources in the business firm? How do regulatory or other constraints influence non-profit behaviour?

My purpose in this paper is to show that the first two of these questions can be answered in the affirmative, that the preliminary evidence tends to support the proposition that the opportunity for discretion does have a systematic effect on resource allocation decisions, and that regulatory constraints are apt to produce particularly strong manifestations of

*   The author acknowledges with thanks the helpful comments of R.M. Cyert, J.G. March, A.H. Meltzer, E.S. Mills, J.F. Muth, L.A. Rapping and H.A. Simon. The study resulting in the paper was made in part under a fellowship granted by the Ford Foundation. However, the conclusions, opinions and other statements in the paper are the author's and are not necessarily those of the Ford Foundation.

non-profit behaviour. Section I introduces the notion of 'expense preference' for translating managerial goals to an operational form, develops the implications of a model constructed around these objectives, and contrasts these with those obtained from the profit-maximization hypothesis. Section II examines some of the preliminary evidence on discretionary behaviour. The effects of regulatory constraints are considered in Section III.

I. SOME MODELS OF BUSINESS BEHAVIOUR[2]

My purpose in this section will be to show how managerial objectives can be introduced into a theory of the firm, to develop the implications of a model responsive to what appears to be the salient motives of managers, and to contrast these with those obtained from short-period and multiperiod versions of the profit-maximization hypothesis.

1. A Managerial Discretion Model

Managerial Objectives. The following list represents a (largely overlapping) composite of the managerial motives identified as the result of the experiences and insights of the organization theorists, Barnard (1962) and Simon (1961), and the study of business leadership of Gordon (1961): salary, security, power, status, prestige, professional excellence.[3] That they are neither equally significant nor entirely independent should be obvious. Rather than attempt a finer discrimination, however, it seems more fruitful to enquire into the behaviour such motives produce.

The usual objection to introducing non-pecuniary elements into the theory of the firm is that such considerations, if not unimportant, are analytically evasive. Since their importance is an empirical question, it can hardly be dismissed so easily. In order, however, to assess their influence, an analytical basis for examining them must be devised. Shifting attention from the motives to the *means* by which the motives are realized provides the necessary connection. That is, rather than attempt to introduce security, power, prestige, and so forth into the theory directly, we ask instead: to what activities do these motives give rise? These activities, rather than the motives, are then made a part of the model.

The essential notion that we propose in order to connect motives with behaviour is that of *expense preference*. That is, the management does not have a neutral attitude towards costs. Directly or indirectly, certain classes of expenditure have positive values associated with them. In particular, staff expense, expenditures for emoluments, and funds available for discretionary investment have value additional to that which derives from their productivity.

Expansion of staff is an activity that offers positive rewards, the benefits of which can be enjoyed quite generally (Marshall, 1932, pp.321-2). Indeed, since promotional opportunities within a fixed-size firm are limited, while increased jurisdiction has the same general effect as promotion but simultaneously produces the chance of advance for all, the incentive to expand staff may be difficult to resist. Not only is it an indirect means to the attainment of salary (Simon, 1957), but is a source of security, power, status, prestige and professional achievement as well.[4]

We use the term 'emoluments' in a somewhat special sense. They refer to that fraction of managerial salaries and perquisites that are discretionary. That is, emoluments represent rewards which, if removed, would not cause the managers to seek other employment. They are economic rents and have associated with them zero productivities. Thus they are not a return to entrepreneurial capacity but rather result from the strategic advantage that the management possesses in the distribution of the returns to monopoly power. Being a source of material satisfaction and an indirect source of status and prestige, they are desirable as a means of satisfying goals in each of these respects.

The management would normally prefer to take these emoluments as salary rather than as perquisites of office since, taken as salary, there are no restrictions on the way in which they are spent, while if withdrawn as corporate personal consumption (such as expense accounts, executive services, office suites, etc.), there are specific limitations on the ways these can be enjoyed. However, there are two considerations that make perquisites attractive. First, for tax purposes it may be advantageous to withdraw some part of discretionary funds as perquisites rather than salary. Second, perquisites are much less visible rewards to the management than salary and hence are less likely to provoke stockholder or labour dissatisfaction.[5] Hence a division of emoluments between salary and perquisites is to be expected.

Although it is difficult to specify what fraction of salary and perquisites is discretionary in the sense defined, it is possible, as we shall show in Section II, to test for the relation of these rewards to competition in the product market and managerial tastes. Thus, they can be identified *ex post* even if not *ex ante*.

The existence of satisfactory profits is necessary to assure the interference-free operation of the firm to the management. Precisely what this level will be involves a complicated interaction of the relative performance of rivals, the historical performance of the firm and special current conditions that affect the firm's performance. Management, however, will find it desirable to earn profits that exceed the acceptable level. For one thing, managers derive satisfaction from self-fulfilment and organizational achievement, and profits are one measure of this success. In addition, profits are a source of discretion (indeed, we define 'discretionary profits' as the difference between actual profits and minimum profits demanded). Discretionary profits represent a source of funds whose allocation may be importantly determined by managerial, in addition to economic, considerations. As with the expansion of staff, the expansion of physical plant and equipment provides general opportunities for managerial satisfaction and for much the same reasons.

The Model. Since these notions will be introduced explicitly into a mathematical model, it will be useful to define them more precisely. The relationships that we shall use are:

R = revenue = $P \cdot X$; $\partial^2 R / \partial X \partial S \geq 0$
P = price = $P(X, S; \epsilon)$; $\partial P / \partial X < 0$; $\partial P / \partial S \geq 0$; $\partial P / \partial \epsilon > 0$
X = output
S = staff (in money terms) or (approximately) general administrative and selling expense
ϵ = the condition of the environment (a demand-shift parameter)
C = production cost = $C(X)$
M = managerial emoluments
π = actual profits = R-C-S
π_R = reported profits = $\pi - M$
π_O = minimum (after tax) profits demanded
T = taxes where t = tax rate and $\bar{T}$ = lump-sum tax
$\pi_R - \pi_O - T$ = discretionary profits
U = the utility function

From our statement of the firm's objectives, the firm is operated so as to

maximize: $U = U[S, M, \pi_R - \pi_O - T]$
subject to: $\pi_R \geq \pi_0 + T$

As formulated, the constraint is of the same form as the last term in the utility function. Hence, assuming that second-order conditions are satisfied and disallowing corner solutions, the constraint becomes redundant so that we can treat the problem as one of straightforward maximization.[6] Substituting the functional relationships for profits into the expression we have:

maximize: $U = U[S, M, (1 - t)(R - C - S - M) - \pi^O]$.

The following first-order results are obtained by setting the partial derivatives of U with respect to X, S, and M equal to zero.[7]

$$\frac{\partial R}{\partial X} = \frac{\partial C}{\partial X} \tag{1}$$

$$\frac{\partial R}{\partial S} = \frac{-U_1 + (1 - t) U_3}{(1 - t) U_3} \tag{2}$$

$$U_2 = (1 - t) U_3. \tag{3}$$

From equation (1) we observe that the firm makes its production decision in the conventional fashion by equating marginal gross revenue to the marginal costs of production. However, equation (2) reveals that the firm will employ staff in the region where the marginal value product of staff is less than its marginal cost. The equation can be written as:

$$\frac{\partial R}{\partial S} = 1 - \frac{1}{(1 - t)} \frac{U_1}{U_3}, \text{ where } \frac{U_1}{U_3}$$

is the marginal rate of substitution between profits and staff. In the profit-maximizing organization, staff has no value other than that associated with its productivity, so that this exchange rate is zero, and the equality of marginal costs and value products obtains. Equation (3) discloses that the firm will absorb some amount of actual profits as emoluments—the amount being dependent on the tax rate.

Having established the equilibrium conditions, the comparative statics properties of the model remain to be developed.[8] That is, we want to find how the system adjusts to a change in the condition of the environment (the demand-shift parameter ϵ), a change in the profit tax rate (t) and a lump-sum tax ($\bar{T}$).

The results for a displacement by each of the parameters are shown in Table 2.1. The direction of adjustment of any particular decision variable to a displacement from its equilibrium value by an increase in a particular parameter is found by referring to the row and column entry corresponding to this pair.

Table 2.1
Responses to displacements from equilibrium for the managerial model

Variable	Parameter		
	ϵ	t	$\bar{T}$
X^O	+	+	−
S^O	+	+	−
M^O	+	+	−

Actually the response to a change in the profits rate is not unambiguous. It can be shown that this response is separable into a net substitution effect and the equivalent of an income effect, where the net substitution effect is always positive and the income effect is always negative. The gross substitution effect is the combination of these two separate effects and hence depends on their relative magnitudes. Under reasonable assumptions, the gross substitution effect will be positive as shown in the table.[9]

2. Entrepreneurial Models

The significance of these responses can best be discussed by comparing them to the corresponding results obtained from profit-maximizing models. Consider first the usual or single-period profit-maximizing model. As is well known, the equilibrium relations for this model require that the firm be operated so as to equate marginal gross revenue with the marginal costs of production and the marginal value product of staff with its marginal cost. The comparative statics responses are shown in Table 2.2.

Table 2.2 Responses to displacements from equilibrium for the short-run profits-maximizing model

Variable	Parameter		
	ϵ	t	$\bar{T}$
X^0	+	0	0
S^0	+	0	0

The differences between the models are more numerous than their similarities. Indeed, it is only with respect to the demand-shift parameter (ϵ) that the two return the same results, and even here the result is not identical. In addition to the increases in staff and output that the profit-maximization model shows, the managerial model also indicates that spending for emoluments will increase as ϵ increases. Moreover, while the qualitative differences with respect to ϵ are not great, quantitative differences may produce sharper discriminations. In general, a profit-maximizing firm will adjust to changes in business conditions within narrower bounds than the utility-maximizing firm. The absence of slack in its operations, as contrasted with the calculated accumulations (and decumulation) of slack by the utility-maximizing firm, is responsible for these quantitative differences.

A more general entrepreneurial model can be obtained by devising a multiperiod or discounted version of the profit-maximization hypothesis.

The variables are subscripted by time periods by i, where $i = 1, 2 \ldots n$, and n is the planning horizon. Letting r be the discount rate, profits in year i will be discounted by $1/(1 + r)^{i-1}$. Let this be represented by α^{i-1}. We make the assumption that production decisions in period k affect costs in no other period or, if there are effects, that these are offsetting. However, staff expenditures in period k are assumed to have a positive influence on future period revenues over the entire planning horizon. Indeed, the length of the 'period' can be defined as the interval beyond which current production decisions have no effect, and the length of the planning horizons as the number of such periods for which current staff expenditures have a positive effect.

Letting π represent the discounted value of profits, the objective is to maximize:

$$\pi = \sum_{i=1}^{n} (1 - t)(R_i - C_i - S_i - \bar{T}_i) \, \alpha^{i-1}.$$

First order conditions for a maximum are obtained by setting the partial derivatives of π with respect to X_1 and S_1 equal to zero. Thus we have:

$$\frac{\partial R_1}{\partial X_1} = \frac{\partial C_1}{\partial X_1} \tag{4}$$

$$\frac{\partial R_1}{\partial S_1} = 1 - \sum_{i=2}^{n} \frac{\partial R_i}{\partial S_1} \alpha^{i-1} \tag{5}$$

Inspection of equation (4) reveals that the firm chooses that value of output for which the marginal gross revenue is equal to the marginal costs of production. Equation (5), however, shows the current marginal value product of staff is less than its current marginal cost.[10] These equilibrium conditions are thus similar to those obtained from the managerial model.

Since the effects when the tax is levied for a period less than the planning horizon are different from those when the tax covers the entire horizon, the tax-rate effect is split into 'temporary' (designated tax rate t') and 'permanent' (designated tax rate t'') types. The comparative statics responses for this model are displayed in Table 2.3.

Table 2.3 Comparative statics responses for the discounted profits-maximizing model

Variable	Parameter			
	ϵ	t'	t''	$\bar{T}$
X_1^0	+	+	0	0
S_1^0	+	+	0	0

Whereas the qualitative responses to a 'temporary' change in the profits tax rate are identical to those obtained from the managerial model, a change in the 'permanent' profits tax or the levy of a lump-sum tax (or bounty) produces no effect in the profits-maximizing organization. A response to both is predicted by the managerial model. Hence a discrimination between the hypotheses on the basis of comparative statics properties is potentially achievable.

II. SOME EVIDENCE

Changes in either the profits tax or a lump-sum tax provide the most direct basis for distinguishing between the utility and profit-maximization theories. Testing the effects of a profits tax, however, requires that a rather advanced type of simultaneous equations model be devised, while lump-sum taxes are hard to come by. The first of these carries us beyond the range of the present analysis, and only preliminary evidence on the effects of the lump-sum tax is available. (See section II (2).)

Fortunately other tests of a less direct but nonetheless meaningful sort can be devised. For one thing, the comparative statics implications are limited to qualitative responses; quantitative differences are neglected. If, therefore, significant quantitative differences between the two theories can be shown to exist, these can be used for making a discrimination where qualitative properties are identical.

Secondly, tests of particular behaviour are available. Thus, the utility-maximizing theory is based on the proposition that opportunities for discretion and managerial tastes will have a decided impact on the expenditures of the firm. More precisely, those expenditures that promote managerial satisfactions should show a positive correlation with opportunities for discretion and tastes. The profit-maximizing theory is somewhat ambiguous on this question. Interpreted as a theory which attends entirely to the stockholders' best interests, it clearly implies that expenditures which, under the utility-maximizing hypothesis, will be positively correlated with measures of discretion and tastes, will instead be uncorrelated with these relationships. Interpreted somewhat more loosely, closer agreement with the utility-maximizing hypothesis can be obtained. Thus, it is possible that the management first selects that physical combination of factors that maximizes profits and then absorbs some amount of actual profits as cost. These absorptions may be correlated with the same measures of discretion and taste as would be expected under the utility-maximizing theory. Hence, evidence that managers respond to opportunities for discretion is not inconsistent with the profit-maximizing theory, but neither is evidence to the contrary; the theory is simply silent on this question. However, the failure of firms to respond to opportunities for discretion constitutes a contradiction of the utility-maximizing hypothesis while observations that firms do display expense-preference behaviour supports it.

The executive compensation and retained-earnings analyses reported in section II (1) below are designed to test for the effects of discretion and taste in management expenditure decisions. The summary of the field studies in section II (2) is concerned with the question of physical magnitudes of adjustment to adversity and provides some indication of what criteria are involved in making expense adjustments as well as what effects a lump-sum tax has on business behaviour.

1. Principal Firm Analysis

If the firm is operated so as to attend to managerial interests, then the classes of expenditure for which expense preference was indicated should be expanded beyond the levels called for by strictly profit considerations. The amount by which such expansions occur should be positively related to the opportunity for discretion and the tastes of the management. More precisely, if X is an expenditure for which a positive expense preference exists, I_1 is an index of the absence of competition, I_2 is an index of management taste, I_3 is an index of stockholder diffusion, and $f(\pi)$ is the level of X which would be supported solely by profit considerations, then under the utility-maximization hypothesis:

$$X = f(\pi)g(I_1,I_2,I_3)$$

where

$$\frac{\partial X}{\partial I_i} > 0.$$

Under the stockholder version of the profit-maximization hypothesis, the partial derivative of X with respect to each of the I_i will be zero.

Since it is in the large corporation that manifestations of discretionary behaviour are alleged to be important, and as complete data are more readily available among larger industrial firms than their smaller counterparts, the tests are restricted to those firms that clearly qualified as 'principal firms'. Among the 26 industries included in the analysis, selection was limited to the two largest firms, ranked according to sales, in each.[11] The tests performed are cross-section tests for the years 1953, 1957 and 1961.

Executive Compensation. George Stigler (1956) has observed that the estimation of the effect of monopoly on profit may be complicated by the absorption of some fraction of 'true' monopoly profit as cost. In particular, 'the magnitude of monopoly elements in wages, executive compensation, royalties, and rents is possibly quite large' (p. 35). Our interest here is limited to testing only a part of this hypothesis. Specifically, we examine the effects of discretion on compensating the top executive.

Focusing on a single representative of management might appear to restrict severely the relevance of our results. If the compensation of the rest of the management group were determined independently of that of the chief executive, this would certainly be the case. However, payments between executive levels are carefully scaled (Baxter, 1938 p.181; Koontz and O'Donnell, 1955, p.320; Simon, 1957). Hence, the factors that influence compensation to the top executive can be presumed to affect the level of staff compensation generally.

Under the utility-maximizing hypothesis, a positive expense preference towards emoluments exists. In particular, executive salaries should be correlated with the opportunities for discretion. Letting W_a be the actual salary of the management and W_c be the competitive salary, we have: $W_a = W_c + (W_a - W_c)$, where $W_a - W_c$ is a measure of the monopoly returns withdrawn by the management (by virtue of its advantageous position) as economic rent.

As indicated above, the hypothesis that discretion influences expenses takes the form $X = f(\pi)g(I_1, I_2, I_3)$, where $f(\pi)$ is the expense incurred strictly on a profit-maximizing basis, and I_1, I_2, and I_3, are indices of the absence of competition, the tastes of the management, and the diffusion of the stockholders respectively. Specifying $f(\pi)$ for purposes of studying executive compensation is somewhat difficult. A measure of hierarchial activity over which the executive in question has responsibility, together with the special abilities required for the position, probably measures this approximately. For the top executive, the level of hierarchical activity is effectively the entire staff structure. Thus, let $f(\pi) = f'(S, Z)$ where S is the level of staff (general administrative and selling expenses)[12] and Z is an index of special ability.

We assume that the index of competitive pressure (I_1) is reflected by the concentration ratio and the entry barrier in each industry. The concentration ratio reflects the influence of realized interdependencies between rivals. Where concentration ratios are high, interdependencies will generally be intimate, and behaviour between rivals will at least be circumspect and may involve explicit agreements. In either case, the influence of competition will be consciously controlled. Hence, an increase in the concentration ratio will tend to widen the opportunities for managerial discretion. Obviously, this measure is defective and there will be exceptions. However we are content merely to account for average rather than exceptional behaviour.

The barrier to entry measure, as developed by Bain (1962), is explicitly designed to estimate the extent to which firms are insulated from the effects of competition. Although concentration and entry conditions are correlated, they are by no means identical. In combination they provide a particularly good measure of the opportunities for discretion. High concentration together with a high barrier to entry will tend to produce substantial discretion, for not only is potential competition limited, but existing rivals are few enough to appreciate their conditions of inter-dependence. Low values for each of these measures will tend to produce the reverse effect, while mixed values, presumably, give rise to mixed effects.

To allay any suspicion that the concentration ratio and entry barriers are merely another measure of size, it might be noted that the product moment correlations between the logarithm of sales and the logarithms of 'staff', concentration and barriers (for the firms included in the sample) are about 0.75, -0.13, and -0.14 respectively. Quite clearly these latter two correlations are small enough that if the concentration and barriers have an effect on compensation, it is not primarily due to their relationship to size.

A sharp measure of managerial tastes (I_2) is not available. However, the composition of the board may act as a proxy measure of the extent to which management desires to operate the firm free from outside interference. Although low proportional representation of the management on the board of directors need not reflect a 'taste' for active outside participation in the affairs of the firm, clearly a high internal representation does reflect the intent of the management to conduct the affairs of the firm free from such outside influence. We hypothesize that as the management representation on the board increases, there tends to be a subordination of stockholder for managerial interests. In this sense, the composition of the board reflects management's attitude towards discretionary resource allocations and a voluntary change in composition reflects a change in these 'tastes'.

An estimate of stockholder diffusion (I_3) was not obtained. Such a measure would probably be correlated with the composition of the board variable. However the association may not be great. Where substantial concentration of ownership exists, there is frequently a tendency towards nepotism. This in turn may produce high internal representation rather than the high outside representation that would otherwise be predicted. If in fact the correlation were zero (and there were no other neglected variable to consider), our estimate of the composition effect would be unbiased. As it is, some bias may result from the lack of a diffusion measure.[13]

The effects of each of the independent variables on executive compensation should be positive. In addition, they are assumed to be multiplicative. Thus we assume that:

$$X_i = \alpha_0 S_i^{\alpha^1} C_i^{\alpha^2} H_i^{\alpha^3} B_i^{\alpha^4} U_i \qquad (6)$$

where
X_i = compensation of the top executive
S_i = administrative, general, and selling expense (i.e. 'staff')
C_i = concentration ratio in the industry
H_i = height of the barrier to entry in the industry
B_i = composition of the board
U_i = a random error term[14]
    and the subscript i refers to the ith firm in the sample.[15]

Taking logarithms of both sides of the equation and using these data to obtain least-squares estimates of the net regression coefficients, we obtain the results shown in Table 2.4.

Table 2.4 Regression of executive compensation on 'staff' concentration ratio, composition of the board, and barriers to entry

| | | *Year* | |
	1953	*1957*	*1961*
'Staff'			
coeff.	0.228[a]	0.240[a]	0.218[a]
s.e.	0.061	0.052	0.054
partial	(0.564)	(0.610)	(0.614)
Concentration			
coeff.	0.503[a]	0.513[a]	0.422[b]
s.e.	0.157	0.143	0.152
partial	(0.517)	(0.517)	(0.470)
Composition			
coeff.	0.137	0.139	0.053
s.e.	0.118	0.101	0.120
partial	(0.213)	(0.224)	(0.084)
Entry Barriers			
coeff.	0.446[a]	0.221[b]	0.200
s.e.	0.110	0.114	0.126
partial	(0.606)	(0.307)	(0.290)
Coeff. of Correl.			
adjusted	0.786	0.724	0.687

Notes:
[a] Significant at the 0.1 per cent level.
[b] Significant at the 2.5 per cent level.

The signs for each of the parameters in all three years are as predicted by the expense-preference hypothesis. Moreover, with the exception of the composition of the board coefficient, which is significant at the 10 per cent level only in 1957, all of the regression coefficients are highly significant—two-thirds being significant at the 2.5 per cent level.[16] Whereas the relation of executive compensation to general administrative and selling expense (i.e. 'staff') is almost certain to be positive and significant, there is no reason to believe that the measures of taste and discretion that we introduce should have the effects shown (unless one endorses the view that management responds to opportunities for discretion in the ways indicated). Since the compensation of the chief executive generalizes to the entire staff structure, these results have broad significance for the resource allocation process within a business firm. Furthermore, we would expect that these same measures of discretion would produce similar effects over the entire range of expenditures on emoluments.

Of course it could be argued that the concentration ratio and entry barrier variables have positive regression coefficients because they are correlated with the profit rate—that this profitability effect is responsible for the results obtained. But obviously the causality runs from concentration and entry barriers to profits rather than the reverse. Thus, by focusing on the market structure the model directs attention to the ultimate determinants of discretionary behaviour (competition in the product market) rather than the apparent determinant (the profit rate). Although these market variables might not perform as well as the profit rate among the smaller firms in the industry, it does not seem inappropriate to use them for studying the behaviour of the two largest firms where the relationship between market structure and behaviour is probably reasonably direct. Indeed, it is of interest to note that: (1) if the profit rate on the stockholders' equity is substituted for the concentration ratio and the entry barrier variables, the coefficient of determination (R^2) falls to two-thirds of the value obtained using these market variables in 1953 and 1961, and yields less than a 10 per cent increase in R^2 in 1957; (2) if the profit rate, concentration ratio and entry barrier variables are all included, the profit rate is significant only in 1957 and has the wrong sign in 1961, while the concentration ratio and entry barrier variables remain significant at the 10 per cent level or better in every year.

Although the profit rate might perform better if a weighted average were used instead of current values, the argument offered above that this is an apparent rather than the ultimate determinant of behaviour still applies. Moreover, the appropriate estimate of the profit rate is the actual rather than the reported rate. But the actual rate is unknown if, as the evidence above suggests, some fraction of actual profits is absorbed as salary and perquisites.

Some feeling for the responsiveness of salary to the independent variables in the regression equation can be obtained by taking the median of the estimates for each parameter and finding the effect on salary of increasing each individual independent variable by a factor of two. In some gross sense we can expect that executive salaries will possibly increase on the order of 17 per cent if the level of staff activity were to double, on the order of 41 per cent if the concentration ratio in the industry were to double, on the order of 10 per cent if the internal representation on the board were to double, and on the order of 25 per cent if the industry of which the firm was a part had a substantial or high barrier to entry rather than a low one. Thus, not only are the signs as predicted by the theory, but the magnitudes are sufficiently large to render somewhat doubtful the contention that discretionary effects are unimportant.

Earnings retention. The composition of the board variable was used in the executive compensation model to reflect the 'tastes' of the management for discretion. Internal representation on the board acts as a proxy for the attitude of the management towards outside influence. As the proportional representation of management on the board increases, it is assumed that stockholder interests tend to be subordinated to managerial objectives. This was manifested in the executive compensation regression by the positive regression coefficient associated with the composition of board variable.

A second test for this effect is to examine the relationship between composition of the board and earnings retention policy. Consistency with our model requires that the earnings retention ratio be directly related to the composition of the board. This follows since retained earnings are a source of discretion and a high internal representation provides the opportunity for management to shift the dividend policy to its advantage.

Alternative theories of the firm that regard managerial objectives as unimportant implicitly predict that there will be no association between the composition of the board and retention policy. Thus, our hypothesis of a direct association is tested against the null hypothesis of no association.

Earnings retention will, of course, be responsive to a number of considerations other than that of the composition of the board. Most important, investment opportunities will differ between industries and these could easily be overriding. If it can be assumed that the firms in the same industry have identical opportunities, however, these effects can be neutralized.

A paired comparison technique was used to neutralize the industry effects. That is, between the two principal firms in each of the 26 industries we compare the composition of the board and earnings retention ratio. The random variable can take on either of two values: 1 if the higher internal representation is paired with the higher earnings retention ratio, and 0 otherwise. Hence it is distributed as a binomial. Under the hypothesis that no association exists, the expected number of times the positive association will occur, divided by the total number of observations, is one half. Thus the null hypothesis is that the binomial parameter p is 0.50. Our model, however, predicts that the positive association will occur more than one half of the time—i.e. that p exceeds 0.50.

The results of each of the three years as well as the pooled results for all three years are shown in Table 2.5. The proposition that internal representation has no effect on the earnings retention policy between pairs of firms in the same industry is unsupported by the data. In every year the proportion of positive observations exceeds 0.50. In 1953 and 1957 the probability that a value as high as that observed if the null hypothesis were true is 0.34 and 0.13 respectively, and in 1961 this drops to 0.02. Clearly we are inclined to reject the hypothesis in favour of the alternative suggested. That is, due to the discretion associated with the retention of earnings and the opportunity to influence the retention policy which arises from representation on the board, the relation that we suggested (namely, that between pairs of firms in the same industry, the higher the internal representation, the higher the earnings retention rate) is supported by the data. Although it is possible that the composition of

Table 2.5 Binomial test for association between composition of board and earnings retention policy

	1953	*1957*	*1961*	*All years*
Number of observations	25	26	26	77
Expected number of positive occurrences under the null hypothesis	12.5 (p=0.50)	13 (p=0.50)	13 (p=0.50)	38.5 (p=0.50)
Actual number of positive occurrences	13.5 ($\hat{p}$=0.54)	16 ($\hat{p}$=0.54)	18 ($\hat{p}$=0.62)	47.5 ($\hat{p}$=0.69)
Probability that a value as high as observed would occur if the null hypothesis were true[a]	0.34	0.13	0.02	0.02

[a] Normal approximation to the binomial was used to obtain the probabilities that the null hypothesis would produce the results observed.

the board is acting only as an intervening variable and that the real explanation for this association lies elsewhere, no simple connection suggests itself.

The strongest evidence in favour of our hypothesis is provided by the pooled results for all three years. Here the observed number of positive occurrences would appear by chance under the null hypothesis with a probability of only 2 times in 100. Before the pooling of the observations can be justified, however, it is first necessary to establish that the observations are independent and that the association observed in one period is simply not carried over to the following period. Since the composition of the board and earnings retention decisions reflect policy considerations that exhibit continuation in consecutive years, lack of independence between consecutive years would be expected. On the other hand, our observations are separated by a period of four years. The association between consecutive years may well be eliminated over this interval. Since this interval can scarcely be resolved on *a priori* grounds, we submit the hypothesis that the observations are independent to test.

A chi-square test for association was used. A low value of χ^2 is consistent with the hypothesis that the observations between successive four-year intervals are independent. The value of χ^2 between 1953 and 1957 is 0.0065, and between 1957 and 1961 is 0.62. Sampling randomly from independent populations, values as high or higher than this would occur 95 per cent and 45 per cent of the time, respectively. Hence the hypothesis of independence is supported, the pooling of the observations is justified, and the best test for the composition of the board effect is that of all three years combined. Here the possibility that the positive association observed has occurred by chance is only 0.02. Indeed, among pairs of principal firms we can expect that the firm with the higher internal representation on the board of directors will have a higher earnings retention ratio about 60 per cent of the time.

The above results are limited to directional effects only and say nothing about the magnitudes involved. This is probably all that the data justify. However, a crude estimate of the quantitative effect is available by an application of the general model suggested above for studying discretionary expenditures. Thus, let

R_{ik} = the retained earnings ratio
ρ_k = the rate of return on investment available to principal firms
C_k = the concentration ratio
H_k = the entry barrier
B_{ik} = the composition of the board of directors
V_{ik} = a random error term[17]

The subscript *i* refers to the firm, and the subscript *k* refers to the industry of which the firm is a part. Then, assuming the retention is multiplicative, we have:

$$R_{ik} = \beta_0[f(\rho_k)]^{\beta_1}C_k^{\beta_2}H_k^{\beta_3}B_k^{\beta_4}V_{ik}. \tag{7}$$

Taking the ratio of retained earnings between the ith and jth principal firms in the same industry yields:

$$\frac{R_{ik}}{R_{jk}} = \left(\frac{B_{ik}}{B_{jk}}\right)^{\beta_4}V'. \tag{8}$$

Taking logarithms of both sides of the equation, the value of β_4 can be estimated by least squares. The resulting estimates for 1953, 1957 and 1961 are 0.17, 0.17 and 0.16 respectively; but only the 1957 estimate is significant at the 10 per cent level.[18] These estimates suggest that the retained earnings ratio would increase by about 12 per cent if the internal representation on the board of directors were to double.

A tenuous connection between the composition of the board and the investment policy of the firm can be obtained by noting the results obtained by Gordon (1961) and Scott (1962) in their studies of investment financing. Gordon remarks that:

The really surprising result is produced by return on investment . . . In both industries there is a statistically significant tendency for the retention rate to fall as the corporation's rate of return increases. We must conclude that either [our estimate] is a poor measure of rate of return on investment or that corporations are not primarily influenced by the price of their stock in setting dividend rates. (1961, pp. 231-2)

And Scott, in a somewhat more broadly-based study of dividend policy, observes that the 'negative correlation of −0.30 between undistributed profits . . . and the subsequent growth of earnings . . . is somewhat surprising. It suggests that stockholders . . . might benefit from more generous dividend distributions' (1962, p.244). For a theory that makes the firm's objectives identical with those of the stockholders, such a result is somewhat disquieting. For an approach such as ours, however, which allows for the subordination of stockholder to managerial objectives, a possible explanation for these results based on the composition of the board analysis can be easily provided.

As was suggested above, high internal representation on the board of directors favours attention to managerial objectives, and this is man-ifested in a high earnings retention rate. The funds thus provided are available to the management for the pursuit of expansionary objectives, and the resulting investment, being based on a combination of profit and expansionary goals, will exceed the amount dictated by profit considerations alone. As a result, the average rate of return in firms whose management is inclined to subordinate objectives can be expected to fall below that in firms where management interests are more nearly those of the stockholders.[19] Thus the tastes of the management, as revealed originally in the composition of the board, make their influence felt through the earnings retention policy and thence on the return on investment. Where these tastes favour expansion, there is an adverse effect on the rate of return on investment. This indirect implication of our theory is precisely the result that Gordon and Scott report. Although conjectural, it suggests the value of including a 'taste' variable, of which the composition of the board is a somewhat imperfect proxy, in future studies of the investment decision.

2. The Evidence from the Field Studies

Simon (1962) has pointed out that 'neither the classical theory of the firm nor any of the amendments to it or substitutes for it . . . have had any substantial amount of empirical testing' (p.8). To remedy this he offers several proposals, one of which is the intensive interview. This has the advantage of permitting detailed observations that are unavailable in the ordinary survey, and these may provide insights into the ways in which the firm perceives its problems and the processes it employs in responding to them.

Unfortunately, field study observations are difficult to summarize. Their relevance derives largely from their detail and, since the observations are few in number, statistical tests are often inappropriate. The field studies reported here are precisely of this kind. They nonetheless produce insights that would be difficult to obtain by other means. Of principal interest from our studies of the response of firms to adversity are the following:

1.   In the face of a sharp drop in profitability, hierarchical expenses typically undergo extensive curtailment. One firm, after a long period of operating in a seller's market, responded to a sharp fall in profits with the following adjustments (Williamson, 1962, pp. 5-11): (a) salaried employment over the entire organization was reduced by 32 per cent; (b) headquarters employment was reduced by 41 per cent; (c) the R & D staff was reduced from 165 personnel to 52 and much of its work was redirected to commercial R & D organizations; (d) the personnel and public relations staff was streamlined from 57 to 7; and (e) a general reduction in emoluments of all kinds was realized. All this occurred with production unchanged. Return on investment over the interval was increased from the 4 per cent level to which it had fallen to 9 per cent.

Further cutbacks in some areas are expected; additions are contingent on changes in volume and are tied to a new set of long-range plans.

Both the type and magnitude of these reductions suggest that the managers were operating the firm so as to attend to other than merely profitability goals in the period preceding the earnings decline. Invoking the notions of expense preference and discretionary spending makes it possible to provide an uncomplicated explanation for the adjustments observed.

2.   The philosophy of management in instituting cutbacks is of particular interest. The chief budgeting officer in one organization made this observation:

In any large organization, certain plants or departments will have found ways to habitually operate more efficiently than others. This may be due to *competitive pressure* which has historically been felt in some products to a greater extent than others. It may be due to differences in *individual management philosophy*. . . . It follows . . . that any approach toward an arbitrary management dictate for an across-the-board slash in all cost areas will inevitably damage necessary functions in some areas, and leave remaining inefficiencies in others. (Cited in Williamson, 1962, p.13)

As a result, cost reductions were tailored to the individual divisions— taking their competitive history and management philosophies into account. Whereas such behaviour is consistent with the managerial model, it is less clear that it should occur in a profit-maximizing organization.

Related observations of interest were the way in which headquarters overheads were allocated to achieve the effects of a lump-sum tax (ibid., pp.53-8) and the discretion that the division management was permitted in the allocation of any earnings in excess of the assigned profit goal (ibid., pp.26-8). In both respects, the behaviour observed is readily accommodated by the managerial model but it is not easily explained by the profit-maximizing hypothesis. In addition, the business literature abounds with descriptions of behaviour that generally conforms to those cited above.[20]

The detail revealed by the field studies, like the relationships found from the principal firm analyses, suggests that in order to explain and predict what appears to be a non-trivial range of business behaviour, it may be necessary to make managerial objectives an integral part of the analysis. To treat them otherwise is to require *ad hoc* explanations for behaviour which, broadly conceived, may be entirely rational and hence subject to systematic analysis and routine explanation.

III. APPLICATION TO REGULATED INDUSTRIES

Armen Alchian and Ruben Kessel (1962) have argued that the presence of a regulatory constraint in the form of a maximum allowable rate of return tends to encourage expenditures on emoluments and other items that yield managerial satisfactions. That is, if above-normal profits cannot be long continued and if super-normal profits will almost certainly invite the early attention of the regulatory commissions, the management of a regulated firm has an incentive to hold profits at or below some 'safe' level by absorbing profits through expanding satisfaction-producing expenses. Alchian and Kessel argue that the behaviour of these firms is best analysed by substituting a general preference function for profits.

Although they do not formalize their argument, the effects they describe appear to be largely in accord with those obtained from the model that we have proposed. Thus, if the utility-maximization model is augmented to include a maximum-profit constraint, it is easily shown that, when the firm encounters the region bounded by the constraint, the profit component in the utility function becomes fixed at this allowable maximum value, and expenditures on staff and emoluments will be increased to assure that this condition is not violated (Williamson, 1963). This is precisely the behaviour they describe. Rather than generalize their argument, however, they restrict the application of their analysis to regulated industries (or others similarly confronted by a maximum profits constraint—such as firms facing potential antitrust action). In all other circumstances, they claim, competition in the product market or competition in the capital market will remove any opportunities for such non-profit behaviour (Alchian and Kessel, 1962, p.160).

The position that competition in the product market will render impotent any tendencies to promote non-profit expenditures is quite unassailable. The mechanism of natural selection enforces conformance to the profit-maximizing norm. However, their belief that, in the absence of competition in the product market, the capital market will assign monopoly powers 'to those who can use them most profitably' (ibid., p.160) lacks an equally efficacious enforcement mechanism. It requires that effective control of monopoly power reside with the stockholders and that this be transferable through financial (capital market) rather than by political (managerial) processes. It has been widely recognized, however, and it has been the force of our argument and evidence above, that the management and not the stockholders are in effective control of the monopoly power in the business firm,[21] and the transference mechanism is one of executive ascension rather than financial exchange. Subject to loose performance constraints imposed by the capital market (both the stockholders and the firm's creditors), the management is largely free to exercise the monopoly power that the firm possesses at its own discretion. Thus, while we fully agree with the Alchian–Kessel discussion on non-pecuniary motives and their suggestion that profits be replaced by a general preference function, we would suggest that regulated industries are merely a special case of the general case where competition in the product market—for reasons of concentration, conglomerate bigness, or barriers to entry—is weak.

IV. CONCLUSIONS

Based on the twin assumptions of self-interest and rational behaviour, a general approach for introducing managerial objectives into a theory of the firm has been suggested. The notion of expense preference constitutes a critical part of the argument. It provides the essential connection for relating managerial objectives to operating behaviour.

In addition to the comparative statics properties that were investigated, the managerial model also provides identical qualitative responses to those of the profit-maximizing model with respect to a sales tax (of either the specific or *ad valorem* variety). Thus the utility maximization hypothesis preserves the main theorems of the profit-maximization hypothesis with respect to shifts in demand and application of a sales tax. Indeed, since there is little dispute concerning the general validity of these implications of the classical theory, it would be distressing to have the managerial model predict differently. However, when it comes to matters where the qualitative implications of the profit-maximizing model have been somewhat suspect, namely the effects of a profits tax and a lump-sum tax, the managerial model registers responses that contradict the classical theory.

The evidence presented is clearly suggestive rather than definitive. Such as it is, it generally supports the implications of the utility-maximization approach. Although it is not strong enough to provide a discrimination between the utility and profit-maximizing theories, it does suggest that either firms are operated as indicated by the managerial model, or if 'actual' profits are maximized, that reported profits are reduced by absorbing some fraction of actual profits in executive salaries and possibly in perquisites of a variety of sorts. This raises a serious question whether studies of monopoly power based on reported profits provide an accurate estimate of the effects of monopoly. It is possible that a non-negligible part of true monopoly profits is absorbed internally.[22]

If subsequent results confirm the present findings concerning the effects of internal representation on the board of directors on executive compensation and dividend policy, the case for an independent board becomes much more compelling. Although Gordon has already argued this position persuasively (1961, pp.343-51), the reasoning has lacked empirical support and there is little indication that his views have been heeded.

A continuing investigation of the effect of discretion on managerial behaviour would appear to be warranted. Indeed, we could not agree more with Becker's view (1962, p.179) that the economist *can* provide non-pecuniary motives with economic content and that 'progress in this field has been hindered not so much by an intractable concept as by the economist's reluctance to take the concept seriously'.

NOTES

1. For an argument that monopoly distortions are not great, see Harberger (1954) and David Schwartzman (1959).
2. The material appearing in this and subsequent sections is developed in more detail in my unpublished doctoral dissertation, 'The Economics of Discretionary Behaviour: Managerial Objectives in a Theory of the Firm' (Carnegie Institute of Technology, 1963). The initial version of the model, which has since been modified, appears in Williamson, 1963.
3. In addition to the factors listed, Barnard and Simon also include expansion as one of the firm's objectives. Indeed Baumol (1962) suggested that the firm is operated so as to maximize the rate of growth of sales (pp.1085-7), which is the dynamic counterpart of his static sales-maximization hypothesis (1959) and preserves the main theorems of his earlier model (1962, p.1087). Although 'expansion' objectives also enter into the model that we propose, it is a somewhat selective variety of expansion that will occur—namely, expansion of those types of activities that most contribute to the satisfaction of the management—rather than a generalized expansion of the entire scale of the firm. Whether this leads to a more fruitful construction is an empirical question and can scarcely be determined on *a priori* grounds. The preliminary evidence that is examined in section II below appears to support the proposition that preferences towards specific varieties of expenses exist (rather than a generalized preference for expansion *per se*), but this is essentially an open question.
4. As has been observed among organization theorists, 'the modern organization is a prolific generator of anxiety and insecurity' [p.24]. This insecurity is partly due to uncertainty with respect to the survival of the organization as a whole and, more important (and more immediately relevant to its individual members), of the parts with which the individuals identify. Attempts to reduce this condition can be expected; indeed, the direction these efforts will take can be anticipated. If the surest guarantee of the survival of the individual parts appears to be size, efforts to expand the separate staff functions can safely be predicted.

   That staff contributes to power, status and prestige should be self-evident. This is true within the organization as well as in the manager's business and social relationships outside the firm. The vast influence that executives in large industrial organisations enjoy arises much more from the perceived control over resources that they possess than from the personal wealth which they have attained.

The 'professional' inducement to expand staff arises from the typical view that a progressive staff is one that is continuously providing more and better service. An aggressive staff will therefore be looking for ways to expand. Although in choosing directions for expansion the relative contribution to productivity will be considered, the absolute effect on profits may be neglected. As long as the organization is able to satisfy its performance requirements, there is a predisposition to extend programme beyond the point where marginal costs equal marginal benefits. The incentive to increase staff, having both natural and legitimate elements, is exceptionally difficult to resist.

5. Historically, whenever stockholder discontent has been rampant, management compensation has been a favourite target (Gordon, 1961, p.164). Likewise in wage negotiations, unions often make a point of executive salary levels. Emoluments, being much less visible, are less readily attacked.

6. Although this is a convenience, it is by no means a necessity. An inequality-constrained maximization could be handled by making use of the Kuhn–Tucker theorem (1951).

7. In these expressions, U_1 is the first partial of the utility function with respect to S, U_2 is the first partial with respect to M, and U_3 is the first partial with respect to $\pi_R - \pi_0 - T$.

8. The procedure we use for obtaining the comparative statics responses is described in Samuelson (1958, pp.12-14).

9. Only when the firm is pressed very hard to satisfy its minimum-profits constraint is a reversal apt to occur.

10. Over the entire horizon, however, the marginal value product of staff equals its marginal cost.

11. Although the sample is a purposive rather than a random sample, the results probably generalize to a somewhat larger population. Based on the *1962 Moody's* listing of major industries (pp.a-16, a-17) 24 additional industries would be added to our list of 26 for a total of 50 major industries and, with two 'principal firms' in each, 100 principal firms.

12. Previous studies of executive compensation have used the total revenue of the firm for this purpose (Roberts, 1950; McGuire *et al*, 1962). This has the advantage of minimizing errors of measurement that arise from differences in accounting practice but is probably not as good as proxy for 'staff' as is general administrative and selling expense. Sales are defective for two reasons. For one thing, they reflect activity at levels below the management hierarchy whereas the size effect would be expected to act largely within the hierarchy (Simon, 1957). Secondly, inter-firm comparisons are complicated by differences in vertical integration policies. As a matter of curiosity, regressions replacing general administrative and selling expense by sales were run—with uniformly adverse results. The objections to using general administrative and selling expense as a proxy for hierarchial expense are largely related to differences in accounting practice among firms. However, the components of general administrative and selling expense very nearly give us a measure of the level of staff activity in the firm (for a list of the functions usually included see Vance (1952, chs 17 and 18). Amounts charged to these accounts are, for the most part, current costs, and hence

ambiguities arising from the use of historical costs are reduced.

13. Alternatively, the composition of the board variable might be interpreted as reflecting the *joint* effects of management tastes and stockholder diffusion. What is really needed, however, are sharper measures that reflect each of these effects separately.

14. U_i includes the effects of special abilities (the Z variable mentioned above), the omitted stockholder-diffusion variable, numbers of years the top executive has held that position, and other neglected factors.

15. The number of observations for each of the years was 26 in 1953, 30 in 1957 and 25 in 1961. Inability to use all 52 of the firms studied (as in the second set of tests reported here) was largely due to the lack of estimates on the condition of entry for many of the industries. The sources of the data were as follows:

    Executive compensation: as a matter of law, publicly-held corporations are required to report executive compensation to the Securities and Exchange Commission. Although these data are a matter of public record, they are not readily available. *Business Week*, however, annually publishes executive compensation figures for a group of principal firms. It was from this source that the data on compensations were obtained.

    General administrative and selling expense and composition of the board: both were obtained from *Moody's Industrials* (supplemented occasionally by other sources when the listing of officers in *Moody's* was incomplete).

    Concentration ratios: data on concentration for 1953 were developed from the 1954 concentration ratios for the four largest firms reported in *Concentration in American Industry* (Washington, DC, 1957). Concentration data for 1957 and 1961 were developed from the 1958 concentration ratios for the four largest firms reported in *Concentration Ratios in Manufacturing Industry 1958,* Part I (Washington, DC, 1962). A weighted average of several of the SIC industry groups was sometimes used to arrive at a concentration ratio for the industries in question. Although such weighting procedures can produce distortions, this is probably not too serious in reasonably narrowly defined industry groups.

    Barrier to entry: Bain's study (1962) provided the estimates of the height of the barrier to entry. In addition, I took the liberty of classifying textiles as an industry with a low-entry barrier since Bain did not include textiles in his analysis, but there is general agreement that the industry has a low-entry barrier. A dummy variable which took on the value 1 (ln 1 = 0) when the barrier to entry was low and e (ln e = 1) when the barrier was high or substantial was used in the regressions. Two dummy variables to represent the substantial and high-entry conditions separately were also tried. Although one might suppose that the parameter for the high-barrier dummy would exceed that of the substantial-barrier dummy, the results were somewhat mixed. As I have suggested elsewhere (Williamson, 1963), however, the principal difference between a substantial and high barrier may be that in the former case the firm expands selling expense beyond its optimal level in order to discourage entry, with the result that the effective condition of entry is the same in substantial- and high-barrier industries. The question requires additional empirical investigation.

16. The tests are one-tailed tests, which are appropriate since the hypothesis specifies that the signs should be positive (which they are). The standard errors shown are corrected for the finite population correction

$$\left(\frac{N-n}{N}\right)^{1/2},$$

where N is 100 in all years and n is 26, 30 and 25 for 1953, 1957 and 1961 respectively.

Whether the results apply to a larger group than these 100 principal firms remains a subject for subsequent investigation.

17. Neglected variables that may influence the retained earnings policy include liquidity measures (such as the current ratio) times interest earned and other financial variables. Among principal firms in the same industry such measures tend to display substantial stability.

18. Since the estimates are sensitive to extreme values of retained earnings (values of $R_{ik} > 0.95$, or < 0.05), and since such extreme values ordinarily represent a transitory condition, these extreme values were removed in making the estimates. Thus the estimated values of β_4 apply to the range of retained earnings between 5 and 95 per cent.

Actually, there is little theoretical reason for including the product market variables in the retained earnings regression. They are included primarily for the purpose of indicating how variables common to both firms can be eliminated by using the ratio device. It is of some interest to note, however, that the estimate of β_4 obtained using only those industries with a high concentration ratio (>50), exceeds that obtained from industries with a low concentration ratio (≤50) in all three years.

19. In addition to the quantity of funds invested and diminishing rate of return effect, there may also be political influences to consider (Cyert and March, 1963). As the amount of available resources increases, the importance of political relative to economic criteria will tend to increase. Any such shift towards political considerations naturally has an adverse effect on the rate of return on investment.

20. For surveys on such behaviour, see Thompson (1958), Friedman (1961) and *Wall Street Journal* (1963).

21. Mason (1960, p.4), for example, takes the position that 'almost everyone now agrees that in the large corporation the owner is, in general, a passive recipient; that typically control is in the hands of management; and the management normally selects its own replacements'. See also Rostow (1960) and Gordon (1961, pp.vi-x).

22. The results obtained by Becker in his study (1957) of the effects of monopoly on discrimination also support this proposition.

REFERENCES

Alchian, A.A. and Kessel, R.A., 'Competition, Monopoly, and the Pursuit of Pecuniary Gain', in *Aspects of Labor Economics*. Princeton, N.J.: 1962.

Bain, J.S., *Barriers to New Competition*. Cambridge, Mass.: 1962.

Baker, J.C., *Executive Salaries and Bonus Plans*. New York: 1938.

Barnard, C.I., *The Functions of the Executive*. Cambridge, Mass.: 1962.

Baumol, W.J., *Business Behaviour, Value and Growth*. New York: 1959.

Baumol, W.J., 'On the Theory of Expansion of the Firm', *American Economic Review, December 1962*, **52**, 1078-87.

Becker, G.S., *The Economics of Discrimination*. Chicago: 1957.
Becker, G.S., 'Competition, Monopoly, and the Pursuit of Pecuniary Gain: Comment', in *Aspects of Labor Economics*. Princeton, N.J.: 1962.
Cyert, R.M. and March, J.G., *A Behavioural Theory of the Firm*. Englewood—Cliffs, N.J.: 1963.
Friedman, J.J. 'Top Management Faces the Cost Challenge', *Dun's Review of Modern Industry*, January 1961, 77, 34-6.
Gordon, R.A., *The Investment, Financing and Valuation of the Corporation*. Homewood, Ill.: 1962.
Gordon, R.A., *Business Leadership in the Large Corporation*. Berkeley: 1961.
Harberger, A.C., 'Monopoly and Resource Allocation', *American Economic Review Proceedings*, May 1954, 44, 78-87.
Kaysen, C., 'The Corporation: How Much Power? What Scope?', in Mason (ed.), 1960.
Koontz, H. and O'Donnell, C., *Principles of Management*. New York: 1955.
Kuhn, H.W. and Tucker, C.W., 'Nonlinear Programming', in *Proceedings of the Second Berkeley Symposium on Mathematical Statistics and Probability*. Berkeley: 1951.
McGuire, J.W., Chiu, J.S.Y. and Elbing, A.C., 'Executive Incomes, Sales and Profits', *American Economic Review*, September 1962, 52, 753-61.
Marshall, A., *Industry and Trade*. London: 1932.
Roberts, D.R., *Executive Compensation*. Glencoe, Ill.: 1959.
Rostow, E.V., 'To Whom and for What Ends is Corporate Management Responsible?' in Mason (ed.), 1960.
Samuelson, P.A., *Foundations of Economics*. Cambridge.: 1958.
Schwartzman, D., 'The Effect of Monopoly on Price', *Journal of Political Economy*, August 1959, 67, 352-62.
Scott, M. Fg., 'Relative Share Prices and Yields', *Oxford Economic Papers*, N.S., October 1962, 14, 218-50.
Simon, H.A., 'The Compensation of Executives', *Sociometry*, March 1957, 20, 32-35.
Simon, H.A., *Administrative Behaviour*. New York: 1961.
Simon, H.A., 'New Developments in the Theory of the Firm', *American Economic Review*, May 1962, 52, 1-15.
Stigler, G.J., 'The Statistics of Monopoly and Merger', *Journal of Political Economy*, February 1956, 64, 33-40.
Thompson, E.T., 'The Cost of Cutting Urge', *Fortune*, May 1958, 57, 118-21.
Thompson, V.A., *Modern Organization*. New York: 1961.
Vance, L.L., *Theory and Technique of Cost Accounting*. Brooklyn: 1952.
Wall Street Journal, 'White Collar Cutback', January 3, 1963, p.1.
Williamson, O.E., 'Managerial Behaviour: The Evidence from the Field Studies', *Behavioural Theory of the Firm Working Paper No. 38*. Pittsburgh: 1962.
Williamson, O.E., 'A Model of Rational Managerial Behaviour', in Cyert and March 1963.
Williamson, O.E., 'Selling Expense as a Barrier to Entry' *Quarterly Journal of Economics*, February 1963, 77, 112-28.

3. Hierarchical Control and Optimum Firm Size*

There is a great deal of evidence that almost all organizational structures tend to produce false images in the decision-maker, and that the larger and more authoritarian the organization, the better the chance that its top decision-makers will be operating in purely imaginary worlds. This perhaps is the most fundamental reason for supposing that there are ultimately diminishing returns to scale.[1]

Although we are quite in agreement with Professor Boulding's judgment that problems of transmitting accurate images across successive levels in a hierarchical organization are fundamentally responsible for diminishing returns to scale, there is less than unanimity on this issue. Indeed, it has long been disputed whether or in what ways the management factor is responsible for a limitation to firm size. Although descriptive treatments of this question have been numerous, these have generally been too imprecise to permit testable implications to be derived. The present analysis attempts a partial remedy for this condition by embedding in a formal model the control loss features of hierarchical organization that have recently been advanced in the bureaucratic theory literature. The background to this discussion of control loss as a limitation to firm size is reviewed in section I. A simple model possessing basic control loss attributes is developed and its properties derived in section II. In section III, we extend and elaborate the model, developing additional implications and indicating some of the problems to expect in empirical testing. The conclusions are given in section IV.

I. BACKGROUND TO THE ANALYSIS

That the question of the optimum size firm presented a serious dilemma for the theory of the firm was noted by Knight in 1933. Thus, he observed:

---

* Research on this paper was supported by a grant to the author from the National Science Foundation and from the Lilly Foundation grant to the University of California, Los Angeles, for the study of the economics of property rights.

The relation between efficiency and size is one of the most serious problems of theory, being in contrast with the relation for a plant, largely a matter of personality and historical accident rather than of intelligible general principles. But this question is peculiarly vital because the possibility of monopoly gain offers a powerful incentive to *continuous and unlimited* expansion of the firm, which force must be offset by some equally powerful one making for decreased efficiency [in the production of money income] with growth in size, if even boundary competition is to exist. (Knight, 1965, p.xxiii).

Within a year, Robinson (1934, 1962) proposed what we believe to be a substantially correct answer, namely, that problems of coordination imposed a static limitation to firm size; and Coase in his classic 1937 article on 'The Nature of the Firm' generally supports this position (1952, pp.340-1). Kaldor (1934), however, argued that problems of coordination vanished under truly static conditions, and hence only declining product demand curves or rising factor supply curves could be responsible for a static limitation to firm size. Only in the context of firm dynamics did coordination problems, in his view, constitute a genuine limitation to firm size. But, as Robinson was quick to point out, Kaldor's argument rested on his peculiar specification of the static condition as one in which the control problem is defined to be absent. This approach to the economics of the firm he found quite uninstructive for, as he pungently noted, 'In Mr. Kaldor's long period we shall not only be dead but in Nirvana, and the economics of Nirvana . . . is surely the most fruitless of sciences' (Robinson, 1934, p.250).

The argument remained there[2] until Ross (1952-53, p.148), in a sweeping attack on the economic treatments of this question, took the position that this whole literature bordered on the irrelevant for its failure to incorporate 'certain aspects of the theory of organization and management'. Recasting the problem in what he regarded as suitable organizational terms, he concluded that 'by appropriate measures of decentralization and control the firm may expand without incurring increasing costs of coordination over a range sufficiently wide to cover all possible cases within the limits imposed by scarcity of resources' (p.154). Starbuck imputes similar views to Andrews, albeit incorrectly,[3] and, in apparent sympathy with Ross, likewise regards the treatment by economists of these issues as entirely too narrow and probably self-serving (Starbuck, 1964, p.343).

Penrose also finds this literature unsatisfactory, observing that 'whether managerial diseconomies will cause long-run increasing costs [requires that] management . . . be treated as a "fixed factor" and the nature of the "fixity" must be identified with respect to the nature of the managerial task of "coordinating". *This identification has never been satisfactorily accomplished*' (Penrose, 1959, p.12 emphasis added). She continues to regard the issue as a vital one, however, but argues with Kaldor that it is the dynamics, not the statics, of coordination that give rise to a limitation to firm size. In their view, expansion is contingent on knowledgeable planning and skilful coordination where these are a function of internal experience. Since experience is available in restricted supply, the rate of growth is thereby necessarily restricted. Variations on this argument have since been developed, and some have come to regard the growth rate as the only limitation to firm size.[4]

It is unfortunate (although understandable) that the static limitation argument should continue to be misunderstood in this way. The difficulty is probably traceable to the distinction between truly static and quasi-static conditions. Those who reject the static limitation argument tend to adopt the former position, while those who advocate it take the latter. This is implicit in the Kaldor–Robinson dispute cited above. Differences of this sort are especially difficult to resolve, but an effort to explicate the quasi-static position may nevertheless be useful.

The problem can be stated in terms of deterministic versus stochastic equilibrium. A steady state is reached in each. But whereas in the former the data are unchanging, in the latter the firm is required to adapt to circumstances which are predictable in the sense that although they occur with stochastic regularity, precise advance knowledge of them is unavailable. Although the deterministic condition provides circumstances in which the usual management functions can be progressively eliminated through the refinement of operations, this is the world of Kaldor's Nirvana and has limited relevance for an understanding of business behaviour. Instead, customers come and go, manufacturing operations break down, distribution systems malfunction, labour and materials procurement are subject to the usual vagaries, all with stochastic regularity, not to mention minor shifts in demand and similar disturbing influences of a transitory nature. Throughout all of this, the management of the firm is required to adapt to the new circumstances: request the relevant data, process the information supplied, and provide the appropriate instructions. Coordination in these circumstances is thus essential. If, simultaneously, a general expansion of operations accompanies these quasi-static adjustments, additional direction would be required. But in no sense is growth a necessary condition for the coordinating function to exist. We, therefore, take the position that bounded rationality[5] imposes a (quasi)-static limitation to firm size through the mechanism of control loss and that growth considerations act mainly to intensify this underlying condition.

In resorting to the notion of bounded rationality, we ally ourselves with Ross in his claim that economic arguments regarding a static limitation to firm size have not taken adequately into account the contributions which organization theory has made to this problem. But rather than resort to the normative literature of administrative management theory as Ross does, we turn instead to the positive theories of bureaucratic behaviour. The former, as March and Simon (1958, pp.22-32) have aptly observed, is a generally vacuous literature in which most of the interesting problems of organizational behaviour are defined away. Although Ross's instincts were correct, his preference for a normative rather than a positive theory put him on the wrong trail and inevitably led to untestable conclusions of the sort cited above.

The aspect of bureaucratic theory that we regard as particularly relevant for studying the question of a static limitation to firm size is what we shall refer to as the 'control loss' phenomenon. It is illustrated daily in the rumour-transmission process and was studied intensively by Bartlett (1932) in his experimental studies of serial reproduction. His experiments involved the oral transmission of descriptive and argumentative passages through a chain of serially linked individuals. Bartlett concludes from a number of such studies that:

It is now perfectly clear that serial reproduction normally brings about startling and radical alterations in the material dealt with. Epithets are changed into their opposites; incidents and events are transposed; names and numbers rarely survive intact for more than a few reproductions; opinions and conclusions are reversed—nearly every possible variation seems as if it can take place, even in a relatively short series. At the same time the subjects may be very well satisfied with their efforts, believing themselves to have passed on all important features with little or no change, and merely, perhaps to have omitted unessential matters. (Bartlett, 1932, p.175).

Bartlett (ibid., pp.180-1) illustrated this graphically with a line-drawing of an owl which—when redrawn successively by eighteen individuals, each sketch based on its immediate predecessor—ended up as a recognizable cat; and the further from the initial drawing one moved, the greater the distortion experienced. The reliance of hierarchical organizations on serial reproduction for their functioning thus exposes them to what may become serious distortions in transmission.

Although this phenomenon is widely experienced, it was not generally regarded as having special theoretical significance until Tullock (1965, pp.142-93) argued that not only was authority leakage possible in a large government bureau, but it was predictable and could be expressed as an increasing function of size. Downs (1966) has since elaborated the argument and summarized it in his 'law of diminishing control: *The larger any organization becomes, the weaker is the control over its actions exercised by those at the top*' (1966, p.109). The cumulative loss of control as instructions and information are transmitted across successive hierarchical levels is responsible for this result.

Thus, assuming that economies of specialization have been exhausted and that superiors are normally more competent than subordinates, a quality–quantity trade-off necessarily exists in every decision to expand. It arises for two reasons, both of which are related to the distance of the top executive from the locus of productive activity. First, expansion of the organization (adding an additional hierarchical level) removes the superior further from the basic data that affect operating conditions; information regarding those conditions must now be transmitted across an additional hierarchical level which exposes the data to an additional serial reproduction operation with its attendant losses. Furthermore, the top executive or peak coordinator (to use Papandreou's term (1952, p.204) cannot have all the information that he had before the expansion plus the information now generated by the new parts (assuming that he was fully employed initially). Thus, he can acquire additional information only by sacrificing some of the detail provided to him previously. Put differently, he trades off breadth for depth in undertaking the expansion; he has more resources under his control, but the quality (serial reproduction loss) and the quantity (bounded capacity constraint) of his information are both less with respect to the deployment of each resource unit. In a similar way, being further removed from the operating situation and having more subordinates means that his instructions to each are less detailed and are passed across an additional hierarchical level. For precisely the same reasons, therefore, the behaviour of the operating units will scarcely correspond as closely to his objectives as it did prior to the expansion. Taken together, this loss in the quality of the data provided to the peak coordinator and in the quality of the instructions supplied to the operating units made necessary by the expansion will be referred to as 'control loss'. It will exist even if the objectives of the subordinates are perfectly consonant with those of their superiors and, *a fortiori*, when subordinate objectives are dissonant.

There are, of course, anti-distortion control devices that the leadership has access to, and Downs (1966, pp.78-90) has examined a number of them. These include redundancy, external data checks, creation of overlapping areas of responsibility, counter-biases, reorganization so as to keep the hierarchy flat, coding, and so on. The problem with all of these is that they are rarely available at zero cost and invariably experience diminishing returns. Hence, eventually, increasing size encounters control loss. Our objective here is to show how this argument, initially developed in the context of the behaviour of government bureaux, has relevance for the static limitation to firm size issue.[6]

II. THE BASIC MODEL

Consider a hierarchically-organized business firm with the following characteristics: (1) only employees at the lowest hierarchical level do manual labour; the work done by employees at higher levels is entirely administrative (planning, forecasting, supervising, accounting, and so on); (2) output is a constant proportion of productive input; (3) the wage paid to employees at the lowest level is w_0; (4) each superior is paid β ($\beta>1$) times as much as each of his immediate subordinates; (5) the span of control (the number of employees a supervisor can handle effectively) is a constant s ($s>1$) across every hierarchical level; (6) product and factor price are parameters; (7) all non-wage variable costs are a constant proportion of output; (8) only the fraction $\bar{\alpha}$ ($0<\bar{\alpha}<1$) of the intentions of a superior are effectively satisfied by a subordinate; and (9) control loss is strictly cumulative (there is no systematic compensation) across successive hierarchical levels.

The first assumption can be restated as: there are no working foremen.[7] This seems quite reasonable and permits us to simplify the analysis of the relation of output to input. Taken together with assumption (2), which assures that there are no economies of specialization in production (in the relevant range), we are able to express output as a constant proportion of productive input. The distinction between direct labour input and productive labour input should be emphasized. The former refers to the total labour input at the lowest hierarchical level. The latter is that part of the direct labour input which yields productive results. The latter is smaller than the former not by reason of labour inefficiencies but because of the cumulative control loss in the transmission of data and instructions across successive hierarchical levels.

Assumption (3) is innocuous; assumption (4) is plausible and appears to correspond with the facts. This is Simon's conclusion in his study (1957b) of the theory and practices of executive compensation. The constant β condition is also reported by a US Department of Labor study (1964, p.8) of salary structures in the large firm, which found that 'the relationship maintained between salary rates for successive grades was more commonly *a uniform percentage spread* between grades than a widening percentage spread' (emphasis added). An independent check of this hypothesis is also possible from the data on executive compensation included in the Annual Report of the General Motors Corporation from 1934 to 1942. This is developed in Appendix A below.

Assumption (5), that the span of control is constant across levels, is also employed in the wage model tested in Appendix A, although the cumulative distribution relation tested does not uniquely imply this relation.[8] Taken in conjunction with the Department of Labor findings on β, however, the fits reported in Appendix A also lend support to the constant span of control assumption. We nevertheless show in section III where this assumption can be relaxed somewhat and the basic results preserved.

Assumption (6) permits us to treat prices in the product and factor markets as parameters. As we shall show, this can also be relaxed without affecting the qualitative character of our results. Assumption (7) is not critical, but permits us a modest simplification. Assumptions (8) and (9) are merely restatements of the earlier argument. They are responsible for the control loss attributes of the model. Since much of the exposition in subsequent parts of the paper will be explicitly concerned with them, we shall say no more about them here.

For the purposes of developing a model around these assumptions, let:

s = span of control
$\bar{\alpha}$ = fraction of work done by a subordinate that contributes to objectives of his superior ($0 < \bar{\alpha} < 1$); it is thus a compliance parameter
N_i = number of employees at the ith hierarchical level = s^{i-l}
n = number of hierarchical levels (the decision variable)
P = price of output
w_0 = wage of production workers
w_i = wage of employees at ith hierarchical level
$\quad = w_0\beta^{n-1}(\beta > 1)$
r = non-wage variable cost per unit output
Q = output
$\quad = \theta(\bar{\alpha}s)^{n-1}$
R = total revenue
$\quad = PQ$
C = total variable cost
$\quad = \Sigma_{i=1}^{n}w_iN_i + rQ$

Without loss of generality, we assume that $\theta = 1$. The objective is to find the value of n (the number of hierarchical levels, and hence the size of the firm) so as to maximize net revenue. This is given by:

$$R - C = PQ - \Sigma_{i=1}^{n} w_iN_i - rQ = P(\bar{\alpha}s)^{n-1} - \Sigma_{i=1}^{n} w_0\beta^{n-i}s^{i-1} - r(\bar{\alpha}s)^{n-1}$$

$$(1)$$

now:

$$\Sigma_{i=1}^{n} w_0\beta^{n-i} s^{i-1} = w_0\left(\frac{\beta^n}{s}\right)\Sigma_{i=1}^{n}\left(\frac{s}{\beta}\right)^i$$

where:

$$\Sigma_{i=1}^{n} \left(\frac{s}{\beta}\right)^{i} = \frac{\left(\frac{s}{\beta}\right)^{n+1} - \left(\frac{s}{\beta}\right)}{\frac{s}{\beta} - 1} \simeq \frac{s^{n+1}}{(s-\beta)\beta^{n}}$$

Thus, we have:

$$R - C = P\,(\bar{\alpha}s)^{n-1} - w_0\,\frac{s_n}{s-\beta} - r\,(\bar{\alpha}s)^{n-1}. \qquad (1')$$

Differentiating this expression with respect to n and setting equal to zero (and letting ln denote natural logarithm), we obtain as the optimal value for n:

$$n^* = 1 + \frac{1}{ln\bar{\alpha}}\left[ln\frac{w_0}{P-r} + ln\frac{s}{s-\beta} + ln\left(\frac{ln\,s}{ln(\bar{\alpha}s)}\right)\right]. \qquad (2)$$

The values of $\bar{\alpha}$ and $w_0/(P-r)$ in this expression are both between zero and unity, while $\beta < s$ and $\bar{\alpha}s > 1$. The condition $\beta < s$ must hold for the approximating relation to apply and is supported by the data.[9] The condition $\bar{\alpha}s > 1$ must hold if there is to be any incentive to hire employees. Not merely diminishing but negative returns would exist were $\bar{\alpha}s < 1$. Since $ln\bar{\alpha} < 0$, the expression in brackets must be negative, a condition which is virtually assured by the stipulation that the firm earn positive profits.[10] Assuming that the appropriate bounds and inequality conditions are satisfied, the following *ceteris paribus* conditions are obtained from the model:

(a) Optimal n increases as the degree of compliance with supervisor objectives ($\bar{\alpha}$) increases.
(b) Optimal n is infinite if there is no loss of intention ($\bar{\alpha}=1$) between successive hierarchical levels. Only a declining product demand curve or rising labour supply curve could impose a (static) limit on firm size in such circumstances.
(c) Optimal n decreases as the ratio of the basic wage to the net price over non-wage variable costs ($w_0/P-r$) increases. Thus, the optimum size for an organization will be relatively small and the optimum shape relatively flat in labour-intensive industries.
(d) Optimal n increases as the span of control (s) increases. Intuition would have led us to expect that flatter organizations (fewer hierarchical levels) would be associated with wider spans of control, but obviously this is not the case.[11]

(e) Optimal n decreases as the wage multiple between levels (β) increases.

Plausible values for $\bar{\alpha}$ can be obtained by substituting estimated values for each of the parameters into equation (2). This is done below. In addition, propositions (c), (d) and (e) can be tested empirically by observing that total employment is given by:

$$N^* = \Sigma_{i=1}^{n^*} N_i = \Sigma_{i=1}^{n^*} s^{i-1} \tag{3}$$

The sum of this series is given by:

$$N^* = \frac{s^{n^*}-1}{s-1} \simeq \frac{s^{n^*}}{s-1}. \tag{4}$$

Taking the natural logarithm and substituting the value of optional n^* given by equation (2), we have:

$$\ln N^* \simeq \ln\left(\frac{1}{s-1}\right) +$$
$$\ln s \left\{1 + \frac{1}{\ln\bar{\alpha}}\left[\ln\frac{w_0}{P-r} + \ln\frac{s}{s-\beta} + \ln\left(\frac{\ln s}{\ln(\bar{\alpha}s)}\right)\right]\right\}. \tag{5}$$

Expressing the optimal size firm in this way avoids the necessity of collecting data by hierarchical levels.

Employment among the 500 largest industrials in the United States generally is between 1000 and 100,000 employees. For values of s between 5 and 10, which is the normal range (Koontz and O'Donnell, 1955, p.88), this implies an optimal n of between 4 and 7. If all of our assumptions were satisfied, if there were no additional factors (risk, growth and so on) acting as limitations to firm size, and for values of β in the range of 1.3 to 1.6 and $w_0/P-r$ in the range $\frac{1}{3}$ to $\frac{2}{3}$, the implied value of $\bar{\alpha}$ is in the neighbourhood of 0.90. Since other factors are likely to act as limitations to some extent, the true value of $\bar{\alpha}$ may generally be higher than this. It is our contention, however, for the reasons given above, that values of $\bar{\alpha}$ less than unity are typical and that the cumulative effects of control loss are fundamentally responsible for limitations to firm size.

III. EXTENSIONS

Although the basic model developed in the preceding section makes evident the critical importance of control loss as a static limitation to firm size in a way which is more precise than was heretofore available and thus both clarifies the issues and expresses them in a potentially testable form, it is obviously a highly special model and may be properly regarded with scepticism for that reason. We attempt in this section to generalize the analysis in such a way as to make clear its wider applicability. First, the possibility of introducing economies of scale, either through the specialization of labour or in the non-labour inputs, to offset diseconomies due to control loss is examined. Second, we develop the properties of a model in which the utility function of the firm includes both profits and hierarchical expense. Next, imperfections in the product market are permitted. Fourth, we allow for the possibility of variations in the span of control at the production level. Finally, the compliance parameter ($\bar{\alpha}$) is expressed as a function of the span of control.

1. Economies of scale

We assume above that economies of scale due to specialization of labour or in the non-labour inputs have been exhausted so that diseconomies of scale due to control loss give rise to increasing average cost conditions in the range of output under consideration. These assumptions can be made more precise here. For this purpose, we express the parameter θ which converts input to output as a function of n. Over the range where economies of specialization exist $\partial\theta/\partial n > 0$, whereas when these have been exhausted $\partial\theta/\partial n = 0$. Thus, average cost can be expressed as:

$$AC = w_0 \frac{s}{s-\beta} \cdot \frac{1}{\theta\bar{\alpha}^{n-1}} - r \qquad (6)$$

and AC will decrease so long as $\partial\theta/\partial n > \theta ln\bar{\alpha}$. When these two are in balance, constant returns to the labour input will prevail, but as $\partial\theta/\partial n$ declines (and eventually goes to zero), diminishing returns due to control loss will set in.

In a similar way, the non-wage variable cost per unit output parameter, r, can be expressed as a function of output, where $\partial r/\partial Q < 0$ initially, but eventually $\partial r/\partial Q = 0$. Thus, average costs will at first decline for this reason as well, but the cumulative effects of control loss will ultimately dominate and the average cost curve will rise. Implicitly, the model in section II assumes that both $\partial\theta/\partial n$ and $\partial r/\partial Q$ are zero, so that economies with respect to both labour and non-labour inputs are assumed to be exhausted in the relevant range. Actually, this is somewhat stronger than is necessary for control loss to impose a limitation to firm size; this result would obtain under the assumptions that $\partial^2\theta/\partial n^2 < 0$ and $\partial^2 r/\partial Q^2 > 0$. This latter, however, would lead only to changes in degree and not in kind from those derived above.

2. A utility-maximizing version

As we have argued elsewhere, a shift from a profit-maximizing to a utility-maximizing assumption seems appropriate where large firm size is involved, since the characteristics of the opportunity set that the management has access to progressively favour non-profit objectives as size increases. In addition, the bureaucratic operations of a large firm may be less attractive to strictly profit-oriented managers than to managers who have broader objectives. Alternatively, if profit-directed managers are typically less adept politicians, they may simply be outmanoeuvred and displaced in circumstances which encourage or permit the pursuit of non-profit goals. In any case, only modest changes in the above model are necessary to transform it to a utility-maximizing form of the sort that we have investigated previously (Williamson, 1964). For this purpose, we assume that the management has a utility function that includes both staff (or hierarchical expense) and profits as principal components. Designating staff expense as H and treating this as all wage expense above the operating level, we have:

$$H=\Sigma_{i=1}^{n-1} w_0\beta^{n-i} s^{i-1}\simeq w_0\frac{\beta s^{n-1}}{s-\beta}. \tag{7}$$

We represent the utility function by U and, given our assumption that staff and profits are the principal components, the objective becomes: maximize

$$U=U(\mathrm{H},\mathrm{R}-C)=U\left[w_0\frac{\beta s^{n-1}}{s-\beta},\ P(\bar{\alpha}s)^{n-1}-w_0\frac{s^n}{s-\beta}-r(\bar{\alpha}s)^{n-1}\right]. \tag{8}$$

Treating n as the only decision variable and all other variables in this expression as parameters, optimal n is now given by:

$$n^*=1+\frac{1}{ln\bar{\alpha}}\left[ln\frac{w_0}{P-r}+ln\ \frac{s-(U_1/U_2)\ \beta}{s-\beta}\ +ln\left(\frac{lns}{ln\bar{\alpha}s}\right)\right]. \tag{9}$$

Comparing this expression with that obtained in equation (2), we observe that the only difference is the presence of a $(U_1/U_2)\ \beta$ term in the brackets of equation (9), where U_1 is the first partial of the utility function with respect to staff, and U_2 is the first partial with respect to profits. Obviously, if staff is valued objectively only for the contribution that it makes to profits, U_1 is zero and (9) becomes identical with (2). If, however, the management displays a positive preference for hierarchical expense so that the ratio U_1/U_2 is not zero, the optimal value of n^* in the utility-maximizing organization will be larger than in the corresponding profit-maximizing organization with identical parameters.[12]

The response of n^* to an increase in each of the parameters is identical with that given previously with the exception of β. Whether n^* will increase or decrease in response to an increase in β depends on whether U_1/U_2 is greater than or less than unity respectively.

3. Imperfection in the product market

If product price is not treated as a parameter but instead $P=P(Q)$, $\partial P/\partial Q<0$, we obtain the following expression for optimal n:

$$n^*=1+\frac{1}{ln\bar{\alpha}}\left\{ln\frac{w_0}{P\left(1-\frac{1}{\eta}\right)-r}+ln\frac{s}{s-\beta}+ln\frac{lns}{ln(\bar{\alpha}s)}\right\}, \qquad (10)$$

where η is the elasticity of demand.

Obviously, in a perfect product market, where $\eta=\infty$, (10) is identical with (2). As is to be expected, the value of optimal n decreases as demand becomes more inelastic.

4. Variation in the span of control over operators

It is assumed in the model developed in section II that the span of control is uniform throughout the organization. Although variations in the span of control among the administrative levels of the organization are generally small, this is frequently untrue between the foremen and operatives. Typically, the span of control is larger here and the reasons are quite obvious: tasks tend to be more highly routinized, and thus the need for supervision and coordination are correspondingly attenuated. Letting σ be the span of control between foremen and operatives, total employment of operatives is now given by the product of σ and the number of foremen, where this latter is s^{n-2}. Productive output is thus the product of control loss, $(\bar{\alpha})^{n-1}$, times σs^{n-2} or $\bar{\alpha}\sigma(\bar{\alpha}s)^{n-2}$. The value of optimal n derived from this version of the model is:

$$n^*=1+\frac{1}{ln\bar{\alpha}}\left\{ln\frac{w_0}{P-r}+ln\left(\frac{\sigma+\beta s/s-\beta}{\sigma}\right)+ln\left[\frac{lns}{ln(\bar{\alpha}s)}\right]\right\}. \qquad (11)$$

Again, it is obvious by comparing this expression with equation (2) that when $\sigma=s$ they are identical and that qualitatively the properties are the same. The additional implication that obtains from this model is that as σ increases, optimal n increases. That is, for $\bar\alpha$ unchanged, increasing the span of control between the foremen and operatives leads to a general increase in the number of levels and, consequently, number of employees in the hierarchical organization, a result which is completely in accord with our intuition.

5. Compliance and span of control interaction

The difficulties associated with the selection of an optimum span of control have been noted by Simon as follows:

> The dilemma is this: in a large organization with interrelations between members, a restricted span of control produces excessive red tape . . . . The alternative is to increase the number of persons who are under the command of an officer . . . . But this, too, leads to difficulty, for if an officer is required to supervise too many employees, his control over them is weakened.
>
> Granted, then, that both the increase and decrease in span of control have some undesirable consequences, what is the optimum point? (Simon, 1957a, p.28).

More precisely, the dilemma can be stated in terms of compliance ($\bar\alpha$) and span of control (s) interaction. Whereas the preceding analysis treats the level of compliance ($\bar\alpha$) and the span of control (s) independently, in fact they are intimately related. Increasing the span of control means that while each supervisor has more productive capability responsive to him he has less time to devote to the supervision of each, and hence a loss of control results. For purposes of examining this behaviour, we let:

$$\bar\alpha=f(s), \quad \partial f/\partial s<0. \tag{12}$$

Given that $\bar\alpha$ is a declining function of s as indicated, the question next arises: What is the optimum value of s and how is this related to size of firm? Now output is given by $Q=(\bar\alpha s)^{n-1}$, so that for any particular level of output, say $\bar Q$, choice of n implies a value for s (and, hence, through equation (12), $\bar\alpha$) and conversely.[13] To determine the relation between optimum s and $\bar Q$, we observe that since gross revenue is fixed given the level of output, the optimization problem can be expressed as one of minimizing labour costs subject to constraint. Thus, the objective is:

minimize

$$C_L=w_0\frac{s^n}{s-\beta}$$

subject to

$$\text{(i) } (\bar{\alpha}s)^{n-1}=\bar{Q}$$
$$\text{(ii) } \bar{\alpha}=f(s). \tag{13}$$

The standard technique for studying the behaviour of this system is to formulate it as a Langrangian and perturb the first order conditions with respect to $\bar{Q}$. Unfortunately, the resulting expressions cannot be signed on the basis of the general functional relation $\bar{\alpha}=f(s)$. Assuming, however, that the function is bell-shaped on the right (which intuitively is the correct general configuration), we can replace equation (12) and hence the second constraint by

$$\bar{\alpha}=e^{-ks^2}. \tag{12'}$$

The value of the exponent k in this expression can be interpreted as a goal-consistency parameter. As goal consistency increases, the value of k decreases and $\bar{\alpha}$ increases at every value of s.

The comparative statics responses of n and s (and hence $\bar{\alpha}$) to changes in firm size (as measured by output) and goal inconsistency (k) are shown in Table 3.1.

Table 3.1 Comparative statics responses

Decision variable	Shift parameter	
	Output	Goal inconsistency
	$(d\bar{Q})$	(dk)
Hierarchical level (dn)	+	+
Span of control (ds)	−	−
Control effectiveness $(d\bar{\alpha})$	+	?

The direction of adjustment of any particular decision variable to a displacement of equilibrium by an increase in either of those parameters is found by referring to the row and column entry corresponding to the decision variable–parameter pair.[14]

That the number of hierarchical levels should increase as output increases is not surprising. That the span of control should decrease, however, is less obvious. Moreover, it contradicts what little data there are on this question. Thus, Starbuck (1964, p.375) concludes his systematic survey of the relevant literature bearing on this issue with the observation that the 'administrative span of control ... probably increases with organizational size'. Unless our model can be somehow extended to explain this condition, it calls seriously into question the validity of the control–loss approach to organizational behaviour. Thus, one of the merits of formalizing this argument as we have is that we can go beyond mere plausibility arguments to discover the less obvious properties of the model and address the relevant evidence to them. Appendix B below concerns itself with this dilemma.

That an increase in k (goal inconsistency) leads to a decrease in the span of control and hence increase in n for a fixed-size organization is entirely in accord with our intuition. Indeed, given that control loss is cumulative across hierarchical levels, we would expect that consistency is relatively high (k is low) and thus the span of control large in large organizations. That organizations such as the Catholic Church successfully operate with relatively flat hierarchical structures is surely partly attributable to the high degree of goal consistency that the organization possesses. Selection and training procedures obviously contribute to this result.

High goal consistency is probably also more likely in business firms that are operated as utility-maximizing rather than profit-maximizing concerns, where the utility function of the former results from the goal consensus among the management, whereas the latter represents a constraint that is rarely identical with underlying managerial objectives (Williamson, 1964, pp.32-7, 153-60). It does not follow, therefore, that requiring strict adherence to a profit goal necessarily leads to maximum profits. Contentious discord can be expected to develop in such circumstances which implies high k and may yield low profits. We thus have the paradox that (within limits) the permissive pursuit of non-profit goals may actually lead to the realization of higher profits.

IV. CONCLUSIONS

The proposition that the management factor is responsible for a limitation to firm size has appeared recurrently in the literature. But the arguments have tended to be imprecise, lacked predictive content, and consequently failed to be convincing. The present paper attempts to overcome some of these shortcomings by developing a formal model in which the control loss phenomenon is made central to the analysis. The importance of control loss to an understanding of bureaucratic behaviour in non-market organizations has been noted previously. Our use of this proposition here is based on one of the fundamental tenets of organization theory: namely, virtually all of the interesting bureaucratic behaviour observed to exist in large government bureaucracies finds its counterpart in large non-government bureaucracies as well, and this is particularly true where the phenomenon in question is a result of the bounded rationality attributes of decision-makers. We, therefore, borrow from the bureaucracy literature the proposition that control loss occurs between successive hierarchical levels (and that this tends to be cumulative) and introduce it into a theory of the firm in which neither declining product demand curves nor rising factor supply curves are permitted to impose a static limit on firm size.

For any given span of control (together with a specification of the state of technology, internal experience, etc.) an irreducible minimum degree of control loss results from the simple serial reproduction distortion that occurs in communicating across successive hierarchical levels. If, in addition, goals differ between hierarchical levels, the loss in control can be more extensive.

The strategy of borrowing behavioural assumptions from the organization theory literature and developing the implications of the behaviour observed within the framework of economic analysis would seem to be one which might find application quite generally. Thus, the organization theory approach to problems tends frequently to be rich in behavioural insights but weak analytically, while economics generally and the theory of the firm literature in particular has a highly developed modelling apparatus but has evidenced less resourcefulness in its use of interesting behavioural assumptions. Combining these two research areas so as to secure access to the strengths of each would thus appear to be quite promising. In any case, it is the strategy followed in this paper and, to the extent we have had any success, suggests itself for possible use elsewhere.

APPENDIX A: TEST OF THE WAGE MODEL

Our basic wage hypothesis is that $w_i = w_0 \beta^{n-i}$, where w_0 is the base level salary, n is the number of hierarchical levels, i is the particular level in question, and β is the wage multiple. Unfortunately, the General Motors' data are reported by wage ranges of unequal size rather than by hierarchical levels. It can nevertheless be used to test our hypothesis by developing the cumulative distribution counterpart of our model.

Taking logarithms of this wage relation, we have $\log w_i = \log w_0 + (n-i)\log\beta$. By assumption (5), the total number of employees at level i is $N_i = s^{i-1}$, where s is the span of control. Taking this logarithm, we obtain $\log N_i = (i-1) \log s$. Solving for i in this second logarithmic expression and substituting into the first we obtain:[15]

$$\log N_i = \log b_0 - \frac{\log s}{\log \beta} \log w_i, \text{ or } N_i = b_0 w_i^{-b_1} \tag{A1}$$

where $\log b_0 = (\log s/\log \beta) \cdot [\log w_0 + (n-1) \log \beta]$ and $b_1 = (\log s/\log \beta)$.

We denote by $N(\bar{w})$ the total number of individuals having a wage greater than $\bar{w}$. This is given by:

$$N(\bar{w}) = \int_{\bar{w}}^{\infty} b_0 w^{-b_1} dw = \left(\frac{b_0}{b_1}\right) \bar{w}^{(-b_1+1)} \qquad (A2)$$

or $N(\bar{w}) = a_0 \bar{w}^{-a_1}$ where $a_0 = b_0/b_1$ and $a_1 = -b_1 + 1$. This cumulative form does not require either information about the hierarchical levels or uniform size classes and hence can be applied to the General Motors' (or any similar class of) wage data. Being derived from our wage employment hypotheses, it should produce a good fit to the data if these hypotheses are substantially close approximations. The results are reported in Table A.1.

Table A.1 Wage model fit to General Motors salary data, 1934–42*

	1934	1936	1938	1940	1942
No. Observations	10	11	6	6	6
$\bar{R}^2$	0.940	0.970	0.956	0.907	0.944
Log $\hat{a}_0$	10.022	10.828	10.688	11.859	10.822
	(0.733)	(0.523)	(0.882)	(1.400)	(1.077)
$\hat{a}^1$	−1.904	−2.067	−2.037	−2.297	−2.045
	(0.160)	(0.116)	(0.193)	(0.306)	(0.236)

Note: * Standard errors are shown in parentheses.

As is quickly apparent from inspecting the Table A.1 results, the wage model given by equation (A2) provides an excellent fit to the data. The coefficients of determination adjusted for degrees of freedom all exceed 0.90, and the estimates of the coefficients are both stable over the entire interval and significantly different from zero in every year. Assuming that General Motors' salary schedules are not atypical (and since General Motors is frequently regarded as a model of better management practices we might expect imitation from other firms in this respect), we have some confidence that the assumptions underlying our wage model are correct at least for the class of large corporations that we are principally concerned with.

APPENDIX B: A DIGRESSION ON DYNAMICS

The analysis in the text has at least two disturbing implications. First, not only does control loss impose a limit to firm size, but once this limit is reached the firm will stabilize at this level. Since continuing expansion of large firms is common, the model appears to be at variance with reality in this aspect. Second, the model predicts that the span of control decreases with firm size, while the evidence points to the contrary. Either the control loss argument must be fundamentally incorrect, or the model must be amended in one or more respects.

We propose an extension, one that mainly involves allowance for dynamic conditions ignored in our static analysis. At least three factors are operative. First, increases in experience lead to refinements, shortcuts and routinization, all of which permit increasing the span of control for a fixed level of control loss. And experience is obviously positively related to firm size. Second, although most of the economies of scale resulting from specialization and indivisibilities are ordinarily exhausted at a relatively modest firm size (Bain, 1956, ch.iii), the economies that result from a large data-processing capability may well extend considerably beyond this size. Since for a given level of control loss increases in information processing capability permit the span of control to be expanded, the association of an increasing span of control and large firm size may be due in part to this information processing and firm size relation. Third, the rate of change of firm size may have an important influence. Penrose (1959, pp.44-8) has argued persuasively that the dynamics of growth require additional hierarchical personnel than are needed when the expansion is completed. Presumably this is because problems of coordination and control are more serious during periods of expansion. Expressing this argument in span of control terms, an inverse relation is to be expected between span and control and the growth rate. The remaining question then is what, if any, association between growth rate and size is to be expected. The data here are scant, but the results from the stochastic, serial correlation growth models of Ijiri and Simon (1964, pp.86-7) are at least suggestive, namely, that 'firms which grow large experience most of their growth [early in their history] . . ., then reach a plateau.' Assuming that this is generally valid, growth rates will tend to be inversely related to firm size. Thus here again we have a dynamic, size-related condition that helps to explain the apparent contradiction between the data relating span of control to firm size and our static analysis.

Taking these dynamic or age-related characteristics into account suggest that, given the value of $\bar{\alpha}$, the optimum span of control be expressed as:

$$s = \varphi(Q, k, t, d, dQ/dt, \ldots) \tag{B1}$$

where

Q = output: $\varphi_Q<0$

k = goal inconsistency parameter; $\varphi_k<0$

t = chronological age (a proxy for experience); $\varphi_t>0$

d = data-processing capability; $\varphi_d>0$

dQ/dt = rate of change of output; $\varphi(dQ/dt)<0$.

Among the advantages of this formulation is that it permits us to accommodate parts of Penrose's theory as a part of our own. Thus, if increases on dQ/dt reduce the span of control, additional hierarchical levels will be required to sustain the level of output. But for a fixed $\bar{\alpha}$, cumulative control loss which is given by $(1-\bar{\alpha}^n)$ now increases. Hence, costs increase as dQ/dt increases, and the optimum growth rate is therefore restricted. Although Penrose's emphasis is on internal experience and no attention is given to notions such as the span of control, the existence of control loss is implicit in her discussion and our model helps make this clear. Similarly, she observes that 'as plans are completed and put into operation, managerial services absorbed in the planning processes will be gradually released' (Penrose, 1959, p.49). Plan realization here implies that dQ/dt decreases, hence the span of control increases and the release of managerial services follows necessarily.

The above information also points up the very real dangers of performing simple correlations between s and Q. For the reasons given above, Q is positively related to t and d, and negatively related to dQ/dt. In as much as φ_t and φ_d are positive while $\varphi dQ/dt$ is negative, the combined effect of these three factors could easily swamp the true effect of Q on s (as predicted by our static model) if simple bivariate analysis were attempted.

NOTES

1. Kenneth E. Boulding, Richard T. Ely Lecture, 78th Annual Meeting of the American Economic Association.
2. Chamberlin (1948, pp.249-50) objected to some aspects of the argument in his treatment of the divisibility question, but nevertheless acknowledged that problems of coordination arising from increasing complexity eventually were responsible for increasing unit costs.
3. According to Starbuck, Andrews takes the position that 'it is impossible to conceive of any human organization too vast for organized efficiency'. Andrews (1949, pp.134-5), however, is quite specific in stating otherwise.
4. Thus, Williamson, J., takes the position that: 'One of the more discredited concepts in the theory of the firm is that of an "optimum size" firm . . . [S]ince firms are not restricted to the sale of a single product or even a particular range of products, there is no more reason to expect profitability to decline with size than there is evidence to suggest that it does. This raises the question

as to what does limit the size of a firm. The answer . . . is that there are important costs entailed in *expanding* the size of a firm, and that these expansion costs tend to increase with the firm's growth rate' (Williamson, J., 1966, p.1).

5. Robinson (1934, p.254) came very close to stating it in these terms, but he failed to formalize the argument and lacked an explanation for the control–loss phenomenon. Hence, Penrose's discontent with his argument as expressed above. For a later discussion of the notion of bounded rationality, see March and Simon (1958, ch.vi). Simon (1957a, p.xxiv) observes that 'it is precisely in the realm where human behaviour is *intendedly* rational, but only *limitedly* so, that there is room for a genuine theory of organization and administration'. The theory advanced here attempts to make explicit the way in which intended but limited rationality operates as a limitation to firm size.

6. Monsen and Downs (1965) have used the argument that control loss varies directly with firm size to examine the self-interest-seeking behaviour of management in the large business firm. However, their analysis is entirely descriptive, and they pass over the optimum firm size issue and focus instead on the implications of control loss for bureaucratic decision-making within the firm.

7. This assumption has been expressed in this way by Mayer (1960).

8. Strictly speaking, the empirical results reported in Table A.1 support the proposition that the ratio $\log s/\log \beta$ is constant across successive hierarchical levels, not that s and β are identical across levels. Letting $\log s/\log \beta = \gamma$, where γ is a constant, implies that $\beta = s^{1/\gamma}$ at every level. Thus, changes in the span of control would be accompanied by changes in the wage multiple according to the relation $\beta_i = s_i^{1/\gamma}$. That β and s are related in this way seems at least as special as to assume that they are constant across levels. Moreover, in view of the US Department of Labor report that β is indeed constant across levels, the constant s condition is implied by our results.

9. If $\beta > s$, then $(\log s/\log \beta) < 1$ and $a_1 = -(\log s/\log \beta) + 1 > 0$. But as the results in Table A.1 show, a_1 is clearly negative, which requires that $s > \beta$, as assumed.

10. The condition that the firm earn positive profits implies that:

$$(P-r)(\bar{\alpha}s)^{n-1} - \frac{s^n}{s-\beta}w_0 > 0,$$

or:

$$\frac{w_0}{P-r} \cdot \frac{s}{s-\beta} \cdot \frac{1}{\bar{\alpha}^{(n+1)}} < 1.$$

This requires that:

$$\left[ln\frac{w_0}{P-r} + ln\frac{s}{s-\beta} + ln\frac{1}{\bar{\alpha}^{(n-1)}} \right] < 0.$$

Since $ln\,[1/\bar{\alpha}^{(n-1)}]$ is approximately of the same magnitude as $ln[ln\,s/ln(\bar{\alpha}s)]$, or if anything is likely to exceed it, the condition that the firm earn positive profits is tantamount to requiring the bracketed term in equation (2) to be negative.

11. This result should be interpreted with some care. It assumed that $\bar{\alpha}$ is unaffected by increasing the span of control. Within any given firm, this is possible only if the increase in the span of control results from a management or technical innovation. Otherwise, increasing the span of control would lead to an increase in control loss. With this caveat in mind, the result indicated in the text is less counter-intuitive. See section III (5).

12. As we argue below, it seems plausible to suppose that $\bar{\alpha}$ will be larger in utility-maximizing organizations in which the goal of the firm represents a consensus among those managers whose preferences count.

13. Actually, two values of s and $\bar{\alpha}$ are consistent with each feasible choice of n: a high $\bar{\alpha}$, low s pair and a low $\bar{\alpha}$, high s pair. Of these two, the high $\bar{\alpha}$, low s position is always preferred since, with output fixed, gross revenues are unaffected by choice of s (and the associated value of $\bar{\alpha}$), while increasing s for a given n leads to higher employment and hence costs increase. More precisely, costs vary roughly in proportion to s^{n-1}, and the lower the value of s the lower the associated labour costs.

14. The responses to changes in k are unambiguous. Those for changes in $\bar{Q}$ hold over all relevant values of $\bar{\alpha}$ (≥ 0.7) and s (≥ 2).

15. The derivation of equation (A1) is similar to Simon (1957b). Simon does not, however, go on to derive the cumulative relationship given by equation (A2), which is ordinarily the only testable version of the model. A similar derivation to ours can, however, be found in Davis (1941, ch.ix).

REFERENCES

Andrews, P.W.S., *Manufacturing Business*. New York: Macmillan, 1949.

Bain, J.S., *Barriers to New Competition*. Cambridge, Mass.: Harvard University Press, 1956.

Bartlett, F.C., *Remembering*. New York: Cambridge University Press, 1932.

Chamberlin, E.H., 'Proportionality, Divisibility and Economies of Scale', *Quarterly Journal of Economics*, LXII, February 1948, 229-62.

Coase, R.H., 'The Nature of the Firm', *Economica,* N.S., IV, 1937, 386-405. Reprinted in George J. Stigler and Kenneth E. Boulding (eds.), *Readings in Price Theory*. Homewood, Ill.: Richard D. Irwin, 1952.

Davis, H.T., *The Analysis of Economic Time Series*. Granville, Ohio: Principia Press, 1941.

Downs, Anthony, *Bureaucratic Structure and Decisionmaking* (RM- 4646- PR). Santa Monica, Calif.: RAND, March 1966.

Ijiri, Yuji and Simon, H.A., 'Business Firm Growth and Size', *American Economic Review*, LIV, March 1964, 77-89.

Kaldor, Nicholas, 'The Equilibrium of the Firm', *Economic Journal*, XLIV, March 1934, 70-1.

Knight, F.H., *Risk, Uncertainty and Profit*. New York: Harper & Row, 1965.

Koontz, H. and O'Donnell, C., *Principles of Management*. New York: McGraw-Hill, 1955.

March, J.G. and Simon, H.A., *Organizations*. New York: John Wiley, 1958.

Mayer, Thomas, 'The Distribution of Ability and Earnings,' *Review of Economics and Statistics*, XLII, May 1960, 189-98.

Monsen, R.J., Jr and Downs, Anthony, 'A Theory of Large Managerial Firms', *Journal of Political Economy,* **LXXIII** (June, 1965), 221-36.

Papandreou, A.G., 'Some Basic Issues in the Theory of the Firm', in B.F. Haley (ed.), *A Survey of Contemporary Economics.* Homewood, Ill.: Richard D. Irwin, 1952.

Penrose, Edith, *The Theory of the Growth of the Firm.* New York: John Wiley, 1959.

Robinson, E.A.G., 'The Problem of Management and the Size of Firms', *Economic Journal,* **XLIV**, June 1934, 240-54.

Robinson, E.A.G., *The Structure of Competitive Industry.* Chicago: University of Chicago Press, 1962.

Ross, N.S., 'Management and the Size of the Firm', *Review of Economic Studies,* **XIX**, 1952–53, 148-54.

Simon, H.A., *Administrative Behaviour.* 2nd ed. New York: Macmillan 1957a.

Simon, H.A., 'The Compensation of Executives', *Sociometry*, March, pp.32-35, 1957.

Starbuck, W.H., 'Organizational Growth and Development', in J.G. March (ed.), *Handbook of Organizations.* Chicago: Rand McNally, 1964.

Tullock, Gordon, *The Politics of Bureaucracy.* Washington: Public Affairs Press, 1965.

US Department of Labor, *Salary Structure Characteristics in Large Firms* (1963). (Bull. no. 1417.) Washington, August 1964.

Williamson, John, 'Profit, Growth and Sales Maximization', *Economica,* **XXXIII**, February 1966, 1-16.

Williamson, O.E., *The Economics of Discretionary Behaviour: Managerial Objectives in a Theory of the Firm.* New York: Prentice-Hall, 1964.

4. Assessing and Classifying the Internal Structure and Control Apparatus of the Modern Corporation

WITH NAROTTAM BHARGAVA

The evolution and economic properties of what Chandler (1966) refers to as the multidivision enterprise have been described by Chandler and by O.E. Williamson (1970). Among the properties that have been imputed to the multidivision (or M-form) structure are that it permits the firm simultaneously to realize strategic responsiveness and operating efficiency and in the process internalize certain failures in the capital market with net beneficial consequences.[1] In order for these effects to be realized, however, attention to more than mere divisionalization is required. It is also necessary that a separation of operating from strategic responsibilities be provided. The former are assigned to the operating divisions while the latter are made the focus of the general management. Moreover, such a partitioning does not by itself assure strategic effectiveness; for this to obtain requires that the general management develop an internal control apparatus, to assess the performance of the operating divisions, and an internal resource allocation capability which favours the assignment of resources to high-yield uses. That divisionalized enterprises sometimes, and perhaps often, fail to meet these stipulations is suggested by Ansoff and Brandenburg, who observe that the performance potential in divisionalized firms frequently goes unrealized because general managements 'either continue to be overly responsive to operating problems [that is, non-strategic but interventionist] or reduce the size of the corporate office to a minimum level at which no capacity exists for strategic and structural decision-making' (1971, p. B-722). The results reported in the Appendix to this chapter are consistent with these propositions.[2]

A major problem thus is posed for testing the 'M-form hypothesis' (Williamson 1970, p.134) in that, if all divisionalized firms are classified as M-form firms, without regard for the related internal decision-making and control apparatus, an over-assignment to the M-form category will result. Some divisionalized firms are essentially holding companies, in that they lack the requisite control machinery, while others are only nominally divisionalized with the general office maintaining extensive involvement in operating affairs. If indeed the M-form designation is to be reserved for those firms that *combine* the appropriate structural and internal operating attributes, as we believe it should, information on both aspects is required.

The difficulty with this is three-fold. First, information on internal operating procedures is less easy to come by than is that on divisonalization. That this can be overcome, however, is at least suggested by the classification efforts reported in the Appendix. Secondly, the appropriate degree of involvement by the general office in the affairs of the operating divisions varies with the nature of the factor or product market interdependencies that exist within the firm and thus need to be 'harmonized'. Divisions that are involved in the exchange of intermediate products (vertical integration) typically face different control needs from those in which such internal, cross-divisional transactions are absent. Similarly, the requisite product market controls are more extensive if operating divisions produce common products than when, by reason of product diversification, such interdependencies are absent.

The third problem is that reaching the M-form structure may require the firm to pass through a transitional stage during which the 'optimum' control relationship, expressed in equilibrium terms, is violated. An appreciation for the natural life-cycle in the M-form enterprise is necessary if these transitional conditions are to be detected and an appropriate classification made. (The issue is addressed in section II(3) below. The sample of firms reported in the Appendix, and the related discussion of the assignments made, go into this as well.)

Although these are the principal difficulties, three further problems ought to be noted. First, whether or not divisionalization is at all indicated depends on firm size. The most efficient way to organize the small, specialized firm is normally along functional lines. Only as the firm expands in size and/or product variety is divisionalization likely to be appropriate. Since, initially, the classification effort will be restricted to the largest 500 industrials in the United States, which firms generally meet the requisite size and variety conditions to support divisionalization, this is not an immediate issue.

Second, the nature of the environment (market structure, demand uncertainty, information technology, etc.) is of critical importance in determining whether activities are more usefully transacted within firms than across markets, whether the divisionalization of those activities which have been internalized is indicated, and the degree to which internal controls in a divisionalized enterprise ought to be extended. These issues have been examined elsewhere (Williamson 1971a, 1971b).

Suffice it to observe here that (1) whether the exchange of intermediate product between technologically separable activities ought to occur within firms or across markets needs to be assessed in terms of the effects of each mode on incentives and, relatedly, the economizing of transaction costs;[3] (2) a low-variety environment makes the choice between firm and market transactions less critical—especially in so far as the optimal degree of vertical integration is concerned;[4] and (3) improvements in the information technology commonly favour internalization and more extensive internal auditing and controls—at least in the short run.[5]

Third, even in a divisionalized enterprise with the appropriate control apparatus, it is possible that the firm will not be operated in a strictly profit-maximizing fashion. The issue is separable into two parts: first, to what goals does the general management aspire; second, in what degree are the goals of the general management shared. Although we feel that the general management is likely naturally to adopt what is essentially a profit-maximizing attitude (Williamson 1970, ch.8), we would concede that shifting from a unitary or holding company structure to adopt an M-form organization mainly assures that (more nearly) least-cost behaviour and a better assignment of resources to high-yield internal uses will be realized. That earnings retention or acquisition biases in support of growth goals may exist cannot be disallowed. Relevant to such an assessment is the efficacy of competition in the capital market. Noteworthy in this connection is that, once a sufficient number of firms have adopted the M-form structure, the *system* can be expected to display superior self-policing properties. Competition in the capital-market forces will better serve to check non-profit-maximizing behaviour under these circumstances (Williamson 1970, pp.138-41).

Even if a general management adopts a fully profit-maximizing attitude, however, there is still a problem of internal implementation to be faced. Some compromises with the operating divisions may, as a matter of political reality, have to be made; what Allen refers to as 'conditional autonomy' (1970, p.26), whereby divisions with favourable performance records develop a degree of internal insularity, obtains. We agree but would suggest that the degree of actual divisional autonomy is less in an M-form firm than is commonly supposed. The recurring nature of the bargaining relationship between the general office and the operating divisions generally redounds to the advantage of the headquarters unit in both informational and effective control senses. As a result, the general management that is disposed to be assertive can expect its preferences to be realized more fully than a short-run focus on 'apparent' divisional autonomy would suggest.

Thus, although the conventional economic theory of the firm may be regarded as defective in that it simply imputes a profit goal and assumes, implicitly, that the firm is staffed by dedicated stewards who accept higher level goals without exception (thereby eliminating any need for an internal auditing apparatus), a more self-conscious examination of internal organization and an assessment of the efficiency properties and systems consequences of the M-form structure lead, from the standpoint of neoclassical analysis, to a somewhat reassuring result.[6]

A brief review of alternative divisionalized types of firms, expressed in terms of technological and market characteristics, is given in section I. Alternative internal control procedures are treated in section II. A classification scheme is proposed in section III. A sketch of some of the research uses to which a classification of the 500 largest industrials by organization form can be put is given in section IV. The Appendix illustrates the application of the resulting classification scheme to a sample of eight companies. The types of documents that have been found useful for such classification purposes and the assignment techniques are discussed.

1. ALTERNATIVE DIVISIONALIZED FIRMS DESCRIBED

It will be convenient in this section to develop the argument in two parts. First, the integrated (mainly single-product) enterprise is described. A discussion of the diversified firm then follows.

1. The Integrated Enterprise

Three general issues are posed within the integrated form: (1) interstage exchange relationships; (2) replication of production units (the multi-plant issue); and (3) marketing. Given that successive processes are *technologically* separable, which even in sequential processes that follow immediately in time and place is commonly satisfied, the question is: What sort of exchange relations ought to obtain between stages? At a minimum, the physical transfer of product ought normally to be metered. Whether indeed the product is separately priced and if so according to what standard need also to be considered. The importance of coordinating the responses of successive stages in reaction to unanticipated changes in the condition of the environment likewise deserves attention.

Aspects of the interstage exchange relation problem have been addressed elsewhere (Williamson 1971a, 1971b). Of relevance to us here are the following two propositions: (1) vertical integration potentially overcomes the incentives to haggle, posture, distort information, etc. that a small-numbers market-exchange relationship predictably poses, but (2) common ownership, without more, merely creates a bilateral internal exchange with the result that, were the respective stages given semi-autonomous divisional standing, antagonistic bargaining would not be relieved greatly. As a consequence, if successive stages of production are to be accorded divisional standing, extensive interstage (cross-divisional) rules may need to be devised.

Divisionalization by successive stages, however, is not the only possibility. More attractive frequently is divisionalization by *replication*—whereby several individually integrated plants are set up and operated in a semi-autonomous fashion. (This assumes, of course, that technological economies of scale are exhausted[7] at modest plant size—at least for most stages.)

The degree of autonomy to be accorded to each of the divisions in the single-product firm that employs replication as the divisionalizing strategy is nevertheless limited by considerations of possible factor-market economies and product–market interactions. Some centralization may be indicated so as to realize factor-purchasing and inventory economies. Often apt to be more crucial, however, is the need to mitigate antagonistic (competitive) marketing activities between the several divisions. Centralized marketing of the combined output of the various plants may be arranged on this account. Alternatively, if the marketing function is not centralized but instead is delegated to the separate divisions, rules to limit competition at the market interfaces presumably need to be designed. Territorialization is frequently resorted to for this purpose.

2. The Diversified Firm

Product diversification, mainly because it avoids or at least mitigates product-market interaction effects in the firm's marketing activities, facilitates diversification. Common early stages of production, however, are consistent with a diversified end-product mix. Thus common materials may be involved, as in many metal-refining and processing industries before the fabrication stage, or common processes may be employed for different materials that then go to distinct end-uses. Also, there may be a common scientific base on which a variety of quite different end-products rely. Early production stages of these kinds may more appropriately be organized as cost than as profit centres, with profit centre divisionalization being reserved for the divergent end-product activities.

To illustrate, suppose there are three activity stages: an early production stage, an intermediate stage in which production is completed, and marketing. Assume that all products originate in a common first stage, that there are four distinct intermediate stage processes, and that there are five distinct final products. That there 'ought' under these circumstances to be five divisions, one associated with each final product, is uncertain. For one thing, the economies of scale at (say) the first stage may be sufficient to warrant that all production originates in a single, indecomposable plant. Second, if for some products economies of scale at the second stage are slight in relation to the size of the market, parallel divisionalization may be feasible. Third, even though products may be distinct, there may be interaction effects to consider. (For example, products may be complements.)

Stage   Stage 2   Product

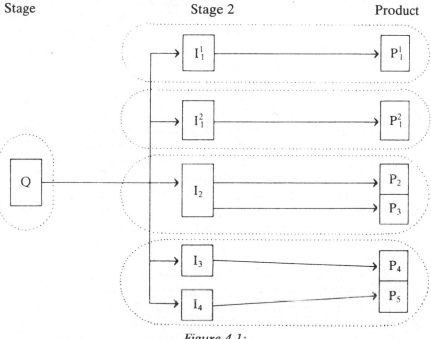

Figure 4.1:

Consider the situation shown in Figure 4.1. Here Q refers to first-stage activity, I_i refers to intermediate stage processing, P_l^m refers to the final product, and the subscript refers to the process (product) type while the superscript (if any) denotes replication. The proposed divisions are shown by the dotted lines.

That it is generally inefficient for the early stage of a production process to transfer product to a later stage at a price that maximizes the profit of the early stage is well known. Rather, so as to discourage the use of inefficient factor proportions in the later stages and avoid the restriction of production, product should be transferred at its marginal cost. But then the early-stage production divisions cannot normally[8] be evaluated in profit centre terms. Rather, Q becomes a cost centre and its performance is assessed in least-cost rather than net revenue terms.

Plants I_1^1 and I_1^2 are assumed to be identical and produce a common product (designated P_1^1 and P_1^2 respectively). Plant I_2 produces two distinct products P_2 and P_3, while plants I_3 and I_4 produce the distinct products P_4 and P_5 respectively. Products P_4 and P_5 while manufactured by separate processes, are assumed to be complements.

The rationale for the divisionalization shown is as follows. First, Q is split off as a cost centre since, for the reasons given above, it cannot efficiently be operated as a profit centre, while to assign it to one of the later stages would place unaffiliated stages at a disadvantage[9] and to combine several later stages leads to over-aggregation (in that such aggregation impairs accountability with the result that internal control is sacrificed in the process) in relation to underlying 'natural' decomposability conditions. Rules to ensure efficient transactional relations between stages 1 and 2 are assumed to be feasible, whence the divisional standing according to Q.

A high degree of coordination between each intermediate state and its corresponding marketing stage is assumed to exist and warrant the joining of each such pair of stages within a division.[10] As indicated, I_1^1 and I_1^2 are replicated production facilities producing the common product P_1. A territorial market is set up for each plant, with the result that $I_1^1-P_1^1$ and $I_1^2-P_1^2$ are both profit centres. Territorialization serves to mitigate intrafirm competition in the product market, but interdivisional 'competition', for performance comparison purposes, in other respects is possible.

Technological scale economies are assumed to be such that separate production facilities for P_2 and P_3 are uneconomical. Also, I_2 is assumed to bear a sole source relation to both P_2 and P_3. Since to split I_2 off as a separate division would require that it be operated as a cost centre (given the sole source assumption) with the attendant difficulties that this poses, and as interstage coordination would be impaired in the process, a single profit centre spanning I_2, P_2, and P_3 is set up instead.

I_3 and I_4 are separate plants between which there is no direct exchange relationship. They supply products P_4 and P_5 respectively. These products are assumed to be complements, however, for which a joint marketing effort is warranted. The resulting profit centre spans I_3, I_4, P_4, and P_5.[11]

II. INTERNAL CONTROLS DESCRIBED

The discussion of internal controls begins with a description of the very limited controls associated with the holding company form of organization. Strategic controls of the sort appropriate to an M-form organization are considered next. Transitional adjustment problems are then examined, after which the involvement of the general office in operating affairs is briefly discussed.

1. Holding Company

What we refer to here as a holding company form of organization is a loosely divisionalized structure in which the controls between the headquarters unit and the separate operating parts are limited and often unsystematic. The divisions thus enjoy a high degree of autonomy under a weak executive structure.[12]

Perhaps the least ambitious type of divisionalization to consider within the holding company classification is that in which the general office is essentially reduced to a clerical agency for the assembly and aggregation of earnings and other financial reports. The holding company in these circumstances serves as a risk-pooling agency, but in this respect is likely to be inferior to a mutual fund. The transaction costs associated with altering the composition of the 'portfolio' of the holding company, by selling off existing divisions and acquiring new operating companies, will ordinarily exceed the costs that a mutual fund of comparable assets would incur by its trading of common stocks (or other securities) so as to adjust its portfolio. Little wonder that those academics who interpret the conglomerate as being a substitute mutual fund report that it has inferior diversification characteristics to mutual funds themselves.[13]

Moreover, it is not clear that just a 'little bit' of additional control from the general office will lead to results that are superior to those that would obtain were the various divisions of the holding company to be free-standing firms in their own right. Being part of a holding company rather than an independent business entity easily has umbrella effects. If the holding company serves as a collection agency for unabsorbed cash flows and uses these to shore up the ailing parts of the enterprise, the resulting insularity may encourage systematic distortions (of a managerial discretion sort) among the divisional managements.[14] Being shielded from the effects of adversity in their individual product markets, slack behaviour sets in.

This is not, of course, a necessary consequence. The general management might consciously refuse to reinvest earnings but mainly pay these out as dividends. Alternatively, it might scrutinize reinvestment decisions every bit as well as the unassisted capital market could. Indeed, because it enjoys an *internal* relationship to the divisions, with all of the constitutional powers that this affords, the general management might be prepared to assume risks that an *external* investor ought properly to decline. (Thus the general management can ordinarily detect distortions and replace the divisional management at lower cost than can an external control agent similarly detect and change the management of a comparable free-standing business entity. The holding company, in this respect, is less vulnerable to the risks of what might be referred to as managerial moral hazard.) Given, however, that the holding company is *defined* to be a divisionalized form in which the general office does not involve itself in strategic controls of the sort described below, it is unclear that the holding company form of organization is socially to be preferred to an arrangement in which the various divisions are each set up as fully independent enterprises instead. Holding companies certainly cannot be expected reliably to yield results that compare favourably with those which we impute to the M-form structure.

2. Strategic Controls

If indeed the firm is to serve effectively as a miniature capital market, which in many respects is what the M-form structure ought to be regarded,[15] a more extensive internal control apparatus than the holding-company form of organization possesses is required. The argument here has been stated elsewhere (Williamson 1970). For purposes of making this paper internally more complete, however, the main points bear repeating.

Manipulation of the incentive machinery. Closer adherence to the goals of the general management can be secured if the special incentive machinery to which organization uniquely has access is consciously exercised to favour operating behaviour that is consistent with the general management's objectives. Both pecuniary and non-pecuniary awards may be employed for this purpose.

That salaries and bonuses can be adjusted to reflect differential operating performances, assuming that such differentials exist and can be discerned, is a familiar application of the incentive machinery. That non-pecuniary rewards, especially status, can also be adjusted for this purpose is less widely recognized but is scarcely novel. Several points might usefully be emphasized, however, in this connection.

First is the trivial proposition that pecuniary and non-pecuniary incentives are substitutes to some degree. This takes on significance mainly in conjunction with the further proposition that the efficacy of non-pecuniary incentives varies with the manner in which economic activity is organized. To the extent that internal organization is better able to confer status than is the market, which in some respects it presumably is, internal organization is favoured in relation to the market because of the substitution of non-pecuniary for pecuniary rewards that it permits. More generally, organizing modes that *economize on pecuniary outlays*—whether by realizing technological economies, mitigating transactional frictions, tax avoidance, substituting non-pecuniary for pecuniary rewards, etc.—will tend to be adopted in a regime where survival is governed mainly by the test of profits.

That non-pecuniary incentives are not costless, however, ought also to be appreciated. In particular, non-pecuniary incentives are commonly less flexible reward and penalty instruments than are pecuniary incentives. As Barnard (1946) observes, 'Loss of status is more than loss of its emoluments; it is more than loss of prestige. It is a serious injury to the personality' (p.69). Since typically non-pecuniary rewards are efficacious only to the extent that they are visible, while this is less true of pecuniary rewards, the attitudes of attachment toward each differ. Presumably the loss of status symbols has announcement effects that 'expose' the individual more severely than would a salary cut. Thus Barnard reports that 'the fear of losing status is what leads some to refuse advancement of status' (p.69) and notes that once status has been conferred, strong resistance to loss of status is to be anticipated (p.78). Although some types of efforts to maintain status presumably have favourable productivity effects, those that take the form of politicizing or anguish are apt to drain energies. Net productivity losses easily result.

Of course, sometimes a change of employment, or at least of position, may be altogether necessary. The division manager may not have the management capacities initially ascribed to him, conditions may change in ways that warrant the appointment of a manager with different qualities, or he may be managerially competent but uncooperative (given, for example, to aggressive sub-goal pursuit in ways that impair overall performance). Changes made for either of the first two reasons reflect simple functional assessments of job requirements in relation to managerial skills. By contrast, to replace a division manager for the third reason involves the deliberate manipulation of the incentive machinery to produce more satisfactory results. The occasion to intervene in this way will presumably be rare, however, if the conditional nature of the appointment is recognized from the outset. Rather, the system becomes self-enforcing in this respect once it is clear that the general management is prepared to replace division managers who regularly defect from general management's goals[16].

Although the general office does not ordinarily become directly involved in the exercise of the incentive machinery within the operating divisions, its indirect influence can be great. The decision to change (replace, rotate) a division manager is often made for the incentive effects this has on lower-level participants. Employment policies—including criteria for selection, internal training procedures, promotions etc.—can likewise be specified by the general office in ways that serve to ensure closer congruence between higher-level goals and the behaviour of the operating parts. A more pervasive incentive impact on lower-level participants who are not directly subject to review by the general office can in these ways be effected.

Internal audits. Adjusting the incentive machinery in any fine-tuning sense to achieve reliable results requires that the changes be made in an informed way. A back-up internal audit that reviews divisional performance and attempts to attribute effects to the several possible causes—distinguishing especially as between those outcomes that are due to changes in the condition of the environment from those that result from managerial decision-making—is useful for this purpose. As Churchill, Cooper and Sainsbury (1964) observe, 'to be effective, an audit of historical actions should have, or at least be perceived as having, the power to go beneath the apparent evidence to determine what in fact did happen' (p.258). Of particular importance in this connection is the recurrent nature of this auditing process. Thus although current variations of actual from projected may sometimes be 'accounted for' in plausible but inaccurate ways, a persistent pattern of performance failure can be explained only with difficulty.

The superior inference capability of an internal audit, as compared with the relatively crude powers of the capital market in this respect, commends internal organization as a substitute for the capital market not merely because discretionary behaviour may thereby be attenuated but also because division managers may be induced to accept risks which in a free-standing firm would be declined[17]. Too often, as Luce and Raiffa (1958) observe, 'the strategist is evaluated in terms of the outcome of the adopted choice rather than in terms of the strategic desirability of the whole risky situation' (p.76). This tendency to rely on outcomes rather than assess their complex situation more completely is especially to be expected of systems with low powers of inference. Managers of free-standing firms, realizing that outcomes rather than decision processes will be evaluated, are naturally reluctant to expose themselves to high-variance undertakings. *Ceteris paribus*, the low-cost access of internal organization to a wider range of sophisticated inference techniques encourages more aggressive risk-taking.

Even if the incentive machinery is not employed in a systematic way so as to give effect to internal audits, the auditing process may by itself serve to induce self-regulatory behaviour of a sort. Moral suasion reinforced by group compliance pressures can, if the results of the audits are internally publicized, have beneficial control consequences. Still, to rely on informal procedures is unnecessarily casual; mobilizing the incentive machinery as a follow-on to the internal audit will more reliably produce intended effects.

A further use to which audits might be put is as a basis for determining when operating divisions could benefit from outside help. The general management may include on its staff what amounts to an internal management consulting unit—to be loaned or assigned to the operating divisions as the need arises. Partly the occasion for such an assignment may be revealed by the internal audit. Thus, although the general management ought not routinely to become involved in operating affairs,[18] having the capability to intervene prescriptively in an informed way under exceptional circumstances serves to augment its credibility as an internal control agent.[19] Again, self-regulatory behaviour by the operating divisions is encouraged.

Cash flow allocation. In addition to policing on internal efficiency matters, and thereby securing a higher level of adherence to profit-maximization than the unassisted capital market could realize (at comparable cost), the general management and its support staff can perform a further capital-market function: assigning cash flows to high-yield uses. Thus cash flows in the M-form are not automatically returned to their sources but instead are exposed to an internal competition. Investment proposals from the several divisions are solicited and evaluated by the general management. The usual criterion is rate of return on invested capital. As an article in *Business Week* (8 April 1972, pp.54-7) put it, the keys to management in the 1970s were 'analysis' and 'control'. Many corporations, accordingly, are assigning financial controllers to the division managers to assist them in assessing and proposing new projects. Again, the recurrent nature of the budgeting relationship serves to assure integrity in the process.

Moreover, because the costs of communicating internally are normally lower than would be incurred in making an investment proposal to the external capital market,[20] it may be practicable to decompose the internal investment process into stages. A sequential decision process (in which additional financing is conditional on prior-stage results) may thus be both feasible and efficient as an internal investment strategy. The transaction costs of reproducing such a process through the capital market, by contrast, are likely to be prohibitive.

In many respects, this assignment of cash flows to high-yield uses is the most fundamental attribute of the M-form enterprise in the comparison of internal with external control processes. It must be appreciated, of course, that the divisionalized firm is able to assign cash flows to only a fairly narrow range of alternatives at any one point in time. Even if the firm is actively acquiring new activities and divesting itself of old, its range of choice is circumscribed in relation to that which general investors, who are interested in owning and trading securities rather than managing real assets, have access to. What the M-form firm does is trade off breadth for depth in this respect. As Alchian and Demsetz (1972) put it, in a similar context, 'Efficient production with heterogeneous resources is a result not of having *better* resources but in *knowing more accurately* the relative productive performances of those resources' (p.29).

Externality adaptation. As noted in section 1, spillovers in production or marketing may occur between some of the operating components of an organization. These spillovers may be mitigated by combining the affected parts within a single division. If, however, the resulting division becomes oversized—in that it is administratively unmanageable and effectively defeats the divisionalization concept, with consequent loss of control in the incentive, auditing and cash flow senses described above—externalities may simply be tolerated or adapted to in other respects. Thus, rather than resort to combination, rules may be devised to attempt to augment positive and attenuate negative spillover effects.

As indicated earlier, interdivisional transfer-pricing rules between successive production stages may sometimes be necessary—especially if the item in question cannot be procured externally at competitive prices. Similarly, the selling and pricing practices of divisions that market products having high cross-elasticity of demand will presumably require mediation by higher-level authority. Divisions that are severely constrained in these or related respects cannot fully be regarded as profit centres—at least in the autonomous degree that this term ordinarily implies.

Divisionalization may nevertheless be meaningful in that *efficiency* performance can still be assessed.[21] Also, although the spillover aspect of investment proposals will require special attention, the allocation of resources to favour high-yield projects can be conducted in the ways described above.

Of course, in circumstances where the affected parts are very richly connected, divisionalization may not be feasible. An 'oversized' unit operating along traditional functional lines may then emerge. Often, however, a more extensive decomposition of the enterprise is possible than the operating parts of a functionally organized firm would concede. Proposals to divisionalize an integrated system rarely originate with those who are deeply involved with managing a 'complex' system in which everything is (or appears to be) connected with everything else. One of the critical functions of the general management is to discover the decomposability properties of the enterprise and, where circumstances permit (that is, the malcoordination losses do not offset the prospective organizational gains), divisionalize accordingly.

3. Transitional Adjustments

The above discussion is conducted mainly in equilibrium terms. For many purposes, this is altogether appropriate. In as much, however, as it may take some time for an organization to recognize the need for reorganization, to effect a major structural change, and then become adapted to its operational consequences (which is to say that organizational learning is involved), the period just prior to, during and immediately following a reorganization along M-form lines is apt to be a disequilibrium interval. Some allowance for the difficulties of adjustment may be needed if the performance consequences of such a change are to be accurately evaluated.

Similarly, the process of effectively integrating new acquisitions within an established M-form enterprise may take time. The incumbent managers of the newly-acquired firm may have been able to negotiate, as a condition of support for the acquisition, that their division be accorded special autonomy. Only as this management is redeployed within the parent organization, reaches retirement, or is otherwise induced to accept a more normal divisionalized relationship can the M-form control apparatus be brought fully to bear. Indeed, as a transitional matter to hasten the divisionalization, the general management may, at its first 'legitimate' opportunity, involve itself more actively in the operating affairs of the newly acquired parts than would, assessed in equilibrium terms, ordinarily be appropriate. The purpose of this effort, presumably, is to effect a more rapid conditioning of attitudes and transformation of procedures than would otherwise obtain—bringing both more nearly into congruence with those existing elsewhere in the firm. Such apparent over-involvement ought not to be regarded as a contradiction to M-form procedures unless the interference is long continued and widely practised throughout the enterprise. Otherwise it is merely a transitional condition and a violation of M-form operations is not implied.

4. Operational Decision-making

The M-form structure is thoroughly corrupted when the general management involves itself in the operating affairs of the divisions in an extensive and continuing way. The separation between strategic and operating issues is sacrificed in the process; the indicated internalization of capital-market functions with net beneficial effects can scarcely be claimed. Accountability is seriously compromised; a substitution of enterprise expansion of profitability goals predictably obtains (Williamson 1970, pp.48-49).

Effective divisionalization thus requires the general management to maintain an appropriate 'distance'. Moreover this holds for the support staff on which the general management relies for internal auditing and management consulting services. Over-involvement upsets the rational allocation responsibilities between short-run operating matters and longer-run planning and resource allocation activities. What March and Simon (1958) refer to as Gresham's law of planning—'Daily routine drives out planning' (p.185)—takes effect when operating and strategic functions are mixed. While the arguments here are familiar and their implications for organizational design reasonably clear, maintaining a separation between these two activities apparently poses severe strain on some managements. A desire to be comprehensively involved is evidently difficult to resist.

5. Optimum Divisionalization

Optimum divisionalization thus involves (1) the identification of separable economic activities within the firm, (2) according quasi-autonomous standing (usually of a profit-centre nature) to each, (3) monitoring the efficiency performance of each division, (4) awarding incentives, (5) allocating cash flows to high-yield uses, and (6) performing strategic planning (diversification, acquisition, etc.) activities in other respects. The M-form structure is one that *combines* the divisionalization concept with an internal control and strategic decision-making capability. The general management of the M-form usually requires the support of a specialized staff to discharge these functions effectively. It bears repeating, however, that care must be exercised lest the general management and its staff become over-involved in operating matters and fail to perform the high-level planning and control functions on which the M-form enterprise relies for its continuing success.

As indicated at the outset of this paper, whether and how to divisionalize depends on firm size, functional separability, and the state of information technology. Also, it should be pointed out that our reference here to 'optimum' is used in comparative-institutional terms. As between otherwise comparable unitary or holding company forms of organization, the M-form structure would appear to possess significant advantages. It cannot, however, be established on the basis of the argument advanced here (and elaborated by Williamson, 1970) that the M-form structure is the best of all conceivable structures. Organizational innovations may even now be in the making that will make it obsolete in part, but which academics will identify as noteworthy only after several years. A keener sensitivity to organizational innovations and their economic importance than has existed in the past should nevertheless help to avoid the long recognition lags before the significance of the M-form structure and its conglomerate variant became apparent.

III. A CLASSIFICATION SCHEME

The above analysis leads to a (tentative) six-way classification of large corporate structures. We expect that experience with the scheme may reveal certain ambiguities and suggest better definitions; the need to devise still additional categories may also become evident. We think it useful nevertheless to get on with the assignment task and make the refinements as we go. Surely enough is known about internal organization at this time to begin such an effort. The following classification scheme is accordingly proposed.

1. Unitary (U-form)
This is the traditional functionally organized enterprise. (It is still the appropriate structure in most small to lower-middle-sized firms. Some medium-sized firms in which interconnections are especially rich may continue to find this the appropriate structure.) A variant on this structure occasionally appears in which the enterprise is mainly of U-form character but where the firm has become diversified in slight degree and the individual parts are given semi-autonomous standing. Unless such diversification accounts for at least a third of the firm's value added, such a functionally organized firm will be assigned to the U-form category.

2. Holding Company (H-form)
This is the divisionalized enterprise for which the requisite internal control apparatus has not been provided. The divisions are often affiliated with the parent company through a subsidiary relationship.

3. Multidivisional (M-form)
This is the divisionalized enterprise in which a separation of operating from strategic decision-making is provided and for which the requisite internal control apparatus has been assembled and is systematically employed.

Two sub-categories should be distinguished: type D_1, which denotes a highly integrated M-form enterprise, possibly with differentiated but otherwise common final products; and type D_2, which denotes the M-form enterprise with diversified final products or services. As between these two, a more extensive internal control apparatus to manage spillover effects is needed in the former.

4. Transitional multidivisional (M'-form)
This is the M-form enterprise that is in the process of adjustment. Organizational learning may be involved or newly-acquired parts may

not yet have been brought into a regular divisionalized relationship to the parent enterprise.

5. Corrupted multidivisional (M̄-form)
The M̄-form enterprise is a multidivisional structure for which the requisite control apparatus has been provided but in which the general management has become extensively involved in operating affairs. The appropriate distance relation thus is missing, with the result that M-form performance, over the long run, cannot reliably be expected.

6. Mixed (X-form)
Conceivably a divisionalized enterprise will have a mixed form in which some divisions will be essentially of the holding-company variety, others will be M-form, and still others will be under the close supervision of the general management. Whether a mixed form is likely to be viable over the long run is perhaps to be doubted. Some 'exceptions' might, however, survive simply as a matter of chance. The X-form classification thus might be included for completeness purposes and as a reminder that organizational survival is jointly a function of rational and chance processes (Alchian, 1958). Over the long pull the rational structures should thrive, but aberrant cases will appear and occasionally persist.

That the X-form lacks for rationality properties, however, is probably too strong. For example, a large U-form firm that enjoys monopoly power in its main market may wish to restrict the reinvestment of cash flows back into this market. At the same time it may discover attractive opportunities to invest some part of these funds in unrelated business activities. Diversification could follow, but not in sufficient degree to warrant disestablishment of the main market from central office control. The diversified parts of the business thus might each be given divisional standing, but the main business retained, for the most part, under its earlier control relationship. Only if the main business itself could be efficiently divided (through product differentiation, geographic territorialization, or other lines), which eventually it may, might divisionalization of this part of the firm's activities be warranted.

IV. RESEARCH OPPORTUNITIES[22]

Once the classification of the largest 500 industrials according to the scheme proposed in section III and illustrated in the Appendix is completed, it would be of interest to investigate the influence of organization form on firm behaviour and performance. Comparative growth and profit rates among rival firms might be studied. Investment behaviour, including marginal rates of return to alternative sources of funds (Baumol *et al.*, 1970; Friend and Husic, 1971), as well as other forms of internal expenditure (hierarchical expense, advertising, R & D, etc.) ought also to be investigated for organization form effects. Executive compensation practices as a function of organization form, following along the lines developed by Masson (1971), should also be examined. Evidence relating to slack (internal inefficiency), as this is influenced by organization form and changes in the condition of the environment, should be studied. Internal operating practices, such as cross-subsidization, and 'offensive' marketing practices, such as reciprocity, could also be investigated to determine whether these are affected by organization form. It is probably important, for the purpose of making each of the types of studies suggested, to make allowance for firm size effects.

Of related interest is the historical evolution of the M-form structure. Chandler (1966) traces much of this in descriptive terms, but a more formal assessment of this organizational innovation would seem useful. Of special interest are the factors that influence the rate of diffusion: What firms with what characteristics were induced to adopt it at what time? It is our impression that the period 1945-50 is the critical period during which the M-form innovation took on quantitative significance, that from 1950-60 it was adopted by many large firms as a defensive measure, and that 1960-70 is the period during which the conglomerate variant of this structure flourished. Historical studies of aggregate business behaviour may, at the least, want to distinguish between pre-war and post-war periods, in the expectation that the latter will conform more nearly with the M-form hypothesis.

Considerations of organization form might also usefully be introduced into the study of bureaucracies more generally, to include non-profit institutions (hospitals, universities etc.) and the public sector.

APPENDIX[23]

Our purpose in the Appendix is to give an illustration of each of the organization form types described in section III and indicate some of the sources that can be used for assigning large corporations quite generally to organization form categories. The firms appearing below were all among the largest 200 industrial corporations in the US (as ranked by 1965 sales in the *Fortune* 500 series).

U-form
The U-form structure is a vanishing breed among large US corporations.

Reynolds Metals Company is one of the last such firms to make the transformation from a unitary to a divisionalized structure. Inspection of their annual reports together with correspondence from Mr Robert L. Teeter (Assistant Director for Corporate Planning) reveals that the company had maintained a U-form structure from its inception in 1929 until 1969. The company indicates in its *1969 Annual Report* that 'In the past year, our corporate structure was reorganized on a divisional, profit centre basis.' However, it is not clear to what extent operating responsibilities have been delegated to the divisions and whether appropriate rules have been made for harmonizing interdivisional interaction effects. Thus, while Reynolds Metals appears definitely to have been a U-form firm up until 1969, its current classification is uncertain. We provisionally assign it to M'-form status.

Quaker Oats Company is another example of a firm that only recently adopted a divisionalized structure. Although it had begun to diversify into chemicals and toys a number of years ago, this was merely incidental to the main business of the firm as a food processor and distributor. In an announcement dated 23 September 1970, President Robert D. Stuart, Jr stated that the company was being changed 'from a centralized functional [U-form] organization to a substantially decentralized one with profit responsibility delegated to a number of Groups and Divisions'. He went on to note that while some of the organizational changes 'will take place very soon, . . . others, such as accounting and management information services, are highly complex and will take longer.' Among the advantages that he imputed to the new structure were that it 'heightens the incentive to succeed by making success at each level more visible . . . [and is] readily adaptable to adding new businesses, either internally or through acquisition'. Thus Quaker Oats, which had a U-form structure until 1970, is provisionally assigned to M'-form status at the moment.

H-form
The Signal Companies Inc. is an example of an H-form firm. In the *1968 Annual Report*, Forrest N. Shumway, President, reported that the firm's name had been changed from Signal Oil and Gas to the Signal Companies, indicated that in 1968 the firm had acquired one company, created two others, and purchased nearly half of another, and characterized the organizational structure of the corporation in the following terms:

Each of the Signal Companies functions within a corporate framework but is essentially on its own in day-to-day operations; each had its own slate of officers and Board of Directors. We weave them together and into the parent company by an interlock of directors, and we draw from directors of Signal and the major affiliates of our Executive Committee. . . .

We have been acquiring superior managements among our affiliates. . . . This permits us to maintain a relatively small corporate staff, which can concentrate on corporate legal and financing matters and serve as a conduit and catalyst for all the companies.

The parent staff also conducts a broadscale corporate advertising and public relations programme to help earn favourable attitudes among the financial community and the general public.

The three major components of the Signal Companies operations are Signal Oil and Gas Company (petroleum, with 1970 sales of $495 million), Mack Trucks, Inc. (heavy-duty trucks and off-highway equipment, 1970 sales of $534 million), and The Garrett Corporation (aerospace, 1970 sales of $379 million). Other smaller Signal Companies are involved in screw compressors, housing, chemicals, computer components, etc., with aggregate 1970 sales of $78 million. Although the corporate staff performed more than a simple financial aggregation function for these various companies, it had neither the intention nor the capacity to perform the management control functions that we associate with the M-form structure. Rather, through its aggressive acquisition period during the 1960s at least, Signal was organized under an H-form structure. We have been unable to ascertain whether the financial difficulties that Signal has experienced more recently have given rise to any later changes in its corporate structure.[24]

M-form

As noted, the M-form structure can be split into two types. Type D_1 is one in which manufacturing and/or marketing spillovers exist since common processes or products are involved. General Motors is illustrative. It was transformed from what was essentially an H-form structure under W.C. Durant's leadership (during the period 1908 to 1920)[25] to an M-form structure under the du Ponts and Alfred P. Sloan, Jr in the early 1920s.

Although General Motors was in 1920 and has since remained a diversified company (producing household appliances, diesel locomotives, military vehicles, etc.), its main business throughout the period from 1920 to the present has been automobiles. Some coordination of manufacturing, but especially marketing, was needed lest the various automobile divisions compete in counterproductive ways (assessed in terms of the effect on corporate profits). The general office in General Motors thus became involved not merely in monitoring and strategic resource allocation (which is characteristic of the general office in any M-form structure), but, being a type D_1 variant, was also engaged in rule-making and related processes designed to mitigate negative and enhance positive spillovers among the divisions (Chandler 1966, pp.182-191).

The recent recentralization of certain manufacturing activities at General Motors may be in response to changing technology, perceived control difficulties with the earlier organization, strategic antitrust considerations, or some combination thereof. We lack the necessary information to determine how this is to be interpreted. At present, however, General Motors is still to be regarded as an M-form structure.

The type D_2 variant is illustrated by Textron.[26] The firm, formerly Atlantic Rayon Company, had been a textile firm. The company engaged in extensive diversification under Royal Little during the 1950s. It appears mainly to have employed an H-form (or incipient M'-form) structure during this period. By 1960 the decentralized management pattern had been established; growth during the 1960s was mainly internal. Concurrently, the general office began to exercise M-form controls. Thus although it maintains a lean central staff (there being only 115 people at the Textron headquarters in 1970), it closely manages resource allocations and in 1969 group controllers were added to the headquarters staff.

Sales among the four industry groups in 1969 were distributed as follows: aerospace, 37 per cent; consumer products, 26 per cent; industrial products, 21 per cent; and metal products, 16 per cent. While these are a diverse mixture of activities, Textron has remained strictly a manufacturing organization and thus enjoys commonality among its divisions in this respect. Group vice-presidents are easily rotated among the operating companies for this reason.

M'-form

Deere & Company illustrates a firm that has recently been through and appears not fully to have completed a transformation from a functional to an M-form enterprise. Deere was originally a farm-equipment manufacturer organized along U-form lines. By 1966, however, it had become diversified and organizationally too complex to be managed along functional lines. The manufacturing and marketing departments were accordingly subdivided into farm equipment, industrial equipment, and consumer products components. This evidently was not wholly successful, however, and the company divisionalized along product lines in 1970.

The Deere & Company management, in an internal memorandum dated 17 February 1970, summarized the changing organization structure of the firm in the following terms:

Some years ago when the business of Deere & Company and its subsidiaries was concentrated almost exclusively in the farm equipment markets of the United States and Canada, an organization based on function, structured primarily on manufacturing, marketing and financial lines, was both appropriate and highly effective. As our business grew, new markets and products became increasingly important to us with our overseas expansion and our addition of industrial equipment and consumer products lines. Each of these additions not only opened new opportunities, but also imposed requirements for new and different ways of operating. In 1966 we began to adjust to those requirements by modifying the original management structure based on functions, adding the Overseas Division and regrouping within the Manufacturing and Marketing Divisions their organizations into farm equipment, industrial equipment and consumer products components.

Another change is now needed: the establishment of operating divisions based on product lines and regional market areas, and the creation of a corporate staff division to provide increasingly effective counsel, services and functional guidance for the operating divisions.

The hoped for benefits of the reorganization include:

1 Greater recognition and scope for corporate staff activities plus improved coordination of these activities. The complexities of modern technology and professional specialization have made staff functions equal in importance with those of operations as a factor in business success.
2 Clear focusing of operating management talents on the development of business opportunities in each of our principal product lines and regional market areas.
3 Closer coordination of the manufacturing and marketing functions within each product line and market area.
4 More opportunities for developing corporate executives with experience in broad general management responsibilities.
5 Divisional accounting to give better knowledge of the return-on-investment performance of the major parts of our business, and to facilitate return-on-investment comparisons among John Deere operating divisions and with other companies in the same industries.

This new management organization clearly is consistent with and gives new emphasis and meaning to the traditional John Deere policy of decentralization of authority and responsibility within a framework of corporate objectives, policies and communications practices. The senior vice-president in charge of each division has full authority and responsibility within such limits and within the limits of the resources allotted to his division.

Whether Deere will fully attain an M-form structure cannot yet be determined. From 1966 to the present, it is assigned to the M'-form category.

M̄-form

Allis-Chalmers Company illustrates a divisionalized firm that possibly might have been intended to be an M-form enterprise but in which the general office became excessively involved in operating affairs. Mr Lee P. Appleton, Assistant Secretary and Treasurer, indicated in a letter dated 18 February 1971 that the company had been divisionalized for 'at least twenty years', but went on to observe that the divisionalization concept had recently undergone great change within Allis-Chalmers—as indeed it has.

The 1952 annual report refers only to General Machinery and Tractor divisions. Partly through acquisition and partly by splitting existing divisions, this had grown to six divisions by 1955: Power Equipment, Industrial Equipment, General Products, Construction Machinery, Farm Equipment, and Buda. Nuclear Power and Defense Products divisions were added subsequently. The 1964 annual report reported a general reorganization out of which 'twelve integrated operating divisions with full management responsibility' were created. The purported autonomy objective, however, was apparently unrealized.

The company subsequently experienced heavy reverses and was subject to repeated takeover threats. Only after the president and chairman of the board resigned and David C. Scott was brought in (from Colt Industries) did the company face up to its actual organizational practices. The 1968 annual report catalogues the problem.

Before year-end 1969, a total of 5000 non-production personnel will have been released throughout the company. Corporate staff employees—that is people not reporting to profit centres—now total 132, a reduction of more than 1300 from this classification in five months. Most of those formerly classified 'corporate staff' have been transferred to profit centres.

Although decentralization moves were made some four years ago, operating divisions were not held to true profit responsibility. In addition to their own operating expenses, each producing division was charged with a proportionate amount of heavy corporate expense. It is our intention to decentralize Allis-Chalmers fully into true profit centres, where each division and department general manager can be accurately measured in his performance of generating profit.

At present, our operations are structured into seven operating groups, each . . . headed by a senior president or vice president, who reports to the President.

The reorganization, however, has not by itself been fully effective. The 13 March 1971 issue of *Business Week* observed that the company apparently had need of fresh talent at top and middle-management levels.

While Allis-Chalmers appears clearly to illustrate the $\bar{M}$-form structure during the 1950s and early 1960s, there is a serious problem of recognizing this corrupted form of an M-form enterprise at the time. Annual reports, press releases, even 'depth' reports in the business magazines, rarely expose over-involvement by a general office in the affairs of the operating divisions. A strong indication that this condition prevails can be deduced from questionnaire responses in which the size of the general office staff is reported. Not all companies are prepared to respond to such a query, however. Moreover, the size of this staff is merely a first indication. Its composition and the characteristics of the firm need also to be considered. (Thus M-form, type D_1 firms will usually require larger staffs than will type D_2; also firms that centralize the R & D function may have what appear to be large staffs, but these may be little involved, in an operating sense, with the operating divisions.)

X-form
Firestone Tire & Rubber Company is one of the most highly integrated firms in the rubber industry. While it had become diversified to the extent that 40 per cent of its sales were in non-rubber products in 1969, its main business has continued to be in tyres. The tyre business is operated along U-form lines, while the other businesses (mainly rubber products, plastics, steel products, and textiles) are set up as product divisions which enjoy quasi-autonomous standing. The X-form classification appears to be appropriate.[27]

NOTES

1. For a somewhat similar discussion of the internal resource allocation effects see Drucker (1970). Also of relevance in this connection are the treatments by Heflebower (1960) and Weston (1970). Certain work at the Harvard Business School also relates to these issues (see Bower 1971 and the references therein; also Allen 1970).
2. More generally, the results of Bhargava's PhD dissertion, on which the Appendix to this chapter is mainly based, support the argument that divisionalization is merely a necessary but not a sufficient condition to classify a firm as an M-form structure.
3. It is important that these assessments be made in a multi-period rather than a single-period context. This is the recurrent behaviour issue discussed in the text below.
4. Even in a low-variety environment, internalization may be favoured by incentive advantages of internal in relation to market organization. Thus capital market failures may be internalized to advantage on this account. The extent to which this advantage exists will, however, vary directly with market uncertainties.
5. New market institutions may develop in the long run, which institutions may permit product market transitions to be consummated more efficiently, in which event vertical integration may be unnecessary, or permit outsiders (mainly stockholders or their agents) more effectively to monitor the affairs of the firm and thus reduce incentives for conglomerate organization.

   Note that our use of internalization, both here and elsewhere in the paper, refers to the shift of a market transaction to an internal transaction. This is a somewhat more narrow use of the term than is common. Others use internalization to refer to any efficient adaptation, market or otherwise, with respect to an externality.
6. A problem not discussed above but which nevertheless warrants acknowledgement is that of limits to firm size. One way of putting this is as follows: Why cannot the large firm do everything the small firm can do and more? If it can, the need for markets vanishes. The issues here have been examined

elsewhere (Williamson 1971b). That large size and diversification experience limits will simply be taken as given for the purposes of this paper.

7. This is somewhat over-strong. Transportation or other factor cost considerations may even dictate that certain single plant technological economies be sacrificed in favour of multiplant operations so as to realize least cost supply at point of delivery.

8. An exception is if the production stage in question is competitively organized by outside suppliers. In such an event, however, there is little incentive to internalize the activity from the outset.

9. This assumes that the later stages are about on a parity in terms of the volume and variety of demands placed on the early stage. If one stage were to be much larger than all of the others and to have special needs for coordinating with the early stage, a combination of these two stages might be warranted.

10. This is clearly arbitrary; a divisional separation between marketing and the prior production stage may sometimes be warranted.

11. That the exercise is hypothetical and over-simple ought to be emphasized. If, however, it serves better to expose the issues, its purpose will have been realized.

12. That this is a somewhat special use of the term 'holding company' ought to be appreciated. (We considered referring to this as the federal form of organization, but decided that this posed at least as many problems.) Essentially what we are after is a category which, for reference purposes, represents divisionalization of a very limited sort.

13. See in this connection Smith and Schreiner (1969) and Westerfield (1970).

14. For a dynamic-stochastic model that is consistent with this prediction, see Williamson (1970), ch.5.

15. The argument is developed more extensively in Williamson (1970), pp.138-50, 176-7. For a somewhat similar view, see Alchian and Demsetz (1972), and Drucker (1970).

16. This assumes that there are no property rights (of an academic tenure, civil service, etc. sort) associated with positions.

17. If the firm is not merely divisionalized but is also diversified, risk-pooling effects will obtain as well. These, however, are not at issue here.

18. The reasons for avoiding operating involvement have been given elsewhere. A comparative study by Allen (1970) of two divisionalized firms broadly supports the general argument. Allen observes that, of the two firms, the high-performing firm had a 'fairly simple but highly selective set of organizational devices to maintain control over its divisions' while the management of the low-performing firm become 'over involved', in relation to its capacity, in the affairs of its operating divisions (p.28).

19. This internal management consulting unit would ordinarily be made available at the request of the operating divisions as well as at the behest of the general management. Such a unit would presumably possess scarce expertise of a high order. It would be uneconomical for each operating division to attempt to replicate such a capability.

20. On the reasons for this, see the discussion in Williamson (1970), pp.114, 119-21; also March and Simon (1958), p.35.

21. These are the cost centres referred to in section 1.

22. For a more extensive development of the matters discussed in this section, including a development of the policy issues, see Williamson (1972), pp.28-31.

23. The Appendix is based mainly on efforts of Bhargava to classify the largest

200 industrial corporations in the US as a part of his PhD dissertation. The assignments made here are provisional. Certain cross-checks on the assignments made have yet to be completed.

24. That crises reveal the need for more comprehensive controls, which may involve transforming an H-form to an M-form structure, is suggested by Richard A. Smith's treatment of Olin Mathieson in his *Corporations in Crisis* (New York, 1963).

25. Chandler (1966) characterizes the early organization of General Motors as 'a loosely-knit federation of many operating enterprises' (p.151). Harlow Curtice observes that prior to 1921, 'Operations were neither integrated nor coordinated' and that in many respects 'the individual units [were] largely out of control'. Sloan and the du Ponts devised and implemented what we refer to in the text as the M-form structure.

26. In addition to the annual report of Textron, a *Business Week* article ('Textron: built to diversify', 17 October 1970) has been useful for our treatment of Textron.

27. A letter from Glenn D. Cross, manager of organizational planning, observes that 'Our organization structure falls mainly within the functional category although one phase of it, concerning our non-tire activities, is of the division type'. The 1969 annual report reports that 'From the very beginning Firestone has been one of the most integrated of businesses. From the ownership of rubber plantations this integration terminates at franchised retail stores dealing exclusively in Firestone manufactures.'

REFERENCES

Alchian, Armen (1958), 'Uncertainty, Evolution, and Economic Theory', *Journal of Political Economy*, **58**, 211-22.

Alchian, Armen and Demsetz, Harold (1972), 'Production, Information Costs and Economic Organization', *American Economic Review*, December, **62**, 777-803.

Allen, Stephen A., Ill (1970), 'Corporate Divisional Relationships in Highly Diversified Firms', in Jay W. Lorsch and Paul R. Lawrence (eds.) *Studies in Organization Design*. (Homewood, Ill.; Irwin), pp.16-35.

Ansoff, H.I. and Brandenburg, R.G., 'A Language for Organizational Design: Part II', *Management Science*, **17**, B-717-31.

Barnard, Chester I. (1946), 'Functions and Pathology of Status Systems in Formal Organizations', in W.F. White (ed.), *Industry and Society*, pp.46-83.

Baumol, W.J., Heim, Peggy, Malkiel, B.G. and Quandt, R.E. (1970), 'Earnings Retention, New Capital, and the Growth of the firm', *Review of Economics and Statistics*, **52**, 345-55.

Bower, Joseph L. (1971), 'Management Decision-Making in Large Diversified Firms', (unpublished manuscript).

Chandler, Alfred D., Jr. (1966), *Strategy and Structure* (New York).

Churchill, N.C., Cooper, W.W. and Sainsbury, T., (1964), 'Laboratory and Field Studies of the Behavioural Effects of Audits', in C.P. Bonini *et al* (ed.), *Management Control: New Directions in Basic Research*. (New York: McGraw-Hill), pp.253-67.

Coase, Ronald H. (1972), 'Industrial Organization: A Proposal for Research', in Victor R. Fuchs (ed.), *Policy Issues and Research Opportunities in Industrial*

Organization, (New York: National Bureau of Economic Research).

Drucker, Peter (1970), 'The New Markets and the New Capitalism', *The Public Interest*, **21**, 44-79.

Friend, Irwin and Husic, Frank, (1971), 'Efficiency of Corporate Investment' (Working Paper No. 4-71) (Rodney L. White Center for Financial Research, University of Pennsylvania).

Heflebower, Richard B. (1960), 'Observations on Decentralization in Large Enterprises', *Journal of Industrial Economics*, **9**, 7-22.

March, J.G. and Simon, H.A. (1958), *Organizations* (New York: Wiley).

Masson, R.T. (1971), 'Executive Motivations, Earnings, and Consequent Equity Performance', *Journal of Political Economy*, **79**, 1278-92.

Smith, D. (1971), 'The Performance of Merging Banks', *Journal of Business* (April).

Smith, K.V. and Schreiner, J.C. (1969), 'A Portfolio Analysis of Conglomerate Diversification', *Journal of Finance*, **24**, 413-29.

Westerfield, Randolph (1970), 'A Note on the Measurement of Conglomerate Diversification', *Journal of Finance*, **25**, 909-14.

Weston, J. Fred (1970), 'Diversification and Merger Trends', *Business Economics*, **5** (January).

Williamson, O.E. (1970), *Corporate Control and Business Behaviour* (Englewood Cliffs, New Jersey: Prentice-Hall).

Williamson, O.E. (1971a), 'The Vertical Integration of Production: Market Failure Considerations', *American Economic Review*, May, **61**, 112-25.

Williamson, O.E. (1971b), 'On the Limits of Internal Organization, with Special Reference to the Vertical Integration of Production' (unpublished manuscript).

Williamson, O.E. (1972), 'Antitrust Enforcement and the Modern Corporation', in V. Fuchs (ed.), *Policy Issues and Research Opportunities in Industrial Organization*, (New York), pp.16-33.

Part II
THE ECONOMICS OF FIRM AND
MARKET ORGANIZATION

5. Introduction

The essays in this section all maintain a comparative institutional orientation. As my introductory remarks to Part I indicate, this approach to economic organization did not come naturally to me and was not reflected in my earlier work. The need to adopt a comparative approach became progressively more evident, however, as the limits of non-comparative 'market failure' analysis were displayed. Coase had put his finger on the problem (1964, p.195):

Contemplation of an optimal system may suggest ways of improving the system, it may provide techniques of analysis that would otherwise have been missed, and, in special cases, it may go far to providing a solution. But in general its effect has been pernicious. It has directed economists' attention away from the main question, which is how alternative arrangements will actually work in practice. It has led economists to derive conclusions for economic policy from a study of an abstract model of a market situation. . . . Until we realize that we are choosing between social arrangements which are all more or less failures, we are not likely to make much headway.

Persuasive though these remarks were upon reading them, the research ramifications did not register until later.

The first essay in Part II had complex origins. I had spent the academic year 1966-67 as Special Economic Assistant to the head of the Antitrust Division of the US Department of Justice and had occasion to review the literature on vertical market structures at that time. Although much of it was instructive, many of the core issues were scarcely touched. The neoclassical model of the firm on which most of this literature relied simply ignored comparative institutional issues of firm and market organization.

I thereafter returned to the University of Pennsylvania and was asked by Julius Margolis to develop an organization theory course for a new public policy programme that he was designing. The course was first offered under the title 'Theories of Institutions'. It attempted to survey the market failure and organization theory literature, with special emphasis on the first. The students and I, upon identifying a market failure, attempted to push it back to its origins. Time after time we arrived at the same behavioural features. The possibility that internal organization was a response to the (comparative) contracting failures of markets was thus suggested.

Not only did this paper interpret vertical integration as a response to the costliness of contracting that attended certain types of market exchange, but it furthermore identified asset specificity as the troublesome feature that was principally responsible for contracting difficulties. If transactions are supported by non-trivial investments in durable transaction-specific assets, then what may have originated as a large-numbers bidding condition at the outset will be transformed into a bilateral exchange relation thereafter. This 'fundamental transformation' has pervasive organizational ramifications. Indeed, this vertical integration story is a paradigm: labour market organization, regulation, corporate governance and even family organization are variations on a theme.

The second essay in this part elaborates on this approach. It is a more thoroughly comparative approach to economic organization. It identifies both the critical dimensions with respect to which transactions differ and the leading organizational structures—or, as I prefer to call them, governance structures—to which transactions might feasibly be assigned. And it attempts to effect a discriminating—mainly transaction cost economizing—match. Although the resulting apparatus is very crude and stands in need of refinement, a systematic approach for operationalizing transaction cost arguments had been put in place. This is crucial to an effort to derive refutable (comparative institutional) implications, thereby to help transaction-cost economics to overcome its tautological reputation.

The next essay returns to an examination of the modern corporation. I attempt to trace the origins, evolution and attributes of the modern corporation. Although complex institutions serve a variety of economic purposes, I argue that the modern corporation is mainly to be understood as the product of a series of organizational innovations that have had the purpose and effect of economizing on transaction costs. Failure to recognize this has been the source of much confusion, to which the 'inhospitality tradition' in antitrust bears testimony. Supplanting the neoclassical conception of the firm as production function by one which regards the firm as governance structure, whence respects organizational form differences, is needed to restore perspectives. Hitherto puzzling features of conglomerate and multinational enterprise are reinterpreted in the process.

The last essay poses the question 'What is transaction-cost economics?'. This was given as the eighth annual Marion O'Kellie McKay lecture at the University of Pittsburgh. The intellectual antecedents (in law, economics and organization) are described first; the behavioural assumptions on which transaction cost economics relies, the critical dimensions for describing transactions, and a sketch of some of the main applications are then examined.

REFERENCE

Coase, Ronald H., 'The Regulated Industries: Discussion', *American Economic Review,* May 1974, **64**, 194-7.

6. The Vertical Integration of Production: Market Failure Considerations*

The study of vertical integration has presented difficulties at both theoretical and policy levels of analysis. That vertical integration has never enjoyed a secure place in value theory is attributable to the fact that, under conventional assumptions, it is an anomaly: if the costs of operating competitive markets are zero, 'as is usually assumed in our theoretical analysis' (Arrow, 1969, p.48), why integrate?

Policy interest in vertical integration has been concerned mainly with the possibility that integration can be used strategically to achieve anti-competitive effects. In the absence of a more substantial theoretical foundation, vertical integration, as a public policy matter, is typically regarded as having dubious if not outright anti-social properties. Technological interdependencies, or possibly observational economies, constitute the principal exceptions.

The technological interdependency argument is both the most familiar and the most straightforward: successive processes which naturally follow immediately in time and place dictate certain efficient manufacturing configurations; these in turn are believed to have common ownership implications. Such technical complementarity is probably more important in flow process operations (chemicals, metals, etc.) than in separable component manufacture. The standard example is the integration of iron and steelmaking, where thermal economies are said to be available through integration. It is commonly held that where 'integration does not have this physical or technical aspect—as it does not, for example, in integrating the production of assorted components with the assembly of those components—the case for cost savings from integration is generally much less clear' (Bain, 1968, p.381).

* Research on this paper was supported by a grant from the Brookings Institution. It is part of the larger study referred to in note 1. Helpful comments from Noel Edelson, Stefano Fenoaltea, Julius Margolis and Almarin Phillips are gratefully acknowledged.

There is, nevertheless, a distinct unease over the argument. This is attributable, probably, to a suspicion that the firm is more than a simple efficiency instrument, in the usual scale economies and least-cost factor proportions senses of the term, but also possesses coordinating potential that sometimes transcends that of the market. It is the burden of the present argument that this suspicion is warranted. In more numerous respects than are commonly appreciated, the substitution of internal organization for market exchange is attractive less on account of technological economies associated with production but because of what may be referred to broadly as 'transactional failures' in the operation of markets for intermediate goods. This substitution of internal organization for market exchange will be referred to as 'internalization'.

The two principal prior contributions on which the argument relies are Coase's seminal discussion on 'The Nature of The Firm' (1937) and Arrow's later review of market versus non-market allocation (1969). As will be evident, I agree with Malmgren (1961), that the analysis of transaction costs is uninteresting under fully stationary conditions and that only when the need to make unprogrammed adaptations is introduced does the market versus internal organization issue become engaging.

But while Malmgren finds that the advantage of the firm inheres in its capacity to control information and achieve plan consistency among interdependent activities, which may be regarded as an information processing advantage, I mainly emphasize the differential incentive and control properties of firms in relation to markets. This is not to suggest that information processing considerations are unimportant, but rather that these incompletely characterize the distinctive properties of firms that favour internal organization as a market substitute.

I. INTERNAL ORGANIZATION: AFFIRMATIVE ASPECTS

A complete treatment of vertical integration requires that the limits as well as the powers of internal organization be assessed. As the frictions associated with administrative coordination become progressively more severe, recourse to market exchange become more attractive, *ceteris paribus*. It is beyond the scope of this paper, however, to examine the organizational failure of the vertical integration question.[1] Rather it is simply asserted that, mainly on account of bounded rationality and greater confidence in the objectivity of market exchange in comparison with bureaucratic processes, market intermediation is generally to be preferred to internal supply in circumstances in which markets may be said to 'work well'.[2]

The properties of the firm that commend internal organization as a market substitute would appear to fall into three categories: incentives, controls and what may be referred to broadly as 'inherent structural advantages'. In an incentive sense, internal organization attenuates the aggressive advocacy that epitomizes arms' length bargaining. Interests, if not perfectly harmonized, are at least free of representations of a narrowly opportunistic sort; in any viable group, of which the firm is one, the range of admissable intra-organizational behaviour is bounded by considerations of alienation. In circumstances, therefore, where protracted bargaining between independent parties to a transaction can reasonably be anticipated, internalization becomes attractive.[3]

Perhaps the most distinctive advantage of the firm, however, is the wider variety and greater sensitivity of control instruments that are available for enforcing intra-firm in comparison with inter-firm activities (Williamson, 1970). Not only does the firm have the constitutional authority and low-cost access to the requisite data which permit it to perform more precise own-performance evaluations (of both a contemporaneous and *ex post* variety) than can a buyer, but its reward and penalty instruments (which include selective use of employment, promotion, remuneration and internal resource allocation processes) are more refined.

Especially relevant in this connection is that, when conflicts develop, the firm possesses a comparatively efficient conflict resolution machinery. To illustrate, fiat is frequently a more efficient way to settle minor conflicts (say, differences of interpretation) than is haggling or litigation. *Inter*organizational conflict can be settled by fiat only rarely, if at all. For one thing, it would require the parties to agree on an impartial arbitrator, which agreement itself may be costly to secure. It would also require that rules of evidence and procedure be established. If, moreover, the occasion for such interorganizational settlements were to be common, the form of organization converges in effect to vertical integration, with the arbiter becoming a manager in fact if not in name. By contrast, *intra*organizational settlements by fiat are common (Whinston, 1964, pp.410-14).

The firm may also resort to internalization on account of economies of information exchange. Some of these may be due to structural differences between firms and markets. Others, however, reduce ultimately to incentive and control differences between internal and market organization. It is widely accepted, for example, that communication with respect to complex matters is facilitated by a common training and experience and if a compact code has developed in the process. Repeated interpersonal interactions may permit even further economies of communication;

subtle nuances may come through in familiar circumstances which in an unfamiliar relationship could be achieved only with great effort. Still, the drawing of an organizational boundary need not, by itself, prevent intensely familiar relations from developing between organizations. Put differently, but for the goal and control differences described above, the informational advantages of internal over market organization are not, in this respect, apparent. Claims of informational economies thus should distinguish between economies that are attributable to information flows *per se* (structure) and those which obtain on account of differential veracity effects (see section II(4)).

II. MARKET FAILURE CONSIDERATIONS

What are referred to here as market failures are failures only in the limited sense that they involve transaction costs that can be attenuated by substituting internal organization for market exchange. The argument proceeds in five stages. The first three are concerned with characterizing a successively more complex bargaining environment in which small-numbers relations obtain. The last two deal with the special structural advantages which, either naturally or because of prevailing institutional rules, the firm enjoys in relation to the market.

1. Static Markets

Consider an industry that produces a multicomponent product, assume that some of these components are specialized (industry-specific), and assume further that among these there are components for which the economies of scale in production are large in relation to the market. The market, then, will support only a few efficient-sized producers for certain components.

A monopolistic excess of price over cost under market procurement is commonly anticipated in these circumstances—although, as Demsetz (1968) has noted, this need not obtain if there are large numbers of suppliers willing and able to bid at the initial contract award stage. Assume, however, that large-numbers bidding is not feasible. The postulated conditions then afford an 'apparent' incentive for assemblers to integrate backward or suppliers to integrate forward. Two different cases can be distinguished: bilateral monopoly (oligopoly) and competitive assembly with monopolistic supply. The former is considered here; the latter is treated in section II(3).

Bilateral monopoly requires that both price and quantity be negotiated. Both parties stand to benefit naturally by operating on rather than off the contract curve—which here corresponds to the joint profit-maximizing quantity (Fellner, 1947). But this merely establishes the amount to be exchanged. The terms at which this quantity will be traded still need to be determined. Any price consistent with non-negative profits to both parties is feasible. Bargaining can be expected to ensue. Haggling will presumably continue until the marginal private net benefits are perceived by one of the parties to be zero. Although this haggling is jointly (and socially) unproductive, it constitutes a source of private pecuniary gain. Being, nevertheless, a joint profit drain, an incentive to avoid these costs, if somehow this could be arranged, is set up.

One possible adaptation is to internalize the transaction through vertical integration; but a once-for-all contract might also be negotiated. In a perfectly static environment (one that is free of disturbances of all kinds), these may be regarded with indifference: the former involves settlement on component supply price while merger requires agreement on asset valuation. Bargaining skills will presumably be equally important in each instance (indeed, a component price can be interpreted in asset valuation terms, and conversely). Thus, although vertical integration may occur under these conditions, there is nothing in the nature of the problem that requires such an outcome.

A similar argument in these circumstances also applies to adaptation against externalities: joint profit considerations dictate that the affected parties reach an accommodation, but integration holds no advantage over once-for-all contracts in a perfectly static environment.

Transforming the relationship from one of bilateral monopoly to one of bilateral oligopoly broadens the range of bargaining alternatives, but the case for negotiating a merger agreement in relation to a once-for-all contract is not differentially affected on this account. The static characterization to the problem, apparently, will have to be relaxed if a different result is to be reached.

2. Contractual Incompleteness

Let the above conditions be enriched to include the stipulation that the product in question is technically complex and that periodic redesign and/or volume changes are made in response to changing environmental conditions. Also relax the assumption that large-numbers bidding at the initial contract award stage is infeasible. Three alternative supply arrangements can be considered: a once-for-all contract, a series of short-term contracts, and vertical integration.

The dilemma posed by once-for-all contracts is this: lest independent parties interpret contractual ambiguities to their own advantage, which differences can be resolved only by haggling or, ultimately, litigation, contingent supply relations ought exhaustively to be stipulated. But exhaustive stipulation, assuming that it is feasible, is itself costly. Thus although, if production functions were known, appropriate responses to final demand or factor price changes might be deduced, the very costliness of specifying the functions and securing agreement discourages the effort. The problem is made even more severe where a changing technology poses product redesign issues. Here it is doubtful that, despite great effort and expense, contractual efforts reasonably to comprehend the range of possible outcomes will be successful. An adaptive, sequential decision process is thus indicated. If, however, contractual revisions or amendments are regarded as an occasion to bargain opportunistically—which predictably they will be—the purchaser will defer and accumulate adaptations, if by packaging them in complex combinations their true value can better be disguised; some adaptations may be forgone altogether. The optimal sequential decision-making process can in these respects be distorted.

Short-term contracts, which would facilitate adaptive, sequential decision-making, might therefore be preferred. These pose problems, however, if either (1) efficient supply requires investment in special-purpose, long-life equipment, or (2) the winner of the original contract acquires a cost advantage, say by reason of 'first mover' advantages (such as unique location or learning, including the acquisition of undisclosed or proprietary technical and managerial procedures and task-specific labour skills).

The problem with condition (1) is that optimal investment considerations favour the award of a long-term contract so as to permit the supplier confidently to amortize his investment. But, as indicated, long-term contracts pose adaptive, sequential decision-making problems. Thus optimal investment and optimal sequential adaptation processes are in conflict in this instance.

It might be argued that condition (2) poses no problems since initial bidders will fully reflect in their original bids all relevant factors. Thus, although anticipated downstream cost advantages (where downstream is used both here and subsequently in the sense of time rather than place) will give rise to small-numbers competition for downstream supply, competition at the initial award stage is sufficient to assure that only competitive returns will be realized over the entire supply interval. One might expect, therefore, that the low bidder would come in at a price below cost in the first period, set price at the level of alternative supply price in later periods, and earn normal returns overall. Appropriate changes can be introduced easily at the recontracting interval.

A number of potential problems are posed, however. For one thing, unless the total supply requirements are stipulated, 'buying-in' strategies are risky. Also, and related, the alternative supply price is not independent of the terms that the buyer may subsequently offer to rivals.

Moreover, alternative supply price is merely an upper bound; an aggressive buyer may attempt to obtain a price at the level of current costs on each round. Haggling could be expected to ensue. Short-term contracts thus experience what may be serious limitations in circumstances where non-trivial first mover advantages obtain.

In consideration, therefore, of the problems that both long and short-term contracts are subject to, vertical integration may well be indicated. The conflict between efficient investment and efficient sequential decision-making is thereby avoided. Sequential adaptations become an occasion for cooperative adjustment rather than opportunistic bargaining; risks may be attenuated; and differences between successive stages can be resolved more easily by the internal control machinery.

It is relevant to note that the technological interdependency condition involving flow process economies between otherwise separable stages of production is really a special case of the contractual incompleteness argument. The contractual dilemma is this: on the one hand, it may be prohibitively costly, if not infeasible, to specify contractually the full range of contingencies and stipulate appropriate responses between stages. On the other hand, if the contract is seriously incomplete in these respects but, once the original negotiations are settled, the contracting parties are locked into a bilateral exchange, the divergent interests between the parties will predictably lead to individually opportunistic behaviour and joint losses. The advantages of integration thus are not that technological (flow process) economies are unavailable to non-integrated firms, but that integration harmonizes interests (or reconciles differences, often by fiat) and permits an efficient (adaptive, sequential) decision process to be utilized. More generally, arguments favourable to integration that turn on 'supply reliability' considerations commonly reduce to the contractual incompleteness issue.[4]

3. Strategic Misrepresentation Risk

Contractual incompleteness problems develop where there is *ex ante* but not necessarily *ex post* uncertainty. Strategic misrepresentation risks are serious where there is uncertainty in both respects. Not only is the future uncertain but it may not be possible, except at great cost, for an outside agency to establish accurately what has transpired after the fact. The advantages of internalization reside in the facts that the firm's *ex post* access to the relevant data is superior, it attenuates the incentives to exploit uncertainty opportunistically, and the control machinery that the firm is able to activate is more selective.

Affirmative Occasions for Integration. Three affirmative occasions to integrate on account of strategic misrepresentation risk and two potentially anticompetitive consequences of integration can be identified.

(a) *Moral Hazard*. The problem here arises because of the conjoining of inharmonious incentives with uncertainty—or, as Arrow puts it (1969, p.55), it is due to the 'confounding of risks and decisions'. To illustrate, consider the problem of contracting for an item the final cost and/or performance of which is subject to uncertainty. One possibility is for the supplier to bear the uncertainty. But he will undertake a fixed price contract to deliver a specified result the costs of which are highly uncertain only after attaching a risk premium to the price. Assume that the buyer regards this premium as excessive and is prepared on this account to bear the risk himself. The risk can easily be shifted by offering a cost-plus contract. But this impairs the incentives of the supplier to achieve least-cost performance; the supplier may reallocate his assets in such a way as to favour other work to the disadvantage of the cost-plus contract.

Thus although if commitments were self-enforcing, it might often be institutionally most efficient to divide the functions of risk-bearing and contract execution (that is, cost-plus contracts would have ideal properties), specialization is discouraged by interest disparities. At a minimum, the buyer may insist on monitoring the supplier's work. In contrast therefore to a fixed-price contract, where it is sufficient to evaluate end-product performance, cost-plus contracts, because they expose the buyer to risks of inefficient (high cost) contract execution, require that *both* inputs and outputs be evaluated.

Internalization does not eliminate the need for input evaluation. Rather, the advantage of internalization, for input monitoring purposes, resides in the differential ease with which controls are exercised. An external agency, by design, lacks recourse to the internal control machinery: proposed remedies require the consent of the contractor and then are highly circumscribed; unrestricted access by the buyer to the contractor's internal control machinery (including selective use of employment, promotion, remuneration and internal resource allocation processes) is apt to be denied. In consideration of the costs and limitations of input monitoring by outsiders, the buyer may choose instead to bear the risk and perform the work himself. The buyer thus internalizes, through backward vertical integration, a transaction which, but for uncertainty, would move through the market. A cost-type contract for *internal procurement* is arranged.

(b) *Externalities/Imputation*. The externality issue can be examined in two parts. First, has a secure, unambiguous, and 'appropriate' assignment of property rights been made? Second, are the accounting costs of imputing costs and benefits substantial? If answers to these questions are affirmative and negative respectively, appropriability problems will not become an occasion for vertical integration. Where these conditions are not satisfied, however, integration may be indicated.

The assignment aspect of this matter is considered in section II(5). Here it is assumed that an efficacious assignment of property rights has been made and that only the expense of imputing costs and benefits is at issue. But indeed this is apt often to be the more serious problem. High imputation expenses which discourage accurate metering introduce ambiguity into transactions. Did party A affect party B, and if so in what degree? In the absence of objective, low-cost standards, opposed interests can be expected to evaluate these effects differently. Internalization, which permits protracted (and costly) disputes over these issues to be avoided, may on this account be indicated.

(c) *Variable Proportions Distortions*. Consider the case where the assembly stage will support large numbers; fewness appears only in component supply. Whether monopolistic supply prices provide an occasion for vertical integration in these circumstances depends both on production technology and policing expense. Variable proportions at the assembly stage afford opportunities for non-integrated assemblers to adapt against monopolistically-priced components by substituting competitively-priced factors (McKenzie, 1951). Although conceivably the monopolistic component supplier could stipulate, as a condition of sale, that fixed proportions in assembly should prevail, the effectiveness of such stipulations is to be questioned—since ordinarily the implied enforcement costs will be great. Where substitution occurs, inefficient factor proportions, with consequent welfare losses, will result. The private (and social) incentives to integrate so as to reduce total costs by restoring efficient factor combinations are evident.

Anti-competitive Consequences. Anti-competitive effects of two types are commonly attributed to integration: price discrimination and barriers to entry (cf. Stigler, 1968, p.303).

(a) *Price discrimination*. The problem here is first to discover differential demand elasticities, and secondly to arrange for sale in such a way as to preclude reselling. Users with highly elastic demands which purchase the item at a low price must not be able to service inelastic demand customers by acting as a middleman; all sales must be final. Although vertical integration may facilitate the discovery of differential elasticities, it is mainly with respect to the non-resale condition that it is regarded as especially efficacious.

Integration, nevertheless, is a relatively extreme response. Moreover price discrimination is clearly practised in some commodities without recourse to vertical integration (witness electricity and telephone service). What are the distinguishing factors? Legality considerations aside, presumably it is the cost of enforcing (policing) terms of the contract that are at issue. Some commodities apparently have self-enforcing properties—which may obtain on account of high storage and repacking costs or because reselling cannot be arranged inconspicuously. The absence of self-enforcing (policing) properties is what makes vertical integration attractive as a means of accomplishing discrimination.

(b) *Entry barrier effects*. That the vertical integration of production might be used effectively to bar entry is widely disputed. Bork (1969, p.148) argues that

In general, if greater than competitive profits are to be made in an industry, entry should occur whether the entrant has to come in at both levels at once or not. I know of no theory of imperfections in the capital market which would lead suppliers of capital to avoid areas of higher return to seek areas of lower return.

But the issue is not one of profit avoidance but rather involves cost incidence. If borrowers are confronted by increasingly adverse rates as they increase their finance requirements, which Hirshleifer suggests is a distinct possibility (1970, pp.200–1), cost may not be independent of vertical structure.

Assuming that vertical integration has the effect of increasing capital requirements, the critical issues are to what extent and for what reasons the supply curve of finance behaves in the way postulated. The following conjecture is offered as a partial explanation: unable to monitor the performance of *large, complex* organizations in any but the crudest way or to effect management displacement easily except on evidence of seriously discreditable error, investors demand larger returns as finance requirements becomes progressively greater, *ceteris paribus*. Thus the costs of policing against the contingency that managers will operate a rival enterprise opportunistically are, on this argument, at least partly responsible for the reputed behaviour of the supply curve of capital. In consideration of this state of affairs, established firms may use vertical integration strategically to increase finance requirements and thereby to discourage entry if potential entrants feel compelled, as a condition of successful entry, to adopt the prevailing structure—as they may if the industry is highly concentrated.

4. Information Processing Effects

As indicated in section I, one of the advantages of the firm is that it realizes economies of information exchange. These may manifest themselves as information impactedness, observational economies, or what Malmgren (1961) refers to as the 'convergence of expectations'.

Information Impactedness. Richardson illustrates the problems of information impactedness by reference to an entrepreneur who was willing to offer long term contracts (at normal rates of return, presumably) but which contracts others were unprepared to accept because they were not convinced that he had 'the ability, as well as the will, to fulfil them. He may have information sufficient to convince himself that this is the case, but others may not' (Richardson, 1960, p.83). He goes on to observe that the perceived risks of the two parties may be such as to make it difficult to negotiate a contract that offers commensurate returns to each; objective risks are augmented by contractual risks in these circumstances. Integration undertaken for this reason is akin to self-insurance by individuals who know themselves to be good risks but are priced out of the insurance market because of their inability, at low cost, to 'reveal' this condition to insurers.

Observational Economies. As Radner indicates, 'the acquisition of information often involves a "set-up cost", i.e. the resources needed to obtain the information may be independent of the scale of the production process in which the information is used' (Radner, 1970, p.457). Although Radner apparently had horizontal firm size implications in mind, the argument also has relevance for vertical integration. If a single set of observations can be made that is of relevance to a related series of production stages, vertical integration may be efficient.

Still, the question might be raised, why common ownership? Why not an independent observational agency that sells information to all comers? Or, if the needed information is highly specialized, why not a joint venture? Alternatively, what inhibits efficient information exchange between successive stages of production according to contract? In relation, certainly, to the range of intermediate options potentially available, common ownership appears to be an extreme response. What are the factors which favour this outcome?

One of the problems with contracts is that of specifying terms. But even if terms could be reached, there is still a problem of policing the agreement. To illustrate, suppose that the common information collection responsibilities are assigned by contract to one of the parties. The purchasing party then runs *a veracity risk*: information may be filtered and possibly distorted to the advantage of the firm that has assumed the information collection responsibility. If checks are costly and proof of contractual violation difficult, contractual sharing arrangements manifestly experience short-run limitations. If, in addition, small numbers prevail so that options are restricted, contractual sharing is subject to long-run risks as well. On this argument, observational economies are mainly to be attributed to strategic misrepresentation risks rather than to indivisibilities.

Convergence of Expectations. The issue to which the convergence of expectations argument is addressed is that, if there is a high degree of interdependence among successive stages of production and if occasions for adaptation are unpredictable yet common, coordinated responses may be difficult to secure if the separate stages are operated independently. March and Simon (1958, p.159) characterize the problem in the following terms:

> Interdependence by itself does not cause difficulty if the pattern of interdependence is stable and fixed. For, in this case, each subprogram can be designed to take account of all the subprograms with which it interacts. Difficulties arise only if program execution rests on contingencies that cannot be predicted perfectly in advance. In this case, coordinating activity is required to secure agreement about the estimates that will be used as the basis for action, or to provide information to each subprogram unit about the activities of the others.

This reduces, in some respects, to a contractual incompleteness argument. Were it feasible exhaustively to stipulate the appropriate conditional responses, coordination could proceed by contract. This is ambitious, however; in the face of a highly variable and uncertain environment, the attempt to programme responses is apt to be inefficient. To the extent that an unprogrammed (adaptive, sequential) decision process is employed instead, and in consideration of the severe incentive and control limitations that long-term contracts experience in these circumstances (see section II(2) above), vertical integration may be indicated.

But what of the possibility of short-term contracts? It is here that the convergence of expectations argument is of special importance. Thus assume that short-term contracts are not defective on account either of investment disincentives or first-mover advantages. It is Malmgren's (1961) contention that such contracts may nevertheless be vitiated by the absence of structural constraints. The costs of negotiations and the time required to bring the system into adjustment by exclusive reliance on market (price) signals are apt to be great in relation to that which would obtain if successive states were integrated and administrative processes employed as well or instead.

5. Institutional Adaptations
Institutional adaptations of two types are distinguished: simple economic and extra-economic.

Simple Economic. As has been noted by others, vertical integration may be a device by which sales taxes on intermediate products are avoided, or a means by which to circumvent quota schemes and price controls

(Coase, 1937, pp.338-9; Stigler, 1968, pp.136-7). But vertical integration may also be undertaken because of the defective specification of property rights.

Although the appropriate assignment of property rights is a complex question, it reduces (equity considerations aside) to a simple criterion: what assignment yields maximum total product (Coase, 1960, p.34)? This depends jointly on imputation and negotiation expenses and on the incentives of the compensated party. So as to focus on the negotiation expense aspect, assume that imputation expenses are negligible and set the incentive question aside for the moment.[5] An 'appropriate' assignment of property rights will here be defined as one which automatically yields compensation in the amount of the external benefit or cost involved, while an 'inappropriate' assignment is one that requires bargaining to bring the parties into adjustment. Thus if A and B are two parties and A's activity imposes costs on B, the appropriate assignment of property rights is to require A to compensate B. If instead property rights were defined such that A is not required to compensate B, and assuming that the externality holds at the margin, efficient adaptation would occur only if B were to bribe A to bring his activity into adjustment—which entails bargaining. Only if the costs of such bargaining are neglected can the alternative specifications of property rights be said to be equivalent. For similar reasons, if A's activity generates benefits for B, the appropriate specification of property rights will be to require B fully to compensate A. Harmonizing the otherwise divergent interests of the two parties by internalizing the transaction through vertical merger promises to overcome the haggling costs which result when property rights are left either undefined or inappropriately specified.

Other. Risk-aversion refers to the degree of concavity in the utility valuation of pecuniary outcomes. Decision-makers who are risk-averse will be concerned not merely with the expected value, but also with the dispersion in outcomes associated with alternative proposals: the greater the dispersion, the lower the utility valuation. *Ceteris paribus*, decision-makers who are the less risk-averse will presumably assume the risk-bearing function. Even, however, if attitudes toward risk were identical—in the sense that every individual (for any given set of initial endowments) would evaluate a proposal similarly—differing initial asset positions among the members of a population could warrant a specialization of the risk-bearing function, with possible firm and market structure effects (Knight, 1965).

Arrow calls attention to norms of social behaviour, including ethical and moral codes. He observes in this connection that

It is useful for individuals to have some trust in each other's word. In the absence of trust, it would become very costly to arrange for alternative sanctions and guarantees, and many opportunities for mutually beneficial cooperation would have to be foregone. (1969, p.62).

One would expect, accordingly, that vertical integration would be more complete in a low-trust than a high-trust culture, *ceteris paribus*.

III. CONCLUSIONS

That product markets have remarkable coordinating properties is, among economists at least, a secure proposition. That product markets are subject to failure in various respects and that internal organization may be substituted against the market in these circumstances is, if somewhat less familiar, scarcely novel. A systematic treatment of market failure as it bears on vertical integration, however, has not emerged.

Partly this is attributable to inattention to internal organization: the remarkable properties of firms that distinguish internal from market coordination have been neglected. But the fragmented nature of the market failure literature as it bears on vertical integration has also contributed to this condition; the extensive variety of circumstances in which internalization is attractive tends not to be fully appreciated.

The present effort attempts both to address the internal organization issue and to organize the market failure literature as it relates to vertical integration in a systematic way. The argument, however, by no means exhausts the issues that vertical integration raises. For one thing, the discussion of market failures may be incomplete in certain respects. For another, a parallel treatment of the sources and consequences of the failures of internal organization as they relate to vertical integration is needed. Third, the argument applies strictly to the vertical integration of production; although much of it may have equal relevance to backward vertical integration into raw materials and forward integration into distribution, it may have to be delimited in significant respects. Fourth, game theoretic considerations, which may permit the indicated indeterminancy of small numbers bargaining situations to be bounded, have been neglected. Finally, nothing in the present analysis establishes that observed degrees of vertical integration are not, from the social welfare standpoint, excessive. It should nevertheless be apparent that a broader *a priori* case for the vertical integration of production exists than is commonly acknowledged.

NOTES

1. I discuss the organizational failure dimension of this issue in *Markets and Hierarchies (1975)*. Policy implications of the argument are also examined there.
2. An intermediate market will be said to work well if, both presently and prospectively, prices are non-monopolistic and reflect an acceptable risk premium, and if market exchange experiences low transaction costs and permits the realization of essential economics. To the extent that the stipulated conditions do not hold, internal supply becomes relatively more attractive, *ceteris paribus*.
3. Common ownership by itself, of course, does not guarantee goal consistency. A holding company form of organization in which purchaser and supplier are independent divisions, each maximizing individual profits, is no solution. Moreover, merely to stipulate joint profit-maximization is not by itself apt to be sufficient. The goal needs to be operationalized, which involves both rule-making (with respect, for example, to transfer pricing) and the design of efficacious internal incentives. For a discussion, see Williamson (1970).
4. It is sometimes suggested that breach of contract risk affords an additional reason for integration: the small supplier of a critical component whose assets are insufficient to cover a total damage claim leaves the purchaser vulnerable. But this is an argument against small suppliers, not contracting quite generally; the large, diversified supplier might well have superior risk-pooling capability to that of the integrated firm. The risks of contractual incompleteness, however, remain and may discourage purchasing from large, diversified organizations. For a discussion of 'ideal' contracts in this connection, see Arrow (1965, pp.52-3).
5. As Coase has emphasized (1960, pp.32-3, 41), compensation can impair the incentives of the compensated party that experiences an external cost to take appropriate protective measures. Parties that are assured of compensation will be content to conduct business as usual. Such a practice easily contributes to greater social cost than would obtain were compensation denied. A sensitivity to what, in a broad sense, might be regarded as contributory negligence is thus required if the system is to be brought fully into adjustment. Clairvoyance with respect to contributory negligence would of course permit the courts to supply those who experience the external cost with requisite incentives to adapt appropriately. Since, however, such clairvoyance (or even, unbiasedness) cannot routinely be presumed, internalizing the transaction through vertical integration may be indicated for this reason as well. (Interestingly, a symmetrical problem is not faced where the externality is a benefit. Stipulating that compensation shall be paid induces Meade's (1952) orchard grower not merely to extend his production appropriately, but also to shift from apples to peaches if this is socially advantageous.)

REFERENCES

Arrow, Kenneth J., *Aspects of the Theory of Risk-Bearing*, Helsinki, 1965.
Arrow, Kenneth J., 'The Organization of Economic Activity: Issues Pertinent to

the Choice of Market versus Nonmarket Allocation' in *The Analysis and Evaluation of Public Expenditure: The PPB System*, vol. 1. Joint Economic Committee, Washington, DC, 1969, pp.47-64.

Bain, Joe S., *Industrial Organization*, New York, 1968.

Bork, Robert H., 'Vertical Integration and Competitive Processes' in J. Fred Weston and Sam Peltzman (eds.), *Public Policy Toward Mergers*, Pacific Palisades, Calif., 1969, pp.139-49.

Coase, Ronald H., 'The Nature of the Firm', *Economica*, November 1937, **4**, 386-405; reprinted in George J. Stigler and Kenneth E. Boulding (eds.). *Readings in Price Theory*, Homewood, Ill., 1952, pp.331-51.

Coase, Ronald H., 'The Problem of Social Cost', *Journal of Law and Economics*, 1960, **3**, 1-44.

Demsetz, Harold, 'Why Regulate Utilities?' *Journal of Law and Economics*, April 1968, **11**, 55-66.

Fellner, William, 'Prices and Wages under Bilateral Oligopoly', *Quarterly Journal of Economics*, August 1947, **61**, 503-32.

Hirshleifer, J., *Investment, Interest and Capital*, Englewood Cliffs, N.J., 1970.

Knight, Frank H., *Risk, Uncertainty and Profit*, New York, 1965.

McKenzie, Lionel, 'Ideal Output and Interdependence of Firms', *Economic Journal*, December 1951, **61**, 785-803.

Malmgren, H.B., 'Information, Expectations and the Theory of the Firm', *Quarterly Journal of Economics*, August 1961, **75**, 399-421.

Meade, James E., 'External Economies and Diseconomies in a Competitive Situation', *Economic Journal*, March 1952, **62**, 54-67.

Radner, Roy, 'Problems in the Theory of Markets under Uncertainty', *American Economic Review*, May 1970, **60**, 454-60.

Richardson, G.B., *Information and Investment*, London, 1960.

Stigler, George J., *The Organization of Industry*, Homewood, Ill., 1968.

Whinston, Andrew, 'Price Guides in Decentralized Organizations', in W.W. Cooper, H.J. Leavitt and M.W. Shelly, II, (eds.), *New Perspectives in Organization Research*, New York, 1964, pp.405-48.

Williamson, Oliver E., *Corporate Control and Business Behaviour*, Englewood Cliffs, N.J., 1970.

Williamson, Oliver E., *Markets and Hierarchies*, New York, 1975.

7. Transaction-Cost Economics: The Governance of Contractual Relations*

The new institutional economics is preoccupied with the origins, incidence, and ramifications of transaction costs. Indeed, if transaction costs are negligible, the organization of economic activity is irrelevant, since any advantages one mode of organization appears to hold over another will simply be eliminated by costless contracting. But despite the growing realization that transaction costs are central to the study of economics,[1] sceptics remain. Stanley Fischer's complaint is typical: 'Transaction costs have a well-deserved bad name as a theoretical device ... [partly] because there is a suspicion that almost anything can be rationalized by invoking suitably specified transaction costs'.[2] Put differently, there are too many degrees of freedom; the concept wants for definition.

Among the factors on which there appears to be developing a general consensus are: (1) opportunism is a central concept in the study of transaction costs;[3] (2) opportunism is especially important for economic activity that involves transaction-specific investments in human and physical capital;[4] (3) the efficient processing of information is an important and related concept;[5] and (4) the assessment of transaction costs is a comparative institutional undertaking.[6] Beyond these general propositions a consensus on transaction costs is lacking.

Further progress in the study of transaction costs awaits the identification of the critical dimensions with respect to which transaction costs differ and an examination of the economizing properties of alternative

* This paper has benefitted from support from the Center for Advanced Study in the Behavioural Sciences, the Guggenheim Foundation, and the National Science Foundation. Helpful comments by Yoram Ben-Porath, Richard Nelson, Douglass North, Thomas Palay, Joseph Sax, David Teece, and Peter Temin and from the participants at seminars at the Yale Law School and the Institute for Advanced Study at Princeton are gratefully acknowledged. The paper was rewritten to advantage after reading Ben-Porath's discussion paper, 'The F-Connection: Family, Friends, and Firms and the Organization of Exchange', and Temin's discussion paper, 'Modes of Economic Behaviour: Variations on Themes of J.R. Hicks and Herbert Simon'.

institutional modes for organizing transactions. Only then can the matching of transactions with modes be accomplished with confidence. This paper affirms the proposition that transaction costs are central to the study of economics, identifies the critical dimensions for characterizing transactions, describes the main governance structures of transactions, and indicates how and why transactions can be matched with institutions in a discriminating way.

I am mainly concerned with intermediate product market transactions. Whereas previously I have emphasized the incentives to remove transactions from the market and organize them internally (vertical integration),[7] the analysis here is symmetrical and deals with market, hierarchical and intermediate modes of organization alike. The question of why there is so much vertical integration remains interesting, but no more so than the question of why there are so many market- (and quasi-market) mediated transactions. A discriminating analysis will explain which transactions are located where and give the reasons why. The overall object of the exercise essentially comes down to this: for each abstract description of a transaction, identify the most economical governance structure—where by governance structure I refer to the institutional framework within which the integrity of a transaction is decided. Markets and hierarchies are two of the main alternatives.

Some legal background to the study of transactions is briefly reviewed in section I. Of the three dimensions for describing transactions that I propose, investment attributes are the least well understood and probably the most important. The special relevance of investments is developed in the context of the economics of idiosyncrasy in section II. A general contracting schema is developed and applied to commercial contracting in section III. Applications to labour, regulation, family transactions and capital markets are sketched in section IV. Major implications are summarized in section V. Concluding remarks follow.

I. SOME CONTRACTING BACKGROUND

Although there is widespread agreement that the discrete transaction paradigm—'sharp in by clear agreement; sharp out by clear performance'[8]—has served both law and economics well, there is increasing awareness that many contractual relations are not of this well-defined kind.[9] A deeper understanding of the nature of contract has emerged as the legal-rule emphasis associated with the study of discrete contracting has given way to a more general concern with the contractual purposes to be served.[10]

Ian Macneil, in a series of thoughtful and wide-ranging essays on contract, usefully distinguishes between discrete and relational transactions.[11] He further supplies twelve different 'concepts' with respect to which these differ.[12] Serious problems of recognition and application are posed by such a rich classificatory apparatus. More useful for my purposes is the three-way classification of contracts that Macneil offers in his article (1978), where classical, neoclassical and relational categories of contract law are recognized.

1. Classical Contract Law

As Macneil observes, any system of contract law has the purpose of facilitating exchange. What is distinctive about classical contract law is that it attempts to do this by enhancing discreteness and intensifying 'presentiation',[13] where presentiation has reference to efforts to 'make or render present in place or time; to cause to be perceived or realized at present'.[14] The economic counterpart to complete presentiation is contingent claims contracting—which entails comprehensive contracting whereby all relevant future contingencies pertaining to the supply of a good or service are described and discounted with respect to both likelihood and futurity.[15]

Classical contract law endeavours to implement discreteness and presentiation in several ways. For one thing, the identity of the parties to a transaction is treated as irrelevant. In this respect it corresponds exactly with the 'ideal' market transaction in economics.[16] Second, the nature of the agreement is carefully delimited, and the more formal features govern when formal (for example, written) and informal (for example, oral) terms are contested. Third, remedies are narrowly prescribed such that 'should the initial presentiation fail to materialize because of non-performance, the consequences are relatively predictable from the beginning and are not open-ended.'[17] Additionally, third-party participation is discouraged.[18] The emphasis, thus, is on legal rules, formal documents and self-liquidating transactions.

2. Neoclassical Contract Law

Not every transaction fits comfortably into the classical contracting scheme. In particular, long-term contracts executed under conditions of uncertainty are ones for which complete presentiation is apt to be prohibitively costly if not impossible. Problems of several kinds arise. First, not all future contingencies for which adaptations are required can be anticipated at the outset. Second, the appropriate adaptations will not be evident for many contingencies until the circumstances materialize. Third, except as changes in states of the world are unambiguous, hard contracting between autonomous parties may well give rise to veridical disputes when state-contingent claims are made. In a world where (at least some) parties are inclined to be opportunistic, whose representations are to be believed?

Faced with the prospective breakdown of classical contracting in these circumstances, three alternatives are available. One would be to forgo such transactions altogether. A second would be to remove these transactions from the market and organize them internally instead. Adaptive, sequential decision-making would then be implemented under common ownership and with the assistance of hierarchical incentive and control systems. Third, a different contracting relation which preserves trading but provides for additional governance structure might be devised. This last brings us to what Macneil refers to as neoclassical contracting.

As Macneil observes, 'Two common characteristics of long-term contracts are the existence of gaps in their planning and the presence of a range of processes and techniques used by contract planners to create flexibility in lieu of either leaving gaps or trying to plan rigidly.'[19] Third-party assistance in resolving disputes and evaluating performance often has advantages over litigation in serving these functions of flexibility and gap filling. Lon Fuller's remarks on procedural differences between arbitration and litigation are instructive:

> there are open to the arbitrator . . . quick methods of education not open to the courts. An arbitrator will frequently interrupt the examination of witnesses with a request that the parties educate him to the point where he can understand the testimony being received. This education can proceed informally, with frequent interruptions by the arbitrator, and by informed persons on either side, when a point needs clarification. Sometimes there will be arguments across the table, occasionally even within each of the separate camps. The end result will usually be a clarification that will enable everyone to proceed more intelligently with the case. There is in this informal procedure no infringement whatever of arbitrational due process.[20]

A recognition that the world is complex, that agreements are incomplete, and that some contracts will never be reached unless both parties have confidence in the settlement machinery thus characterizes neoclassical contract law. One important purposive difference in arbitration and litigation that contributes to the procedural differences described by Fuller is that, whereas continuity (at least completion of the contract) is presumed under the arbitration machinery, this presumption is much weaker when litigation is employed.[21]

3. Relational Contracting

The pressures to sustain ongoing relations 'have led to the spin-off of many subject areas from the classical, and later the neoclassical, contract law system, e.g. much of corporate law and collective bargaining.'[22] Thus, progressively increasing the 'duration and complexity' of contract has resulted in the displacement of even neoclassical adjustment processes of a more thoroughly transaction-specific, ongoing, administrative kind.[23] The fiction of discreteness is fully displaced as the relation takes on the properties of 'a minisociety with a vast array of norms beyond those centred on the exchange and its immediate processes.'[24] By contrast with the neoclassical system, where the reference-point for effecting adaptations remains the original agreement, the reference-point under a truly relational approach is the 'entire relation as it has developed . . . [through] time. This may or may not include an "original agreement"; and if it does, may or may not result in great deference being given it.'[25]

II. THE ECONOMICS OF IDIOSYNCRASY

Macneil's three-way discussion of contracts discloses that contracts are a good deal more varied and complex than is commonly realized.[26] It furthermore suggests that governance structures—the institutional matrix within which transactions are negotiated and executed—vary with the nature of the transaction. But the critical dimensions of contract are not expressly identified, and the purposes of governance are not stated. Harmonizing interests that would otherwise give way to antagonistic sub-goal pursuits appears to be an important governance function, but this is not explicit in his discussion.

That simple governance structures should be used in conjunction with simple contractual relations and complex governance structures reserved for complex relations seems generally sensible. Use of a complex structure to govern a simple relation is apt to incur unneeded costs, and use of a simple structure for a complex transaction invites strain. But what is simple and complex in contractual respects? Specific attention to the defining attributes of transactions is evidently needed.

As developed in section III, the three critical dimensions for characterizing transactions are (1) uncertainty, (2) the frequency with which transactions recur, and (3) the degree to which durable transaction-specific investments are incurred. Of these three, uncertainty is widely conceded to be a critical attribute;[27] and that frequency matters is at least plausible.[28] The governance ramifications of neither, however, have been fully developed—nor can they be until joined with the third critical dimension: transaction-specific investments. In as much as a considerable amount of the 'action' in the study of governance is attributable to investment differences, some explication is needed.

1. General

The crucial investment distinction is this: to what degree are transaction-specific (non-marketable) expenses incurred. Items that are unspecialized among users pose few hazards, since buyers in these circumstances can easily turn to alternative sources, and suppliers can sell output intended for one order to other buyers without difficulty.[29] Non-marketability problems arise when the *specific identity* of the parties has important cost-bearing consequences. Transactions of this kind will be referred to as idiosyncratic.

Occasionally the identity of the parties is important from the outset, as when a buyer induces a supplier to invest in specialized physical capital of a transaction-specific kind. In as much as the value of this capital in other uses is, by definition, much smaller than the specialized use for which it has been intended, the supplier is effectively 'locked into' the transaction to a significant degree. This is symmetrical, moreover, in that the buyer cannot turn to alternative sources of supply and obtain the item on favourable terms, since the cost of supply from unspecialized capital is presumably great.[30] The buyer is thus committed to the transaction as well.

Ordinarily, however, there is more to idiosyncratic exchange than specialized physical capital. Human-capital investments that are transaction-specific commonly occur as well. Specialized training and learning-by-doing economies in production operations are illustrations. Except when these investments are transferable to alternative suppliers at low cost—which is rare—the benefits of the set-up costs can be realized only so long as the relationship between the buyer and seller of the intermediate product is maintained.

Additional transaction-specific savings can accrue at the interface between supplier and buyer as contracts are successively adapted to unfolding events, and as periodic contract renewal agreements are reached. Familiarity here permits communication economies to be realized: specialized language develops as experience accumulates and nuances are signalled and received in a sensitive way. Both institutional and personal trust relations evolve. Thus the individuals who are responsible for adapting the interfaces have a personal as well as an organizational stake in what transpires. Where personal integrity is believed to be operative, individuals located at the interfaces may refuse to be a part of opportunistic effects to take advantage of (rely on) the letter of the contract when the spirit of the exchange is emasculated. Such refusals can serve as a check upon organizational proclivities to behave opportunistically.[31] Other things being equal, idiosyncratic exchange relations which feature personal trust will survive greater stress and display greater adaptability.

Idiosyncratic goods and services are thus ones where investments of transaction-specific human and physical capital are made and, contingent upon successful execution, benefits are realized. Such investments can and do occur in conjunction with occasional trades where delivery for a specialized design is stretched out over a long period (for example, certain construction contracts). The transactions that I wish to emphasize here, however, are exchanges of the recurring kind. Although large numbers competition is frequently feasible at the initial award stage for recurring contracts of all kinds, idiosyncratic transactions are ones for which the relationship between buyer and supplier is quickly thereafter *transformed* into one of bilateral monopoly—on account of the transaction-specific costs referred to above. This transformation has profound contracting consequences.

Thus, whereas recurrent spot contracting is feasible for standardized transactions (because large numbers competition is continuously self-policing in these circumstances), such contracting has seriously defective investment incentives where idiosyncratic activities are involved. By assumption, cost economies in production will be realized for idiosyncratic activities only if the supplier invests in a special-purpose plant and equipment or if his labour force develops transaction-specific skills in the course of contract execution (or both). The assurance of a continuing relation is needed to encourage investments of both kinds. Although the requisite incentives might be provided if long-term contracts were negotiated, such contracts are necessarily incomplete (by reason of bounded rationality). Appropriate state-contingent adaptations thus go unspecified. Intertemporal efficiency nevertheless requires that adaptations to changing market circumstances be made.

How to effect these adaptations poses a serious contracting dilemma, though it bears repeating that, absent the hazards of opportunism, the difficulties would vanish—since then the gaps in long-term, incomplete contracts could be faultlessly filled in an adaptive, sequential way. A general clause, to which both parties would agree, to the effect that 'I will behave responsibly rather than seek individual advantage when an occasion to adapt arises', would, in the absence of opportunism, suffice. Given, however, the unenforceability of general clauses and the proclivity of human agents to make false and misleading (self-disbelieved) statements, the following hazard must be confronted: joined as they are in an idiosyncratic condition of bilateral monopoly, both buyer and seller are strategically situated to bargain over the disposition of any incremental gain whenever a proposal to adapt is made by the other party. Although both have a long-term interest in effecting adaptations of a joint profit-maximizing kind, each also has an interest in appropriating as much of the gain as he can on each occasion to adapt. Efficient adaptations which would otherwise be made thus result in costly haggling or even go unmentioned, lest the gains be dissipated by costly sub-goal pursuit. Governance structures which attenuate opportunism and otherwise infuse confidence are evidently needed.

2. Examples

Some illustrations may help to motivate what is involved in idiosyncratic transactions. Specialized physical capital is relatively straightforward. Examples are (1) the purchase of a specialized component from an outside supplier or (2) the location of a specialized plant in a unique, proximate relation to a downstream processing stage to which it supplies vital input.

Thus assume (a) that special-purpose equipment is needed to produce the component in question (which is to say that the value of the equipment in its next-best alternative use is much lower); (b) that scale economies require that a significant, discrete investment be made, and (c) that alternative buyers for such components are few (possibly because of the organization of the industry, possibly because of special design features). The interests of buyer and seller in a continuing exchange relation are plainly strong under these circumstances.

Plant proximity benefits are attributable to transportation and related flow process (inventory, thermal economy, and so on) economies. A specialized plant need not be implied but long life and a unique location are. Once made, the investment pre-empts the unique location and is not thereafter moveable (except at prohibitive cost). Buyer and supplier again need to satisfy themselves that they have a workable, adaptable exchange agreement.[32]

Idiosyncratic investments in human capital are in many ways more interesting and less obvious than are those in physical capital. Polanyi's discussion of 'personal knowledge' is illuminating:

The attempt to analyze scientifically the established industrial arts has everywhere led to similar results. Indeed even in the modern industries the indefinable knowledge is still an essential part of technology. I have myself watched in Hungary a new, imported machine for blowing electric lamp bulbs, the exact counterpart of which was operating successfully in Germany, failing for a whole year to produce a single flawless bulb.[33]

And he goes on to observe with respect to craftsmanship that:

an art which has fallen into disuse for the period of a generation is altogether lost. ... It is pathetic to watch the endless efforts—equipped with microscopy and chemistry, with mathematics and electronics—to reproduce a single violin of the kind the half-literate Stradivarius turned out as a matter of routine more than 200 years ago.[34]

Polanyi's discussion of language also has a bearing on the argument advanced above that specialized code words or expressions can and do arise in the context of recurring transactions and that these yield economies. As he puts it, 'Different vocabularies for the interpretation of things divide men into groups which cannot understand each other's way of seeing things and acting upon them.'[35] And subsequently he remarks that:

To know a language is an art, carried on by tacit judgments and the practice of unspecified skills. . . . Spoken communication is the successful application by two persons of the linguistic knowledge and skill acquired by such apprenticeship, one person wishing to transmit, the other to receive, information. Relying on what each has learnt, the speaker confidently utters words and the listener confidently interprets them, while they mutually rely on each other's correct use and understanding of these words. A true communication will take place if, and only if, these combined assumptions of authority and trust are in fact justified.[36]

Babbage reports a remarkable example of transaction-specific value in exchange that occurred in the early 1800s. Although he attributes the continuing exchange in the face of adversity to values of 'established character' (trust), I believe there were other specialized human and physical investments involved as well. In any event, the circumstance which he describes is the following:

The influence of established character in producing confidence operated in a very remarkable manner at the time of the exclusion of British manufactures from the Continent during the last war. One of our largest establishments had been in the habit of doing extensive business with a house in the centre of Germany; but, on the closing of the continental ports against our manufacturers, heavy penalties were inflicted on all those who contravened the Berlin and Milan decrees. The English manufacturer continued, nevertheless, to receive orders, with directions how to consign them, and appointments for the time and mode of payment, in letters, the handwriting of which was known to him, but which were never signed, except by the Christian name of one of the firm, and even in some instances they were without any signature at all. These orders were executed; and in no instance was there the least irregularity in the payments.[37]

While most of these illustrations refer to technical and commercial transactions, other types of transactions also have an idiosyncratic quality. Justice Rhenquist refers to some of these when speaking of the general class of cases where 'the litigation of an individual's claim of deprivation of a right would bring parties *who must remain in a continuing relationship* into the adversarial atmosphere of a courtroom'[38]—which atmosphere he plainly regards as detrimental to the quality of the relationship. Examples that he offers include reluctance to have the courts mediate collective bargaining disputes[39] and to allow children to bring suit against parents.[40]

But surely we must ask what is distinctive about these transactions. I submit that transaction-specific human capital is central to each. Why also would it take the Hungarians so long to operate the German light-bulb machine? And what else explains the loss of Stradivarius's craftsmanship? Likewise the understanding and trust which evolve between Babbage's transmitter and receiver are valued human assets which, once developed, will be sacrificed with reluctance. And the disruption of continuing relationships to which Justice Rhenquist refers occasions concern precisely because there are no adequate substitutes for these idiosyncratic relations.[41]

The general argument of this paper is that special governance structures supplant standard market-cum-classical contract exchange when transaction-specific values are great. Idiosyncratic commercial, labour and family relations are specific examples.

III. COMMERCIAL CONTRACTING

The discussion of commercial contracting begins with a brief statement on economizing. The proposed schema for characterizing transactions and their governance is then developed, including the relation of the schema with Macneil's three-way classification of contract.

1. Economizing

The criterion for organizing commercial transactions is assumed to be the strictly instrumental one of cost economizing. Essentially this takes two parts: economizing on production expense and economizing on transaction costs.[42] To the degree that transaction costs are negligible, buying rather than making will normally be the most cost-effective means of procurement.[43] Not only can static scale economies be more fully exhausted by buying rather than making, but the supplier who aggregates uncorrelated demands can realize collective pooling benefits as well. Since external procurement avoids many of the bureaucratic hazards of internal procurement (which hazards, however, are themselves of a transaction cost kind),[44] external procurement is evidently warranted.[45]

As indicated, however, the object is to economize on the *sum* of production and transaction costs. To the degree production cost economies of external procurement are small and/or the transaction costs associated with external procurement are great, alternative supply arrangements deserve serious consideration. Economizing on transaction costs essentially reduces to economizing on bounded rationality while simultaneously safeguarding the transactions in question against the hazards of opportunism. Holding the governance structure constant, these two objectives are in tension, since a reduction in one commonly results in an increase in the other.[46]

Governance structures, however, are properly regarded as part of the optimization problem. For some transactions, a shift from one structure to another may permit a simultaneous reduction in both the expense of writing a complex contract (which economizes on bounded rationality) and the expense of executing it effectively in an adaptive, sequential way (by attenuating opportunism). Indeed, this is precisely the attraction of internal procurement for transactions of a recurrent, idiosyncratic kind. Not only are market aggregation economies negligible for such transactions—since the requisite investments are transaction-specific— but market trading in these circumstances is shot through with appropriable quasi-rent hazards. The issues here have been developed elsewhere.[47] The object of this paper is to integrate them into a larger contractual framework.

Note in this connection that the prospect of recovering the set-up costs associated with specialized governance structures varies with the frequency with which transactions recur. Specialized governance structures are much easier to justify for recurrent transactions than for identical transactions that occur only occasionally.

2. Characterizing Transitions

I asserted earlier that the critical dimensions for describing contractual relations are uncertainty, the frequency with which transactions recur, and the degree to which investments are idiosyncratic. To simplify the exposition, I shall assume uncertainty exists in some intermediate degree and focus initially on frequency and the degree to which the expenses incurred are transaction-specific. The separate importance of uncertainty will then be developed in section III(4). Three frequency and three investment categories will be recognized. Frequency can be characterized as one-time, occasional and recurrent; and investments are classed as non-specific, mixed and idiosyncratic. To simplify further the argument, the following assumptions are made: (1) suppliers intend to be in business on a continuing basis, thus the special hazards posed by fly-by-night firms can be disregarded; (2) potential suppliers for any given requirement are numerous—which is to say that *ex ante* monopoly in ownership of specialized resources is assumed away; (3) the frequency dimension refers strictly to buyer activity in the market;[48] and (4) the investment dimension refers to the characteristics of investments made by suppliers.[49]

Although discrete transactions are intriguing—for example, purchasing local spirits from a shopkeeper in a remote area of a foreign country to which one never again expects to visit nor to refer his friends—few transactions have this totally isolated character. For those that do not, the difference between one-time and occasional transactions is not apparent. Accordingly, only occasional and recurrent frequency distinctions will be maintained. The two-by-three matrix shown in Figure 7.1 thus describes the six types of transactions to which governance structures need to be matched. Illustrative transactions appear in the cells.

		Investment Characteristics		
		Non-specific	*Mixed*	*Idiosyncratic*
Frequency	*Occasional*	Purchasing standard equipment	Purchasing customized equipment	Constructing a plant
	Recurrent	Purchasing standard material	Purchasing customized material	Site-specific transfer of intermediate product across successive stages

Figure 7.1: Illustrative commercial transactions

3. Governance Structures

Three broad types of governance structures will be considered: non-transaction-specific, semi-specific and highly specific. The market is the classic non-specific governance structure within which 'faceless buyers and sellers . . . meet . . . for an instant to exchange standardized goods at equilibrium prices.'[50] By contrast, highly specific structures are tailored to the special needs of the transaction. Identity here clearly matters. Semi-specific structures naturally fall in between. Several propositions are suggested immediately: (1) Highly standardized transactions are not apt to require specialized governance structure; (2) only recurrent transactions will support a highly specialized governance structure;[51] (3) although occasional transactions of a non-standardized kind will not support a transaction-specific governance structure, they require special attention none the less. In terms of Macneil's three way classification of contract, classical contracting presumably applies to all standardized transactions (whatever the frequency), relational contracting develops for transactions of a recurring and non-standardized kind, and neoclassical contracting is needed for occasional, non-standardized transactions.

Market governance: Classical contracting. Market governance is the main governance structure for non-specific transactions of both occasional and recurrent contracting. Markets are especially efficacious when recurrent transactions are contemplated, since both parties need only consult their own experience in deciding to continue a trading relationship or, at little transitional expense, turn elsewhere. Being standardized, alternative purchase and supply arrangements are presumably easy to work out.

Non-specific but occasional transactions are ones for which buyers (and sellers) are less able to rely on direct experience to safeguard transactions against opportunism. Often, however, rating services or the experience of other buyers of the same good can be consulted. Given that the good or service is of a standardized kind, such experience rating, by formal and informal means, will provide incentives for parties to behave responsibly.

To be sure, such transactions take place within and benefit from a legal framework. But such dependence is not great. As Lowry puts it, 'the traditional economic analysis of exchange in a market setting properly corresponds to the legal concept of *sale* (rather than contract), since sale presumes arrangements in a market context and requires legal support primarily in enforcing transfers of title.'[52] He would thus reserve the concept of contract for exchanges where, in the absence of standardized market alternatives, the parties have designed 'patterns of future relations on which they could rely'.[53]

The assumptions of the discrete contracting paradigm are rather well satisfied for transactions where markets serve as a main governance mode. Thus the specific identity of the parties is of negligible importance; substantive content is determined by reference to formal terms of the contract; and legal rules apply. Market alternatives are mainly what protect each party against opportunism by his opposite.[54] Litigation is strictly for settling claims; concentrated efforts to sustain the relation are not made because the relation is not independently valued.[55]

Trilateral governance: Neoclassical contracting. The two types of transactions for which trilateral governance is needed are occasional transactions of the mixed and highly idiosyncratic kinds. Once the principals to such transactions have entered into a contract, there are strong incentives to see the contract through to completion. Not only have specialized investments been put in place, the opportunity cost of which is much lower in alternative uses, but the transfer of these assets to a successor supplier would pose inordinate difficulties in asset valuation.[56] The interests of the principals in sustaining the relation are especially great for highly idiosyncratic transactions.

Market relief is thus unsatisfactory. Often the set-up costs of a transaction-specific governance structure cannot be recovered for occasional transactions. Given the limits of classical contract law for sustaining these transactions, on the one hand, and the prohibitive cost of transaction-specific (bilateral) governance, on the other, an intermediate institutional form is evidently needed.

Neoclassical contract law has many of the sought-after qualities. Thus rather than resorting immediately to strict reliance on litigation—with its transaction rupturing features—*third-party assistance* (arbitration) in resolving disputes and evaluating performance is employed instead. The use of the architect as a relatively independent expert to determine the content of form construction contracts is an example.[57] Also, the expansion of the specific performance remedy in past decades is consistent with continuity purposes—though Macneil declines to characterize specific performance as the 'primary neoclassical contract remedy'.[58] The section of the Uniform Commercial Code which permits the 'seller aggrieved by a buyer's breach . . . unilaterally to maintain the relation'[59] is yet another example.

Transaction-specific governance: Relational contracting. The two types of transactions for which specialized governance structures are commonly devised are recurring transactions of the mixed and highly idiosyncratic kinds. The non-standardized nature of these transactions makes primary reliance on market governance hazardous, while their recurrent nature permits the cost of the specialized governance structure to be recovered.

Two types of transaction-specific governance structures for intermediate production market transactions can be distinguished: bilateral structures, where the autonomy of the parties is maintained; and unified structures, where the transaction is removed from the market and organized within the firm subject to an authority relation (vertical integration). Bilateral structures have only recently received the attention they deserve and their operation is least well understood.

(a) Bilateral governance: obligational contracting. Highly idiosyncratic transactions are ones where the human and physical assets required for production are extensively specialized, so there are no obvious scale economies to be realized through inter-firm trading that the buyer (or seller) is unable to realize himself (through vertical integration). In the case, however, of mixed transactions, the degree of asset specialization is less complete. Accordingly, outside procurement for these components may be favoured by scale economy considerations.

As compared with vertical integration, outside procurement also is good in eliciting cost control for steady-state supply. Problems, however, arise when adaptability and contractual expense are considered. Whereas internal adaptations can be effected by fiat, outside procurement involves effecting adaptations across a market interface. Unless the need for adaptations had been contemplated from the outset and expressly provided for by the contract, which often is impossible or prohibitively expensive, adaptations across a market interface can be accomplished only by mutual, follow-on agreements. In as much as the interests of the parties will commonly be at variance when adaptation proposals (originated by either party) are made, a dilemma is evidently posed.

On the one hand, both parties have an incentive to sustain the relationship rather than to permit it to unravel, the object being to avoid the sacrifice of valued transaction-specific economies. On the other hand, each party appropriates a separate profit stream and cannot be expected to accede readily to any proposal to adapt the contract. What is needed, evidently, is some way for declaring admissible dimensions for adjustment such that flexibility is provided under terms in which both parties have confidence. This can be accomplished partly by (1) recognizing that the hazards of opportunism vary with the type of adaptation proposed, and (2) restricting adjustments to those where the hazards are least. But the spirit within which adaptations are effected is equally important.[60]

Quantity adjustments have much better incentive compatibility properties than do price adjustments. For one thing, price adjustments have an unfortunate zero-sum quality, whereas proposals to increase, decrease or delay delivery do not. Also, except as discussed below, price adjustment proposals involve the risk that one's opposite is contriving to alter the terms within the bilateral monopoly trading gap to his advantage. By contrast, a presumption that exogenous events rather than strategic purposes are responsible for quantity adjustments is ordinarily warranted. Given the mixed nature of the exchange, a seller (or buyer) simply has little reason to doubt the representations of his opposite when a quantity change is proposed.

Thus buyers will neither seek supply from other sources nor divert products obtained (at favourable prices) to other uses (or users)—because other sources will incur high set-up costs and an idiosyncratic product is non-fungible across uses and users. Likewise, sellers will not withhold supply because better opportunities have arisen, since the assets in question have a specialized character. The result is that quantity representations for idiosyncratic products can ordinarily be taken at face value. Since inability to adapt both quantity and price would render most idiosyncratic exchanges non-viable, quantity adjustments occur routinely.

Of course, not all price adjustments pose the same degree of hazard. Those which pose few hazards will predictably be implemented. Crude escalator clauses which reflect changes in general economic conditions are one possibility. But since such escalators are not transaction-specific, imperfect adjustments often result when these escalators are applied to local conditions. We should therefore consider whether price adjustments that are more closely related to local circumstances are feasible. The issue here is whether interim price adjustments can be devised for some subset of conditions such that the strategic hazards described above do not arise. What are the preconditions?

Crises facing either of the parties to an idiosyncratic exchange constitute one class of exceptions. Faced with a viability crisis which jeopardizes the relationship, *ad hoc* price relief may be permitted. More relevant and interesting, however, is whether there are circumstances whereby interim price adjustments are made routinely. The preconditions here are two: first, proposals to adjust prices must relate to exogenous, germane and easily verifiable events; and second, quantifiable cost consequences must be confidently related thereto. An example may help to illustrate. Consider a component for which a significant share of the cost is accounted for by a basic material (copper, steel). Assume, moreover, that the fractional cost of the component in terms of this basic material is well specified. An exogenous change in prices of materials would under these circumstances pose few hazards if partial but interim price relief were permitted by allowing pass-through according to formula. A more refined adjustment than aggregate escalators would afford thereby obtains.

It bears emphasis, however, that not all costs so qualify. Changes in overhead or other expenses for which validation is difficult and which, even if verified, bear an uncertain relation to the cost of the component will be passed through in a similar way. Recognizing the hazards, the parties will simply forgo relief of this kind.

(b) Unified governance: internal organization. Incentives for trading weaken as transactions become progressively more idiosyncratic. The reason is that, as the specialized human and physical assets become more specialized to a single use, and hence less transferable to other uses, economies of scale can be as fully realized by the buyer as by an outside supplier.[61] The choice of organizing mode then turns on which mode has superior adaptive properties. As discussed elsewhere, vertical integration will invariably appear in these circumstances.[62]

The advantage of vertical integration is that adaptations can be made in a sequential way without the need to consult, complete or revise inter-firm agreements. Where single ownership entity spans both sides of the transactions, a presumption of joint profit-maximization is warranted. Thus price adjustments in vertically integrated enterprises will be more complete than in inter-firm trading. And quantity adjustments, of course, will be implemented at whatever frequency serves to maximize the joint gain to the transaction.

Unchanging identity at the interface coupled with extensive adaptability in both price and quantity is thus characteristic of highly idiosyncratic transactions which are vertically integrated. Obligational contracting is supplanted by the more comprehensive adaptive capability afforded by administration.

The match of governance structures with transactions that results from these economizing efforts is shown in Figure 7.2.

4. Uncertainty

Transactions conducted under certainty are relatively uninteresting. Except as they differ in the time required to reach an equilibrium exchange configuration, any governance structure will do. More relevant are transactions where uncertainty is present to an intermediate or high degree. The foregoing has dealt with the first of these. The question here is how the governance of transactions is affected by increasing the degree of uncertainty.

		Investment Characteristics		
		Non-specific	*Mixed*	*Idiosyncratic*
Frequency	*Occasional*	Market governance (Classical contracting)	Trilateral governance (neoclassical contracting)	
	Recurrent		Bilateral governance (Relational contracting)	Unified governance

Figure 7.2. Matching governance structures with commercial transactions

Recall that non-specific transactions are ones for which continuity has little value, since new trading relations are easily arranged. Increasing the degree of uncertainty docs not alter this. Accordingly, market exchange continues and the discrete contracting paradigm (classical contract law) holds across standardized transactions of all kinds, whatever the degree of uncertainty.

Matters are different with transaction-specific investments. Whenever investments are idiosyncratic in non-trivial degree, increasing the degree of uncertainty makes it more imperative that the parties devise a machinery to 'work things out'—since contractual gaps will be larger and the occasions for sequential adaptations will increase in number and importance as the degree of uncertainty increases. This has special relevance for the organization of transactions with mixed investment attributes. Two possibilities exist. One would be to sacrifice valued design features in favour of a more standardized good or service. Market governance would then apply. The second would be to preserve the design but surround the transaction with an elaborated governance apparatus, thereby facilitating more effective adaptive, sequential decision-making. Specifically, a more elaborate arbitration apparatus is apt to be devised for occasional non-standard transactions. And bilateral governance structures will often give way to unified ones as uncertainty is increased for recurrent transactions.

Reductions in uncertainty, of course, warrant shifting transactions in the opposite direction. To the extent that uncertainty decreases as an industry matures (which is the usual case) the benefits that accrue to integration presumably decline. Accordingly, greater reliance on obligational market contracting is commonly feasible for transactions of recurrent trading in mature industries.

IV. OTHER APPLICATIONS

The three dimensions for describing transactions—frequency, investment idiosyncrasy and uncertainty—apply to transactions of all kinds. The same general considerations that apply to governance structures for commercial transactions carry over as well. The specific governance structures for organizing commercial transactions do not, however, apply without modification to the governance of other types of transactions. Applications of the framework to the study of labour markets, regulation, family law and capital markets are briefly sketched here.

1. Labour
Occasional labour-market transactions typically take the form of repair or replacement services—the plumber, electrician, and so forth. Especially in older homes or structures, these transactions can take on an idiosyncratic quality. Although such transactions can be interesting, the transactions on which I want to focus are recurrent labour-market transactions of the non-specific, mixed and idiosyncratic kinds.

Summers' examinations of collective agreements in relation to the law of contracts disclosed that, while the collective bargain differed greatly from the ordinary bargain of commerce, collective agreements are nonetheless a part of the 'mainstream of contract'.[63] He suggested that the study of contract proceed on two levels: the search for an underlying framework and, within that framework, an examination of the distinctive institutional attributes that distinguish each type of transaction. With respect to the first of these he conjectured that 'the principles common to the whole range of contractual transactions are relatively few and of such generality and competing character that they should not be stated as legal rules at all.'[64]

I am persuaded that Summers' two-part strategy for studying contract leads to a deeper understanding of the issues. And I believe that the frame-work set out in the preceding sections of this paper provides much of the underlying unity called for by Summers. What differs as one moves across various contracting activities is the institutional infrastructure.

Non-specific transactions. Non-specific labour-market transactions are ones where employer and employee are largely indifferent to the identity of each: migrant farm labour is an example. Although an unchanging employment association between firm and worker may be observed to continue over long intervals for some of these employees, each party is essentially meeting bids in the spot market. A valuable ongoing relationship, in which specific training and on-the-job learning yield idiosyncratic benefits, is thus not implied. Both wages and employment are variable and market governance applies to transactions of this kind. Consider, therefore, mixed and idiosyncratic labour-market transactions.

Mixed transactions. Probably the most interesting labour-market transactions are those where large numbers of workers acquire an intermediate degree of firm-specific skill. Note that, in as much as the degree of idiosyncracy is a design variable, firms would presumably redesign jobs to favour more standardized operations if it were impossible to devise governance structures which prevented antagonistic bargaining relations from developing between firms and idiosyncratically-skilled employees. Although least-cost production technologies would be sacrificed in the process, net gains might nevertheless be realized since incumbent workers would realize little strategic advantage over otherwise qualified but inexperienced outsiders.

Justice Rhenquist has observed that 'Adjudicatory review of the decisions of certain institutions, while perhaps insuring a "better" decision in some objective sense, can only disrupt on-going relationships within the institution and thereby hamper the institution's ability to serve its designated societal function.'[65] Examples of adjudicatory review with respect to which he counsels caution include collective bargaining agreements.

The reasons for this are that adjudicatory review is not easily apprised of the special needs of the transaction and the prospect of such review impairs the incentive of the parties to devise bilateral governance structure. The *Vaca* v. *Stipes* holding, which Justice Rhenquist cites, is fully consistent with this interpretation. There the Court held that an individual could not compel his union to take his grievance to arbitration, since if the law were otherwise 'the settlement machinery provided by the contract would be substantially undermined, thus . . . [introducing] the vagaries of independent and unsystematic negotiations.'[66] Archibald Cox elaborates as follows:[67]

giving the union control over all claims arising under the collective agreement comports so much better with the functional nature of a collective bargaining agreement. . . . Allowing an individual to carry a claim to arbitration whenever he is dissatisfied with the adjustment worked out by the company and the union . . . discourages the kind of day-to-day cooperation between company and union which is normally the mark of sound industrial relations—a relationship in which grievances are treated as problems to be solved and contracts are only guideposts in a dynamic human relationship. When . . . the individual's claim endangers group interests, the union's function is to resolve the competition by reaching an accommodation or striking a balance.

The practice described by Cox of giving the union control over arbitration claims plainly permits group interests—whence the concern for system viability—to supersede individual interests, thereby curbing small-numbers opportunism.

General escalator or predetermined wage adjustments aside, wages are unchanging under collective bargaining agreements.[68] Interim adaptations are nonetheless essential. These take three forms: (1) quantity adjustments, (2) assignment changes, and (3) refinement of working rules as a result of grievances.

Quantity adjustments are made in response to changing market opportunities. Either the level or the mix of employment is adjusted as economic events unfold. Given that valuable firm-specific training and learning reside in the workers, layoffs with a presumption of re-employment when conditions improve are common. Conformably, the degree to which the machinery governing access to jobs is elaborated ought to vary directly with the degree to which jobs in a firm are idiosyncratic. Thus promotion ladders in firms where a succession of interdependent jobs are highly idiosyncratic should be long and thin, with access mainly restricted to the bottom, whereas promotion ladders in non-idiosyncratic activities should be broadly structured.[69] Likewise, promotion on merit ought to be favoured over promotion strictly by seniority in firms where jobs are more idiosyncratic.[70]

Highly idiosyncratic transactions. Recall that idiosyncratic transactions involve not merely uniqueness but uniqueness of a transaction-specific kind. Also recall that our concern in this section is with recurring transactions. Thus, although there are many uniquely skilled individuals (artists, athletes, researchers, administrators), unique skills are rarely of a transaction-specific kind. On the contrary, most of these individuals could move to another organization without significant productivity losses.

The exceptions are those where the benefits which accrue to experience (inside knowledge) and/or team interaction effects are great. Whereas commercial transactions of a highly idiosyncratic nature are unified under a common ownership, limits on indenture foreclose this option for labour-market transactions. Instead of 'merger', complex contracts designed to tie the interests of the individual to the organization on a long-term basis are negotiated. Severe penalties are provided should either party seek unilateral termination. Non-vested, long-term, contingent reward schemes are devised. More generally, transaction-specific infrastructure will be highly individuated for such transactions.

2. Regulation of Natural Monopoly

Again the argument is that specialized governance structure is needed to the degree that efficient supply necessarily joins buyers and sellers in a bilateral trading relation of a continuing nature. And again, the object of governance is (1) to protect the interests of the respective parties and (2) adapt the relationship to changing circumstances.

Although differing in details, both Goldberg[71] and I[72] have argued that specialized governance structure is needed for services for which natural monopoly features are great. Such structure presumably has the purpose of providing sellers (investors) and buyers with security of expectations, which is a protective function, while at the same time facilitating adaptive, sequential decision-making. Rate-of-return regulation with periodic review has these features. To the extent, however, that such regulation is observed in conjunction with activities where transaction-specific investments are insubstantial (as, for example, in the trucking industry), the case for regulation is not at all apparent—or, if it is to be made, must appeal to arguments very different from those set out here.

3. Family Law

The issue here is whether the role of adjudication should be *expanded* to help govern family relationships. Granting that adjudication as ultimate relief can and often does serve a useful role for sustaining family relations, such relations are plainly idiosyncratic to an unusual degree and a specialized governance structure is surely the main mode of governance. As the role of adjudication is expanded, reliance upon internal structure is apt to be reduced. Therefore, except when individual rights are seriously threatened, withholding access to adjudication may be indicated.

Justice Rhenquist's remarks concerning the corrosive effects of adversary hearings on the family are apposite: 'Any sort of adversary hearing which pits parent against child is bound to be disruptive, placing stresses and tensions on the intra-familial relationships which in turn weaken the family as an institution.'[73] Whether, as this suggests, parent-child family relations are optimized where adjudication is zero or negligible is beyond the scope of this paper. It suffices for my purposes merely to note that valued family relations are recurrent and idiosyncratic and that a specialized, transaction-specific governance structure must be encouraged lest the parties withhold investing heavily in the institution.[74]

4. Capital Market Transactions

The ease of verification is critical to the operation of capital markets.[75] Where verification is easy, markets work well and additional governance is unnecessary. Where verification is difficult or very difficult, however, additional governance may be indicated. Occasional transactions are apt to benefit from third-party assistance, while recurring transactions are ones for which bilateral governance will presumably be observed. Assessing capital market transactions within the proposed framework is thus accomplished by substituting 'ease of verification' for 'degree of transaction-specific investment'. Once this is done, the governance structures appropriate to capital markets are broadly similar to those within which commercial transactions are organized.

V. IMPLICATIONS

Dimensionalizing transactions and examining the costs of executing different transactions in different ways generate a large number of institutional implications. Some of these are summarized here.

1. General

1. Non-specific transactions, either occasional or recurrent, are efficiently organized by markets.
2. Occasional transactions that are non-standardized stand most to benefit from adjudication.
3. A transaction-specific governance structure is more fully developed where transactions are (a) recurrent, (b) entail idiosyncratic investment, and (c) are executed under greater uncertainty.

2. Commercial Transactions

1. Optimization of commercial transactions requires simultaneous attention to (a) production economies, (b) transaction-cost economies, and (c) component design.

2. The reason why Macaulay observes so few litigated cases in business[76] is because markets work well for non-specific transactions, while recurrent, non-standard transactions are governed by bilateral or unified structures.

3. As uncertainty increases, the obligational market contracting mode will not be used for recurrent transactions with mixed investment features. Such transactions will either be standardized and shifted to the market, or organized internally.

4. As generic demand grows and the number of supply sources increases, exchange that was once transaction-specific loses this characteristic and greater reliance on market-mediated governance is feasible. Thus vertical integration may give way to obligational market contracting, which in turn may give way to markets.

5. Where inventory and related flow-process economies are great, site-specific supply and transaction-specific governance (commonly vertical integration) will be observed. Generic demand here has little bearing.

6. The organization of the interface between manufacturing and distribution reflects similar investment considerations: goods and services that can be sold without incurring transaction-specific investment will be distributed through conventional marketing channels while those where such investments are great will be supported by specialized—mainly bilateral (for example, franchising) or unified (forward integration) governance structures.

7. The governance of technical change poses special difficulties. The frequently noted limits of markets[77] often gives way to more complex governance relations, again for the same general reasons and along the same general lines as are set out here.[78]

3. Other Transactions

1. The efficiency benefits of collective organization are negligible for non-specific labour. Accordingly, such labour will be organized late, often only with the assistance of the political process.

2. Internal labour markets become highly individuated as jobs become more varied and idiosyncratic.

3. Regulation can be interpreted in part as a response to the transactional dilemma posed by natural monopoly.

4. A transaction-cost justification for regulating activities for which transaction-specific investments are lacking (for example, trucking) is not

apparent. The possibility that politics is the driving consideration in such industries warrants consideration.

5. Adjudication should proceed with caution in the area of family law lest valued transaction-specific investments be discouraged.

6. Ease of verification is the capital market counterpart of transaction-specific investments. Upon making this substitution, the organization of capital markets and intermediate product markets is broadly similar.

VI. CONCLUDING REMARKS

Transaction cost economics is an interdisciplinary undertaking that joins economics with aspects of organizational theory and overlaps extensively with contract law. It is the modern counterpart of institutional economics and relies heavily on comparative analysis.[79] Frictionless ideals are useful mainly for reference purposes.

Although mathematical economics captures only a fraction of the transaction cost phenomena of interest,[80] this has not been the only obstacle. Headway with the study of transaction cost issues has been impeded by lack of verbal definitions. Identifying the critical dimensions with respect to which transactions differ has been a significant omission.

This paper attempts to rectify this deficiency and identifies uncertainty, frequency of exchange, and the degree to which investments are transaction-specific as the principal dimensions for describing transactions. The efficient organization of economic activity entails matching governance structures with these transactional attributes in a discriminating way.

Although the main applications in this paper are to commercial contracting, the proposed approach generalizes easily to the study of labour contracts. It also has ramifications for understanding both public utility regulation and family relations. A unified approach to contract thus emerges.

The fact that the broad features of so many varied transactions fit within the framework is encouraging. The importance of transaction costs to the organization of economic activity is thus confirmed. But the world of contract is enormously complex,[81] and the simple economizing framework proposed here cannot be expected to capture more than main features. Elaborating the framework to deal with microanalytic phenomena, however, should be feasible. And extending it to include additional or substitute dimensions (of which the ease of verification, in the case of capital-market transactions, is an example) may sometimes be necessary.

NOTES

1. Ronald Coase has forcefully argued the importance of transaction costs at 20-year intervals. See R.H. Coase, 'The Nature of the Firm', **4**, *Economica* 386 (n.s. 1937), reprinted in *Readings in Price Theory*, 331 (George J. Stigler and Kenneth E. Boulding (eds.), 1952) and R.H. Coase, 'The Problem of Social Cost,' *Journal of Law and Economics,* **3** (1) (1960). Much of my own work has been 'preoccupied' with transaction costs during the past decade. See especially Williamson, *Markets and Hierarchies: Analysis and Antitrust Implications* (1975). Other works in which transaction costs are featured include: Guido Calabresi, Transaction Costs, Resource Allocation, and Liability Rules: A Comment, *Journal of Law and Economics,* **11** (67) (1968); Victor P. Goldberg, 'Regulation and Administered Contract' *Bell Journal of Economics,* **7** (426) (1976); Benjamin Klein, Robert G. Crawford, and Armen A. Alchian, 'Vertical Integration, Appropriable Rents, and the Competitive Contracting Process, *Journal of Law and Economics,* **21** (297) (1978); and Carl J. Dahlman, 'The Problem of Externality' *Journal of Law and Economics,* **22** (141) (1979). For an examination of Pigou in which transaction costs are featured, see Victor P. Goldberg, *Pigou on Complex Contracts and Welfare Economics* (1979) (unpublished manuscript).
2. S. Fischer, 'Long-Term Contracting, Sticky Prices, and Monetary Policy: Comment', *Journal of Monetary Economics*, **3**, (317, 322), n.5 (1977).
3. Opportunism is a variety of self-interest seeking but extends simple self-interest seeking to include self-interest seeking with guile. It is not necessary that all agents be regarded as opportunistic in identical degree. It suffices that those who are less opportunistic than others are difficult to ascertain *ex ante* and that, even among the less opportunistic, most have their price. For a more complete discussion of opportunism, see Williamson, 7-10, 26-30. For a recent application see Klein, Crawford, and Alchian, (1978) *op cit.*
4. The joining of opportunism with transaction-specific investments (or what Klein, Crawford and Alchian refer to as 'appropriable quasi-rents') is a leading factor in explaining decisions to integrate vertically. See Oliver E. Williamson, 'The Vertical Integration of Production: Market Failure Considerations' *American Economic Review,* **61** (112) (Papers and Proceedings, May 1971); Williamson (1975), pp. 16-19, 91-101; and Klein, Crawford, and Alchian, *op cit.*
5. But for the limited ability of human agents to receive, store, retrieve and process data, interesting economic problems vanish.
6. See Dahlman, *op cit.*
7. See note 4 above.
8. I.R. Macneil, 'The Many Futures of Contract' *Southern Californian Law Review*, **47**, (691, 738) (1974).
9. With respect to commercial contracts, see Karl N. Llewellyn, 'What Price Contract?—An Essay in Perspective', *Yale Law Journal,* **40** (704) (1931); Harold C. Havighurst, *The Nature of Private Contract* (1961); Lon L. Fuller, 'Collective Bargaining and the Arbitrator', *Wisconsin Law Review*, 3, (1963), and *The Morality of Law* (1964); Stewart Macaulay, 'Non-Contractual Relations in Business', *American Sociological Review*, **28** (55) (1963); Lawrence M. Friedman, *Contract Law in America* (1965); Arthur Allen Leff, 'Contract as a Thing', *American Univ. Law Review*, **19** (131) (1970); Macneil, *op cit.*; and 'Contracts: Adjustment of Long-Term Economic Relations

under Classical, Neoclassical, and Relational Contract Law', *Northwestern Univ. Law Review*, **72**, (854) (1978) and Victor P. Goldberg, 'Toward an Expanded Economic Theory of Contract', *Journal of Economic Issues*, **10**, 45 (1976). Labour lawyers have made similar observations regarding contracts governing the employment relationship. See Archibald Cox, 'The Legal Nature of Collective Bargaining Agreement', *Michigan Law Review*, **57** (1) (1958); Clyde W. Summers, 'Collective Agreements and the Law of Contracts', *Yale Law Journal,*, **78** (525) (1969); and David E. Feller, 'A General Theory of the Collective Bargaining Agreement', *Californian Law Review*, **61** (663) (1973).

10. The technical versus purposive distinction is made by Summers, *op cit*. He distinguishes between 'black letter law', on the one hand (pp.539, 543, 548, 566) and a more circumstantial approach to law, on the other (pp.549-51, 561, 566). 'The epitome of abstraction is the *Restatement*, which illustrates its black letter rules by transactions suspended in mid-air, creating the illusion that contract rules can be stated without reference to surrounding circumstances and are therefore generally applicable to all contractual transactions' (p.566). He observes that such a conception does not and cannot provide a 'framework for integrating rules and principles applicable to all contractual transactions' (p.566) but that this must be sought in a more affirmative view of the law in which effective governance relations are emphasized. Contract interpretation and completing contracts are among these affirmative functions.

11. See especially Macneil (1974, 1978) *op. cit.* and references to related work of his cited therein.

12. Macneil (1974), pp.738-40; Macneil (1978), pp.902-05.

13. Macneil (1978), p.862.

14. Ibid, p.863, n. 25.

15. For a discussion of complex contingent claims contracting and its mechanics, see Kenneth J. Arrow, *Essays in the Theory of Risk Bearing* (1971), pp.121-34; J.E. Meade, *The Controlled Economy* (1971), pp.147-88 and Oliver E. Williamson (1975), pp.20-40.

16. As Lester G. Telser and Harlow N. Higinbotham put it: 'In an organized market the participants trade a standardized contract such that each unit of the contract is a perfect substitute for any other unit. The identities of the parties in any mutually agreeable transaction do not affect the terms of exchange. The organized market itself or some other institution deliberately creates a homogeneous good that can be traded anonymously by the participants or their agents.' 'Organized Futures Markets: Costs and Benefits' *Journal of Political Economy*, **85**, (969, 997) (1977).

17. Macneil (1978), p.864.

18. Ibid.

19. Ibid., p.865.

20. Fuller, *op. cit.*, pp.11-12.

21. As Friedman (1965) observes, relationships are effectively fractured if a dispute reaches litigation, *op. cit.*, p.205.

22. Macneil (1978), p.885.

23. Ibid., p.901.

24. Ibid.

25. Ibid., p.890.

26. To be sure, some legal specialists insist that all of this was known all along. There is a difference, however, between awareness of a condition and an

understanding. Macneil's treatment heightens awareness and deepens the understanding.

27. For a recent study of contractual relations in which uncertainty is featured, see Peter Temin, 'Modes of Economic Behaviour: Variations on Themes of J.R. Hicks and Herbert Simon' (March 1979) (Working Paper No. 235, MIT Department of Economics.)

28. Gordon Whinston emphasizes frequency in his 'Note on Perspective Time: Goldberg's Relational Exchange, Repetitiveness, and Free Riders in Time and Space' (October 1978) (unpublished paper).

29. See Telser and Higinbotham, *op. cit.* also Yoram Ben-Porath, 'The F-Connection: Families, Friends, and Firms and the Organization of Exchange' (December 1978) (Report No. 29/78, The Hebrew University of Jerusalem) and Yoram Barzel, 'Measurement Cost and the Organization of Markets' (April 1979) (unpublished paper). Note that Barzel's concern with standardization is mainly in connection with final-product markets, whereas I am more interested in non-standard investments. The two are not unrelated, but identical quality can often be realized with a variety of inputs. I am concerned with specialized (transaction-specific) inputs.

30. This assumes that it is costly for the incumbent supplier to transfer specialized physical assets to new suppliers. On this, see Oliver E. Williamson, 'Franchise Bidding for Natural Monopolies—in General and with Respect to CATV', *Bell Journal of Economics*, 7 (73) (1976). Klein, Crawford, and Alchian use the term 'appropriable quasi-rent' to refer to this condition. Use versus user distinctions are relevant in this connection: 'The quasi-rent value of the asset is the excess of its value over its salvage value, that is, its value in its next best *use* to another renter. The potentially appropriable specialized portion of the quasi rent is the portion, if any, in excess of its value to the second highest-valuing *user*'. p.298.

31. Thorstein Veblen's remarks on the distant relation of the head of a large enterprise to transactions are apposite. He observes that under these impersonal circumstances 'The mitigating effect which personal conduct may have in dealings between man and man is . . . in great measure eliminated. . . . Business management [then] has a chance to proceed . . . untroubled by sentimental considerations of human kindness or irritation or of honesty.' *The Theory of Business Enterprise*, 53 (1927). Veblen evidently assigns slight weight to the possibility that those to whom negotiating responsibilities are assigned will themselves invest the transactions with integrity.

32. The *Great Lakes Carbon* case is an example of the latter: 1970-1973 Trade Reg. Rep. Transfer Binder, para. 19,848 (FTC 8805).

33. Michael Polanyi, *Personal Knowledge: Towards a Post-Critical Philosophy*, 52 (2nd edn, 1962).

34. Ibid., p.53.

35. Ibid., p.112.

36. Ibid., p.206.

37. Charles Babbage, *On the Economy of Machinery and Manufacturers* (1832) p.220-1. More recent examples of contracts wherein private parties can and evidently do 'ignore' the law, even at some peril, when the law and the interests of the parties are at variance are offered by Stewart Macaulay, 'The Use and Nonuse of Contracts in the Manufacturing Industry', *Practical Lawyer*, 9, (13, 16) (1963): 'Requirements contracts probably are not legally enforceable in Wisconsin and a few other States. Yet, chemicals, containers, and a number of other things are still bought and sold there on the basis of

requirements contracts.

Decisions of the United States Court of Appeals for the Seventh Circuit indicate that a clause calling for a 'seller's price in effect at time and place of delivery' makes a contract unenforceable. The Wisconsin cases are not clear. Yet steel and steel products usually are sold in this way.

38. Remarks of Mr Justice Rhenquist, 'The Adversary Society', Baron di Hirsch Meyer Lecture, University of Miami School of Law, 2 February 1978, (emphasis added).

39. Ibid., pp.11-13.

40. Ibid., pp.16-19.

41. As Ben-Porath puts it, 'the most important characteristic of the family contract is that it is embedded in the identity of the partners without which it loses its meaning. It is thus specific and non-negotiable or nontransferable.' Yoram Ben-Porath, *op. cit.*, p.6.

42. More generally, the economizing problem includes choice between a special-purpose and a general-purpose good or service. A general-purpose item affords all of the advantages of market procurement, but possibly at the sacrifice of valued design or performance characteristics. A special-purpose item has the opposite features: valued differences are realized but market procurement here may pose hazards. For the purposes of this paper, intermediate-product characteristics are mainly taken as given and I focus principally on production and transaction cost economies. A more general formulation would include product characteristics in the optimization.

43. This ignores transient conditions, such as temporary excess capacity. (In a zero transaction cost world, such excesses vanish as assets can be deployed as effectively by others as they can by the owner.)

44. On these hazards and their transaction-cost origins, see Williamson (1975), pp.117-31.

45. Dennis Carlton shows that economies of 'vertical integration' can frequently be realized in a market where absent integration, buyers and suppliers are randomly paired. As he defines vertical integration, however, this can be accomplished as effectively by long-term contract as it can by in-house production. Dennis W. Carlton, 'Vertical Integration in Competitive Markets under Uncertainty' *Journal of Industrial Economics*, **27**, (189) (1979).

46. Thus a reduction in monitoring commonly gives rise to an increase in opportunism. Monitoring the employment relation, however, needs to be done with special care. Progressively increasing the intensity of surveillance can elicit resentment and have counterproductive (for example, work-to-rule) results. Such perversities are less likely for interfirm trading.

47. See note 30 above.

48. This seems reasonable for most intermediate product market transactions.

49. Production aspects are thus emphasized. Investments in governance structure are treated separately.

50. Yoram Ben-Porath, *op. cit.*, p.7.

51. Defence contracting may appear to be a counter-example, since an elaborate governance structure is devised for many of these. This reflects in part, however, the special disabilities of the government as a production instrument. But for this, many of these contracts would be organized in-house. Also, contracts that are very large and of long duration, as many defence contracts are, do have a recurring character.

52. S. Todd Lowry, 'Bargain and Contract Theory in Law and Economics', *Journal of Economic Issues*, **10**, (1, 12) (1976).
53. Ibid., p.13.
54. Although recurrent, standard transactions are ones for which an active spot market commonly exists, term contracting may also be employed—especially as planning economies are thereby realized by the parties. See Dennis W. Carlton, 'Price Rigidity, Forward Contracts, and Market Equilibrium' *Journal of Political Economy* (1979). The duration of these contracts will not be long, however, since the assets in question can be employed in other uses and/or in the service of other customers. The result is that changing market circumstances will be reflected relatively quickly in both price and quantity and relatively stringent contracting attitudes may be said to prevail.
55. 'Generally speaking, a serious conflict, even quite a minor one such as an objection to a harmlessly late tender of the delivery of goods, terminates the discrete contract as a live one and leaves nothing but a conflict over money damages to be settled by a lawsuit. Such a result fits neatly the norms of enhancing discreteness and intensifying . . . presentation.' Macneil (1978), p.877.
56. See the articles cited in note 30 above.
57. Macneil (1978), p.866.
58. Ibid., p.879.
59. Ibid., p.880. The rationale for this section of the Code is that 'identification of the goods to the contract will, within limits, permit the seller to recover the price of the goods rather than merely damages for the breach . . ., ([where the] latter may be far less in amount and more difficult to prove).' (Ibid.)
60. As Macaulay observes, 'Disputes are frequently settled without reference to the contract or to potential or actual legal sanctions. There is a hesitancy to speak of legal right or to threaten to sue in . . . negotiations' where continuing business is valued. Macaulay, *op. cit.*, p.61.

    The material which follows in this subsection was originally developed in connection with the study of inflation. See Michael L. Wachter and Oliver E. Williamson, 'Obligational Markets and the Mechanics of Inflation', *Bell Journal of Economics*, **9**, (549) (1978).
61. This assumes that factor prices paid by buyer and outside supplier are identical. Where this is not true, as in some unionized forms, buyers may choose to procure outside because of a differential wage rate. This is a common problem in the automobile industry, which has a very flat and relatively high wage scale.
62. See the references in note 4 above.
63. Summers, *op. cit.*, p.527.
64. Ibid., p.568.
65. Remarks of Mr Justice Rhenquist, *op. cit.*, p.4.
66. 386 US 171, 191 (1967).
67. Cox, *op. cit.*, p.24.
68. The reason, of course, is that it is very costly and apt to be unproductive to reopen wage bargaining during the period covered by a contract. Since to reopen negotiations for one type of job is to invite it for all, and as objective differences among jobs may be difficult to demonstrate, wage bargaining is foreclosed except at contract renewal intervals.
69. Wachter and Williamson, *op. cit.*, p.567.

70. Thus although both non-idiosyncratic and idiosyncratic jobs may be organized collectively, the way in which the internal labour markets associated with each are organized should reflect objective differences between them. Additionally, the incentive to provide an orderly governance structure varies directly with the degree to which efficiencies are attributable thereto. *Ceteris paribus*, non-idiosyncratic jobs ought to be organized later and the governance structure less fully elaborated than for idiosyncratic jobs. Both propositions are borne out by the evidence.
71. Goldberg, *op. cit.*
72. Williamson, (1976).
73. Remarks of Mr Justice Rhenquist, *op. cit.*, p.19.
74. For a more extensive discussion of family transactions, see Yoram Ben-Porath, *op. cit.*, pp.4-7.
75. This feature was called to my attention by Sandford Grossman.
76. Macaulay, *op. cit.*
77. Kenneth J. Arrow, 'Economic Welfare and the Allocation of Resources for Invention', in *The Rate and Direction of Economic Activity*, (1962), p.609.
78. Aspects are discussed in Williamson (1975), pp.203-5.
79. Reliance on comparative analysis has been repeatedly emphasized by Coase, *op. cit.*
80. See Dahlman, *op. cit.*, pp.144-7.
81. Klein, Crawford and Alchian, *op. cit.* p.325.

8. The Modern Corporation: Origins, Evolution, Attributes*

There is virtual unanimity with the proposition that the modern corporation is a complex and important economic institution. There is much less agreement on what its attributes are and on how and why it has successively evolved to take on its current configuration. While I recognize that there have been numerous contributing factors, I submit that the modern corporation is mainly to be understood as the product of a series of organizational innovations that have had the purpose and effect of economizing on transaction costs.

Note that I do not argue that the modern corporation is to be understood exclusively in these terms. Other important factors include the quest for monopoly gains and the imperatives of technology. These mainly have a bearing on market shares and on the absolute size of specific technological units; but decisions to make or buy, which determine the distribution of economic activity, as between firms and markets, and the internal organization (including both the shape and the aggregate size) of the firm are not explained, except perhaps in trivial ways, in these terms. In as much as these are core issues, a theory of the modern corporation that does not address them is, at best, seriously incomplete.

Specifically, the study of the modern corporation should actively concern itself with and provide consistent explanations for the following features of the organizations of economic activity: What are the factors that determine the degree to which firms integrate—in backward, forward, and lateral respects? What economic purposes are served by the widespread adoption of divisionalization? What ramifications, if any, does internal organization have for the long-standing dilemma posed by

* This paper benefited from the very helpful comments of Moses Ambramovitz, Alfred Chandler, Sanford Grossman, Paul Joskow, Scott Masten, Richard Nelson and Douglass North. Parts of it were given at Rice University as a 1981 Peterkin Lecture, and comments of the faculty and students in attendance were also helpful. For related recent assessments of the modern corporation which, however, emphasize somewhat different aspects, see Richard Caves (1980), Robin Marris and Dennis Mueller (1980), and Richard Cyert and Charles Hedrick (1972).

the separation of ownership from control? Can the 'puzzle' of the conglomerate be unravelled? Do similar considerations apply in assessing multinational enterprise? Can an underlying rationale be provided for the reported association between innovation and direct foreign investment?

It is my contention that transaction-cost economizing figures prominently in explaining these (as well as related) major features of the business environment. Since transaction-cost economizing is socially valued, it follows that the modern corporation serves affirmative economic purposes. But complex institutions often serve a variety of purposes—and the corporation can and sometimes is used to pursue anti-social objectives. I submit, however, that (1) objectionable purposes can normally be recognized and dealt with separately and (2) failure to understand the main purposes of the corporation has been the source of much confusion and ill-conceived public policy.[1] Specifically, anti-social purposes have often been attributed where none existed.

In as much as a sensitivity to transactions and transaction-cost economizing can be traced to the 1930s (Commons, 1934; Coase, 1937), it is somewhat surprising that the importance of the modern corporation as a means of reducing transaction costs has been so long neglected. The main reason is that the origins of transaction costs must often be sought in influences and motives that lie outside the normal domain of economics. Accordingly, a large gap separated an identification of transaction costs, as the main factor to which the study of the organization of economic activity must repair, and efforts to give operational content to that insight.

This paper is organized in two parts. Sections 1 and 2 sketch the background and set forth the arguments that are subsequently employed to interpret a series of organizational innovations that have successively yielded the modern corporation. Sections 3 and 4 deal with these changes. My discussion of organizational innovation begins with the latter half of the nineteenth century. In this regard, I follow Alfred Chandler who traces the origins of complex hierarchical forms of business organization to this period (1977). To be sure, others have identified interesting organizational developments in both Japanese[2] and English[3] business history that pre-date, if not prefigure, those in the US. But these earlier developments were not widely adopted by other firms—and in any event represent very primitive forms of divisionalization.[4] As a consequence, these earlier developments were of isolated economic importance and are properly distinguished from the general transformation of American industry that began in the nineteenth century and has continued since.

Key legal features of the corporation—limited liability and the transferability of ownership—are taken as given. Failure to discuss these does not reflect a judgement that these are either irrelevant or uninteresting. The main focus of this essay, however, is on the internal organization of the corporation. Since any of a number of internal structures is consistent with these legal features, an explanation for the specific organizational innovations that were actually adopted evidently resides elsewhere. Among the more significant of these innovations, and the ones addressed here, are: the development of line-and-staff organization by the railroads; selective forward integration by manufacturers into distribution; the development of the multidivisional corporate form; the evolution of the conglomerate; and the appearance of the multinational enterprise. The first three of these changes have been studied by business historians, the contributions of Chandler (1962, 1977) being the most ambitious and notable.

I. SOME BACKGROUND

1. General

Assessing the organization of economic activity in an advanced society requires that a bewildering variety of market, hierarchical and mixed modes be evaluated. Economists, organization theorists, public policy specialists and historians all have an interest and each have offered interpretations of successive organizational innovations. A coherent view, however, has not emerged.

Partly this is because the principal hierarchical structure to be assessed—the modern corporation—is formidably complex in its great size, diversity and internal organization. The natural difficulties which thereby resulted would have been overcome sooner, however, had it not been for a number of conceptual barriers to an understanding of this institution. Chief among these are the following: (1) the neoclassical theory of the firm, which is the main referent to which economists appeal, is devoid of interesting hierarchical features; (2) organization theorists, who are specialists in the study of internal organization and unencumbered by an intellectual commitment to neoclassical economic models, have been preoccupied with hierarchy to the neglect of market modes of organization and the healthy tension that exists between markets and hierarchies; (3) public policy analysts have maintained a deeply suspicious attitude toward non-standard or unfamiliar forms of economic organization; and (4) organizational innovation has been relatively neglected by business and economic historians.

To be sure, this indictment sweeps too broadly. As discussed in section I(2) below, there have been important exceptions. The main features, however, are as I have described. Thus neoclassical theory treats the firm as a production function to which a profit-maximization objective has been ascribed. Albeit useful for many purposes, such a construction is unhelpful in attempting to assess the purposes served by hierarchical modes of organization. The firm as production function needs to make way for the view of the *firm as governance structure* if the ramifications of internal organization are to be accurately assessed. Only recently has this latter orientation begun to make headway—and is still in a primitive state of development.

The preoccupation of organization theory specialists with internal organization is a potentially useful corrective. An understanding of the purposes served by internal organization has remained elusive, however, for at least two reasons. First, efficiency analysis plays a relatively minor role in the studies of most organization theory specialists—many of whom are more inclined to emphasize power. The economizing factors that are crucial to an understanding of the modern corporation are thus effectively suppressed. Second, and related, firms and markets are treated separately rather than in active juxtaposition with one another. The propositions that (1) firms and markets are properly regarded as alternative governance structures to which (2) transactions are to be assigned in discriminating (mainly transaction-cost economizing) ways are unfamiliar to most organization theory specialists and alien to some.

Public policy analysts with an interest in the modern corporation might also have been expected to entertain a broader view. In fact, however, many of these likewise adopted a production function orientation—whereby markets were regarded as the 'natural, hence efficient' way by which to mediate transactions between technologically-separable entities. This was joined by a pervasive sense that the purposes of competition are invariably served by maintaining many autonomous traders. Even sensitive observers were trapped by this combined technological/atomistic logic. Thus Donald Turner, at a time when he headed the Antitrust Division, expressed scepticism over non-standard business practices by observing that 'I approach territorial and customer restrictions not hospitably in the common law tradition, but inhospitably in the tradition of antitrust law.'[5] The possibility that efficiency might be served by imposing restraints on autonomous market trading was evidently thought to be slight. This inhospitality tradition also explains ingrained public policy animosity towards vertical integration and conglomerate organization; more generally, industrial organization specialists were encouraged to discover what were often fanciful 'distortions' at the expense of a more basic understanding of the modern corporation in economizing terms.

The neglect of organizational innovations by business and economic historians has been general but by no means complete and shows recent signs of being corrected.[6] Mainly, however, interpretation has played a secondary role to description in most historical studies of organizational change—which, while understandable, contributes to the continuing confusion over the purposes served by the changing organizational features of the corporation.

This essay attempts to provide a coherent view of the modern corporation by (1) augmenting the model of the firm as production function to include the concept of the firm as governance structure, (2) studying firms and markets as alternative governance structures in a comparative institutional way, (3) supplanting the presumption that organizational innovations have anti-competitive purposes by the rebuttable presumption that organizational innovations are designed to economize on transaction costs, and (4) interpreting business history from a transaction-cost perspective. Such an approach to the study of the modern corporation (and, more generally, to the study of organizational innovation) owes its origins to antecedent contributions of four kinds.

2. Antecedents

Theory of Firms and Markets. The unsatisfactory state of the theory of the firm was recognized by Coase in his classic 1937 article on 'The Nature of the Firm'. As he observed:

Outside the firm, price movements direct production, which is coordinated through a series of exchange transactions on the market. Within a firm, these market transactions are eliminated and in place of the complicated market structure with exchange transactions is substituted the entrepreneur-coordinator, who directs production. It is clear that these are *alternative means of coordinating production.* (1952, p.333; emphasis added).

Coase went on to observe that firms arose because there were costs of using the price system (pp.336-8). But internal organization was no cost panacea, since it experienced distinctive costs of its own (pp.340-2). A balance is struck when the firm has expanded to the point where 'the costs of organizing an extra transaction within the firm become equal to the costs of carrying out the same transaction by means of an exchange in the open market or the costs of organizing in another firm' (p.341).

Related insight on the study of firms and markets was offered by Hayek, who dismissed equilibrium economics with the observation that 'the economic problem of society is mainly one of adaptation to changes in particular circumstances of time and place' (1945, p.524), and who held that the 'marvel' of the price system was that it could accomplish this without 'conscious direction' (p.527). Setting aside the possibility that

Hayek did not make adequate allowance for the limitations of the price system, three things are notable about these observations. First in his emphasis on change and the need to devise adaptive institutional forms. Second, his reference to particular circumstances, as distinguished from statistical aggregates, reflects a sense that economic institutions must be sensitive to dispersed knowledge of a microanalytic kind. And third was his insistence that attention to the details of social processes and economic institutions was made necessary by the 'unavoidable imperfection of man's knowledge' (p.530).

The organization of firms and markets has been a subject to which Arrow had made repeated contributions. He has addressed himself not only to the economics of the internal organization (Arrow, 1964), but also to an assessment of the powers and limits of markets (Arrow, 1969). Like Coase, he expressly recognizes that firms and markets are alternative modes of organizing economic activity (Arrow, 1974). Moreover, whereas the limits of markets were glossed over by Hayek, Arrow specifically traces these to transaction cost origins: 'market failure is not absolute; it is better to consider a broader category, that of transaction costs, which in general impede and in particular cases block the formation of markets' (1969, p.48)—where, by transaction costs, Arrow has reference to the 'costs of running the economic system' (1969, p.48).

Organization Theory. Although organization theorists have not in general regarded efficiency as their central concern, there have been notable exceptions. The early works of Barnard (1938) and Simon (1947) both qualify.

Barnard was a businessman rather than a social scientist and he addressed internal organizational issues that many would regard as outside the scope of economics. Economizing was nevertheless strongly featured in his approach to the study of organizations. Understanding the employment relation was among the issues that intrigued him. Matters that concerned him in this connection included: the need to align incentives, including non-economic inducements, to achieve enterprise viability; the importance of assent to authority; a description of the authority relation within which hierarchical organizations operate; and the role of 'informal organization' in supporting the working rules upon which formal organization relies. The rationality of internal organization, making due allowance for the attributes of human actors, was a matter of continuous concern to Barnard.

Simon expressly relies on Barnard and carries rationality analysis forward. A more precise vocabulary than Barnard's is developed in the process. Simon traces the problem of organization to the joining of rational purposes with the cognitive limits of human actors: 'it is precisely in the realm where human behaviour is *intendedly* rational, but only *limitedly* so, that there is room for a genuine theory of organization and administration' (1957, p.xxiv). Intended rationality supplies purpose, but meaningful economic and organizational choices arise only in a limited (or bounded) rationality context.

Simon makes repeated reference to the criterion of efficiency (pp.14, 39-41, 172-97), but he also cautions that organizational design should be informed by 'a knowledge of those aspects of the social sciences which are relevant to the broader purposes of the organization' (p.246). A sensitivity to sub-goal pursuit, wherein individuals identify with and pursue local goals at the possible expense of global goals[7] (p.13), and the 'outguessing' or gaming aspects of human behaviour (p.252) are among these.

Although Simon examines the merits of centralized versus decentralized modes of organization (1947, pp.234-40), it is not until his later writing that he expressly addresses the matter of factoring problems according to rational hierarchical principles (Simon, 1962). The issues here are developed more fully in section II.

Non-strategic Purposes. The 'inhospitality tradition' referred to above maintained a presumption of illegality when non-standard or unfamiliar business practices were brought under review. These same practices, when viewed 'through the lens of price theory'[8] by Aaron Director (and his students and colleagues at Chicago), were regarded rather differently. Whereas Turner and others held that anti-competitive purposes were being served, Director and his associates reported instead that tie-ins, resale price maintenance and the like were promoting more efficient resource allocation.

In fact, non-standard business practices (such as tie-ins) are anomalies when regarded in the full information terms associated with static price theory. Implicitly, however, Chicago was also relying on the existence of transaction costs—which, after all, were the reason why comprehensive price discrimination could not be effected through simple contracts unsupported by restrictive practices from the outset.[9] Be that as it may, Chicago's insistence that economic behaviour be assessed with respect to its economizing properties was a healthy antidote and encouraged further scrutiny of these same matters—with the eventual result that an economizing orientation is now much more widely held. Indirectly, these views have spilled over and influenced thinking about the modern corporation as an economizing, rather than mainly a monopolizing, entity.[10]

Business History. The study of organizational innovation has been relatively neglected by business and economic historians. Aside from the Research Center in Entrepreneurial History at Harvard, which was established in 1948 and closed its doors a decade later, there has not been a concerted effort to work through and establish the importance of organizational innovation. Probably the most important reason for this neglect is that business history has not had 'the support of an established system of theory' (Larson, 1948, p.135).

Despite this general neglect, notable contributions have nevertheless been made. The works of Davis and North (1971) and of Chandler (1962, 1977) have been especially important. The first of these takes a sweeping view of institutional change and employs a market failure theory for assessing successive changes. It pays only limited attention, however, to the corporation as a unit whose attributes need to be assessed.[11]

Chandler, by contrast, is expressly and deeply concerned with the organization form changes which, over the past 150 years, have brought us the modern corporation as we know it. The story is told in two parts, the first being the evolution of the large, multifunctional enterprise (Chandler, 1977), the second being the subsequent divisionalization of these firms (Chandler, 1962). Both of these transformations are described and interpreted in section II, (3) and (4) below. Suffice it to observe here that (1) Chandler's is the first treatment of business history that describes organizational changes in sufficient detail to permit a transaction-cost interpretation to be applied: (2) Chandler's 1962 book was significant not only for its business history contributions but because it clearly established that organization form had an important impact on business performance—which neither economics nor organization theory had done (nor, for the most part, even attempted) previously: and (3) although Chandler is more concerned with the description than with the interpretation of organizational change, his careful descriptions are nevertheless suggestive of the economic factors that are responsible for the changes observed.

II. TRANSACTION COST ECONOMICS

Each of the antecedent literatures just described has a bearing on the transaction-cost approach to the study of economic institutions in general and the modern corporation in particular. Following Commons (1934), the transaction is made the basic unit of analysis. Specifically, attention is focused on the transaction costs of running the economic system (Coase, 1937; Arrow, 1969), with emphasis on adaptation to unforeseen, and often unforeseeable, circumstances (Hayek, 1945). The issues of special interest are connected with the changing structure of the corporation over the past 150 years (Chandler, 1962; 1977). Rather than regard these inhospitably, the new approach maintains the rebuttable presumption that the evolving corporate structure has the purpose and effect of economizing on transaction costs. These transaction cost and business history literatures are linked by appeal to selective parts of the (mainly older) organizational theory literature.

As Barnard (1938) emphasized, differences in internal organization often had significant performance consequences and could and should be assessed from a rationality viewpoint. Simon (1947) extended and refined the argument that internal organization mattered and that the study of internal organization needed to make appropriate allowance for the attributes of human actors—for what Frank Knight has felicitously referred to as 'human nature as we know it' (1965, p.270). Then, and only then, does the comparative institutional assessment of alternative organizational forms take on its full economic significance.

1. Comparative Institutional Analysis

The costs of running the economic system to which Arrow refers can be usefully thought of in contractual terms. Each feasible mode of conducting relations between technologically-separable entities can be examined with respect to the *ex ante* costs of negotiating and writing, as well as the *ex post* costs of executing, policing, and, when disputes arise, remedying the (explicit or implicit) contract that joins them.

A transaction may thus be said to occur when a good or service is transferred across a technologically-separable interface. One stage of processing or assembly activity terminates and another begins. A mechanical analogy, while imperfect, may nevertheless be useful. A well-working interface, like a well-working machine, can be thought of as one where these transfers occur smoothly.

In neither case, however, is smoothness desired for its own sake: the benefits must be judged in relation to the cost. Both investment and operating features require attention. Thus extensive prior investment in finely-tuned equipment and repeated lubrication and adjustment during operation are both ways of attenuating friction, slippage, or other loss of mechanical energy. Similarly, extensive pre-contract negotiation that covers all relevant contingencies may avoid the need for periodic intervention to realign the interface during execution so that a contract may be brought successfully to completion. Simultaneous attention to both investment (pre-contract costs) and operating expenses (harmonizing costs) is needed if mechanical (contractual) systems are to be designed effectively. The usual study of economizing in a production function framework is thus extended to include an examination of the *comparative costs of planning, adapting and monitoring task completion under alternative governance structures*—where by governance structure I have reference to the explicit or implicit contractual framework within which a transaction is located (markets, firms, and mixed modes—e.g. franchising—included).

The study of transaction-cost economizing is thus a comparative institutional undertaking which recognizes that there are a variety of distinguishably different transactions on the one hand, and a variety of alternative governance structures on the other. The object is to match governance structures to the attributes of transactions in a discriminating way. Microanalytic attention to differences among governance structures and microanalytic definition of transactions are both needed in order for this to be accomplished.

Although more descriptive detail than is associated with neoclassical analysis is needed for this purpose, a relatively crude assessment will often suffice. As Simon has observed, comparative institutional analysis commonly involves an examination of discrete structural alternatives for which marginal analysis is not required: 'In general, much cruder and simpler arguments will suffice to demonstrate an inequality between two quantities than are required to show the conditions under which these quantities are equated at the margin' (1978, p.6).

2. Behavioural Assumptions

Human nature as we know it is marvellously rich and needs to be reduced to manageable proportions. The two behavioural assumptions on which transaction-cost analysis relies—and without which the study of economic organization is pointless—are bounded rationality and opportunism. As a consequence of these two assumptions, the human agents that populate the firms and markets with which I am concerned differ from economic man (or at least the common caricature thereof) in that they are less competent in calculation and less trustworthy and reliable in action. A condition of bounded rationality is responsible for the computational limits of organization man. A proclivity for (at least some) economic agents to behave opportunistically is responsible for their unreliability.

The term bounded rationality was coined by Simon to reflect the fact that economic actors, who may be presumed to be 'intendedly rational', are not hyper-rational. Rather, they experience limits in formulating and solving complex problems and in processing (receiving, storing, retrieving, transmitting) information (Simon, 1957, p.198). Opportunism is related to but is a somewhat more general term than the condition of 'moral hazard' to which Knight referred in his classic statement of economic organization (1965, pp.251-6).[12] Opportunism effectively extends the usual assumption of self-interest seeking to make allowance for self-interest seeking with guile.

But for the *simultaneous* existence of both bounded rationality and opportunism,[13] all economic contracting problems are trivial and the study of economic institutions is unimportant. Thus, but for bounded rationality, all economic exchange could be effectively organized by contract. Indeed, the economic theory of comprehensive contracting has been fully worked out.[14] Given bounded rationality, however, it is impossible to deal with complexity in all contractually relevant respects (Radner, 1968). As a consequence, incomplete contracting is the best that can be achieved.

Ubiquitous, albeit incomplete, contracting would nevertheless be feasible if economic agents were completely trustworthy. Principals would simply extract promises from agents that they will behave in a stewardship fashion, while agents would reciprocally ask principals to behave in good faith. Such devices will not work, however, if some economic actors (either principals or agents) are dishonest (or, more generally, disguise attributes or preferences, distort data, obfuscate issues, and otherwise confuse transactions) and it is very costly to distinguish opportunistic from non-opportunistic types *ex ante*.

Although the dual assumptions of bounded rationality and opportunism complicate the study of economic behaviour and may be inessential for some purposes, the study of alternative modes of organization does not qualify as an exception. To the contrary, failure to recognize and make allowance for both is virtually to invite mistaken assessments of alternative modes.[15] Taking these two behavioural assumptions into account, the following compact statement of the problem of economic organization is suggested: assess alternative governance structures in terms of their capacities to economize on bounded rationality while simultaneously safeguarding transactions against opportunism. This is not inconsistent with the imperative 'maximize profits', but it focuses attention somewhat differently.

3. Dimensionalizing

As Coase observed in 1972, his 1937 paper was 'much cited but little used' (1972, p.63). The reasons for this are many, including a preoccupation by economists with other matters during the intervening 35 years. The main reason, however, is that transaction costs had not been operationalized, and it was not obvious how this could be accomplished.

The post-war market failure literature, especially Arrow's insight (1969) that market failures had transaction costs origins, served to focus attention on the troublesome issues. A recognition that market (and internal) failures of all kinds could be ultimately traced to the human factors described above was a second step. The remaining step was to identify the critical dimensions with respect to which transactions differ.

The attributes of transactions that are of special interest to the economics of organization are: (1) the frequency with which transactions recur, (2) the uncertainty to which transactions are subject,[16] and (3) the degree to which transactions are supported by durable, transaction-specific investments (Williamson, 1979). A considerable amount of explanatory power turns on the last.[17]

Asset specificity can arise in any of three ways: site specificity, as when successive stations are located in cheek-by-jowl relation to each other so as to economize on inventory and transportation expenses; physical asset specificity, as where specialized dies are required to produce a component; and human asset specificity that arises in a learning-by-doing fashion. The reason why asset specificity is critical is that, once the investment has been made, buyer and seller are effectively operating in a bilateral (or at least quasi-bilateral) exchange relation for a considerable period thereafter. In as much as the value of highly-specific capital in other uses is, by definition, much smaller than the specialized use for which it has been intended, the supplier is effectively 'locked into' the transaction to a significant degree. This is symmetrical, moreover, in that the buyer cannot turn to alternative sources of supply and obtain the item on favourable terms, since the cost of supply from unspecialized capital is presumably great. The buyer is thus committed to the transaction as well. Accordingly, where asset specificity is great, buyer and seller will make special efforts to design an exchange relation that has good continuity properties. Autonomous contracting gives way to more complex forms of market contracting and sometimes to internal organization for this reason.

4. Three Principles of Organizational Design

The criterion for organizing commercial transactions is assumed to be the strictly instrumental one of cost economizing. Essentially this takes two parts: economizing on production expense and economizing of transaction costs. In fact, these are not independent and need to be addressed simultaneously. The study of the latter, however, is much less well developed and is emphasized here.

The three principles of organizational design employed here are neither exhaustive nor refined. They nevertheless offer considerable explanatory power in dealing with the main changes in corporate organization reported by Chandler and addressed here. Transaction-cost reasoning supports all three, although only the first, the asset-specificity principle, is tightly linked to dimensionalizing. Bounded rationality and opportunism, however, operate with respect to all three.

The asset-specificity principle turns on the above described transformation of an exchange relation from a large-numbers to a small-numbers condition during the course of contract execution. The second, the externality principle, is often discussed under the heading of 'free-rider' effects. The more general phenomenon, however, is that of sub-goal pursuit; that is, in the course of executing contracts, agents also pursue private goals which may be in some degree inconsistent with the contract's intended purpose. These two principles influence the choice of contracting form (mainly firm or market). In fact, however, the efficacy of internal organization depends on whether sound principles of internal organizational design are respected, which is to say that the details of internal organization matter. The hierarchical decomposition principle deals with this last.

It will be convenient to assume that transactions will be organized by markets unless market exchange gives rise to serious transaction costs. In the beginning, so to speak, there were markets. Both bureaucratic and production cost considerations favour this presumption. The bureaucratic argument is simply this: market exchange serves to attenuate the bureaucratic distortions to which internal exchange is subject. (Although the reasons for this have been set out elsewhere—Thompson, 1967, pp.152-54; Williamson, 1975, Ch.7—the study of firm and market organization is greatly in need of a more adequate theory of bureaucracy.) The production cost advantages of market procurement are three: static scale economies can be more fully exhausted by buying rather than making if the firm's needs are small in relation to the market; markets can aggregate uncorrelated demands, thereby to realize risk-pooling benefits; and markets may enjoy economies of scope[18] in supplying a related set of activities of which the firm's requirements are only one. Accordingly, transactions will be organized in markets *unless* transaction-cost disabilities appear.[19]

Asset Specificity Principle (All Transactions). Recall that transactions are described in terms of three attributes: frequency, uncertainty and asset specificity. Although interesting organizational issues are posed when transactions are of only an occasional kind (Williamson, 1979, pp.245-54), this paper deals entirely with the governance of recurring transactions. Also, it will facilitate the analysis to hold uncertainty constant in intermediate degree—which is to say that we are dealing neither with steady state nor highly uncertain events. Accordingly, asset specificity is the transactional dimension of special interest. The first principle of efficient organizational design is this: *the normal presumption that recurring transactions for technologically separable goods and services will be efficiently mediated by autonomous market contracting is progressively weakened as asset specificity increases.*

The production cost advantages of markets decrease and the (comparative) governance costs of markets increase as assets become progressively more specific. Thus as assets become more fully specialized to a single use or user, hence are less transferable to other uses and users, economies of scale can be as fully realized when a firm operates the asset under its own internal direction as when its services are obtained externally by contract. And the market's advantage in pooling risks likewise shrinks. Simultaneously, the transactions in question take on a stronger bilateral character, and the governance costs of markets increase relatively.

The distinction between *ex ante* and *ex post* competition is essential to an understanding of this condition. What may have been (and commonly is) an effective large numbers bidding situation at the outset is sometimes *transformed* into a bilateral trading relation thereafter. This obtains if, despite the fact that large numbers of qualified bidders were prepared to enter competitive bids for the initial contract, the winning bidder realizes advantages over non-winners at contract renewal intervals because non-trivial investments in durable specific assets are put in place (or otherwise accrue, say in a learning-by-doing fashion) during contract execution. As set out elsewhere (Williamson, 1979), the efficient governance of recurring transactions will vary as follows: classical market contracting will be efficacious wherever assets are non-specific to the trading parties; bilateral or obligational market contracting will appear as assets become semi-specific; and internal organization will displace markets as assets take on a highly specific character.[20]

Internal organization enjoys advantages over market contracting for transactions that are supported by highly specific assets at both contract writing and contract execution stages. Since highly specific assets cannot be redeployed without sacrificing productivity, both suppliers and purchasers will insist upon contractual safeguards before undertaking such projects. Writing and negotiating such contracts is costly. Additionally, implementation problems need to be faced. The internal direction of firms confers execution advantages over bilateral trading in three aspects. First, common ownership reduces the incentives of the trading units to pursue local goals. Second, and related, internal organization is able to invoke fiat to resolve differences whereas costly adjudication is needed when an impasse develops between autonomous traders. Third, internal organization has easier and more complete access to the relevant information when disputes must be settled. The incentive to shift bilateral transactions from markets to firms also increases as uncertainty increases, since the costs of harmonizing a relation among parties vary directly with the need to adjust to changing circumstances.

Externality Principle (Forward Integration). Whereas the asset-specificity principle refers to transactions that are transformed from large to small-numbers bidding situations—as buyers, who initially obtained assets or their services in a competitive market, subsequently face suppliers with some degree of monopoly power—the externality principle involves no such market transformation. Also, the asset-specificity principle applies to backward, forward and lateral integration; by contrast, the externality principle mainly applies to distribution stages.

The externalities of concern are those that arise in conjunction with the unintended debasement of quality for a branded good or service. As discussed below, such debasement is explained by costly metering. The externality is thus a manifestation of the measurement problems to which North refers in his discussion of transaction costs (1978, p.972). It appears mainly at the interface between production and distribution. The differential ease of inspecting, and thereby controlling, the quality of components and materials that are purchased from earlier-stage and lateral suppliers as compared with the cost of exercising quality controls over distributors is responsible for this condition.[21]

End-games and fly-by-night distributors aside, the unintended debasement of quality by distributors poses a problem only where the activities of individual distributors affect one another, as when one retailer's poor service in installation or repair injures a product's reputation for performance and limits the sales of other retailers. More generally, if the quality enhancement (debasement) efforts of distributors give rise to positive (negative) externalities, the benefits (costs) of which can be incompletely appropriated by (assigned to) the originators, failure to extend quality controls over distribution will result in sub-optimization. Autonomous contracting thus gives way to obligational market contracting (e.g. franchising) if not forward integration into distribution[22] as demand interaction effects become more important. More generally, the second principle of efficient organizational design is this: *the normal presumption that exchange between producers of differentiated goods and distribution stages will be efficiently mediated by autonomous contracting is progressively weakened as demand externalities increase.*

Product differentiation is a necessary but not a sufficient condition for troublesome demand externalities to appear. Manufacturers can sometimes insulate a product against deterioration by special packaging (say, by selling the item in hermetic containers with an inert atmosphere and providing replacement guarantees). If, however, such safeguards are very costly, and if follow-on checks and penalties to discourage distributors from debasing the quality image of a product are likewise expensive, autonomous trading will give way to forms of distribution that have superior quality control properties.

Hierarchical Decomposition Principle (Internal Organization).[23] Merely to transfer a transaction out of the market into the firm does not, by itself, assure that the activity will be effectively organized thereafter. Not only are bounded rationality and opportunism ubiquitous, but the problems presented by both vary with changes in internal organization. Accordingly, a complete theory of value will recognize that firm structure as well as market structure matters.

Simon makes provision for bounded rationality effects in arguing that the organizational division of decision-making labour is quite as important as the neoclassical division of production labour, where, from 'the information processing point of view, division of labour means factoring the total system of decisions that need to be made into relatively independent subsystems, each one of which can be designed with only minimal concern for its interactions with the others' (Simon, 1973, p.270). This applies to both vertical and horizontal aspects of the organization. In both respects the object is to recognize and give effect to conditions of near decomposibility. The vertical slice entails grouping the operating parts into separable entities, the interactions within which are strong and between which are weak. The horizontal slice has temporal ramifications of a strategic versus operating kind. Problems are thus factored in such a way that the higher frequency (or short-run dynamics) are associated with the operating parts while the lower frequency (or long run dynamics) are associated with the strategic system (Simon, 1962, p.477). These operating and strategic distinctions correspond with the lower and higher levels in the organizational hierarchy, respectively. Internal incentives and information flows need, of course, to be aligned, lest distortions be deliberately or inadvertently introduced into the internal information summary and transmittal processes.

The hierarchical decomposition principle can thus be stated as follows: *internal organization should be designed in such a way as to effect quasi-independence between the parts, the high-frequency dynamics (operating activities) and low-frequency dynamics (strategic planning) should be clearly distinguished, and incentives should be aligned within and between components* so as to promote both local and global effectiveness.

Each of these three principles of organizational design is responsive to considerations of both bounded rationality and opportunism. Thus asset specificity would pose no problems if comprehensive contracting were feasible (which is tantamount to unbounded rationality) or if winning bidders could be relied upon to behave in an utterly reliable and trustworthy fashion (absence of opportunism). The externality principle is mainly a reflection of opportunism (autonomous distributors permit their suppliers' reputations to be degraded because they bear only part of the costs), but, of course, quality control checks would be unneeded if all relevant information could be costlessly displayed and assessed. The hierarchical decomposition principle recognizes the need to divide problems into manageable units and at the same time prevent agents from engaging in dysfunctional pursuit of local goals, which reflect bounded rationality and opportunism concerns, respectively.

A more comprehensive analysis would embed these principles of organization within a larger optimizing framework where demand as well as cost consequences are recognized and where production versus transaction costs trade-offs are made explicit.[24] For the purposes at hand, however, which take product design as given and focus on distinguishably different rather than close cases, such refinements do not appear to be necessary.

III. THE NINETEENTH-CENTURY CORPORATION

The 1840s mark the beginning of a great wave of organizational change that has evolved into the modern corporation (Chandler, 1977). According to Bruchey, the fifteenth-century merchant of Venice would have understood the form of organization and methods of managing men, records and investment used by Baltimore merchants in 1790 (1956, pp.370-1). These practices evidently remained quite serviceable until after the 1840s. The two most significant developments were the appearance of the railroads and, in response to this, forward integration by manufacturers into distribution.

1. The Railroads
Although a number of technological developments—including the telegraph (Chandler, 1977, p.189), the development of continuous process machinery (ibid., pp.252-3), the refinement of interchangeable parts manufacture (ibid., pp.75-7), and related mass manufacturing techniques (ibid., ch.8)—contributed to organizational changes in the second half of the nineteenth century, none was more important than the railroads (Porter and Livesay, 1971, p.55). Not only did the railroads pose distinctive organizational problems of their own, but the incentive to integrate forward from manufacturing into distribution would have been much less without the low-cost, reliable, all-weather transportation afforded by the railroads. Forward integration is discussed in section III(2); the railroads are treated here.

The appearance and purported importance of the railroads have been matters of great interest to economic historians. But with very few exceptions, the organizational—as opposed to the technological— significance of the railroads has been neglected. Thus Fogel (1964) and Fishlow (1965) 'investigated the railroad as a construction activity and as a means of transport, but not as an organizational form. As with most economists, the internal workings of the railroad organizations were ignored. This appears to be the result of an implicit assumption that the organization form used to accomplish an objective does not matter' (Temin, 1980, p.3).

The economic success of the railroads entailed more, however, than the substitution of one technology (rails) for another (canals). Rather, organizational aspects also required attention. As Chandler puts it:

> [the] safe, regular, reliable movement of goods and passengers, as well as the continuing maintenance and repair of locomotives, rolling stock, and track, roadbed, stations, roundhouses, and other equipment, required the creation of a sizeable administrative organization. It meant the employment of a set of managers to supervise these functional activities over an extensive geographical area; and the appointment of an administrative command of middle and top executives to monitor, evaluate, and coordinate the work of managers responsible for the day-to-day operations. It meant, too, the formulation of brand new types of internal administrative procedures and accounting and statistical controls. Hence, the operational requirements of the railroads demanded the creation of the first administrative hierarchies in American business. (1977, p.87)

The 'natural' railroad units, as these first evolved, were lines of about 50 miles in length. These roads employed about 50 workers and were administered by a superintendent and several managers of functional activities (ibid., p.96). This was adequate as long as traffic flows were uncomplicated and short hauls prevailed. The full promise of the railroads could be realized, however, only if traffic densities were increased and longer hauls introduced. How was this to be effected?

In principle, successive end-to-end systems could be joined by contract. The resulting contracts would be tightly bilateral in negotiation, interpretation and execution, however, since investments in site-specific assets by each party were considerable. Severe contractual difficulties would, therefore, predictably arise.[25] Unless supporting governance structure were simultaneously created,[26] the potential of the railroads for long-haul and high density traffic would evidently go unrealized. One possibility was for heavily travelled end-to-end links to be joined under common ownership.

But while the consolidation of ownership reduced the restraints on long-haul operations, it did not guarantee that the end-to-end systems would work smoothly. Indeed, early operation of the Western and Albany road, which was just over 150 miles in length and was built in three sections, each operated as a separate division with its own set of functional managers, quickly proved otherwise (ibid., pp.96-7). As a consequence, a new organizational structure was fashioned whereby the first 'formal administrative structure manned by full-time salaried managers' in the US appeared (pp.97-8).

This structure was progressively perfected, and the organizational innovation that the railroads eventually evolved is characterized by Chandler as the 'decentralized line-and-staff concept of organization'. This provided that 'the managers on the line of authority were responsible for ordering men involved with the basic function of the enterprise, and other functional managers (the staff executives) were responsible for setting standards' (p.106). Geographic divisions were defined and the superintendents in charge were held responsible for the 'day-to-day movement of trains and traffic by an express delegation of authority' (p.102). These division superintendents were on the 'direct line of authority from the president through the general superintendent' (p.106), and the functional managers within the geographic divisions— who dealt with transportation, motive power, maintenance of way, passenger, freight and accounting—reported to them rather than to their functional superiors at the central office (pp.106-7).

Confronted, as they were by the contractual dilemmas that arise when highly specific assets are in place and by complexities that exceeded, perhaps by several orders of magnitude, those that had been faced by earlier business enterprise, the managements of the railroads supplanted markets by hierarchies of a carefully crafted kind. Although military organizations had earlier devised similar structures, the railroad innovators brought engineering rather than military backgrounds to the task (ch.3.). The hierarchical structure that they evolved was consistent, at least broadly, with the hierarchical principles stated by Simon. Thus support activities (lower-frequency dynamics) were split off from operations (higher-frequency dynamics), and the linkages within each of these classes of activity were stronger than the linkages between. This organizational innovation, in Chandler's judgement, paved the way for modern business enterprise. As with most significant organizational developments, it evolved in a piecemeal rather than a full-blown way (Nelson and Winter, 1981). Failure to recognize the opportunities for decomposition of functions and to perfect the hierarchical governance structures by which these could be realized would have arrested the development of the modern corporation at a very primitive stage.

2. Forward Integration

Forward integration by manufacturers into distribution was one of the significant consequences of the appearance of the railroads. Low-cost transportation combined with telegraph and telephone communication permitted manufacturers efficiently to service a larger market and, as a consequence, realize greater economies of scale in production. The points of connection between manufacturing, wholesaling and retailing, however, also required attention. Forward integration was a common but by no means uniform response. To the contrary, it was highly selective rather than comprehensive, and it is this selectivity that is the matter of special interest to this paper.

At least four degrees of forward integration can be recognized. From least to most, these are:

(a) None—in which event traditional wholesale and retail distribution was continued (many grocery, drug, hardware, jewellery, liquor, and dry goods items were of this kind) (Porter and Livesay, 1971, p.214).
(b) Minor—efforts to pre-sell product and to monitor wholesale inventories, but not to include the ownership and operation of wholesale plants, are examples. Certain branded non-durables (soups, soaps), especially those for which staling was a problem (cigarettes, cereals), are included.
(c) Wholesale—this was undertaken for perishable, branded items that required special handling;[27] often specialized investments in refrigeration were involved (meat and beer are examples) (Chandler, 1977, p.299).
(d) Retail—integration into retail was rare and was reserved for 'new, complex, high-priced machines that required specialized marketing services—demonstration, installation, consumer credit, after-sales service and repair' (Chandler, 1977, p.288). Certain consumer durables (sewing machines, automobiles) and producer durables (some electrical machinery and office machines) were of this kind.

Actually, there is a variant of this fourth category that I shall designate 'mistaken' retail integration. Such integration involved none of the transaction-specific investments in sales and service referred to above, but had the purpose of foreclosing rivals. The ill-fated efforts of American Tobacco to integrate forward into the wholesaling and retailing of cigars (Porter and Livesay, 1971, p.210) and of American Sugar Refining to 'drive its competitor John Arbuckle out of business by buying into wholesale and retail houses' (ibid., p.211, 52) are examples.[28]

The question is how to interpret these developments. Although the data that would be needed for a quantitative analysis have yet to be worked up, a systematic qualitative interpretation along the lines of the discussion in sections II(2) and (3) is nevertheless feasible. The attributes of the five integration classes are set out in Table 8.1, where ++ denotes considerable, + denotes some, ~ is uncertain, and 0 is negligible.

Markets remain the main mode for effecting distribution for classes A and B. Markets enjoy substantial economies of scope for these products while asset specificity is negligible and externalities are dealt with by monitoring inventory. Integration into wholesale occurs for products that involve some asset specificity (refrigeration) and the reputation of branded products needs protection. Integration into retail does not occur, however, until asset specificity at the retail level is great (and these are products for which separate sales and service entails negligible loss of scope economies).[29] Finally, mistaken retail integration involves the sacrifice of scope economies without offsetting governance cost benefits (externalities and asset specificity are negligible). This pattern of integration is broadly consistent with transaction-cost reasoning and explains why forward integration occurred selectively rather than comprehensively in response to the transportation and communication infrastructure.[30]

Table 8.1.

Integration class	Economies of scope	Externalities	Asset specificity
A: none	++	0	0
B: minor	+	+	0
C: wholesale	~	+	+
D_1 retail/viable	0	+	++
D_2 retail/mistaken	+	0	0

IV. THE TWENTIETH CENTURY CORPORATION

Three developments are particularly noteworthy in the evolution of the modern corporation in the twentieth century. The first of these was the appearance of the multidivisional (or M-form) organization. Later developments are the conglomerate and the multinational corporation.

1. The Multidivisional Structure

The most significant organizational innovation of the twentieth century was the development in the 1920s of the multidivisional structure. Surprisingly, this development was little noted or widely appreciated as late as 1960. Leading management texts extolled the virtues of 'basic departmentation' and 'line and staff authority relationships', but the special importance of multidivisionalization went unremarked.[31]

Chandler's pathbreaking study of business history, *Strategy and Structure*, simply bypassed this management literature. He advanced the thesis that 'changing developments in business organization presented a challenging area for comparative analysis' and observed that 'the study of [organizational] innovation seemed to furnish the proper focus for such an investigation' (1966, p.2). Having identified the multidivisional structure as one of the more important of such innovations, he proceeded to trace its origins, identify the factors that gave rise to its appearance, and describe the subsequent diffusion of this organizational form. It was uninformed and untenable to argue that organization form was of no account after the appearance of Chandler's book.

The leading figures in the creation of the multidivisional (or M-form) structure were Pierre S. du Pont and Alfred P. Sloan; the period was the early 1920s; the firms were Du Pont and General Motors; and the organizational strain of trying to cope with economic adversity under the old structure was the occasion to innovate in both. The structures of the two companies, however, were different.

Du Pont was operating under the centralized functionally departmentalized or unitary (U-form) structure. General Motors, by contrast, had been operated more like a holding company by William Durant—whose genius in perceiving market opportunities in the automobile industry (Livesay, 1979, pp.232-4) evidently did not extend to organization. Chandler summarizes the defects of the large U-form enterprise in the following way:

The inherent weakness in the centralized, functionally departmentalized operating company . . . became critical only when the administrative load on the senior executives increased to such an extent that they were unable to handle their entrepreneurial responsibilities efficiently. This situation arose when the operations of the enterprise became too complex and the problems of coordination, appraisal, and policy formulation too intricate for a small number of top officers to handle both long-run, entrepreneurial, and short-run, operational administrative activities. (1966, pp.382-3).

The ability of the management to handle the volume and complexity of the demands upon it became strained and even collapsed. Unable meaningfully to identify with or contribute to the realization of global goals, managers in each of the functional parts attended to what they perceived to be operational sub-goals instead (ibid., p.156). In the language of transaction-cost economics, bounds on rationality were reached as the U-form structure laboured under a communication overload while the pursuit of sub-goals by the functional parts (sales, engineering, production) was partly a manifestation of opportunism.

The M-form structure fashioned by du Pont and Sloan involved the creation of semi-autonomous operating divisions (mainly profit centres) organized along product, brand or geographic lines. The operating affairs of each were managed separately. More than a change in decomposition rules were needed, however, for the M-form to be fully effective. Du Pont and Sloan also created a general office 'consisting of a number of powerful general executives and large advisory and financial staffs' (Chandler, 1977, p.460) to monitor divisional performance, allocate resources among divisions, and engage in strategic planning. The reasons for the success of the M-form innovation are summarized by Chandler as follows:;

The basic reason for its success was simply that it clearly removed the executives responsible for the destiny of the entire enterprise from the more routine operational activities, and so gave them the time, information, and even psychological commitment for long-term planning and appraisal . . .
  [The] new structure left the broad strategic decisions as to the allocation of existing resources and the acquisition of new ones in the hands of a top team of generalists. Relieved of operating duties and tactical decisions, a general executive was less likely to reflect the position of just one part of the whole. (1966, pp.382-3)

In contrast with the holding company—which is also a divisionalized form but has little general office capability and hence is little more than a corporate shell—the M-form organization adds (1) a strategic planning and resource allocation capability, and (2) monitoring and control apparatus. As a consequence, cash flows are reallocated among divisions to favour high-yield uses, and internal incentive and control instruments are exercised in a discriminating way. In short, the M-form corporation takes on many of the properties of (and is usefully regarded as) a miniature capital market,[32] which is a much more ambitious concept of the corporation than the term holding company contemplates.

Although the structure was imitated very slowly at first, adoption by US firms proceeded rapidly during the period 1945 to 1960. Acceptance of this structure by European firms came later. Franko (1972) reports that most large European companies administered their domestic operations through U-form or holding company structures until late in the 1960s, but that rapid reorganization along M-form lines has occurred since. The advent of zero tariffs within the European Economic Community and the post-war penetration of European markets by American multinationals were, in his judgement, important contributing factors.

As Ashby has observed, it is not sufficient to determine the behaviour of a whole machine to know the behaviour of its parts: 'only when the details of coupling are added does the whole's behaviour become determinate' (1956, p.53). The M-form structure represented a different solution to the coupling problem than the earlier unitary form structure. It effected decomposability along product or brand lines to which profit centre standing could be assigned and it more clearly separated operating from strategic decision-making. It carried Simon's hierarchical decomposition principles to a higher degree of refinement.[33]

As compared with the U-form organization of the same activities, the M-form organisation of the large, complex corporation served both to economize on bounded rationality and attenuate opportunism. Specifically:

Operating decisions were no longer forced to the top but were resolved at the divisional level, which relieved the communication load. Strategic decisions were reserved for the general office, which reduced partisan political input into the resource allocation process. And the internal auditing and control techniques which the general office had access to served to overcome information impactedness conditions and permit fine timing controls to be exercised over the operating parts (Williamson, 1975, pp.137-8).

2. The Conglomerate

Chandler's studies of organizational innovation do not include the conglomerate and multinational form of corporate enterprise. These are more recent developments, the appearance of which would not have been feasible but for the prior development of the M-form structure. In as much as transaction-cost economizing is socially valued and has been relatively neglected by prior treatments, my discussion of both of these emphasizes affirmative aspects. But this is intended to redress an imbalance and should not be construed to suggest either that a transaction-cost interpretation is fully adequate or that conglomerates and multinationals pose no troublesome public policy issues.[34] Unrelieved hostility to these two forms of organization, however, is clearly inappropriate. Specifically, conglomerates that have the capacity to allocate resources to high-valued uses and multinationals that use the M-form to facilitate technology transfer warrant more sympathetic assessments.

Although diversification as a corporate strategy certainly predates the 1960s, when general awareness of the conglomerate began to appear, the conglomerate is essentially a post-world war II phenomenon. To be sure, General Electric's profit centres number in the hundreds and GE has been referred to as the world's most diversified firm. Until recently, however, General Electric's emphasis has been the manufacture and distribution of electrical appliances and machinery. Similarly, although General Motors was more than an automobile company, it took care to limit its portfolio. Thus Sloan remarked that 'tetraethyl lead was clearly a misfit for GM. It was a chemical product, rather than a mechanical one. And it had to go to market as part of the gasoline and thus required a gasoline distribution system' (Burton and Kuhn, 1979, p.6). Accordingly, although GM retained an investment position, the Ethyl Corporation became a free-standing entity rather than an operating division (Sloan,

1965, p.224). Similarly, although Durant had acquired Frigidaire, and Frigidaire's market share of refrigerators exceeded 50 per cent in the 1920s, the position was allowed to deteriorate as rivals developed market positions in other major appliances (radios, ranges, washers, etc.) while Frigidaire concentrated on refrigerators. The suggestion that GM get into air conditioners 'did not register on us, and the proposal was not . . . adopted' (ibid., 361). As Burton and Kuhn conclude, GM's 'deep and myopic involvement in the automobile sector of the economy, [prevented] product diversification opportunities in other market areas— even in product lines where GM had already achieved substantial penetration—[from being] recognized' (1979, pp.10-11).

The conglomerate form of organization, whereby the corporation consciously took on a diversified character and nurtured its various parts, evidently required a conceptual break in the mind-set of Sloan and other pre-war business leaders. This occurred gradually, more by evolution than by grand design (Sobel, 1974, p.377); and it involved a new group of organizational innovators—of which Royal Little was one (ibid.). The natural growth of conglomerates, which would occur as the techniques for managing diverse assets were refined, was accelerated as antitrust enforcement against horizontal and vertical mergers became progressively more severe. Conglomerate acquisitions—in terms of numbers, assets acquired, and as a proportion of total acquisitions—grew rapidly with the result that 'pure' conglomerate mergers, which in the period 1948-53 constituted only 3 per cent of the assets acquired by merger, had grown to 49 per cent by 1973-77 (Scherer, 1980, p.124).

Adelman's (1961) explanation for the conglomerate is that this form of organization has attractive portfolio diversification properties. But why would the conglomerate appear in the 1960s rather than much earlier? After all, holding companies, which long predated the conglomerate, can accomplish portfolio diversification. And individual stockholders, through mutual funds and otherwise, are able to diversify their own portfolios. At best the portfolio diversification thesis is a very incomplete explanation for the post-war wave of conglomerate mergers.[35]

The Federal Trade Commission also ventured an early assessment of the conglomerate in which organization form features were ignored. The conglomerate was a natural target for the inhospitality tradition. Thus the FTC Staff held that the conglomerate had the following properties:

With the economic power which it secures through its operations in many diverse fields, the giant conglomerate corporation may attain an almost impregnable economic position. Threatened with competition in any one of its various activities, it may sell below cost in that field, offsetting its losses through profits made in its other lines—a practice which is frequently explained as one of meeting competition. The conglomerate corporation is thus in a position to strike out with great force against smaller business in a variety of different industries. (1948, p.59)

I submit that some phenomena, of which changing internal organization is one, need to be addressed on their own terms. Adopting this view, the conglomerate is best understood as a logical outgrowth of the M-form mode for organizing complex economic affairs. Thus once the merits of the M-form structure for managing separable, albeit related, lines of business (e.g. a series of automobile or a series of chemical divisions) were recognized and digested, its extension to manage less closely related activities was natural. This is not to say that the management of product variety is without problems of its own. But the basic M-form logic, whereby strategic and operating decisions are distinguished and responsibilities are separated, carried over. The conglomerates in which M-form principles of organization are respected are usefully thought of as internal capital markets whereby cash flows from diverse sources are concentrated and directed to high-yield uses.

The conglomerate is noteworthy, however, not merely because it permitted the M-form structure to take this diversification step. Equally interesting are the unanticipated systems consequences which developed as a byproduct. Thus once it was clear that the corporation could manage diverse assets in an effective way, the possibility of takeover by tender offer suggested itself. In principle, incumbent managements could always be displaced by waging a proxy contest. In fact, this is a very expensive and relatively ineffective way to achieve management change (Williamson, 1970, ch.6). Moreover, even if the dissident shareholders should succeed, there was still a problem of finding a successor management.

Viewed in contractual terms, the M-form conglomerate can be thought of as substituting an administrative interface between an operating division and the stockholders where a market interface had existed previously. Subject to the condition that the conglomerate does not diversify to excess, in the sense that it cannot competently evaluate and allocate funds among the diverse activities in which it is engaged, the substitution of internal organization can have beneficial effects in goal pursuit, monitoring, staffing and resource allocation respects. The goal pursuit advantage is that which accrues to M-form organizations in general: since the general management of an M-form conglomerate is disengaged from operating matters, a presumption that the general office favours profits over functional goals is warranted. Relatedly, the general office can be regarded as an agent of the stockholders whose purpose is to monitor the operations of the constituent parts. Monitoring benefits are realized in the degree to which internal monitors enjoy advantages over external monitors in access to information—which they arguably do

(Williamson, 1975, pp.145-8). The differential ease with which the general office can change managers and reassign duties where performance failures or distortions are detected is responsible for the staffing advantage. Resource-allocation benefits are realized because cash flows no longer return automatically to their origins but instead revert to the centre, thereafter to be allocated among competing uses in accordance with prospective yields.[36]

This has a bearing on the problem of separation of ownership from control, noted by Adolph Berle and Gardiner C. Means in 1932. Thus they inquired, 'have we any justification for assuming that those in control of a modern corporation will also choose to operate it in the interests of the stockholders?' (1932, p.121). The answer, then as now, is almost certainly no. Indeed, the evident disparity of interest between managers and stockholders gave rise in the 1960s to what has become known as the managerial discretion literature (Baumol, 1959; Marris, 1964; Williamson, 1964).

There are important differences, however, between the U-form structure, which was the prevailing organization form at the time Berle and Means were writing, and the M-form structure, which in the US was substantially in place by the 1960s. For one thing, as argued above, U-form managers identified more strongly with functional interests and hence were more given to sub-goal pursuit. Secondly, and related, there was a confusion between strategic and operating goals in the U-form structure which the M-form served to rectify—with the result that the general office was more fully concerned with enterprise goals, of which profits is the leading element. Third, the market for corporate control, which remained ineffectual so long as the proxy contest was the only way to challenge incumbent managements, was activated as conglomerates recognized that tender offers could be used to effect corporate takeovers. As a consequence, managements that were otherwise secure and would have permitted managerial preferences to prevail were brought under scrutiny and induced to self-correct against egregious managerial distortions.

To be sure, managerial preferences (for salary and perquisites) and stockholder preferences for profits do not become perfectly consonant as a result of conglomerate organization and the associated activation of the capital market. The continuing tension between management and stockholder interests is evident in the numerous efforts that incumbent managements have taken to protect target firms against takeover (Cary, 1969; Williamson, 1979; George Benston, 1980). Changes in internal organization have nevertheless relieved these concerns. A study of capitalist enterprises which makes no allowance for organization form changes and their capital market ramifications will naturally overlook the possibility that the corporate control dilemma posed by Berle and Means has since been alleviated more by *internal* than it has by regulatory or external organizational reforms.

Not all conglomerates respected M-form principles when they were first organized. The above argument applies only to those where rational decomposition principles were observed and leads to the following testable proposition: conglomerates that were organized along holding company rather than M-form lines (as many were initially) would be less able to cope when adversity appeared, at which time they would be reorganized as M-form firms. Voluntary divestiture is also an interesting conglomerate phenomenon. Such a rationalization of assets is commonly accompanied by internal organizational reforms. Growth maximization theories are mainly at a loss to explain such behaviour.

3. Multinational Enterprise

The discussion of the multinational enterprise (MNE) that follows deals mainly with recent developments and, among these, emphasizes organizational aspects—particularly those associated with technology transfer in manufacturing industries. As Wilkins has reported, direct foreign investment by American firms has a long history: the book value of cumulative US direct foreign investment, expressed as a percentage of GNP, was in the range of 7 to 8 per cent in 1914, 1929 and 1970 (Wilkins, 1974, p.437). Both the character of this investment and, relatedly, the organization structure within which this investment takes place have been changing, however. It is not accidental that the term MNE was coined neither in 1914 nor 1929, but is of much more recent origin.

Thus whereas the ratio of the book value of US foreign investments in manufacturing as compared with all other (petroleum, trade, mining, public utilities) was 0.47 in 1950, this had increased to 0.71 in 1970 (ibid., p.329). Also, 'what impressed Europeans about American plants in Europe and the United States [in 1929] was mass production, standardization, and scientific management; in the 1960s, Europeans were remarking that America's superiority was based on technological and managerial advantage . . . [and] that this expertise was being exported via direct investment' (ibid., p.436).

The spread of the multinational corporation in the post-world war II period has given rise to considerable scrutiny, some puzzlement, and even some alarm (Tsurumi, 1977, p.74). One of the reasons for this unsettled state of affairs is that transaction-cost economizing and organization form issues have been relatively neglected in efforts to assess MNE activity. An important exception is the work of Buckley and Casson (1976).

Organization form is relevant in two related respects. First is the matter of US based as compared with foreign-based investment rates. Tsurumi reports in this connection that the rate of foreign direct investments by US firms increased rapidly after 1953, peaked in the mid-1960s, and has levelled off and declined since (Tsurumi, 1977, p.97). The pattern of foreign direct investments by foreign firms, by contrast, has lagged that of the US by about a decade (pp.91-2).

Recall that the conglomerate uses the M-form structure to extend asset management from specialized to diversified lines of commerce. The MNE counterpart is the use of the M-form structure to extend asset management from a domestic base to include foreign operations. Thus the domestic M-form strategy for decomposing complex business structures into semi-autonomous operating units was subsequently applied to the management of foreign subsidiaries. As noted in section IV(1), the transformation of the corporation along M-form lines came earlier in the US than in Europe and elsewhere. US corporations were for this reason better qualified to engage in foreign direct investments at an earlier date than were foreign-based firms. Only as the latter took on the M-form structure did this multinational management capability appear. The pattern of foreign direct investments recorded by Tsurumi and reported above is consistent with the temporal differences of US and foreign firms in adopting the M-form structure.

That US corporations possessed an M-form capability earlier than their foreign counterparts does not, however, establish that they used it to organize foreign investment. Stopford and Wells have studied this issue. They report that while initial foreign investments were usually organized as autonomous subsidiaries, divisional status within an M-form structure invariably appeared as the size and complexity of foreign operations increased (Stopford and Wells, 1972, p.21). This transformation usually followed the organization of domestic operations along M-form lines (p.24). The adoption of a 'global' strategy or 'worldwide perspective'— whereby 'strategic planning and major policy decisions' are made in the central office of the enterprise—could only be accomplished within a multidivisional framework (p.25).

Even more interesting than these organization form issues is the fact that foreign direct investments by US firms have been concentrated in a few industries. Manufacturing industries that have made substantial foreign direct investments include chemicals, drugs, automobiles, food processing, electronics, electrical and non-electrical machinery, non-ferrous metals and rubber. Tobacco, textiles and apparel, furniture, printing, glass, steel and aircraft have, by comparison, done little foreign direct investment (Tsurumi, 1977, p.87).

Stephen Hymer's 'dual' explanation for the multinational enterprise is of interest in this connection. Thus Hymer observes that direct foreign investment 'allows business firms to transfer capital, technology, and organizational skill from one country to another. It is also an instrument for restraining competition between firms of different nations' (1970, p.443).

Hymer is surely correct that the MNE can service both of these purposes and examples of both kinds can doubtlessly be found. It is nevertheless useful to ask whether the overall character of MNE investment, in terms of its distribution among industries, is more consistent with the efficiency purposes to which Hymer refers (transfer of capital, technology and organizational skill) or with the oligopolistic restraint hypothesis. Adopting a transaction cost orientation discloses that the observed pattern of investment is more consistent with the efficiency part of Hymer's dual explanation.

For one thing, oligopolistic purposes can presumably be realized by portfolio investment coupled with a limited degree of management involvement to segregate markets. Put differently, direct foreign investment and the organization of foreign subsidiaries within an M-form structure are not needed to effect competitive restraints. Furthermore, if competitive restraints were mainly responsible for these investments, then presumably all concentrated industries—which would include tobacco, glass and steel—rather than those associated with rapid technical progress would be active in MNE creation. Finally, although many of the leading US firms that engaged in foreign direct investment enjoyed 'market power' this was by no means true for all.

By contrast, the pattern of foreign direct investments reported by Tsurumi appears to be consistent with a transaction-cost economizing interpretation. Vernon's 1970 study of the *Fortune* 500 corporations disclosed that 187 of these firms had a substantial multinational presence. R&D expenditures as a percentage of sales were higher among these 187 than among the remaining firms in the *Fortune* 500 group. Furthermore, according to Vernon, firms that went multinational tended to be technological innovators at the time of making their initial foreign direct investments.

This raises the question of the attributes of firms and markets for accomplishing technology transfer. The difficulties with transferring technology across market interface are of three kinds: recognition, disclosure and team organization (Arrow, 1962; Williamson, 1975, pp.31-3, 203-7; Teece, 1977).[37] Of these three, recognition is probably the least severe. To be sure foreign firms may sometimes fail to perceive the opportunities to apply technological developments originated elsewhere. But enterprising domestic firms that have made the advance can be expected to identify at least some of the potential applications abroad.

Suppose, therefore, that recognition problems are set aside and consider disclosure. Technology transfer by contract can break down if convincing disclosure to buyers effectively destroys the basis for exchange. A very severe information asymmetry problem exists, on which account the less informed party (in this instance the buyer) must be wary of opportunistic representations by the seller.[38] Although sometimes this asymmetry can be overcome by sufficient *ex ante* disclosure (and veracity checks thereon), this may shift rather than solve the difficulty. The 'fundamental paradox' of information is that 'its value for the purchaser is not known until he has the information, but then he has in effect acquired it without costs' (Arrow, 1971, p.152).

Suppose, *arguendo*, that buyers concede value and are prepared to pay for information in the seller's possession. The incentive to trade is then clear and for some items this will suffice. The formula for a chemical compound or the blueprints for a special device may be all that is needed to effect the transfer. Frequently, however, and probably often, new knowledge is diffusely distributed and is poorly defined (Nelson, 1981). Where the requisite information is distributed among a number of individuals all of whom understand their speciality in only a tacit, intuitive way, a simple contract to transfer the technology cannot be devised. See Polanyi (1962).

Transfer need not cease, however, because simple contracts are not feasible. If the benefits of technology transfer are sufficiently great, exchange may be accomplished either by devising a complex trade or through direct foreign investment. Which will be employed depends on the circumstances. If only a one-time (or very occasional) transfer of technology is contemplated, direct foreign investment is a somewhat extreme response.[39] The complex contractual alternative is to negotiate a tie-in sale whereby the technology and associated know-how are transferred as a package. Since the know-how is concentrated in the human assets who are already familiar with the technology, this entails the creation of a 'consulting team' by the seller to accompany the physical technology transfer—the object being to overcome start-up difficulties and to familiarize the employees of the foreign firm, through teaching and demonstration, with the idiosyncrasies of the operation.[40]

In as much as many of the contingencies that arise in the execution of such contracts will be unforeseen, and as it will be too costly to work out appropriate *ex ante* responses for others, such consulting contracts are subject to considerable strain. Where a succession of transfers is contemplated, which is to say, when the frequency shifts from occasional to recurring, complex contracting is apt to give way to direct foreign investment. A more harmonious and efficient exchange relation—better disclosure, easier reconciliation of differences, more complete cross-cultural adaptation, more effective team organization and reconfiguration—all predictably result from the substitution of an internal governance relation for bilateral trading under these recurrent trading circumstances for assets, of which complex technology transfer is an example, that have a highly specific character.[41]

The upshot is that while puzzlement with and concerns over MNEs will surely continue, a transaction-cost interpretation of this phenomenon sheds insight on the following conspicuous features of multinational investment: (1) the reported concentration of foreign direct investment in manufacturing industries where technology transfer is of special importance; (2) the organization of these investments within M-form structures; and (3) the differential timing of foreign direct investment between US and foreign manufacturing enterprises (which difference also has organization form origins). I furthermore conjecture that the application of transaction cost reasoning will lead to a deeper understanding of other specific features of MNE activity as these are discovered and/or become subject to public policy scrutiny.

V. CONCLUDING REMARKS

There is widespread agreement, among economists and non-economists alike, with the proposition that the modern corporation is an important and complex economic institution. Such agreement is mainly explained by the obtrusive size of the largest firms—running to tens of billions of dollars of assets and sales, with employment numbering in the hundreds of thousands. The economic factors that lie behind the size, shape and performance of the modern corporation, however, are poorly understood.

This puzzlement is not of recent origin. Mason complained over 20 years ago that 'the functioning of the corporate system has not to date been adequately explained. . . . The man of action may be content with a system that works. But one who reflects on the properties or characteristics of this system cannot help asking why it works and whether it will continue to work' (1960, p.4). The predicament to which Mason refers is, I submit, largely the product of two different (but not unrelated) intellectual traditions. The first of these holds that the structural features of the corporation are irrelevant. This is the neoclassical theory of the firm that populates intermediate theory textbooks. Structural differences are suppressed as the firm is described as a production function to which a profit-maximization objective has been assigned. The second has public policy roots; this is the inhospitality tradition that I referred to earlier. In this tradition, distinctive structural features of the corporation are believed to be the result of unwanted (anti-competitive) intrusions into market processes.

The transaction-cost approach differs from both. Unlike neoclassical analysis, internal organization is specifically held to be important. Unlike the inhospitality tradition, structural differences are assumed to arise primarily in order to promote economy in transaction costs. The assignment of transactions between firms and markets and the economic ramifications of internal structure both come under scrutiny in these terms. The application of these ideas to the study of transactions in general and of the modern corporation in particular requires that (1) the transaction be made the principal unit of analysis; (2) an elementary appreciation for 'human nature as we know it' supplant the fiction of economic man; (3) transactions be dimensionalized; (4) rudimentary principles of market and hierarchical organization be recognized; and (5) a guiding principle of comparative institutional study be the hypothesis that transactions are assigned to and organized within governance structures in a discriminating (transaction-cost economizing) way.

The view that the corporation is first and foremost an efficiency instrument does not deny that firms also seek to monopolize markets, sometimes by engaging in strategic behaviour, or that managers sometimes pursue their own goals to the detriment of system goals. But specific structural preconditions need to be satisfied if strategic behaviour is to be feasible[42]—and most firms do not qualify, which is to say that strategic behaviour is the exception rather than the rule. Furthermore, most firms will be penalized if efficiency norms are seriously violated for extended periods of time—which serves to curb managerial discretion. The strongest argument favouring transaction-cost economizing, however, is that this is the only hypothesis that is able to provide a discriminating rationale for the succession of organizational innovations that have occurred over the past 150 years and out of which the modern corporation has emerged.

To recapitulate, although railroad mergers between parallel roads can have monopolizing purposes, the joining of end-to-end systems under common management is explained by transaction-cost economics. The hierarchical structures evolved by the railroads were the outcome of internal efforts to effect coordination across interfaces to which common operating responsibilities had been assigned. Older and simpler structures were unable to manage such complex networks, while coordination by end-to-end contracts between successive stations was prohibitively costly.

Forward integration out of manufacturing into distribution was widespread at the turn of the century. More interesting, however, than this general movement is the fact that forward integration was selective—being extensive in some industries (e.g. sewing machines), negligible in others (e.g. dry goods), and mistaken in still others (e.g. sugar). This selective pattern is predicted by and consistent with transaction-cost reasoning—whereas no other hypothesis makes comparably detailed predictions.

The efficiency incentive to shift from the earlier U-form to the M-form structure is partly explained in managerial discretion terms: the older structure was more subject to distortions of a managerial discretion kind—which is to say that opportunism had become a serious problem in the large U-form firm. Equally, and probably more, important, however, is that the managerial hierarchy in the U-form enterprise was simply over-burdened as the firm became large and complex. The M-form structure represented a more rational decomposition of the affairs of the firm and thereby served to economize on bounded rationality.[43] The subsequent diffusion of this structure was hastened by a combination of product market (pressure on rivals) and capital market (takeover) competition.

The M-form structure, which was originally adopted by firms in relatively specialized lines of commerce, was subsequently extended to manage diversified assets (the conglomerate) and foreign direct investments (MNE). A breadth-for-depth trade-off is involved in the former case, as the firm selectively internalizes functions ordinarily associated with the capital market. MNE activity has also been selective—being concentrated in the more technologically progressive industries where higher rates of R&D are reported and technology transfer arguably poses greater difficulties than is true of technologically less progressive industries. This pattern of foreign direct investment cannot be explained as the pursuit of monopoly but is consistent with transaction-cost reasoning.

The upshot is that a transaction-cost approach to the study of the modern corporation permits a wide variety of significant organizational events to be interpreted in a coherent way.[44] It links up comfortably with the type of business history studies that have been pioneered by Chandler. It has ramifications for the study of regulation (Goldberg, 1976; Williamson, 1976) and for antitrust enforcement. Applications to aspects of labour economics and comparative systems have been made, and others would appear to be fruitful. More generally, while there is room for and need for refinement, a comparative approach to the study of economic institutions in which the economy of transaction costs is the focus of analysis appears to have considerable promise.

NOTES

1. This argument is elaborated in Williamson (1981). It is briefly discussed below in conjunction with what is referred to as the 'inhospitality tradition' within antitrust. See section 1.
2. Sadao Takatera and Nobaru Nishikawa, in an unpublished manuscript (undated), discuss the 'Genesis of Divisional Management and Accounting Systems in the House of Mitsui, 1710-1730'.
3. Gary Anderson, Robert E. McCormick, and Robert D. Tollison, in an unpublished manuscript (May 1981), describe the 'East India Company as a Multi-divisional Enterprise' early in the eighteenth century.
4. Primitive divisionalization is often confused with but needs to be distinguished from multidivisionalization. See Sloan (1965) and Chandler (1962) for a discussion of the origins of the M-form structure in the twentieth century.
5. The quotation is attributed to Turner by Stanley Robinson (1968), NY State Bar Association, Antitrust Symposium, p.29.
6. For an interesting commentary and contribution, see Douglass North (1978). The earlier Lance Davis and North book, however, gave relatively little attention to institutional changes that occurred within firms (1971, p.143).
7. The term 'local goals' subsumes both the functional goals of a sub-unit of the enterprise and the individual goals of the functional managers. In a perfectly harmonized system, private goals are consonant with functional goals, the realization of which in turn promotes global goals. Frequently, however, managers become advocates for parochial interests that conflict with global goal attainment. If, for example, R&D claims a disproportionate share of resources—because of effective but distorted partisan representations from the management and staff of this group—profits (global goals) will suffer. Aggressive sub-goals (or local goal) pursuit of this kind is a manifestation of opportunism (see section II(2)).
8. The phrase is Richard Posner's (1979, p.928).
9. For a discussion of this point, see Williamson (1975, pp.11-13, 109-10).
10. Although the non-strategic tradition inspired by Aaron Director makes insufficient allowance for anti-competitive behaviour, it was a useful counterweight to the inhospitality tradition to which it was paired. For a critique of the more extreme versions of this non-strategic—or, as Posner (1979, p.932) puts it, the 'diehard Chicago'—tradition, see Williamson (1981).
11. Davis and North make repeated reference to the limited liability and unlimited life features of the corporate form and explicitly discuss the importance of organizational changes made by the railroads (1971, pp.143-4). Their treatment of organization form changes in manufacturing, however, emphasizes economies of scale, monopolization (cartelization), protection against foreign competition, and resistence to regulation (pp.167-90). A sense that the corporation is progressively refining structures that economize on transaction costs—in labour, capital and intermediate-product markets—is nowhere suggested.

   Although this is partly recitified in North's later survey paper, where he observes that recent organizational changes have had transaction-cost origins, he defines transaction costs narrowly in terms of the 'measurement of the separable dimensions of a good or services' (1978, p.971). As developed below, measurement is only one aspect—and not, in my judgement, the most important one—for understanding the modern corporation.

12. Moral hazard is a technical term with a well-defined meaning in the insurance literature. It refers to an *ex post* insurance condition and is clearly distinguished from adverse selection, which is responsible for a troublesome *ex ante* insurance screening problem. Opportunism is a less technical but more general term that applies to a wide set of economic behaviour—of which adverse selection and moral hazard are specific kinds. Unless, therefore, moral hazard is given a broader meaning, the substitution of moral hazard for opportunism focuses attention on a subset of the full range of human and economic conditions of concern.

13. The co-existence of cunning and bounded rationality is troublesome to some. How can economic agents simultaneously be more clever and less competent than the hyper-rational man that populates neoclassical models? Is he a maximizer or is he not? This is not a useful dichotomy. Maximizing is an analytical convenience the use of which is often justified by the fact that human agents are '*intendedly* rational' (Simon, 1957b, p.xxiv). As discussed in the text, however, comprehensive contracting, which is an ambitious form of maximizing, is infeasible. Opportunism has important economic ramifications for this reason.

14. I have reference, of course, to the Arrow-Debreu contracting model.

15. The argument that effective *ex ante* competition for the right to supply service (franchise bidding) vitiates the need to regulate decreasing-cost-industries sometimes goes through but not always. Incomplete contracting (bounded rationality) coupled with the hazards of *ex post* opportunism place great strain on the franchise bidding mode if assets are durable and specific. For a critique of what I believe was a mistaken assessment of the feasibility of using franchise bidding for CATV, see Williamson (1976).

16. As Knight observes: 'With uncertainty entirely absent, every individual being in possession of perfect knowledge of the situation, there would be no occasion for anything of the nature of responsible management or control of productive activity' (1965, p.267).

17. Williamson (1979). See also Klein, Crawford and Alchian (1978) for an illuminating discussion of transaction-specific investments in the context of what they refer to as 'appropriable quasi-rents'.

18. Whereas scale economies refer to declining average costs associated with increasing output of a single line of commerce, scope economies are realized 'where it is less costly to combine two or more product lines in one firm rather than to produce them separately' (Panzar and Willig, 1981, p.268). Retail outlets that carry many products and brands (drug stores, department stores) presumably enjoy significant economies of scope in the retailing function.

19. Bureaucratic disabilities aside, any given firm could realize all of these production benefits for itself by an appropriate increase in the scale and scope of its activities. Pursuit of this logic, however, leads to the following anomaly: all firms, of which there will be few, will be comprehensively integrated and diversified in sufficient degree to obviate the need for market exchange. The fact that we do not observe comprehensive integration—as Coase puts it, 'Why is not all production carried on by one big firm?' (1952, p.340)— suggests that the bureaucratic disabilities of internal organization are very serious. But since we do observe that some transactions are organized within firms, this poses the question of which and why. The answer resides in the transaction-cost disabilities of markets that arise when asset specificity and demand externalities appear.

20. Note that the nature of the asset specificity matters. If the assets in question are mobile and the specificity is due to physical but not human asset features, market procurement may still be feasible. This can be accomplished by having the buyer own the specific assets (e.g. dies). He puts the business up for bid and awards it to the low bidder, to whom he ships the dies. Should contractual difficulties arise, however, he is not locked into a bilateral exchange. He reclaims the dies and reopens the bidding. This option is not available if the specific assets are of a human asset kind or if they are non-mobile. See Teece (1980) for a related discussion.
21. Manufacturers may, of course, decide to integrate into components if work-in-process inspections are much cheaper than final inspections.
22. Franchising will be more prevalent if aggregation economies are present at the distribution stage. It will be inefficient in these circumstances for a single-product firm to integrate forward into distribution.
23. The hierarchical decomposition principle is due to Simon (1962, 1973). As he observes, the anatomy of an organization can be viewed either in terms of the groupings of human beings or the flows and transformations of symbols (1973, p.270). He emphasizes the latter, which is in the spirit of transaction-cost analysis.
24. Thus, whereas I argue that the object is to minimize the sum of production and transaction costs, taking output and design as given, the more general problem is to maximize profits, treating output and design as decision variables. A rudimentary statement of the optimizing problem, for a given organization form (f), is to choose output (Q) and design (D) so as to maximize:

$$\pi(Q,D;f) = P(Q,D) \cdot Q - C_f(Q,D;S) - G_f(Q,D),$$

where π denotes profit, $P(Q,D)$ is the demand curve, S denotes combinatorial economies of scope, and C_f and G_f are the production costs and governance (transaction) costs of mode f. Transaction costs become relatively more important to this calculus as the assets needed to support specialized designs become progressively more specific—which they normally will as designs become more idiosyncratic.

Plainly the trade-offs that run through this optimizing relation are more extensive than my earlier discussion discloses, but a detailed assessment of these is not needed for the types of purposes to which the asset-specificity principle is herein applied. Both the externality and hierarchical decomposition principles should likewise be qualified to recognize trade-offs. Again, however, second-order refinements are not needed for the comparative institutional purposes to which these are applied below.

25. Problems of two kinds would need to be faced. Not only would the railroads need to reach agreement on how to deal with a series of complex operating matters—equipment utilization, costing and maintenance; adapting cooperatively to unanticipated disturbances; assigning responsibility for customer complaints, breakdown, etc.—but problems of customers contracting with a set of autonomous end-to-end suppliers would need to be worked out. Plainly, complex contracting issues proliferate.
26. Railroad regulation can be interpreted, in part, as an effort to deal with these contractual difficulties by inventing specialized governance structures. Pursuit of these matters is beyond the scope of this paper. Aspects of the general problem are dealt with in Williamson (1976) and Goldberg (1976).

27. The Whitman candy case involved the use of two different merchandizing methods. Wholesalers were bypassed in the sale of high-grade, packaged candies. Small, inexpensive, bar and packaged candies, by contrast, were sold through the usual jobber and wholesale grocer network. Control of the wholesaling function for the former was arguably more important for quality control purposes. These high-grade items were 'sold directly to retailers so that the company could regulate the flow of the perishable items and avoid alienating customers', (Porter and Livesay, p.220)—who were presumably prepared to pay a premium to avoid stale candy.

28. This is not to say that foreclosure will never be successful unless accompanied by transaction-specific investments. But it should not entail sacrifice of scale economies. Forward integration by the motion picture producers into theatres may have been a viable means of foreclosing entry into the production stage because theatre ownership by major producers entailed little or no sacrifice of scale economies.

29. Concessions in department stores are devices for effecting retail sales for products that are efficiently marketed in conjunction with others but which nevertheless require transaction specific investments. Chandler does not discuss such products, but a more comprehensive microanalytic analysis would, I conjecture, disclose the existence of some where mixed modes arise because aggregation economies and asset specificity are simultaneously present.

30 For a more complete assessment, on which the above is based, see Williamson (1980).

31. The treatment of these matters by Koontz and O'Donnell (1955) is representative.

32. Others who reported that the modern corporation was assuming capital market resource allocation and control functions include Heflebower (1960) and Alchian (1969).

33. Moreover, whereas the line-and-staff structure that the railroads adopted in the 1850s could be said to have been prefigured by the military, there is no such military precedent for the M-form. Rather, the reorganization of the military after World War II has certain M-form attributes.

34. For a discussion of the public policy issues posed by conglomerates, see Williamson (1975, pp.163-71).

35. The diversification of personal portfolios is not a perfect substitute for conglomerate diversification because bankruptcy has real costs that the firm, but not individuals, can reduce by portfolio diversification. Bankruptcy costs have not sharply increased in the past 30 years, however, hence these differences do not explain the appearance of the conglomerate during this interval.

36. To be sure, this substitution of internal organization for the capital market is subject to trade-offs and diminishing returns. Breadth—that is, access to the widest range of alternatives—is traded off for depth—that is, more intimate knowledge of a narrower range of possible investment outlets (Alchian and Demsetz, 1972, p.29), where the general office may be presumed to have the advantage in the latter respect. The diminishing returns feature suggests that the net benefits of increased diversity eventually become negative. Were further diversification thereafter to be attempted, effective control would pass back into the hand of the operating divisions with problematic performance consequences.

37. The material that follows is based on Williamson and Teece (1979). Our argument is similar to that advanced by Buckley and Casson (1976).
38. Markets for information are apt to be especially costly and/or hazardous when transmission across a national boundary is attempted. Language differences naturally complicate the communication problem, and differences in the technological base compound these difficulties. If, moreover, as is commonly the case, cultural differences foster suspicion, the trust that is needed to support informational exchange may be lacking. Not only will contract negotiations be more complex and costly on this account, but execution will be subject to more formal and costly procedures than would obtain under a regime of greater trust.
39. This is an implication of transaction-cost reasoning in which the frequency dimension has explanatory power (Williamson, 1979, pp.245-54).
40. On the importance of on-site observation and of teaching-by-doing, see Polanyi (1962), Doeringer and Piore (1971, pp.15-16), and Williamson, Wachter and Harris (1975).
41. The argument can be extended to deal with such observations as those of Mansfield, Romeo and Wagner (1979), who report that firms use subsidiaries to transfer their newest technology overseas but rely on licensing or joint ventures for older technology. The transaction-cost argument is that the latter are more well defined, hence are more easily reduced to contract and require less firm specific know-how to effect successful transfer.
42. For a discussion of these preconditions—mainly high concentration coupled with high barriers to entry—see Joskow and Klevorick (1979) and Williamson (1981).
43. Had 'normal' managerial preferences prevailed, the U-form, which favoured the exercise of those preferences, would presumably have been retained.
44. Recent contributions to the theory of the firm that are held to have a bearing on the study of the modern corporation are Alchian and Demsetz (1972) and Jensen and Meckling (1976). Both, however, deal with a microcosm much smaller than the modern corporation. Thus Alchian and Demsetz focus on the reasons why technological non-separabilities give rise to team organization. Although small groups may be explained in this way (manual freight loading, whereby two men are required to lift coordinately, is the standard example), the existence of complex hierarchies cannot be explained in terms of the imperatives of such non-separabilities. (The largest work group which, to my knowledge, qualifies is the symphony orchestra.)

   Similarly, while the Jensen and Meckling paper is an important contribution to the principal–agent literature, it does not generalize to the modern corporation—as they expressly acknowledge (1976, p.356). Although they conjecture that their analysis can be applied to the large, diffusely owned corporation whose managers own little or no equity (ibid., p.356), I have serious doubts.

REFERENCES

Adelman, M.A., 'The Antimerger Act, 1950-1960', *American Economic Review*, May 1961, **51**, pp.136-44.

Alchian, A.A., 'Corporate Management and Property Rights', in *Economic*

Policy and Regulation of Corporate Securities, ed. H.G. Manne. Washington: American Enterprise Institute for Public Policy Research, 1969, pp.337-60.

Alchian, A.A., Demsetz, H., 'Production, Information Costs, and Economic Organization', *American Economic Review*, December 1972, **62**(5), pp.777-95.

Arrow, Kenneth J., 'Economic Welfare and the Allocation of Resources of Invention', in *The Rate and Direction of Incentive Activity: Economic and Social Factors*, ed. National Bureau of Economics Research. Princeton: Princeton University Press, 1962, pp.609-25.

Arrow, Kenneth, 'Control in Large Organizations', *Management Science*, April 1964, **10**(3), pp.397-408.

Arrow, Kenneth, 'The Organization of Economic Activity: Issues Pertinent to the Choice of Market Versus Nonmarket Allocation', in *The Analysis and Evaluation of Public Expenditure: The PPB System*, vol. 1. US Joint Economic Committee, 91st Congress, 1st Session, US Government Printing Office, 1969, pp.59-73.

Arrow, Kenneth, *Essay in the Theory of Risk-bearing*. Chicago: Markham, 1971.

Arrow, Kenneth, *The Limits of Organization*, 1st edition. New York: W.W. Norston 1974.

Ashby, W.R., *An Introduction to Cybernetics*. New York: John Wiley, 1956.

Barnard, C.I., *The Functions of the Executive*. Cambridge, Mass: Harvard University Press, 1938.

Baumol, W.J., *Business Behaviour, Value and Growth*. New York: Macmillan, 1959; Harcourt, Brace & World, 1967.

Benston, George J., *Conglomerate Mergers: Causes, consequences and remedies*. Washington DC: American Enterprise Institute for Public Policy Research, 1980.

Berle, A.A. and Means, G.C., *The Modern Corporation and Private Property*. New York: Macmillan, 1932.

Bruchey, Stuart W., *Robert Oliver, Merchant of Baltimore, 1783-1819*. Baltimore: Johns Hopkins University Press, 1956.

Buckley, P.J. and Casson, M., *The Future of Multinational Enterprise*. New York: Holmes & Meier, 1976.

Burton, R.H. and Kuhn, A.J., 'Strategy Follows Structure; The Missing Link of Their Intertwined Relation', Working Paper no. 260, Fugua School of Business, Duke University, May 1979.

Cary, W., 'Corporate Devices Used to Insulate Management from Attack', *Antitrust Law Journal*, 1969-70, **39**(1), pp.318-24.

Caves, R.E., 'Corporate Strategy and Structure', *Journal of Economic Literature*, March 1980, **18**(1), pp.64-92.

Chandler, A.D., Jr., *Strategy and Structure: Chapters in the history of the industrial enterprise*. Cambridge, Mass.: MIT Press, 1962; Garden City, N.J.: Doubleday, 1966.

Chandler, A.D., *The Visible Hand: The managerial revolution in American business*. Cambridge, Mass.: Belknap Press, 1977.

Coase, R.H., 'The Nature of the Firm', *Economica N.S.*, 1937, **4**, pp.386-405; and in *Readings in Price Theory*, ed. G.J. Stigler and K.E. Boulding. Chicago: Richard D. Irwin for the American Economic Association, 1952.

Coase, R.H., 'Industrial Organization: A Proposal for Research', in *Policy Issues and Research Opportunities in Industrial Organization: Economic research: Retrospect and prospect*, ed. Victor R. Fuchs. New York: NBER; distributed by Columbia University Press, New York and London, 1972, pp.59-73.

Commons, Johns R., *Institutional Economics: its place in political economy*. New York: Macmillan [1934], 1951.

Cyert, Richard M. and Hedrick, Charles L., 'Theory of the Firm: Past, Present, and Future; An Interpretation' *Journal of Economic Literature*, June 1972, **10**(2), pp.398-412.

Davis, Lance E. and North, Douglass C., *Institutional Change and American Economic Growth*. Cambridge: Cambridge University Press, 1971.

Doeringer, P. and Piori, M., *Internal Labour Markets and Manpower Analysis*. Boston: D.C. Heath, 1971.

Drucker, P., *Management: Tasks, responsibilities, practices*. New York: Harper & Row, 1974.

Fishlow, Albert, *American Railroads, and the Transformation of the Antebellum Economy*. Cambridge, Mass.: Harvard University Press, 1965.

Fogel, William R., *Railroads and American Economic Growth: Essays in econometric history*. Baltimore: Johns Hopkins University Press, 1964.

Franko, Lawrence G., 'The Growth, Organizational Efficiency of European Multinational Firms: Some Emerging Hypotheses', *Colloques International aux C.N.R.S.*, 1972, pp.335-66.

Goldberg, V P 'Regulation and Administered Contracts' *Bell Journal of Economics*, Autumn 1976, **7**(2), pp.426-52.

Hayek, F.'The Use of Knowledge in Society', *American Economic Review*, September 1945, **35**, pp.519-30.

Heflebower, R.B., 'Observation on Decentralization in Large Enterprises', November 1960, **9**, pp.7-22.

Hymer, S., 'The Efficiency (Contradictions) of Multinational Corporations', *American Economic Review*, May 1970, **60**(2), pp.441-48.

Jensen, M.C. and Meckling, W.H., 'Theory of the Firm: Managerial Behaviour, Agency Costs and Ownership Structure', *Journal of Finance and Economics*, Oct. 1976, **3**(4), pp.305-60.

Joskow, Paul L. and Klevorick, Alvin K., 'A Framework for Analyzing Predatory Pricing Policy', *Yale Law Journal*, December 1979, **89**, pp.213-70.

Klein, B., Crawford, R.A. and Alchian, A.A., 'Vertical Integration, Appropriable Rents, and the Competitive Contracting Process,' *Journal of Law Economics, October 1978*, **21**(2), pp.297-326.

Knight, Frank, H., *Risk, Uncertainty and Profit*. New York: Harper & Row, [1921], 1965.

Koontz, H. and O'Donnell, C., *Principles of Management; An analysis of managerial functions*. New York, McGraw-Hill, 1955.

Larson, Henrietta M., *Guide to Business History; Materials for the study of American business history and suggestions for their use*. Cambridge, Mass. Harvard University Press, 1948.

Livesay, H.C., *American Made: Men who shaped the American economy*, 1st edition. Boston: Little, Brown, 1979.

Mansfield, E., Romeo, A. and Wagner, S., 'Foreign Trade and US Research and Development', *Review of Economics and Statistics*, February 1979, **61**(1), pp.49-57.

Marris, R., *The Economic Theory of Managerial Capitalism*. New York: Free Press, 1964.

Marris, R. and Mueller, D.C., 'The Corporation, Competition, and the Invisible Hand', *Journal of Economic Literature*, March 1980, **18**(1), pp.32-63.

Marschak, J. and Radner, R., *Economic Theory of Teams*. New Haven: Yale University Press, 1972.

Mason, E.S., 'Introduction', in *The Corporation in Modern Society*, ed. E.S. Mason, Cambridge, Mass.: Harvard University Press, 1960, pp.1-24.

Nelson, R.R., 'Assessing Private Enterprise: An Exegisis of Tangled Doctrine', *Bell Journal of Economics*, Spring 1981, **12**(1), pp.93-111.

Nelson, R.R. and Winter, S.G., *An Evolutionary Theory of Economic Behaviour and Capabilities*. Cambridge, Mass.: Harvard University Press, 1981.

North, D.C., 'Structure and Performance: The Task of Economic History', *Journal of Economic Literature*, September 1978, **16**(3), pp.963-78.

Panzar, John C. and Willig, Robert D., 'Economies of Scope', *American Economic Review, Papers and Proceedings*, May 1981, **71**(2), pp.268-72.

Polyani, M., *Personal Knowledge: Towards a post-critical philosophy*. New York: Harper & Row, 1962.

Porter, G. and Livesay, H.C., *Merchants and Manufacturers: Studies in the changing structure of nineteenth-century marketing*. Baltimore: Johns Hopkins University Press, 1971.

Posner, R.A., 'The Chicago School of Antitrust Analysis', *University Pennsylvania Law Review*, April 1979, **127**(4), pp.925-48.

Radner, Roy, 'Competitive Equilibrium Under Uncertainty', *Econometrica*, January 1968, **36**(1), pp.31-58.

Scherer, F.M., *Industrial Market Structure and Economic Performance*. 2nd edition. Chicago: Rand McNally, 1980.

Simon, H.A., *Models of Man: Social and rational mathematical essays on rational human behaviour in a social setting*. New York: John Wiley, 1957a.

Simon, H.A., *Administrative Behaviour; a study of decision-making processes in administrative organization*, 2nd edition. New York: Macmillan [1947], 1957b.

Simon, H.A., 'The Architecture of Complexity', *Proceedings of the American Philosophical Society*, December 1962, **106**(6), pp.467-82.

Simon, H.A., 'Applying Information Technology to Organization Design', *Public Administration Review*, May-June 1973, **33**(3), pp.268-78.

Simon, H.A., 'Rationality as Process and as Process of Thought', *American Economic Review*, May 1978, **68**(2), pp.1-16.

Sloan, A.P., Jr., *My years with General Motors*. New York: MacFadden-Bartell, [1963], 1965.

Sobel, R., *The Entrepreneurs: Explorations within the American business tradition*, New York: Weybright & Talley, 1974.

Stopford, John M. and Wells, Louis T., Jr., *Managing the Multinational Enterprise: Organization of the firm and ownership of the subsidiaries*. New York: Basic Books, 1972.

Teece, D.J., 'Technology Transfer by Multinational Firms', *Economic Journal*, June 1977, **87**, pp.242-61.

Teece, D.J., 'Economies of Scope and the Scope of the Enterprise', *Journal of Economic Behavior Organization* 1980, **1**(3), pp.223-45.

Temin, P., 'The Future of the New Economic History,' *Journal of Interdisciplinary History*, Autumn 1981, **12**(2), pp.179-97.

Thompson, James D., *Organizations in Action: Social science bases of administrative theory*. New York: McGraw-Hill, 1967.

Tsurumi, Y., *Multinational Management: Business strategy and government policy*. Cambridge, Mass.: Ballinger, 1977.

US Federal Trade Commission, *Report of the Federal Trade Commission on the Merger Movement: A summary report*, Washington, DC, US Government

Printing Office, 1948.

Vernon, R., *Sovereignty at Bay: The multinational spread of US enterprises*. New York: Basic Books, 1971.

Wilkins, Mira, *The Maturing of Multinational Enterprise: American business abroad from 1914 to 1970*. Cambridge, Mass.: Harvard University Press, 1974.

Williamson, O.E., *The Economics of Discretionary Behavior: Managerial Objectives in a theory of the firm*. Englewood Cliffs, N.J.: Prentice-Hall, 1964.

Williamson, O.E., *Corporate Control and Business Behavior*. Englewood Cliffs, N.J. Prentice-Hall, 1970.

Williamson, O.E., *Markets and Hierarchies: Analysis and antitrust implications: A study in the economics of internal organization*. New York: Free Press, 1975.

Williamson, O.E., Franchise Bidding for Natural Monopolies—in General and with Respect to CATV', *Bell Journal of Economics*, Spring 1976, 7(1), pp.73-104.

Williamson, O.E., 'Transaction-Cost Economics: The Governance of Contractual Relations', *Journal of Law Economics*, October 1979, 22(2), pp.233-61.

Williamson, O.E., 'On the Governance of the Modern Corporation', *Hofstra Law Review*, Fall 1979, 8(1), pp.63-78.

Williamson, O.E., 'Organizational Innovation: The Transaction-Cost Approach', Discussion Paper no. 82, Center for the Study of Organizational Innovation, University of Pennsylvania, September 1980.

Williamson, O.E., 'Antitrust Enforcement: Where It's Been; Where It's Going', Discussion Paper no. 102, Center for the Study of Organizational Innovation, University of Pennsylvania, May 1981.

Williamson, O.E., and Teece, D.J., 'European Economic and Political Integration: The Markets and Hierarchies Approach', in *New Approaches to European Integration*, ed. P. Salmon.

Williamson, O.E., Wachter, Michael L. and Harris, Jeffrey, E., 'Understanding the Employment Relation: The Analysis of Idiosyncratic Exchange', *Bell Journal of Economics*, Spring 1975, 6(1), pp.50-280.

9. What is Transaction Cost Economics?

Transaction cost economics adopts a contractual approach to the study of economic organization. It maintains that any issue that can be formulated as a contracting problem can be investigated to advantage in transaction-cost economizing terms. Every exchange relation qualifies. Many other issues which, at the outset, appear to lack a contracting aspect turn out, upon scrutiny, to have an implicit contracting quality (the cartel problem is an example). The upshot is that the actual and potential scope of transaction cost economics is very broad.

As compared with other approaches to the study of economic organization, transaction cost economics (1) is more microanalytic; (2) is more self-conscious about its behavioural assumptions; (3) introduces and develops the economic importance of asset specificity; (4) relies more on comparative institutional analysis; (5) regards the business firm as a governance structure rather than a production function; and (6) places greater weight on the *ex post* institutions of contract, with special emphasis on private ordering (as compared with court ordering). A large number of refutable implications obtain upon addressing problems of economic organization in this way.

My discussion of transaction-cost economics proceeds in four parts. Some of the background is briefly sketched in section I. The bounded rationality/opportunism/asset-specificity nexus is examined in section II. A simple contracting schema which applies to the study of non-standard contracting in all its forms is set out in section III. Some applications of this approach are sketched in section IV. Concluding remarks follow.

I. SOME BACKGROUND

1. Antecedents
Although significant transaction cost economics insights in law, econo-

---

* An earlier version of this paper was presented as the Eighth Annual Marion O'Kellie McKay Lecture at the University of Pittsburgh, 9 March, 1984.

mics and organization can be traced to the 1930s, this approach to the study of economic organization resisted operationalization and languished for over 30 years.[1] My own interest in the subject of economic organization originated with my work as a graduate student at Carnegie in the 1960s. I quickly fell under the influence—some say, came under the spell—of Herbert Simon, Richard Cyert and James March. This is a condition from which I have yet to recover, and for which the prognosis is said to be grim.

As Simon has repeatedly acknowledged, his interest in the study of organization owes a great deal to the earlier work of Chester Barnard, whose pathbreaking book, *The Functions of the Executive*, was published in 1938. Whether it was a coincidence or otherwise, the fact is that important and related research that has helped to shape transaction cost economics was being fashioned during the 1930s in law and economics as well.

Karl Llewellyn's prescient treatment of contract law (1931) is especially noteworthy. He took exception with the prevailing approach, which emphasized legal rules and their literal application to the writing and enforcement of contract, and insisted that attention be shifted instead to an examination of the purposes to be served. Under this alternative conception, less emphasis was placed on form and more on substance. Llewellyn distinguished between 'iron rules' and 'yielding rules' (1931, p.729) and held that:

the major importance of legal contract is to provide a framework for well-nigh every type of group organization and for well-nigh every type of passing or permanent relations between individuals and groups . . . —a framework highly adjustable, a framework which almost never accurately indicates real working relations, but which affords a rough indication around which such relations vary, an occasional guide in cases of doubt, and a norm of ultimate appeal when the relations cease in fact to work (pp.736-7).

This is a profoundly disturbing concept of contract. It disputes the legal centralism tradition whereby legal rules and court ordering are presumed to be efficacious, and advances the proposition that institutions of private ordering are crucial to an understanding of contract. Such a shift posed a serious threat to the convenient and prevailing view among economists that the courts settled contract disputes in an informed, effective and low-cost manner.

The principal economic contributions were those of John R. Commons and Ronald Coase. Commons advanced the proposition that the transaction is properly regarded as the basic unit of analysis (1934, pp.4-8). He furthermore recognised that technology is not determinative of economic organization. A leading purpose of organization is to harmonize relations

between parties who are engaged in exchange (1934, p.6). Lest cooperation in a complex contracting context needlessly founder or fracture,
economics should expressly concern itself with matters of governance.

Coase's classic paper 'On the Nature of the Firm' (1937) explicitly
posed the issue of economic organization in comparative institutional
terms. Rather than regard the boundaries of firms as technologically
determined, Coase proposed that firms and markets be considered
alternative means of economic organization (1952, p.333). Whether
transactions were organized within a firm (hierarchically) or between
autonomous firms (across a market) was thus a decision variable. Which
mode was chosen depended on the transaction costs that attended
each.

2. Frictionlessness

Kenneth Arrow has defined transaction costs as the 'costs of running the
economic system' (1969, p.48). Such costs are to be distinguished from
production costs, which is the cost category with which neoclassical
analysis has been preoccupied. Transaction costs are the economic
equivalent of friction in physical systems. The manifold successes of
physics in ascertaining the attributes of complex systems by assuming the
absence of friction scarcely require recounting here. Such a strategy has
had obvious appeal to the social sciences. Unsurprisingly, the absence of
friction in physical systems is cited to illustrate the analytic power
associated with 'unrealistic' assumptions (Friedman, 1953, pp.16-19).

But whereas physicists were quickly reminded by their laboratory
instruments and the world around them that friction was pervasive and
often needed to be taken expressly into account, economists did not have
a corresponding appreciation for the costs of running the economic
system. There is, for example, no reference whatsoever to transaction
costs, much less to transaction costs as the economic counterpart of
friction, in Milton Friedman's famous methodological essay (1953) or in
other post-war treatments of positive economics.[2] Thus although positive
economics admitted that frictions were important in principle, it had no
language to describe frictions in fact.

This neglect of transaction costs had numerous ramifications, not the
least of which was the way in which non-standard modes of economic
organization were interpreted. Until express provision for transaction
costs was made, the possibility that non-standard modes of
organization—customer and territorial restrictions, tie-ins, block book-
ing, franchising, vertical integration, and the like—operate in the service
of transaction-cost economizing was little appreciated. Instead, post-war
economists invoked monopoly explanations whenever confronted with

non-standard contracting practices: 'if an economist finds something—a business practice of one sort or another—that he does not understand, he looks for a monopoly explanation' (Coase, 1972, p.67). Donald Turner's views are representative: 'I approach customer and territorial restrictions not hospitably in the common law tradition, but inhospitably in the tradition of antitrust.'[3] The prevailing firm as production function orientation encouraged this inhospitality attitude among students of antitrust. Also, as Coase observed, this applied price theory orientation informed the two leading texts—the one by Joe Bain (1958), the other by George Stigler (1968)—in industrial organization (1972, pp.61-3).

II. THE WORLD OF CONTRACT

1. Alternative Conceptions of Contract

The world of contract is variously described as one of (1) planning, (2) promise, (3) competition, and (4) governance (or private ordering). Which of these descriptions is most applicable depends on the behavioural assumptions which pertain to an exchange and on the economic attributes of the good or service in question.

The manner in which economic organization is studied turns critically on two behavioural assumptions. What cognitive competencies and what self-interest-seeking propensities are ascribed to the human agents who are engaged in exchange? Transaction cost economics assumes that human agents are subject to bounded rationality, whence behaviour is *intendedly* rational, but only *limitedly* so' (Simon, 1961, p.xxiv), and are given to opportunism, which is a condition of self-interest-seeking with guile. Transaction cost economics further maintains that the most critical dimensions for describing transactions is the condition of asset specificity. Parties who are engaged in a trade that is supported by non-trivial investments in transaction-specific assets are effectively operating in a bilateral trading relation with one another. Harmonizing the contractual interfaces that join the parties, thereby to effect adaptability and promote continuity, becomes the source of real economic value.

Transaction-cost economics thus relies on the conjunction of (1) bounded rationality, (2) opportunism, and (3) asset specificity. Absent any one of these conditions, the world of contract is vastly simplified.

Thus consider transactions where parties are opportunistic and assets are specific but economic agents have unrestricted cognitive competence. This essentially describes the mechanism design literature (Hurwicz, 1972, 1973; Holmstrom, 1983). Thus although the condition of opportunism requires that contracts be written in such a way as to respect private information, whence complex incentive alignment issues are posed, all of the relevant issues of contract are settled at the *ex ante* bargaining stage. Given unbounded rationality, a comprehensive bargain is struck at the outset, according to which appropriate adaptations to subsequent (publicly observable) contingent events are fully described. Contract execution problems thus never arise (or defection from such agreements is deterred) because court adjudication of all disputes is assumed to be efficacious (Baiman, 1982, p.168). Contract, in the context of unbounded rationality, is therefore described as a world of planning.

Consider alternatively the situation where agents are subject to bounded rationality and transactions are supported by specific assets, but the condition of opportunism is assumed to be absent. This last implies that the word of an agent is as good as his bond. Thus although gaps will appear in these contracts, because of bounded rationality, these can be covered by recourse to a self-enforcing general clause. Each party to the contract simply pledges at the outset to execute the contract efficiently (in a joint profit-maximizing manner) and to seek only fair returns at contract renewal intervals. Strategic behaviour is thereby denied. Parties to a contract thus extract all such advantages as their endowments entitle them when the initial bargain is struck. Thereafter, contract execution goes efficiently to completion because promises of the above described kind are, in the absence of opportunism, self-enforcing. Contract in this context, reduces to a world of promise.[4]

Consider then the situation where agents are subject to bounded rationality and are given to opportunism, but asset specificity is presumed to be absent. Parties to such contracts have no continuing interests in the identity of one another. This describes the world where discrete market contracting is efficacious, where markets are fully contestable,[5] where franchise bidding for natural monopoly goes through. In as much as fraud and egregious contract deceits are deterred by court ordering,[6] contract, in this context, is described by a world of competition.

The full catastrophe appears when bounded rationality, opportunism and asset specificity are joined. Planning here is necessarily incomplete (because of bounded rationality), promise predictably breaks down (because of opportunism), and the pairwise identity of the parties now matters (because of asset specificity). This is the world of governance in which court ordering is no longer assumed to be effective. The institutions of private ordering thus command centre stage. This is the world with which transaction cost economics is concerned. The organizational imperative that emerges in these circumstances is this: *organize transactions so as to economize on bounded rationality while simultaneously safeguarding them against the hazards of opportunism.* Such a statement supports a different and larger conception of the economic problem than does the imperative 'maximize profits!'

2. The Fundamental Transformation

It is common to distinguish between fixed and variable costs, but this is merely an accounting distinction. More relevant to the study of contracting is whether assets are redeployable or not (Klein and Leffler, 1981). Many assets that accountants regard as fixed are in fact redeployable—centrally-located, general-purpose buildings and equipment being examples. Durable but mobile assets such as general-purpose trucks and aeroplanes are likewise redeployable. Other costs which accountants treat as variable often have a large non-salvageable part, firm-specific human capital being an illustration. Figure 9.1 helps to make the distinction.

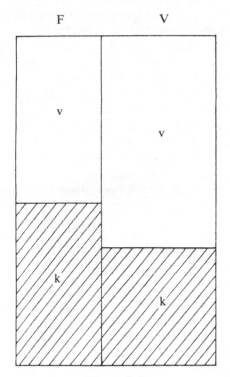

Figure 9.1

Thus costs are distinguished as to fixed (F) and variable (V) parts. But they are furthermore classified as to the degree of specificity, of which only two kinds are recognized: highly specific (k) and non-specific (v).

The shaded region at the bottom of the figure is the troublesome one for purposes of contracting. This is where the specific assets are located. But for such specificity, the world of contract would be enormously simplified.

But for asset specificity, recurrent spot contracting would be feasible. If the identity of the parties does not matter, then each can go his separate way without cost to the other. Contracts can thus be made for short duration, adaptations can be made at contract renewal intervals, and the contracting process operates continuously under the iron discipline of competition.

Transaction-cost economics accepts this as a broadly accurate description of neoclassical exchange. But it insists that many trades are not of this kind. Contrary to earlier practice, transaction cost economics holds that a condition of large-numbers bidding at the outset does not necessarily imply that a large-numbers bidding condition will obtain thereafter. Whether *ex post* competition is fully efficacious or not depends on whether the good or service in question is supported by durable investments in transaction-specific human or physical assets. Where no such specialized investments are incurred, the initial winning bidder realizes no advantage over non-winners. Although it may continue to supply for a long period of time, this is only because, in effect, it is continuously meeting competitive bids from qualified rivals. Rivals cannot be presumed to operate on a parity, however, once substantial investments in transaction-specific assets are put in place. Winners in these circumstances enjoy advantages over non-winners, which is to say that parity is upset. Accordingly, what was a large-numbers bidding condition at the outset is effectively transformed into one of bilateral supply thereafter. The reason why significant reliance investments in durable, transaction-specific assets introduces contractual asymmetry—between the winning bidder on the one hand, and non-winners on the other—is because economic values would be sacrificed if the ongoing supply relation were to be terminated.

A 'fundamental transformation' thus occurs in conjunction with contracts that are supported by transaction-specific investments. Preserving the continuity of the trading relation here takes on real economic value. Accordingly, designing governance structures in which the parties to an exchange have mutual confidence becomes crucial to the study of economic organization where a condition of non-trivial asset specificity obtains. The institutions of private ordering thus take their place alongside the courts. Albeit without reference to asset specificity, this was Llewellyn's point in 1931. Galanter has more recently put it as follows: 'In many instances the participants can devise more satisfactory solutions to their disputes than can professionals constrained to apply general rules on the basis of limited knowledge of the dispute' (1981, p.4). Legal centralism thus gives way to the study of the *ex post* institutions of contract—of which vertical market restrictions and other non-standard contracting practices are examples—in all of their forms.

The importance of asset specificity to economic organization was originally set out in my treatment of vertical integration (1971). It was subsequently elaborated in conjunction with labour-market organization (Williamson, Wachter and Harris, 1975), the regulation of natural monopolies (Williamson, 1976), and, more generally, of complex or non-standard forms of contracting (Williamson, 1975, 1979, 1983). Klein, Crawford, and Alchian (1978) have reference to this same condition in their discussion of 'appropriable quasi-rents'. Indeed, Alchian now holds that, contrary to the position that he held previously, asset specificity has pervasive ramifications for the study of economic organization. (Thus whereas he had once argued that 'long-term contracts between employer and employee are not the essence of the organization we call a firm' (Alchian and Demsetz, 1972, p.777), he now acknowledges that asset specificity is the central feature (Alchian, 1984).) Albeit slowly, this viewpoint has progressively gained ascendancy.

3. Recapitulation
To recapitulate, therefore, the world of contract is variously described as (1) planning, (2) promise, (3) competition, and (4) private ordering. Transaction-cost economics maintains that economic agents are characterized by bounded rationality (which precludes comprehensive planning) and opportunism (which limits promise), and that conditions of asset specificity are widespread (which limits the efficacy of competition).[7] The systematic study of private ordering is thus proposed.

III. A SIMPLE CONTRACTING SCHEMA

Assume that there are two alternative technologies. One is a general-purpose technology, the other a special-purpose technology. The special-purpose technology requires greater investment in transition-specific durable assets and is more efficient for servicing steady-state demands.

Using k as a measure of transaction-specific assets, transactions that use the general-purpose technology are ones for which $k=0$. When transactions use the special-purpose technology, by contrast, a $k>0$ condition obtains. Assets here are specialized to the particular needs of the parties. Productive values would therefore be sacrificed if transactions of this kind were to be terminated prematurely; the bilateral monopoly condition described in section II(2) applies to these.

Whereas classical market contracting—'sharp-in by clear agreement; sharp-out by clear performance' (Macneil, 1974, p.738)—suffices for transactions of the $k=$ kind, unassisted market governance poses hazards whenever non-trivial transaction-specific assets are placed at risk. Parties have an incentive to devise safeguards to protect investments in transactions of the latter kind. Let s denote the magnitude of any such safeguards. An $s=0$ condition is one in which no safeguards are provided; a decision to provide safeguards is reflected by an $s>0$ result.

Refusal to provide a contractual safeguard will, of course, show up in the price. If $p=\bar{p}$ is the price at which the firm procures a good or service under an $s=0$ condition, and $p=\hat{p}$ is the price for the same good or service when $s>0$, then $\bar{p}>\hat{p}$, *ceteris paribus*.

By the way of summary, therefore, the nodes A, B and C in the contractual schema set out in Figure 9.2 have the following properties:

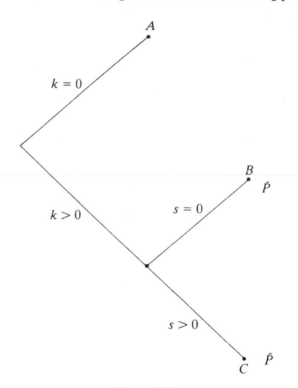

Figure 9.2

(1) Transactions that are efficiently supported by general purpose assets ($k=0$) are located at node A and do not need protective governance structures. Discrete market contracting suffices; the world of competition obtains.

(2) Transactions that involve significant investments of a transaction specific kind ($k>0$) are ones for which the parties are effectively engaged in bilateral trade.

(3) Transactions located at node B enjoy no safeguards ($s=0$), which condition is reflected in the price $\bar{p}>\hat{p}$. Such transactions are apt to be unstable contractually. They may revert to node A (in which event the special-purpose technology would be replaced by the general-purpose ($k=0$) technology) or be relocated to node C (by introducing contractual safeguards that would encourage the continued use of the $k>0$ technology).

(4) Transactions located at node C incorporate safeguards ($s>0$) and thus are protected against expropriation hazards.

(5) In as much as price and governance are linked, parties to a contract should not expect to have their cake (low price) and eat it too (no safeguard). More generally, it is important to study contracting in its entirety. *Ex ante* terms and the manner in which contracts are thereafter executed vary with both *the asset characteristics and the associated governance structure of a transaction.*

The protective safeguards to which I refer normally take on one or more of three forms. The first is to realign incentives, which commonly involves some type of severance payment or penalty for premature termination. The second is to create and employ a specialized governance structure to which to refer and resolve disputes. The use of arbitration, rather than litigation in the courts, is thus characteristic of node C governance. The third is to introduce regularities which support and signal continuity intentions. Expanding a trading relation from unilateral to bilateral exchange—through the concerted use, for example, of reciprocity—thereby to effect an equilibration of trading hazards is an example of this last (Williamson, 1983).

IV. APPLICATIONS

The application of transaction cost economics sketched here are developed more extensively elsewhere. The object is merely to demonstrate that transaction cost economics makes contact with, and is the source of, numerous refutable implications regarding many of the issues that are of central interest to applied microeconomics.

1. Non-standard Contracting, General

Whereas it was once common to approach customer and territorial restrictions and related forms of non-standard contracting as presumptively anti-competitive, transaction cost economics maintains the rebuttable presumption that such practices have the purpose of safeguarding transactions. The contracting schema in section III discloses that firms in which specific assets are placed at hazard ($k>0$) have an incentive to devise protective governance ($s>0$), thereby to locate at node C. Many of the non-standard practices, of which customer and territorial restrictions are examples, serve precisely this purpose.

Thus suppose that a firm develops a distinctive good or service and distributes this through franchisees. Assume further that the incentive to promote this good or service experiences externalities: some franchisees may attempt to free-ride on the promotional efforts of others; or franchisees that service a mobile population may cut costs, allow quality to deteriorate, and shift the reputation effect on to the system. Franchisors thus have an incentive to extend their reach beyond the initial franchise award to include constraints on the condition of supply.

Transparent though this may be, it was not always so. Consider the position of the US Government in arguing the Schwinn case before the Supreme Court:

a rule that treats manufacturers who assume the distribution function more leniently than those who impose restraints on independent distributors merely reflects the fact that, although integration in distribution sometimes benefits the economy by leading to cost savings, agreements to maintain resale prices or to impose territorial restrictions of limited duration or outlet limitations of the type involved here have never been shown to produce comparable economies.[8]

This clear preference for internal over market modes of organization is consonant with the then prevailing preoccupation with technological features and the associated disregard for the benefits of contractual safeguards. In terms of the contracting schema set out above, the government implicitly assumed that all trades were of a node A kind— whence any efforts to impose restrictions were presumptively anti-competitive.

Or consider price discrimination. The Robinson–Patman Act has been interpreted as an effort 'to deprive a large buyer of [discounts] except to the extent that a lower price could be justified by reason of a seller's diminished cost due to *quantity* manufacture, delivery, or sale, or by reason of the seller's good faith effort to meet a competitor's equally low price.'[9] Again, this assumes a node A transaction. If, however, a seller is operating on the $k>0$ branch and is selling to buyers one of whom offers a contractual safeguard while the other refuses, it is unrealistic to expect that product will be sold to both at an identical price. Instead, the node B buyer must pay a premium ($\bar{p}>\hat{p}$) to reflect his refusal to safeguard the hazard.

2. Regulation/deregulation

Monopoly supply is efficient where economies of scale are large in relation to the size of the market. But as Friedman laments, 'There is unfortunately no good solution for technical monopoly. There is only a choice among three evils: private unregulated monopoly, private monopoly regulated by the state, and government operation' (1962, p.128).

That Friedman characterized private unregulated monopoly as an evil is because he assumed that private monopoly ownership implied pricing on monopoly terms. As subsequently argued by Demetz (1968), Stigler (1968) and Posner (1972), however, a monopoly price outcome can be avoided by using *ex ante* bidding to award the monopoly franchise to the firm that offers to supply product on the best terms. Demsetz advances the franchise bidding for natural monopoly argument by stripping away 'irrelevant complications',—such as equipment durability and uncertainty (1968, p.57); Stigler contends that 'customers can auction off the right to sell electricity, using the state as an instrument to conduct the auction .... The auction ... consists of ... [franchise bids] to sell cheaply' (1968, p.19); and Posner agrees and furthermore holds that franchise bidding is an efficacious way by which to award and operate CATV franchises.

Transaction cost economics recognizes merit in the argument, but insists that both *ex ante* and *ex post* contracting features be examined. Only if competition is efficacious at *both* stages does the franchise bidding argument go through. The attributes of the good or service to be franchised are crucial to the assessment. Specifically, if the good or service is to be supplied under conditions of uncertainty and if non-trivial investments in specific assets are involved, the efficacy of franchise bidding is highly problematic. Indeed, the implementation of a franchise bidding scheme under these circumstances essentially requires the progressive elaboration of an administrative apparatus that differs mainly in name rather than in kind from that which is associated with rate of return regulation. It is elementary that a *change in name lacks comparative institutional significance*.

This is not, however, to suggest that franchise bidding for goods or services that are supplied under decreasing cost conditions is never feasible or to imply that extant regulation or public ownership can never be supplanted by franchise bidding with net gains. Examples include local service airlines and, possibly, postal delivery. The winning bidder for each can be displaced

without posing serious asset valuation problems—since the base plant (terminals, post office, warehouses, etc.) can be owned by the government and other assets (planes, trucks, etc.) will have an active second-hand market. It is not, therefore, that franchise bidding is totally lacking in merit, but that those who have favoured this mode have been insufficiently discriminating in their endorsement of it. (Williamson, 1976, pp.102-3)

The selective application of the argument thus has clear ramifications for deregulation—where such reforms are feasible and where they are not (Joskow and Schmalensee, 1983).

3. Labour-market organization

Consider nodes *A, B* and *C* in figure 9.2. The transaction-cost approach to labour organization predicts the following:

(1) Labour-market transactions located at node *A* are ones for which human assets are non-specific. Accordingly:

    (a) Specialized governance structure for these labour transactions is unneeded. Discrete market contracting will characterize transactions of this kind; migrant farm labour is an example.

    (b) Since the organization of non-specific (fungible) labour affords no economies, management (acting as the agent of capital) will normally resist efforts to unionize. Unions, if they appear at all, will be organized late in such industries and often will require the support of the political process.

    (c) The governance structures (ports of entry, promotion ladders, grievance procedures, seniority rules, and the like) will be relatively primitive whether labour of this kind is organized or not.

(2) Labour-market transactions of the node *B* kind expose specialized human assets to expropriation hazards and are unstable.

    (a) Workers will accept such jobs only upon payment of a wage premium.

    (b) Jobs of this kind are apt to be redesigned. Either the idiosyncratic attributes will be sacrificed (in which case the job will revert to node *A*) or protective governance structure will be devised (the attributes will be protected under node *C*).

(3) Labour-market transactions of the node *C* kind are those for which collective organization (often in the form of a union) has been mutually agreed to. As set out elsewhere (Williamson, Wachter and Harris, 1975), such structure protects labour against expropriation hazards, protects management against unwanted quits, and permits adaptations to changing circumstances to be made in an uncontested (mainly cooperative) way.

    (a) Jobs of this kind are candidates for early unionization, since mutual gains can thereby be realized.

(b) The governance structures associated with such jobs will be highly elaborated.

4. Other applications

Other applications of transaction cost economics include (1) vertical integration;[10] (2) corporate governance, where the contractual schema just applied to labour-market organization is, with variation, repeated;[11] (3) other non-standard modes of intermediate-product market contracting, including an assessment of the uses and misuses of reciprocity;[12] (4) the evolution of work modes;[13] (5) family organization;[14] (6) the limits of bureaucracy;[15] (7) the influence of organization form on corporate performance;[16] (8) competition in the capital market;[17] (9) multinational enterprise;[18] and (10) has numerous applications to antitrust, including an assessment of oligopoly and of strategic behaviour.[19]

V. CONCLUDING REMARKS

Transaction-cost economics relies on and develops the following propositions:

(1) The transaction is the basic unit of analysis.
(2) Any problem that can be posed directly or indirectly as a contracting problem is usefully investigated in transaction-cost economizing terms.
(3) Transaction-cost economies are realized by assigning transactions (which differ in their attributes) to governance structures (which are the organizational frameworks within which the integrity of a contractual relation is decided) in a discriminating way. Accordingly:
   (a) the defining attributes of transactions need to be identified;
   (b) the incentive and adaptive attributes of alternative governance structures need to be described.
(4) Although marginal analysis is sometimes employed, implementing transaction-cost economics mainly involves a comparative institutional assessment of discrete institutional alternatives—of which classical market contracting is located at one extreme, centralized, hierarchical organization is located at the other, and mixed modes of firm and market organization are located in between.
(5) Any attempt to deal seriously with the study of economic organization must come to terms with the *combined* ramifications of bounded rationality and opportunism in conjunction with a condition of asset specificity.

As Georgescu-Roegen puts it, 'the purpose of science in general is not prediction, but knowledge for its own sake'. But prediction is nevertheless 'the touchstone of scientific knowledge' (Georgescu-Roegen, 1971, p.37). As compared with other approaches to the study of economic organization, transaction cost economics is the source of numerous refutable implications. Many of these can and should be tightened up, however, and much of the data remain to be developed. It is nevertheless encouraging that the correspondence between the data and the predictions appears to be broadly corroborative. And it is furthermore gratifying that so many of these applications are variations on a theme. As Friedrick Hayek observed, 'whenever the capacity of recognizing an abstract rule which the arrangement of these attributes follows has been acquired in one field, the same master mould will apply when the signs for those abstract attributes are evoked by altogether different elements' (1967, p.50). Although I was aware that the contractual approach to vertical integration that I developed in 1971 would have other applications, little did I imagine that labour-market organization, regulation, non-standard modes of contracting and corporate governance would all yield to the same type of analysis upon restating the issues in contracting terms.

It can be argued, with cause, that transaction cost economics will benefit from efforts to make it 'more rigorous'. Some of this has been occurring,[20] and more is in prospect. Formalization is not, however, warranted at any cost. Forced or premature formalization could stunt the development of this approach, and formalization in which 'the parameters added to the system are largely unmeasured and unmeasurable' is problematic (Simon, 1978, p.8).

NOTES

1. The lack of progress is reflected in Ronald Coase's remark that his 1937 paper was 'much cited and little used' some 35 years later (Coase, 1972, p.63).
2. Herbert Simon's treatments of decision-making in economics focus mainly on individual rather than institutional features of economic organization (1959, 1962).
3. The quotation is attributed to Turner by Stanley Robinson, 1968, NY State Bar Association, Antitrust Symposium, p.29.
4. For an elaboration of contract in the absence of opportunism, see Williamson (1975, pp.26-8, 90-3).
5. Differences between transaction-cost economics and 'contestability theory' (Baumol, Panzer and Willig, 1982) in asset-specificity respects are noteworthy. Both approaches to the study of economic organization acknowledge the importance of asset specificity, but they view it from opposite ends of the telescope. Thus contestability theory reduces asset specificity to insignifi-

cance, whence hit-and-run entry is easy. Transaction-cost economics, by contrast, magnifies the condition of asset specificity. The existence of durable, firm-specific assets is held to be widespread and, accordingly, that hit-and-run entry is often infeasible.

6. The assumption that court ordering is efficacious in a regime of bounded rationality and opportunism is plainly gratuitous, but it is the maintained assumption none the less.
7. See note 5, supra.
8. Brief for the United States at 58, *United States v. Arnold, Schwinn & Co.*, 388 US 365 (1967).
9. *FTC v. Morton Salt Co.*, 334 US 37 (1948): emphasis added.
10. See Williamson (1971, 1975, 1979, 1982), and Klein, Crawford and Alchian (1979).
11. See Williamson, (1984).
12. See Goldberg (1978), Klein and Leffler (1981) and Williamson (1983b).
13. See Williamson (1980).
14. See Ben-Porath (1980) and Robert Pollak (1983).
15. See Williamson (1985).
16. See Williamson (1975).
17. See Williamson (1981).
18. See Williamson (1981).
19. See Williamson (1975, 1983a).
20. See Scott Masten (1982), Michael Riordan and Oliver Williamson (1983), and Sanford Grossman and Oliver Hart (1984).

REFERENCES

Alchian, Armen, 'Specificity, Specialization, and Coalitions', *Journal of Economic Theory and Institutions*, forthcoming.

Arrow, Kenneth, 'The Organization of Economic Activity', *The Analysis and Evaluation of Public Expenditure: The PPB System.* Joint Economic Committee, 91st Congress 1st session, 1969, 59-73.

Baiman, Stanley, 'Agency Research in Managerial Accounting: A Survey' *Journal of Accounting Literature*, 1982, **1**, 154-213.

Bain, Joe, *Barriers to New Competition*, Cambridge, Mass.: Harvard University Press, 1976.

Bain, Joe, *Industrial Organization*, New York: John Wiley, 1958.

Barnard, Chester, *The Functions of the Executive*, Cambridge, Mass.: Harvard Uninversity Press, 1938.

Baumol, William, Panzer, John, and Willig, Robert, *Contestable Markets*, New York: Harcourt, Brace, Jovanovich, 1982.

Ben-Porath, Yoram, 'The F-Connection: Families, Friends, and Firms and the Organization of Exchange', *Population and Development Review*, March 1980, **6**, 1-30.

Coase, Ronald, 'The Nature of the Firm', *Economica* N.S. 1937, **4**, 386-405; reprinted in George J. Stigler and Kenneth E. Boulding (eds.) *Readings in Price Theory*. Homewood, Ill.: Richard D. Irwin, 1952.

Coase, Ronald, 'Industrial Organization: A Proposal for Research', in Victor R. Fuchs (ed.) *Policy Issues and Research Opportunities in Industrial Organization*. New York: National Bureau of Economic Research, 1972, pp.59-73.

Commons, John R., *Institutional Economics*, Madison: University of Wisconsin Press, 1934.

Demsetz, Harold, 'Why Regulate Utilities?', *Journal of Law and Economics*, April 1968, **11**, 55-66.

Friedman, Milton, *Essays in Positive Economics*, Chicago: University of Chicago Press, 1953.

Friedman, Milton, *Capitalism and Freedom*, Chicago: University of Chicago Press, 1962.

Galanter, Marc, 'Justice in Many Rooms: Courts, Private Ordering, and Indigenous Law', *Journal of Legal Pluralism*, **19**, 1981, 1-47.

Georgescu-Roegen, Nicholas, *The Entropy Law and Economic Process*, Cambridge, Mass.: Harvard University Press, 1971.

Goldberg, Victor. 'Toward an Expanded Economic Theory of Contract', *Journal of Economic Issues*, January 1976, **10**, 45-61.

Grossman, Sanford and Hart, Oliver, 'The Costs and Benefits of Ownership: A Theory of Vertical Integration', unpublished manuscript, March 1984.

Hayek, Friedrich, *Studies in Philosophy, Politics and Economics*, London: Routledge & Kegan Paul, 1967.

Joskow, Paul and Schmalensee, Richard, *Markets for Power*, Cambridge, Mass.: MIT Press, 1983.

Holmstrom, Bengt, 'Differential Information, the Market, and Incentive Compatability', in Kenneth Arrow and Seppo Hankapocha, eds., *Frontiers in Economics*, London: Basil Blackwell, 1984.

Klein, Benjamin, Crawford, Robert, and Alchian, Armen, 'Vertical Integration, Appropriable Rents, and the Competitive Contracting Process,' *Journal of Law and Economics*, October 1978, **21**, 297-326.

Klein, Benjamin, and Leffler, Keith, 'The Role of Market Forces in Assuring Contractual Performance' *Journal of Political Economy*, August 1981, **89**, 615-41.

Llewellyn, Karl N., 'What Price Contract?—An Essay in Perspective', *Yale Law Journal*, May 1931, **40**, pp.704-51.

Macneil, Ian R., 'The Many Futures of Contract', *University of California Law Review*, May 1974, **67**, 691-816.

Masten, Scott, 'Transaction Costs, Institutional Choice, and the Theory of the Firm', unpublished PhD dissertation, University of Pennsylvania, 1982.

Meade, James, *The Controlled Economy*, London: George Allen & Unwin, 1971.

Pollack, Robert, 'A Transaction Cost Approach to Households', unpublished manuscript, September 1983.

Posner, Richard, *Economic Approach to Law*, Boston: Little, Brown, 1972.

Posner, Richard, 'The Appropriate Scope of Regulation in the Cable Television Industry', *Bell Journal of Economics*, Spring 1972, **3**, 98-129.

Riordan, Michael and Williamson, Oliver, 'Asset Specificity and Economic Organization', *International Journal of Industrial Organization*, forthcoming.

Simon, Herbert, *Models of Man*, New York: John Wiley, 1957.

Simon, Herbert, 'Theories of Decision-Making in Economic and Behavioural Science', *American Economic Review*, June 1959, **49**, 253-83.

Simon, Herbert, *Administrative Behaviour*, 2nd edn. New York: Macmillan, 1961.

Simon, Herbert, 'New Developments in the Theory of the Firm', *American Economic Review*, March 1962, **52**, 1-16.

Simon, Herbert, 'Rationality as Process and Product of Thought', *American Economic Review*, May 1978, **68**, 1-16.

Stigler, George, *The Organization of Industry*, Homewood, Ill.: Richard D. Irwin, 1968.

Williamson, Oliver E., 'The Vertical Integration of Production: Market Failure Considerations', *American Economic Review*, May 1971, **61**, 112-23.

Williamson, Oliver E., *Markets and Hierarchies: Analysis and Antitrust Implications*, New York: Free Press, 1975.

Williamson, Oliver E., 'Franchise Bidding for Natural Monopolies—in General and with Respect to CATV', *Bell Journal of Economics*, Spring 1976, 7, 73-104.

Williamson, Oliver E., 'Transaction-Cost Economics: The Governance of Contractual Relations', *Journal of Law and Economics*, October, 1979, **22**, 233-61.

Williamson, Oliver E., 'The Organization of Work', *Journal of Economic Behaviour and Organization*, March 1980, **1**, 5-38.

Williamson, Oliver E., 'The Modern Corporation: Origins, Evolution, Attributes', *Journal of Economic Literature*, December 1981, **19**, 1537-68.

Williamson, Oliver E., 'Organization Form, Residual Claimants and Corporate Control', *Journal of Law and Economics*, June 1983, **26**, 351-66.

Williamson, Oliver E., 'Credible Commitments: Using Hostages to Support Exchange', *American Economic Review*, September 1983, **73**, 519-40.

Williamson, Oliver E., 'Corporate Governance', *Yale Law Journal*, June 1984, **93**, 1197-1230.

Williamson, Oliver E., *The Economic Institutions of Capitalism*, New York: The Free Press, 1985.

Part III
PUBLIC POLICY

10. Introduction

Although public concerns surface in all of the essays in Part II, these concerns are central to the three essays in Part III.

My examination of the economics of antitrust takes issue with the then prevailing view that applied microeconomics, in either pure or appreciative form, was wholly adequate to the needs of public policy in this area. To be sure, Ronald Coase had forcefully taken exception with the applied price theory tradition earlier (1972). There was little indication, however, that his views had been heeded: to the contrary, they were more often ignored.

I successively address issues of price discrimination, vertical integration, oligopoly and conglomerate organization from applied price theory and transaction cost economics points of view—with emphasis on the latter. I argue that a correct assessment of the net benefits of price discrimination can only be made upon making explicit allowance for transaction costs. My assessment of vertical integration in transaction cost economics terms discloses that both the benefits and the costs of vertical integration are different from those reached by more conventional modes of analysis. The oligopoly discussion is interesting partly because I had once thought that oligopoly problems fell outside the ambit of transaction cost economics. Upon formulating the oligopoly problem in contracting terms, however, numerous applications became evident. Finally, whereas the conglomerate mode of organization is an anomaly when viewed through the lens of price theory, the transaction cost economics perspective is much more successful in engaging the issues.

The second essay advances the optimistic view that 'ideas, not vested interests' have been responsible for a series of antitrust enforcement reforms during the past decade. Although this opinion is not universally shared and is advanced with caution, a growing sensitivity to efficiency, in all of its forms, has plainly developed.

My examination of regulation in the last essay addresses the efficacy of franchise bidding for natural monopoly. This solution to the problem of natural monopoly was originated by Harold Demsetz (1968), endorsed by George Stigler (1968), and applied to CATV by Richard Posner (1972). Rather than regard natural monopoly as a 'choice among three evils: private unregulated monopoly, private monopoly regulated by the state, and government operation' (Friedman, 1962, p.128), a fourth alternative—franchise bidding—is invented by moving the analysis back to the contract award stage. If there are many qualified suppliers *ex ante*, and if competitive bids for the right to serve the market are solicited, then the oppressive hand of regulation, unregulated monopoly prices and the burdens of government ownership can all be avoided by awarding the franchise to the bidder who offers to supply for the lowest per unit price.

My assessment of the efficacy of franchise bidding for natural monopoly examines microanalytic contracting features that were regarded as irrelevant or were otherwise eschewed by those who originated and endorsed the franchise bidding solution. As it turns out, these details prove to be essential. This applies both to an assessment of franchise bidding in general and to the award of CATV licences.

That franchise bidding has severe limitations does not, however, imply that it should be dismissed. To the contrary, it works well in precisely those same situations where deregulation has merit. And it experiences difficulties where shifts from regulated to deregulated status are problematic. Franchise bidding thus needs to be delimited, lest it be misapplied. Subject to that caveat, it is a useful additional alternative to consider in the regulatory scheme of things. Comparative institutional analysis is the richer for it.

REFERENCES

Coase, Ronald H., 'Industrial Organization: A Proposal for Research', in V.R. Fuchs (ed.), *Policy Issues and Research Opportunities in Industrial Organization*. New York: National Bureau of Economic Research, 1972, pp.59-73.

Demsetz, Harold, 'Why Regulate Utilities?', *Journal of Law and Economics*, Vol. 11 (April 1968), pp.55-66.

Friedman, Milton, *Capitalism and Freedom*, Chicago, University of Chicago Press, 1962.

Posner, Richard, 'The Appropriate Scope of Regulation in the Cable Television Industry', *The Bell Journal of Economics and Management Science*, vol. 3, No. 1 (Spring 1972), pp.98-129.

Stigler, George, *The Organization of Industry*. Chicago: University of Chicago Press, 1968.

11. The Economics of Antitrust: Transaction Cost Considerations*

Economic analysis is commonly, though somewhat arbitrarily, divided into macroeconomic and microeconomic categories. The former is concerned with highly aggregative economic issues—such as national income, employment and inflation—while the latter deals with the behaviour of individual consumers, firms and markets. To the extent that economics is thought to have a bearing on antitrust analysis and policy, the firm and market models of received microtheory are thought, by economists and lawyers alike, to supply the relevant foundations.[1]

Although I am in general agreement with this position, I contend that received microtheory sometimes needs to be augmented by introducing transaction-cost considerations. Failure or refusal to make allowance for transaction costs, in circumstances where these are arguably non-negligible, can lead to error. Not only is an understanding of the issues impaired, but incorrect policy prescriptions will sometimes result.

One of the attractive attributes of the transaction-cost approach[2] is that it reduces, essentially, to a study of contracting—which means that the contracting expertise of lawyers developed in other contexts can be drawn upon. Issues such as the following are addressed: When will a related set of transactions be completed most efficaciously by negotiating contracts between firms (across a market), and when will merger or integration (internal organization) be preferred? In what respects, if any, do pre-existing firm and market structures impede or facilitate the ability of new firms to negotiate the necessary market contracts for labour, capital, materials and intermediate products to effectuate successful entry? While these types of issues can be addressed in an unconvoluted way using the transaction-cost apparatus, the models of received microtheory, in which transaction costs are suppressed, are often ill suited and sometimes misleading.

* Research on this article supported by a grant from the National Science Foundation. Parts of the article are based on a lecture given at the University of California, Los Angeles on 10 January 1974 in conjunction with the Major Issue Lecture Series programme. 'Large-Scale Enterprise in a Changing Society'.

197

I begin with a brief review of received microtheory before setting out the elements of the transaction-cost approach. The examination of vertical integration, oligopoly and conglomerate organization from the transactional point of view suggests antitrust policies somewhat different from those advanced by scholars employing the conventional micro-theory approach. Although not exhausting the applications of the transaction-cost approach to the study of antitrust issues,[3] the article will hopefully give the reader a sense of the relevance of this approach to the antitrust area.

I. THE BASIC APPROACHES

It is widely thought that 'the economic background required for under-standing antitrust issues seldom requires detailed mastery of economic refinements'[4]—meaning, presumably, that the standard economic models of firms and markets found in intermediate microtheory textbooks will normally be sufficient for antitrust purposes. I doubt that this is the case. Conventional analysis sometimes needs to be augmented and at other times supplanted by express consideration of transactional problems.

1. Received Microtheory[5]

Demand curves (average revenue curves), average cost curves, and the marginal curves of revenue and cost drawn to each of these constitute the basic modelling apparatus for most antitrust treatments of firms and markets. Implicit in this model are efficiency assumptions of two kinds. First, it is assumed that the firm realizes the maximum output of product from each feasible combination of factor inputs (mainly labour and capital). That is, it operates on its production function. Failure to operate on the production function would imply wasteful use of inputs; this is assumed away. Second, given the prices of productive factors, it is assumed that the firm chooses the least-cost combination of factors for each possible level of output. The total cost curve, from which average and marginal cost curves are derived, is constructed in this way.

In circumstances where economies of scale are large in relation to the size of the market, a condition of natural monopoly (or perhaps oligo-poly) may be said to exist. The monopolist or the oligopolists who supply goods and services in such a market will be sufficiently large that small percentage changes in their output will perceptibly affect the market price. Price is thus subject to strategic determination. However, in circumstances where economies of scale are exhausted at firm sizes that are small in relation to the market, each firm will regard price as given[6] and a condition of competitive market supply, in which price will be equal to marginal cost, will obtain.

Intermediate types of markets, such as duopoly or oligopoly, are modelled by making appropriate assumptions about the nature of the technology and the inter-firm relations which develop.[7] Depending on the underlying technology and the behavioural assumptions that are employed, the prices and outputs that will be associated with alternative market structures can be succinctly derived. The social welfare implications of each, moreover, can be established by characterizing the benefits and costs resulting from the structure in question in appropriate social welfare terms.[8] The types of trade-offs that antitrust must contend with in circumstances where monopoly power and production economies both obtain can then be displayed in a relatively straightforward manner.[9]

Implicit throughout most analyses of this kind is that the nature of the firm—with respect, for example, to what it will make and what it will buy—is simply taken as given. Matters of internal organization (hierarchical structure, internal control processes) are likewise ignored. The firm is thereby reduced to little more than a production function to which a profit-maximization objective has been assigned. That many interesting problems of firms and markets are suppressed or neglected as a result should come, perhaps, as no surprise.

2. The Transaction Cost Approach[10]

The transactional approach may be stated compactly as follows: (1) markets and firms are alternative instruments for completing a related set of transactions; (2) whether a set of transactions ought to be executed between firms (across markets) or within a firm depends on the relative efficiency of each mode; (3) the costs of writing and executing complex contracts across a market vary with the characteristics of the human decision-makers who are involved with the transaction on the one hand, and the objective properties of the market on the other; (4) although the human and transactional factors which impede exchanges between firms (across a market) manifest themselves somewhat differently within the firm, the same set of factors applies to both. A symmetrical analysis of trading, therefore, requires that the transactional limits of internal organization as well as the transactional sources of market failure be acknowledged. Moreover, just as market structure matters in assessing the efficacy of trades in the market-place, so internal structure matters in assessing internal organization.

The transaction-cost approach is interdisciplinary, drawing extensively on contributions from both economics and organization theory. The market failure,[11] contingent claims contracting,[12] and recent organizational design[13] literatures supply the requisite economic background. The administrative man[14] and strategic behaviour[15] literatures are the main contributions from organization theory.

With this basis the transaction-cost approach attempts to identify a set of market or *transactional factors* which together with a related set of *human factors* explain the circumstances under which complex contracts involving contingent claims will be costly to write, execute and enforce. Faced with such difficulties, and considering the risks that simple, and therefore incomplete, contingent claims contracts pose,[16] the firm may decide to bypass the market and resort to hierarchical modes of organization. Transactions that might otherwise be handled in the market would then be performed internally and governed by administrative processes.

Uncertainty and small-numbers exchange relations, in which one party's choice of trading partners is restricted, are the transactional factors to which market failure is ascribed. Unless joined by a related set of human factors, however, such transactional conditions need not impede market exchange. The pairing of uncertainty with bounded rationality and the joining of small numbers with what I shall refer to as opportunism are especially important.

Consider first the pairing of bounded rationality with uncertainty. The principle of bounded rationality has been defined by Herbert Simon as follows: '*The capacity of the human mind for formulating and solving complex problems is very small compared with the size of the problems whose solution is required for objectively rational behaviour in the real world*',[17] It refers both to neurophysiological limits on the capacity to receive, store, retrieve and process information without error,[18] and to definitional limits inherent in language. If these limits make it very costly or impossible to identify future contingencies and to specify, *ex ante*, appropriate adaptations thereto, long-term contracts may be supplanted by internal organization. Recourse to the internal organization of transactions permits adaptations to uncertainty to be accomplished by administrative processes as each problem arises. Thus, rather than attempt to anticipate all possible contingencies from the outset, the future is permitted to unfold. Internal organization in this way economizes on the bounded rationality attributes of decision-makers in circumstances where prices are not 'sufficient statistics'[19] and uncertainty is substantial.

Rather, however, than resort to internal organization when long-term contingent claims contracts are thought to be defective (too costly or perhaps infeasible), why not employ short-term contracts instead? Appropriate adaptations to changing market circumstances can then be introduced at the contract renewal interval, thereby avoiding the prohibitive costs of *ex ante* specification. The pairing of opportunism with small-numbers exchange relations, however, creates other obstacles to market transactions.

Developing this set of issues is somewhat involved and the interested reader is referred to discussions elsewhere of the types of contracting problems that give rise to vertical integration.[20] Suffice it to observe here that (1) opportunism refers to a lack of candour or honesty in transactions, to include self-interest-seeking with guile; (2) opportunistic inclinations pose little risk to trading partners as long as competitive (large-numbers) exchange relations obtain; (3) many transactions which at the outset involve a large number of qualified bidders are transformed in the process of contract execution—often because of economies of scale and accrued cost-advantages attributable to successful bidders learning more about the job as they perform their work (learning-by-doing)—so that a small-numbers supply condition effectively obtains at the contract renewal interval; and (4) short-term contracting is costly and risky when opportunism and small-numbers relations are joined. The argument will be developed further in other sections of this article.

In consideration of the problems that both long and short-term contracts are subject to—by reason of bounded rationality and uncertainty in the first instance and the pairing of opportunism with small-numbers relations in the second—internal organization may be used instead. With internal organization, issues are handled as they arise rather than in an exhaustive contingent planning fashion from the outset.[21] The resulting adaptive, sequential decision-making process is the internal organizational counterpart of short-term contracting and serves to economize on bounded rationality. That opportunism does not pose the same difficulties for such internal, sequential supply relations that it does when negotiations take place across a market is because (1) internal divisions do not have pre-emptive claims on profit streams, but act under common ownership and supervision more nearly to maximize joint profits instead, and (2) the internal incentive and control machinery is much more extensive and refined than that which obtains in market exchanges.[22] The firm is thereby better able to take the long view for investment purposes (and hence is more prepared to put specialized plant and equipment in place) while simultaneously adjusting to changing market circumstances in an adaptive, sequential manner.

Having said this, I hasten to add that if internal organization serves frequently to attenuate bounded rationality and opportunism problems, it does not eliminate either condition. Of special relevance in this connection are two propositions: (1) the limitations of internal organization in both bounded rationality and opportunistic respects vary directly with firm size, organization form held constant,[23] but (2) organization form—that is, the way in which activities in the firm are hierarchically structured—matters.[24] The import of this latter proposition is developed in the discussion of conglomerates in section IV.

Moreover the choice between firm and market ought not to be

regarded as fixed. Both firms and markets change over time in ways which may render an initial assignment of transactions to firm or market inappropriate. The degree of uncertainty associated with the transactions in question may diminish; market growth may support large numbers of suppliers in competition with one another, and information disparities between the parties often shrink. Also, changes in technology may occur, altering the degree to which bounded rationality limits apply. Thus, the efficacy of completing transactions by hierarchies or markets should be reassessed periodically.

3. An Example: Price Discrimination

The differences between received microtheory and the transaction-cost approach can be illustrated by examining the familiar problem of price discrimination. As will be evident, the transaction-cost approach does not abandon but rather augments the received microtheory model.

Assume for this illustration that the market in question is one in which economies of scale are large in relation to the size of the market, in which case the average cost curve falls over a considerable output range. Assume, in particular, that demand and cost conditions are as shown in Figure 11.1.

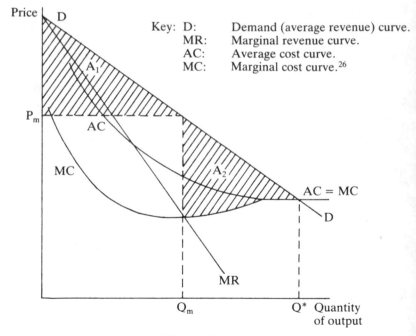

Figure 11.1

The unregulated monopolist who both maximizes profits and sells his output at a single, uniform price to all customers will restrict output below the social optimum[25] (shown by Q^* in Figure 11.1)[26] at which marginal cost equals price. Instead, the monopolist will produce only to the point (Q_m) at which marginal cost equals marginal revenue so that an excess of price over marginal cost obtains.

It is sometimes argued, however, that price discrimination will correct the allocative efficiency distortion in a monopoly situation. The monopolist who can segregate his market in such a way that each customer is made to pay his full valuation (given by the demand curve) for each unit of output has the incentive to add successive units of output until the price paid for the last item sold just equals the marginal cost. The fully discriminating monopolist will thus be led to expand output from the restricted position of a non-discriminating monopolist (Q_m) to the social optimum point (Q^*). Although income distribution will be affected in the process (in possibly objectionable ways), the output distortion is removed and an allocative efficiency gain is realized.[27]

Evaluating this allocative efficiency claim gives us our first opportunity to contrast the conventional analysis of received microtheory with a transactions-cost approach. Implicit in the above conventional microtheory argument is an assumption that the costs of both discovering true customer valuations for the product and of enforcing restrictions against resale (so that there can be no arbitrage) are negligible and can be disregarded. Such costs vanish, however, only if either (1) customers will honestly self-reveal preferences and self-enforce non-sale promises (no opportunism), or (2) the seller is omniscient (a strong variety of unbounded rationality). In as much as assumptions of both kinds are plainly unrealistic, the question naturally arises: Is there an allocative efficiency gain if non-trivial transaction costs must be incurred to discover true customer valuations and/or to police non-resale restrictions? Unfortunately for received microtheory, the outcome is uncertain when these transaction costs are introduced.

To see this, assume (for simplicity) that the transaction costs of accomplishing full price discrimination are independent of the level of output: the costs are either zero, in which event no effort to price discriminate is made, or T, in which case customer valuations become fully known and enforcement against cheating is complete.[28] Price discrimination will of course be attractive to the monopolist if a net profit gain can be shown—which will obtain if the additional revenues (which are given by the two shaded regions, A_1 and A_2, in Figure 11.1) exceed the costs of achieving discrimination, T. What is interesting for social welfare evaluation purposes is that an incremental gross welfare gain is realized only on output that exceeds Q_m. This gain is given by the lower triangle (A_2). Consequently the net social welfare effects will be positive only if A_2 exceeds the transaction costs, T. An allocative efficiency loss, occasioned by high transaction costs, but a private monopoly gain, derived from price discrimination applied to the output that would have been produced even without discrimination (this revenue gain being shown by A_1), is therefore consistent with fully discriminatory pricing in circumstances where non-trivial transaction costs are incurred in reaching the discriminatory result. More precisely, if T is less than A_1 plus A_2 but more than A_2 alone, the monopolist will be prepared to incur the customer information and policing costs necessary to achieve the discriminatory outcome, because *his* profits will be augmented ($A_1+A_2>T$), but these same expenditures will give rise to a net *social* welfare loss ($A_2<T$).[29]

In circumstances where T is zero or negligible, of course, this contradiction does not arise. But the results of received microtheory rest crucially on such an assumption. If, arguably, the assumption is not satisfied, transaction costs need expressly to be taken into account before a welfare assessment is ventured.

II. VERTICAL INTEGRATION

The discussion of market exchange versus internal organization has attractive properties in circumstances where long-term contracts are not feasible, because contractual contingencies overwhelm the limited planning capacities of parties subject to bounded rationality, and where short-term contracts pose hazards, because of the conjunction of opportunism with a small-numbers exchange condition. Prospective inter-firm contracting difficulties are thus responsible for the decision to integrate. The details of such a transactional approach to vertical integration have been worked out elsewhere.[30]

It should be appreciated, however, that this has not been the prevailing rationale for vertical integration among economists. More often the argument runs in terms of technological considerations. Two such arguments are examined below and are rejected in favour of the transactional approach. The possibility that vertical integration might inhibit potential entry is then explored and the incentive to integrate as a means by which to circumvent government controls (taxes, quotas) is briefly treated. I conclude this section with a statement of the antitrust enforcement implications of the argument.

1. A Life-Cycle Analysis
George Stigler deduces, from his explication of Adam Smith's theorem

that the division of labour is limited by the extent of the market, that vertical integration is related to an industry's life-cycle: vertical integration will be extensive in firms in young industries; disintegration will be observed as an industry grows; and reintegration will occur as an industry passes into decline.[31] These life-cycle effects are illustrated by reference to a multi-process product in which each process involves a separable technology and hence its own distinct cost function.[32] Some of the processes display falling cost curves, others curves that rise continuously, and still others U-shaped cost curves.

Stigler then asks, why does the firm not exploit the decreasing cost activities by expanding them to become a monopoly? He answers by observing that, at the outset, the decreasing cost functions may be 'too small to support a specialized firm or firms.'[33] But, unless the argument is meant to be restricted to global or local monopolies, for which there is no indication, resort to a specialized firm does not exhaust the possibilities. Assuming that there are at least several firms in the business, why does one of them not exploit the available economies, to the mutual benefit of all the parties, by producing the entire requirement for the group? The reasons, I submit, turn on transaction costs inherent in inter-firm rivalry.

If, for example, the exchange of specialized information between the parties is involved (Stigler specifically refers to 'market information' as one of the decreasing cost possibilities) strategic misrepresentation issues are posed. The risk here is that the specialist firm will disclose information to its rivals in an incomplete and distorted manner. Because the party buying the information can establish its accuracy only at great cost, possibly by collecting the original data itself, the exchange fails to go through. If, however, rivals were not given to opportunism, the risk of strategic distortion would vanish and the technologically efficient specialization of information could proceed.

The exchange of physical components that experience decreasing costs is likewise discouraged where both long-term and short-term contracts incur prospective transactional difficulties. Long-term contracts are principally impeded by bounded rationality considerations: the extent to which uncertain future events can be expressly taken into account—in the sense that the cost of appropriate adaptations can be estimated and contractually specified—is simply limited. Since, given opportunism, incomplete long-term contracts predictably pose interest conflicts between the parties, other arrangements are apt to be sought.

Spot market (short-term) contracting is an obvious alternative. Such contracts, however, are hazardous if there are only a small number of suppliers, which (by assumption) holds true for the circumstances described by Stigler. The buyer then incurs the risk that the purchased product or service will, at some later time, be supplied under monopolis-

tic terms. Industry growth, moreover, need not eliminate the tension of
small numbers bargaining if the item in question is one for which learning
by doing is important and if the market for human capital is imperfect.[34]
Delaying own-production until own-requirements are sufficient to exhaust scale economies would, considering the learning costs of undertaking own-production at this later time, incur substantial transition costs.
It may, under these conditions, be more attractive from the outset for
each firm to produce its own requirements—or, alternatively, for the
affected firms to merge.[35] Absent present or prospective transaction costs
of the sorts described, however, specialization by one of the firms
(monopoly supply), to the mutual benefit of all, would presumably occur.
Put differently, technology is no bar to contracting; it is transactional
considerations that are decisive.

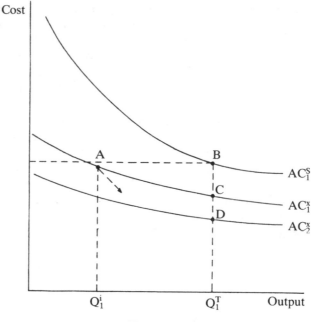

Figure 11.2

Aspects of the above argument can be illustrated with the help of
Figure 11.2. The average costs of supplying the item in question by a
specialized outside supplier at time 1 are shown by the curve AC_1^s. Firms
that are already in the industry can supply the same item at the average
costs shown by AC_1^X. The curve AC_1^s is everywhere above the curve AC_1^X
because firms already in the industry avoid the set-up costs which a
specialized outside supplier would incur. Each of the firms in the industry

generates requirements for the item at time 1 of Q_1^i. The total industry requirement at time 1 is Q_1^T.

The implicit comparison that Stigler makes in his explanation for vertical integration is point A versus point B. Thus although having a specialized supplier service the whole industry (produce Q_1^T) would permit economies of scale to be more fully exploited, the declining cost advantage is more than offset by the set-up costs. Therefore, the average costs of the specialized supplier (at B) exceed the average costs that each individual firm would incur by supplying its own requirements (at A). My argument, however, is that point A should also be compared with point C—where point C shows the average costs of supplying the requirements for the entire industry by one of the firms that is *already in* the industry. Such a firm does not incur those set-up costs which disadvantage the outside specialist supplier. Given the decreasing cost technology that Stigler assumes, the average costs at C are necessarily less than those at A. Why then not have one of the firms already in the industry supply both itself and all the others? The impediments, I submit, are the hazards of inter-firm contracting (of both long-term and spot market types) that have been described above.

The comparison, moreover, can be extended to include a consideration of the curve AC_2^X, which represents the average costs that will be incurred by a firm at time 2 that has been supplying continuously during the interval from time 1 to time 2. The curve AC_2^X is everywhere lower than AC_1^X by reason of advantages gained from learning-by-doing. To the extent that such learning advantages are not or cannot be shared with others,[36] they will accrue only to firms that have undertaken own–production during the period in question. Thus if one of the firms in the industry becomes the monopoly supplier to all others at time 1, and if at time 2 the other firms become dissatisfied with the monopoly supplier's terms, the buying firms cannot undertake to supply their own requirements at a later date on cost parity terms because they have not had the benefit of learning by doing.

Note finally the arrow that points away from point A toward point D. If the industry is expected to grow (plainly the case for the circumstances described by Stigler) and if each of the firms in the industry can be expected to grow with it, then each firm, if it supplies its own requirements (Q_1^i) at time 1 and incurs average costs of A, can, by reason of both growth and learning by doing, anticipate declining own-supply costs— perhaps to the extent that each substantially exhausts the economies of scale that are available. Since supplying its own requirements avoids the transactional hazards of procuring its supply from a market with only a few trading partners, vertical integration of the items with a decreasing cost technology is all the more to be expected.

2. Technological Interdependency

Of the various rationales for vertical integration that have been advanced, the technological interdependency argument is both the most familiar and straightforward: successive processes which naturally follow immediately in time and place dictate certain efficient manufacturing configurations; these, in turn, are held to have common ownership implications. Such technical complementarity is probably more important in flow process operations, such as chemicals and metals, than in separable component manufacture. The standard example is the integration of the making of iron and steel, where thermal economies are said to be available through integration. It is commonly held that where 'integration does not have this physical or technical aspect—as it does not, for example, in integrating the production of assorted components with the assembly of those components—the case for cost savings from integration is generally much less clear'.[37]

I submit, however, that such technological interdependency is neither essential for cost savings to be realized by integration nor typical of most integrated activities. Consider Adam Smith's pin-making example.[38] Pin manufacture involved a series of technologically distinct operations such as wire straightening, cutting, pointing and grinding. In principle, each of these activities could be performed by an independent specialist and work passed from station to station by contract. The introduction of buffer inventories at each station, moreover, would decrease the coordination requirements and thereby reduce contractual complexity. Each worker could then proceed at his own pace, subject only to the condition that he maintain his buffer inventory at some minimum level. A series of independent entrepreneurs rather than a group of employees, each subject to an authority relation, would thus perform the tasks in question.

Transaction costs militate against such an organization of tasks, however. For one thing, it may be possible to economize on buffer inventories by having the entire group act as a unit, under common direction, with respect to such matters as work breaks and variable rates of production. Although rules could be worked out in advance and made explicit in the contract, or the authority to make such decisions could be rotated among the members of the group, coordination might usefully be assigned to a 'boss', who oversees the entire operation and can more easily judge the fatigue and related work attitudes in the group.

The more pressing reasons for replacing autonomous contracting by an employment relation, however, turn on adaptability considerations. Suppose one of the individuals becomes ill (real or feigned) or becomes injured. Who nominates and chooses a replacement, or otherwise arranges to pick up the slack, and how is compensation determined? Reaching agreements on such matters is apt to be relatively costly compared with having a boss reassign the work among the members of the group or make other *ad hoc* arrangements on the group's behalf. Similarly, what is to be done if an individual declines to deliver the requisite quantity or quality to the next station? How are penalties determined? Litigation is apt to be costly and time consuming, and to what avail if the individual lacks the requisite assets to compensate for the losses attributable to his deviant behaviour? Again, remedies and adaptations under an employment relation, where an individual has much weaker property claims to a work station, are likely to be quicker and less costly to effectuate.

The problem, more generally, is that autonomous contracting in small numbers circumstances is fraught with difficulties if unforeseen events requiring adaptation frequently appear, especially if the parties are given to opportunism. Rather than endure the costs that can be expected to arise when a series of bilateral contracts are negotiated among a group of individuals each of whom enjoys, in the short run at least, a monopoly position, a firm will integrate such related activities instead. Central ownership of the work stations and an employment relation between the workers and entrepreneur will facilitate adaptation.[39]

3. The Condition of Entry

Stigler observes that 'it is possible that vertical integration increases the difficulty of entry by new firms, by increasing the capital and knowledge necessary to conduct several types of operation rather than depend on rivals for supplies or markets'.[40] Others, however, take exception to this argument. Robert Bork, for example, contends that 'In general, if greater than competitive profits are to be made in an industry, entry should occur whether the entrant has to come in at both levels or not. I know of no theory of imperfections in the capital market which would lead suppliers of capital to avoid areas of higher return to seek areas of lower return'.[41] Similarly, Ward Bowman observes that 'difficulties of access to the capital market that enable X to offer a one dollar inducement (it has a bankroll) and prevent its rivals from responding (they have no bankroll and, though the offering of the inducement is a responsible business tactic, for some reason cannot borrow the money) . . . [have] yet to be demonstrated'.[42] As I hope to make apparent, these and related arguments of the received microtheory variety go through only if transaction-cost considerations are suppressed. The pairing of bounded rationality with uncertainty and the joining of opportunism with a condition of 'information impactedness' (where one party to a transaction has access to information that the other party can obtain only at some expense, if at all) are the neglected factors.[43]

The phenomenon to be explained is not merely an increase of the financial requirements, as Stigler indicates, but an adverse alteration of the terms under which capital becomes available. Borrowing by the firm to finance additional plant and equipment is, of course, unlike borrowing by the consumer to purchase a house. The firm borrows funds in anticipation of realizing a prospective stream of earnings. These prospective earnings, as well as the resale value of the assets in question, are used to support the loan in question. The homeowner, by contrast, is not ordinarily able to augment his earnings by purchasing a house. Thus, whereas the householder who successively increases the size of his mortgage eventually incurs adverse capital costs, because the risks of default are greater, the firm need not likewise be impeded. Why then, if at all, does vertical integration by established firms disadvantage prospective entrants on account of capital market 'defects'?

An assessment of the issues will be facilitated by setting out the specific alternatives. Suppose that two distinct stages of production can be identified in the industry in question (designated I and II respectively). Assume further that stage I in the industry is essentially monopolized while stage II may or may not be integrated. The question now is whether a potential entrant who has developed a technologically satisfactory stage I substitute and has an established reputation in activity related to stage I will be unaffected by the integrated condition of stage II. Consider, in particular, the following contrasting conditions: (1) the monopolistic stage I producer is not integrated, in which case the prospective new entrant can come into stage I only and sell his product to stage II producers (suitably expanded, if that is necessary for absorption of the additional stage I production); and (2) the monopolistic stage I producer is integrated into stage II so that either (a) the new entrant himself must come in at both stages, or (b) independent new entrants appear simultaneously at both stages. If Bork and Bowman are correct, the cost of capital ought to be independent of these conditions.

To contend that the terms of finance are the same under condition 2(a) as they are under condition I implies that the capital market has equal confidence in the new entrant's qualifications to perform stage II activities as it does in firms that are already experienced in the business. Except in circumstances where experienced firms are plainly inept, this is tantamount to saying that experience counts for nought. This, however, is implausible for transactions that involve large, discrete investments rather than small but recurring commitments of funds. Thus, although a series of small, recurring transactions can be monitored reasonably effectively on the basis of *ex post* experience, this is much less easy for transactions of the large, discrete variety—which are the kind under consideration here. Reputation, which is to say prior experience, is of special importance in establishing the terms of finance for transactions that involve large, discrete commitments of funds.

The significance that lenders and investors attach to reputation can be traced in part to the incompleteness of information regarding the qualifications of applicants for financing. Faced with incomplete information, suppliers of capital are vulnerable to opportunist representations. Unable to distinguish between those unknown candidates who have the capacity and the will to execute the project successfully from the opportunists who assert that they are similarly qualified, when objectively (omnisciently) thay are not, the terms of finance are adjusted adversely against the entire group. Furthermore, and of special relevance to the issue at hand, if lenders are not omniscient then, as between two candidates for financing, both of whom would be judged by an omniscient assessor to have identical capacities and wills to execute the project, but only one of whom has a favourable and widely known performance record, the unknown candidate will find that he is disadvantaged.[44]

Moreover, where both candidates are equally suspect, but one has access to internal sources of financing while the other does not, the candidate requiring outside financing may be unable to proceed. In this connection, timing can be of critical significance. If one firm moves to the integrated structure gradually and finances the undertaking out of internal funds, while the second firm perceives the market opportunity later but, to be viable, must move immediately to a comparably integrated structure, the second firm may have to contend with adverse capital market rates.

The learning-by-doing conditions referred to earlier[45] are also germane to an assessment of the earnings opportunities of an integrated versus non-integrated new entrant. By assumption, the prospective entrant is well qualified in stage I processes. If learning-by-doing yields significant cost advantages and if the prospective entrant has no special qualifications in stage II processes, will his incentive to enter be any the less keen if, by reason of the integration of his competitors, he must now come in at both stages? I submit that if the knowledge gleaned from experience is deeply impacted, which is to say that it is not generally known or easily made knowable to those who lack experience, and if it is very costly to hire away the requisite experienced personnel from the integrated firm,[46] the prospective entrant is plainly at a disadvantage. Information impactedness and imperfect labour markets thus combine to explain the cost disadvantage of the otherwise qualified new entrant in relation to the experienced firm. Were the monopolistic stage I producer not to have integrated into stage II so that the prospective entrant could come in at stage I only and could rely on already experienced stage II firms to acquire the necessary capital to expand appropriately and service his stage II needs, capital costs would be lower and the prospect of entry thereby enhanced.[47]

The problems, moreover, do not vanish if the new entrant comes in at stage I only and relies on independent entry into stage II to occur (condition 2(b)). Not only is the cost of capital adjusted adversely against potential new processors in stage II, by reason of the lack of experience referred to above, but simultaneous yet independent entry into both stages may be impeded because of 'non-convergent expectations'[48] such that interdependent decisions between stages will fail to be made in a compatible way. Lack of common information among independent stage I and II specialists with respect to the market opportunities which they confront and doubts regarding the true investment intentions and contractual reliability of other parties are the apparent impediments to effective coordination. Ultimately, however, the problems are to be attributed to the human and transactional factors described in section I.

To be sure, the argument has no special significance to analysis of monopoly power unless the industry in question is already very concentrated[49] or, in less concentrated markets, conditions of effective collusion, which include collective refusal to deal, obtain. In such circumstances, however, inter-firm rivalry, by itself, cannot be expected to self-police the market in a way that reliably assures the competitive outcome. Accordingly, potential competition has an important market policing role to play. If potential entrants regard imitation of prevailing vertical structures as contributing importantly to the prospect of successful entry (as they may in highly concentrated industries), vertical restrictions that require funds to be raised by less, rather than more, experienced firms can impede entry.

The financing issue, then, is not that capital markets perversely avoid earnings opportunities, the test proposed by Bork, or that financing cannot be arranged under any terms whatsoever, the condition referred to by Bowman. Rather, the cost of capital is at issue. If a prospective new entrant has the self-financing to come in at one stage (or can raise the capital at reasonable terms, perhaps because of a proven capability at this stage of operations) but lacks the self-financing (and incurs adverse terms should he attempt to raise the capital) to come in at the second stage, the condition of entry can clearly be affected by pre-existing vertical restrictions.[50]

4. Circumventing Regulation

As Ronald Coase[51] and George Stigler[52] have both pointed out, vertical integration is sometimes employed as a device by which to evade sales taxes, quota schemes and other methods of non-price rationing. Since such efforts by the government to interfere with the price mechanism typically apply to market-mediated but not to internal transactions, the shift of such transactions from the market to the firm serves to circumvent these regulatory schemes.[53] This is perfectly straightforward and is derived from received microtheory without appeal to transaction-cost considerations.

Conventional microtheory can also be made to address the following issue: can a regulated firm that is permitted only a 'fair' rate of return in supplying a final good or service effectively evade the regulatory restraint by integrating backward into supply of its own equipment? As David Dayan[54] has shown, such backward integration will permit the regulated industry to earn monopoly profits if either equipment transfer prices or the rate of return at the equipment supply stage is unregulated.

While I do not wish to minimize the importance of such considerations in individual industries, I submit that these are rather special cases and that the main incentive for vertical integration is that integration serves to economize on transaction costs and/or is undertaken for the strategic purpose of impeding entry. The types of issues raised in the discussion of the transactional approach in section I and in the earlier parts of this section are the root causes for integration.

5. Policy Implications

Vertical integration raises serious antitrust issues only in those circumstances where otherwise qualified actual or potential rivals can be said to be disadvantaged by it. The two situations in which disadvantage to rivals may arise are dominant firm (or otherwise very concentrated) industries and moderately concentrated industries where collusion has been successfully effected. For the reasons given in section III, such collusion is usually difficult to achieve. Accordingly, very concentrated industries in which the bulk of production is accounted for by integrated firms constitute the subset of principal interest for antitrust policy.

Even in concentrated industries, vertical integration cannot be held to be objectionable *per se*. Two cases can be distinguished. The easiest to deal with is the case where, but for vertical integration by the leading firms in stage I of the industry, stage II would be competitively organized. The objection to vertical integration here is twofold. For one thing, the residual (non-integrated) sector of the stage II market is so reduced that only a few firms of efficient size can service the stage II market. Firms that would otherwise be prepared to enter stage I may therefore be discouraged from coming in by the prospect of having to engage in small numbers bargaining, with all the hazards that this entails, with these few non-integrated stage II firms. Moreover, integrated entry may be rendered unattractive if prospective stage I entrants lack experience in stage II-related activity, and therefore would incur high capital costs were they to enter both stages themselves. The integration of stages I and II by leading firms is anti-competitive then, in entry aspects at least, if severing the vertical connection would permit competitive (large numbers) stage II activity to develop without loss of scale economies.

The second case is that where economies of scale at both stages are large in relation to the size of the total (not merely the residual) market. The advantage of severing the vertical connection in these circumstances is that potential entrants into one of the states will be less deterred from entering that stage, because they will not also have to incur the adverse capital costs attached to entry at the unfamiliar stage. Whether a welfare gain will thereby result depends, however, on off-setting factors of two kinds. First, with only a small number of firms at each stage, frequent haggling over contractual terms, imposing preparatory and negotiating costs on each side, may be expected between stage I and stage II firms. But even if these transaction costs do not obtain, the prospect is that goods and services will not be transferred between the stages at marginal cost prices.[55] Assuming that the technologies in question are of the variable proportions types, inefficient factor utilization results.[56] The question then is whether costs of these two types are more than offset by the gains of facilitating entry accomplished by severing a vertical connection.

Vertical integration in industries with low to moderate degrees of concentration does not, however, pose these same problems. Here a firm entering either stage can expect to strike competitive bargains with firms in the other stage, whether they are integrated or non-integrated.[57] The reasons are that no single integrated firm enjoys a strategic advantage with respect to such transactions and that collusion by the collection of integrated firms (in supply or demand respects) is difficult to effectuate. Vertical integration rarely poses an antitrust issue, therefore, except when the industry in question is highly concentrated or, in less concentrated industries, collective refusals to deal are observed.[58] But for such circumstances, vertical integration is apt to be of the efficiency promoting kind.[59]

III. OLIGOPOLY

The treatment of oligopoly in this section is less an analysis of oligopoly as such than an explication of why oligopoly can be expected to differ in non-trivial ways from monopoly. Although this difference may seem obvious, it has not always been so; the view that dissolution into oligopoly is no remedy for monopoly is widely held.[60] Don Patinkin contends that unless there are 'enough independent firms resulting from the dissolution to make the operation of competition possible . . . we will replace monopoly with some oligopolistic situation, and it is quite possible that we would be as badly off as under monopoly.'[61]

I take exception to that position here. It fails to make allowance for the advantages of internal organization as compared with contracting in adaptational respects, and it gives insufficient standing to the different incentives, and the related propensity to cheat, that distinguish internal from inter-firm organization.

1. Economic Antecedents of the Transactional Approach[62]

Fellner on Qualified Joint Profit-Maximization. William Fellner contends that it is impossible to deduce determinate prices and outputs for oligopoly markets on the basis of demand and supply functions that are derived from technological data and utility functions.[63] Rather, fewness carries with it a range of indeterminacy. Thus, although received price theory is useful for establishing the region of indeterminacy, notions of 'conjectural interdependence' are needed to ascertain how choice is made within these limits. As he sees it 'all problems of conjectural interdependence are essentially problems of bargaining—provided we interpret bargaining in the broader sense, including the "implicit" variety'.[64]

Within the range of indeterminacy, Fellner identifies four factors which determine relative bargaining power. The first two are concerned with social and political limits on bargaining and need not detain us here. The second two are more situation-specific: the ability of the parties to take and to inflict losses during stalemates; and toughness, in the sense of unwillingness to yield.[65]

He notes that quasi-agreements (bargains) will change in response to shifts in relative strength among the parties, and that changing market circumstances make it necessary for oligopolistic rivals to adapt their behaviour appropriately.[66] Such quasi-agreements, moreover, 'do not usually handle *all* economic variables entering into the determination of aggregate gains'.[67] Although this is partly because of 'administrative circumstances', where these are left undefined, 'it is largely a consequence also of uncertainty due to which various persons and organizations discount their own future possibilities. . . . This is especially true of those variables that require skill and ingenuity in handling (such as those directly connected with advertising, product variation, technological change, and so forth)'.[68] Later he indicates that the use of strategic variables of these kinds requires inventiveness,[69] and indicates that 'the present value of this future flow of inventiveness cannot be calculated with sufficient accuracy' for the relative strength of the parties to be established.[70] This in turn prevents the corresponding quasi-agreement from being reached. As an industry 'matures', however, and particularly if new entrants do not appear, the degree of competition with respect to non-price variables may be attenuated.[71]

Fellner indicates that profit pooling would not be necessary to reach a full-blown joint profit-maximization result in those oligopolies where (1) the product is undifferentiated, and (2) all firms have identical horizontal cost curves.[72] In these circumstances a simple market-sharing agreement will suffice to achieve this result. Such conditions, however, represent a very special case. Even here, moreover, there is the need to reach agreement on what adjustments to make to changing demand conditions: who decides? how are differences reconciled?

In the more usual case where cost differences and/or product differentiation exist, joint profit-maximization requires inter-firm cash flows. Complete pooling in these circumstances implies that 'no attention is paid to how much profit each participant earns directly on the market but only to how much the aggregate of the participants earns. Each participant is compensated from the pool of earnings according to his share'.[73] Profit pooling, however, is held to be hazardous both for antitrust reasons and, even more, because some firms will be at a 'substantial disadvantage if the agreement is terminated and aggressive competition is resumed'.[74] Consequently, only qualified joint profit-maximization among oligopolists is to be expected.

Stigler on Oligopoly. Stigler takes as given that oligopolists wish, through collusion, to maximize joint profits[75] and attempts to establish the factors which affect the efficacy of such aspirations. While he admits that 'colluding firms must agree upon the price structure appropriate to the transaction classes which they are prepared to recognize',[76] his analysis is focused entirely on the problem of policing such a collusive agreement. 'A price structure of some complexity'[77], one which makes 'appropriate' provision for heterogeneity among products and buyers and for the hazard of activating potential entrants, is simply imputed to oligopolists.[78]

Stigler notes that since secret violations of such agreements commonly permit individual members of an oligopoly to gain larger profits[79] than they would gain by strict adherence to the agreement, a mechanism to enforce agreements is needed. Enforcement for Stigler 'consists basically of detecting significant deviations from the agreed-upon prices. Once detected, the deviations will tend to disappear because they are no longer secret and will be matched by fellow conspirators if they are not withdrawn'.[80] Accordingly, a weak conspiracy is one in which 'price cutting is detected only slowly and incompletely'.[81]

Since an audit of transaction prices reported by sellers is unlawful, and in any event may be unreliable,[82] transaction prices paid by buyers are needed to detect secret price-cutting. Stigler contends, in this connection, that statistical inference techniques are the usual way in which such price cutting is discovered. In particular, the basic method of detecting a price-cutter is that he is getting business that he would not otherwise obtain.[83] Among the implications of this statistical inference approach to oligopoly are that (1) collusion is more effective in markets where buyers correctly report prices tendered (as in government bidding),[84] (2) collusion is limited if the identity of buyers is continuously changing (as in the construction industries)[85] and (3) elsewhere the efficacy of collusion varies inversely with the number of sellers, the number of buyers, and the proportion of new buyers, but directly with the degree of inequality of firm size among sellers.[86]

2. Legal Antecedents of Transactional Analysis

Turner on Conscious Parallelism. Donald Turner's basic position on conscious parallelism is that such behaviour, by itself, does not imply agreement. It needs to be buttressed by additional evidence that the observed parallelism is not simply 'identical but unrelated responses by a group of similarly situated competitors to the same set of economic facts'.[87] He illustrates the argument by posing an 'extreme hypothetical' in which there are only two or three suppliers—each of identical size, producing an identical product at identical costs—and markets are static.[88] He contends, in these circumstances, that 'the "best" price for each seller would be precisely the same, would be known to be the same by all, and would be charged without hesitation in absolute certainty that the others would price likewise'.[89] Although he is not explicit on this, the price that he appears to have in mind is the joint profit-maximizing (monopoly) price.[90]

Turner then goes on to note that the hypothetical is rather unrealistic. Products are rarely fully homogeneous, cost differences will ordinarily exist, and adaptations will need to be made to changing market circumstances.[91] He accordingly holds that 'for a pattern of non-competitive pricing to emerge . . . requires something which we could, not unreasonably, call a "meeting of the minds".'[92] He declines, however, to regard this as unlawful. Absent explicit collusion, this is merely rational price-making in the light of all market facts.[93] 'If monopoly and monopoly pricing are not unlawful *per se*, neither should oligopoly and oligopoly pricing, absent agreement of the usual sort, be unlawful *per se*.'[94]

Because the behaviour in question cannot be rectified by injunction ('What specifically is to be enjoined?'),[95] relief would presumably have to take the form of dissolution or divestiture.[96] This, however, is to admit that the fundamental issue is structure, not remediable conduct. Unless structural monopoly is to be subject to dissolution, structural oligopoly ought presumably to be permitted to stand. Although Turner declined in 1962 to propose a structural remedy for either condition, he has since altered his position on both.[97]

Posner on Oligopoly. Richard Posner takes exception to Turner's position that oligopolistic interdependence of a natural and non-collusive sort explains the price excesses in oligopolistic industries.[98] Rather, a small numbers condition is held to be merely a necessary but not a sufficient condition for such price excesses to appear.[99] Because 'interdependence theory does not explain . . . how oligopolistic sellers establish a supracompetitive price',[100] including adjustment to changing market conditions, Posner suggests that the study of oligopoly proceed in terms of cartel theory instead.[101]

Posner's basic argument is that 'voluntary actions by the sellers are necessary to translate the rare condition of an oligopoly market into a situation of non-competitive pricing'.[102] Effective cartel behaviour is, moreover, costly to effectuate; costs of bargaining, adaptation and enforcement must all be incurred.[103] The upshot is that because 'tacit collusion or non-competitive pricing is *not inherent* in an oligopolistic market structure but, like conventional cartelizing, requires additional, voluntary behaviour by sellers,[104] a conduct remedy under section one of the Sherman Act[105] is held to be appropriate.[106] Once the oligopolist is faced with the prospect of severe penalties for collusion, tacit or otherwise, Posner concludes that the rational oligopolist will commonly decide not to collude but will expand his output until competitive returns are realized.[107]

3. The Transaction-Cost Approach

To focus attention on what I believe to be the critical issues, I shall assume, initially, that oligopolistic agreements are lawful, in that there is no legal bar to collusion, but that oligopolists cannot appeal to the courts for assistance in enforcing the terms of an oligopolistic agreement. The oligopolists themselves, however, can take punitive actions to bring deviant members into line, provided that laws such as those prohibiting libel or the destruction of property are respected. Entry is assumed to be difficult; also, I shall assume that profit-pooling is permitted but that horizontal mergers between the firms are disallowed.[108]

I shall argue that oligopolists will commonly have difficulty in reaching, implementing and enforcing agreements under these circumstances, but this argument does not mean that laws regarding oligopoly are of no account. The stipulations that horizontal mergers are disallowed and that collusive agreements are unenforceable in the courts are both important in this connection. If, however, it can be shown that monopolistic outcomes are difficult to effectuate even when the law permits collusion, then the performance differences between monopolies (dominant firm markets) and oligopolies are not to be attributed principally to the unlawfulness of collusion among oligopolists.[109] It follows, of course, that if express and lawful agreements are difficult for oligopolists to reach and implement, tacit agreements are even less reliable instruments for achieving collusion.

An agreement between two or more parties will be attractive in the degree to which (1) the good, service or behaviour in question is amenable to specification in writing; (2) joint gains from collective action are potentially available; (3) implementation in the face of uncertainty does not occasion costly haggling; (4) monitoring the agreement is not costly; and (5) detected non-compliance carries commensurate penalties at low enforcement expense. Consider the application of the transaction cost approach proposed in section I to each of these conditions in an oligopolistic agreement.

Specification of Terms. Recall that oligopolistic collusion is assumed to be lawful. The parties to the collusive arrangement can therefore negotiate openly and express the details of the agreement in writing without exposing themselves to prosecution. The question to be assessed here is whether the latitude thus afforded will permit a comprehensive collusive agreement to be specified.

I submit that, except in rather special and unlikely circumstances, a comprehensive agreement to maximize joint profits (but not entailing merger) will rarely be feasible because of transaction costs. A comprehensive statement of this kind would require an inordinate amount of knowledge about the cost and product characteristics of each firm, the interaction effects between the decision variables within each firm, and the interaction effects of decision variables between firms. Not only is the relevant information costly to come by, to say nothing of digesting it and devising the appropriate responses for each of the firms to make but, if anything approximating a complete agreement is to be written, this information gathering and analysis needs to be done *ex ante* for a whole series of contingent future events, most of which will never materialize.

The point is that joint profit-maximization, even as an abstract exercise, is very difficult to accomplish once one departs from the simplest sort of textbook exercise. Homogeneous products, identical linear and horizontal cost curves, and static markets constitute the 'ideal'. Maintaining these product and cost assumptions in the face of changing demand does not greatly complicate the abstract analysis, in that the conditions of joint profit-maximization are easy to display, but the operational problems become somewhat more difficult in the face of uncertainty, which will be discussed below.[110]

In more realistic circumstances, involving differentiated products, product and process innovation, organization form[111] changes, and revisions in selling expense and financial strategies, the resulting complexity becomes impossibly great in relation to the bounded rationality of planners. When, in addition, the optimization problem is cast in a multiperiod framework under conditions of uncertainty, abstract analysis breaks down.[112] One concludes, accordingly, that the absence of legal prohibitions to collusive agreements is not what prevents comprehensive collusion.[113] Rather, it is prevented by elementary considerations of bounded rationality.[114]

Joint Gains. Suppose, *arguendo*, that it were possible to specify the joint profit-maximizing strategy. Would the parties then be prepared to make such an agreement? I submit that, but for the simple textbook cases referred to above, the parties would commonly decline to accept comprehensive joint profit-maximization of the profit-pooling kind.

Partly disagreement might arise, as Fellner suggests, on account of differences between the parties concerning the appropriate discount rates to be used in evaluating future prospects. Surely more fundamental, however, are the risks and monitoring expenses that profit-pooling entails. As Fellner notes, some of the parties must accede to reductions in relative output and to contractions in relative firm size if the joint profit-maximizing result is to be realized. This, however, is hazardous. Firms which are authorized to expand relatively as a result of the agreement will be powerfully situated to demand a renegotiated settlement at a later date. Wary of such opportunism, firms for which retrenchment is indicated will decline from the outset to accept a full-blown profit-pooling arrangement. Moreover, even setting such concerns aside, monitoring the profit-pooling agreement will be costly because of the pairing of opportunism with information impactedness. This will be discussed below.[115]

Implementation under Uncertainty.[116] Implementing an agreement under conditions of uncertainty requires that the parties agree, when changes in the environment occur, on what new state of the world obtains. Problems can arise if, for any true description of the state of the world (1) some parties would realize benefits if a false state were to be declared; and either (2) information regarding the state of the world is dispersed among the parties and must be pooled, or (3) despite the possession of identical information by all the parties, definitive agreement must still be reached.

Consider condition (3). Even though all parties have identical information with respect to the true condition of the environment, they need not agree on what state of the world has actually been realized. Unless the parties have stipulated fully how observations are to be interpreted as state-of-the-world descriptions, differences in opinion can be anticipated. If some parties stand to benefit from having one state declared, but others would benefit if another state were declared, and if each side can make a plausible case for its position, opportunistic representations in support of each outcome can be expected. Costly haggling may then ensue.

To illustrate, suppose that demand on day t is known to be a function only if the mean temperature on day $t-1$: if the mean temperature on day $t-1$ exceeds T_0, demand on day t is of type D_1; otherwise it is of type D_2. Suppose also that all firms have free access to temperature readings on day $t-1$ at 4.00 a.m., noon and 8.00 p.m. If on date t the unit weighted average of the temperatures on the preceding day is well above or well below T_0, the declaration of demand types is made without difficulty. Suppose, however, that the unit weighted average of day $t-1$ temperatures just slightly exceeds T_0 while weights of 0.95, 1.10 and 0.95 would reduce it to below T_0. If some parties benefit if demand is declared to be of type D_2 even though it is actually D_1, they may then assert that 'everyone knows' that the noon-time temperature deserves to be assigned a greater weight in computing the daily mean. Protracted haggling could ensue. Moreover, in the usual circumstances where the state of the world is multidimensional, the occasion for such disputes naturally increases.[117]

The problems are compounded if condition (2) obtains. Here the necessary information to ascertain the true state of the world is dispersed and pooling of the data is required. An agreement on how to interpret the data is to little purpose if the parties selectively disclose or distort the information to which they have preferential access. The pairing of opportunism with information impactedness thus poses serious implementation problems to the oligopolists.

Monitoring Execution of the Agreement. As Stigler points out, and as is widely recognized, oligopolists have an incentive to cheat on price-fixing agreements if they believe that cheating will go, for a time at least, undetected. Given that information about individual sales is impacted, in that the seller knows exactly what the terms were but, given uncertainty, his rivals do not and can establish the terms only at some cost, the individual seller can often cut prices below the agreed level to the disadvantage of the other parties to the conspiracy. The pairing of opportunism (here manifested as cheating) with information impactedness makes oligopolistic agreements difficult to police.

This argument, moreover, applies to oligopolistic collusion with respect to considerations other than price as well. If anything, agreeing to collude with respect to marketing expense, R&D efforts, and similar business practices is even more hazardous than price collusion for non-opportunistic parties who are prepared to abide by the agreements. Although it is easy to establish after the fact that a rival has made significant design changes or introduced a new product in violation of the agreement, such information may come too late. If recovery from a large shift in market share attributable to, for example, an 'illicit' innovation is inordinately expensive, the detection of such a violation is to little avail—unless, of course, all firms have maintained a defensive posture against such contingencies, in which case collusion in these non-price respects can scarcely be said to be operative.

As mentioned above, profit-pooling is also subject to problems of monitoring.[118] Even if firms were prepared to enter into agreements in which all profits are pooled and each participant is assigned a share of the total, there is still the problem of determining what the contribution of each firm to the pool should be. Individual firms have an incentive to understate true profits in these circumstances.

Moreover, merely auditing the earnings of each firm, even to the extent that *all* sources of revenue and cost are fully disclosed, is not sufficient to avoid distortion. An assessment of individual expense items must also be made. The problems facing the auditor here are akin to those facing the defence agencies in monitoring cost-plus (or more generally, cost-sharing) defence contracts.[119] Unless it can be established that certain types or amounts of actual costs are unwarranted, and hence will be disallowed, each firm has an incentive to incur excessive costs.

Expense excesses can take any of several forms. Perhaps the simplest is to allow some operations to run slack so that the management and workers in the firm take part of their rewards as on-the-job leisure. A second way is to allow emoluments to escalate, in which case corporate personal consumption expenditures exceed levels which, from a profit-maximizing standpoint, would be incurred. Third, and most important, firms may incur current costs which place them at a strategic advantage in future periods. Developing new and improved technology or training the workforce are examples of this sort of cost. Evaluating individual firm performance in these several respects is at least an order of magnitude more difficult than simple audits of revenue and cost streams. Profit-pooling, therefore, poses severe enforcement problems, even assuming that the agreement itself were legal.

Penalizing Violations. Recall that it was assumed that while collusive agreements are not unlawful, the participants in such agreements cannot call upon the courts to help enforce the agreement. Instead, violators must be determined and penalties must be administered by the parties to the contract. Problems of two types arise in connection with penalties. First, do the penalties, if implemented, constitute an effective deterrent to the would-be violator? Second, even if penalties can be devised that would be efficacious, will the parties to the conspiracy be prepared to impose them?

Because the conspirators lack legal standing, conventional penalties such as fines and jail sentences are presumably unavailable. Rather, penalties are *exacted in the market-place* by confronting the violator with unusually adverse circumstances. Price reductions are matched and perhaps even undercut. Normal types of inter-firm cooperation (e.g. supply of components) are suspended. Key employees may be raided. Except, however, as deviant firms are highly dependent on rivals for vital supplies, such market reactions may well be ones that the deviant is prepared to risk.

For one thing, the contract violator is not the only firm to be adversely affected by exacting these penalties in the market-place. The firms meting out the penalties also incur costs.[120] Second, and related, securing the collective action needed to punish the violator may be difficult. Thus, although all firms may agree both that a violation has taken place and that the violator deserves to be punished, not all may be prepared to participate in administering it. Defectors (e.g. those willing to supply the deviant with the essential component, perhaps at a premium price), which is to say opportunists, who refuse to incur the costs of punishing the violator, naturally reduce the costs of being detected in violation of the agreement. Where such defection is deemed likely, collusive agreements are all the less probable.[121]

4. Policy Implications: Dominant Firms versus Oligopolistic Interdependence

The monopolistic (or dominant firm) enjoys an advantage over oligopolists in adaptational respects because he does not have to write a contract in which future contingencies are identified and appropriate adaptations thereto are devised. Instead, he can face the contingencies when they arise; each bridge can be crossed when it is reached, rather than having to decide *ex ante* how to cross all bridges that one might conceivably face.[122] Put differently, the monopolist can employ an adaptive, sequential decision-making procedure, which greatly economizes on bounded rationality demands, without exposing himself to the risks of contractual incompleteness which confront a group of conspiring oligopolists. Adaptation within a firm (in contrast to that between firms) is also promoted by the more complete development of efficient, albeit often informal, communication codes and an associated trust relationship between the parties.[123] Thus, while I do not mean to suggest that there are no costs whatsoever to dissolution,[124] and, accordingly, do not propose it as an automatic remedy, to suggest that oligopolists will be able easily to replicate the (joint) profit-maximization strategy of a monopolist is simply unwarranted. Even if cheating on a specific agreement were not a problem, there is still the need among oligopolists to reach the specific agreement. The high cost of exhaustively complete specification of agreements discourages efforts toward comprehensiveness—in which case, because actual oligopolistic contracts are of the incomplete coordination kind, competition of a non-price sort predictably obtains.

To assume, moreover, that oligopolists will voluntarily adhere to whatever limited agreements they reach is plainly unreasonable. Cheating is a predictable consequence of oligopolistic conspiracy; the record is replete with examples.[125] The pairing of opportunism with information impactedness explains this condition.

The monopolist, by contrast, does not face the same need to attenuate opportunism. Even within the monopoly firm in which semi-autonomous operating divisions have been created, with each operated as a profit centre, interdivisional cheating on agreements will be less than inter-firm cheating because: (1) the gains can be less fully appropriated by the defector division; (2) the difficulty of detecting cheating is much less; and (3) the penalties to which internal organization has access (including dismissing opportunist division managers) are more efficacious. Unlike independently-owned oligopoly firms, the operating divisions do not have fully pre-emptive claims on their profit streams (so the inclination to cheat is less) and, unlike oligopolies, they are subject to detailed audits, including an assessment of internal efficiency performance. Also, where oligopolists can usually penalize defectors only by incurring losses themselves (e.g. by matching or over-matching price cuts), the monopoly firm has access to a powerful and delicately conceived internal incentive system that does not require it to incur market penalties of a price-cutting sort.[126] It can mete out penalties to groups and individuals in the firm in a quasi-judicial fashion and in this way it assumes some of the functions of a legal system. Altogether, the opportunism which threatens agreements among oligopolists is a less severe problem for the dominant firm.

More generally, my argument comes down to this; it is naive to regard oligopolists as shared monopolists *in any comprehensive sense*— especially if they have differentiated products, have different cost experiences, are differently situated with respect to the market by virtue of size, and plainly lack the machinery by which oligopolistic coordination, except of the most primitive variety, is accomplished and enforced. Except, therefore, in highly concentrated industries producing homogeneous products, with non-trivial barriers to entry, and at a mature stage of development oligopoly is unlikely to pose antitrust issues for which dissolution is an appropriate remedy. In the usual oligopoly situation efforts to achieve collusion are unlikely to be successful or, if they are, will require sufficient explicit communication that normal remedies against price-fixing, including injunctions not to collude, will suffice.

Where, however, the industry is of the special type just described, recognized interdependency may be sufficiently extensive to permit tacit collusion to succeed. Injunctive remedies, as Turner noted, are unsatisfactory in such circumstances.[127] Accordingly, dissolution ought to be actively considered. The recent case brought by the Antitrust Division against the major firms in the gypsum industry affords a current example of a case in which, assuming the charges can be proved, dissolution would appear to be warranted.[128] By contrast, the cereal case brought by the Federal Trade Commission is not one for which comprehensive collusion seems likely.[129]

This does not, however, imply that the cereal industry poses no public policy problems whatsoever. Simply because the shared monopoly model does not fit well does not mean that public policy concerns vanish. But I would urge that attention be focused on those specific practices in the industry which are thought to be objectionable. If, for example, excessive advertising in the cereal industry can be reasonably established, this can be dealt with directly. Selective attention to specific wasteful practices, rather than grand conspiracy theories, are called for.

A related implication of the argument is that dissolution of dominant firms is not an idle economic exercise done to reduce large aggregations of corporate power for political or social purposes alone but unlikely to have significant economic performance consequences. For all the reasons developed above, several independent entities cannot realize the same degree of coordination between their policies in price and non-price respects as can a single firm.[130] Moreover, the price and non-price differences that predictably arise[131] will typically redound to the consumer's benefit.[132] Accordingly, a more assertive antitrust policy with regard to the dissolution of dominant firms is indicated.[133]

IV. CONGLOMERATE ORGANIZATION

1. Received Microtheory versus Transactional Interpretations

As the remarks of Bork and Bowman cited earlier make clear,[134] received microtheory is loath to concede that capital markets may fail to operate frictionlessly. Partly for this reason, the fiction that managers operate firms in fully profit-maximizing ways is maintained. It is argued that any attempt by opportunist managers to promote their own goals at the expense of corporate profitability would occasion intervention through the capital market. Effective control of the corporation would be transferred to those parties who perceived the lapse; profit-maximizing behaviour would then be quickly restored.

Parties responsible for the detection and correction of deviant behaviour in the firm would, of course, participate in the greater profit which the reconstituted management would realize. This participation would not, however, be large. One reason is that incumbent managements, by assumption, have little opportunity for inefficiency or malfeasance because any tendency towards waywardness would be quickly detected and costlessly extinguished. Accordingly, the incremental profit gain occasioned by takeover would be small. Moreover, the market for corporate control is presumably one in which large numbers of qualified takeover agents are non-collusively organized. Competitive offers assure that the takeover gains mainly redound to the stockholders.

Shorey Peterson's sanguine views on corporate behaviour are roughly of this kind. He characterizes the latitude to disregard the profit goal as 'small',[135] and goes on to observe that '[f]ar from being an ordinary election, a proxy battle is a *catastrophic* event whose mere possibility is a threat, and one not remote when affairs are in *conspicuous* disarray.'[136] Indeed, even 'stockholder suits . . . may be provoked by evidence of *serious* self-dealing.'[137] On the principle that the efficacy of legal prohibitions is to be judged 'not by guilt discovered but by guilt discouraged', he concludes that such suits, albeit rare, may have accomplished much in helping to police the corporate system.[138]

While I do not mean to suggest that such deterrence has not been important, Peterson's observations appear to me to be *consistent* with the proposition that traditional capital markets are beset by serious problems of information impactedness and incur non-trivial displacement costs if the incumbent management is disposed to resist the takeover effort. Why else the reference to catastrophic events, conspicuous disarray, and serious self-dealing? Systems that are described in these terms are not ones for which a delicately conceived control system can be said to be operating. As recent military history makes clear, controls that involve a large and discrete shock to the system are appropriate only when an offence reaches egregious proportions. The scope for opportunism, accordingly, is wider than Peterson seems prepared to concede.

The reasons why traditional control of management performance by the capital market is relatively crude are that internal conditions in the firm are not widely known or easy to discover (information impactedness) and that those seeking to gain control of the firm (takeover agents) might well take opportunistic advantage of the shareholders' bounded rationality. Information impactedness means that outsiders cannot make confident judgements that the firm has departed from profit-maximizing standards, except with difficulty. The firm is a complex organization and its performance is a joint consequence of exogenous economic events, rival behaviour and internal decisions. Causal inferences are correspondingly difficult to make and hence opportunism is costly to detect. Moreover, once detected, convincing interested stockholders that a displacement effort ought to be supported encounters problems. In as much as time and the analytical capacity of stockholders are not free goods (which is to say that the limits imposed by bounded rationality must be respected) the would-be takeover agent cannot simply display all of his evidence and expect stockholders to evaluate it and reach the 'appropriate' conclusion. Rather, any appeal to the stockholders must be made in terms of highly digested interpretations of the facts. Although this helps to overcome the stockholders' bounded rationality problem, it poses another: How is the interested stockholder (or his agent) to distinguish between bona fide and opportunistic takeover agents?

The upshot of these remarks is that the transaction costs associated with *traditional* capital market processes for policing management, of the sort described by Peterson, are considerable. Correspondingly, the range of discretionary behaviour open to incumbent managements is rather wider than Peterson and other supporters of the fiction of the frictionless capital market concede.[139]

One of the more attractive attributes of the conglomerate form of organization (of the appropriate kind)[140] is that it serves to overcome certain of these limitations of traditional capital markets. The argument, which I shall develop below, essentially reduces to the proposition that conglomerate firms (of the appropriate kind) function as miniature capital markets with consequences for resource allocation which are, on balance, beneficial.

This poses, however, the following paradox: under conventional assumptions that more choices are always preferred to fewer, the banking system ought to have superior resource-allocation properties to any miniature imitation thereof. Put differently, why should a miniature capital market ever be preferred to the real thing? As might be anticipated, transaction-cost considerations supply the resolution. If decision-makers could be easily apprised of an ever-wider range of alternatives and choose intelligently among them, there would be no occasion to supplant the traditional market. But it is elementary that, where complex events have to be evaluated, information processing capacities are quickly reached. As a result, expanding the range of choice may not only be without purpose but can have net detrimental effects. A trade-off between breadth of information, in which respect the banking system may be presumed to have the advantage, and depth of information, which is the advantage of the specialized firm,[141] is involved. The conglomerate can be regarded as an intermediate form that ideally optimizes with respect to the breadth-depth trade-off.[142] Although the number of alternatives considered by a conglomerate's management is limited, its knowledge (*ex post* and *ex ante*) with respect to each remains relatively deep. Operating as it does as an internal control agent, its auditing powers are more extensive and its control instruments are more selective than an external control agent can employ. Information impactedness is reduced as a result and opportunism is attenuated in the process.

2. Objections to the Conglomerate

The failure on the part of the received microtheory to regard the internal organization of the firm as interesting is, I believe, responsible for what Posner has called 'the puzzle of the conglomerate corporations'.[143] This puzzle has not, however, deterred those who most rely on received microtheory from venturing the opinion that the conglomerate is inno-cent of anti-competitive purpose or potential and ought not to be an object of antitrust prosecution.[144] But an affirmative rationale for the conglomerate, based on received microtheory, has yet to appear.[145]

The populist critics of the conglomerate have not allowed this lapse to go unnoticed. Robert Solo's views are perhaps representative. He contends that

when faced with a truly dangerous phenomenon, such as the conglomerate mergers of the 1960s, produced by financial manipulators making grist for their security mills, the professional antitrust economists were silent. Like other realities of a modern enterprise, this phenomenon, which will probably subvert management effectiveness and organizational rationale for generations, is out-side their conceptual framework.[146]

Several things should be said in this connection. First, in defence of antitrust economists, I would point out that financial manipulation is not their main concern. This is the principal business of the Securities and Exchange Commission rather than the Antitrust Division. Although Solo might object with cause that economists are excessively narrow, never-theless, as matters are divided up currently, it is the security specialists who are presumably at fault. Second, and more important, Solo's sweeping changes leave the particular dangers of the conglomerate phenomenon completely unspecified. Third, I agree that an understand-ing of the conglomerate requires an extension of the conventional framework. Nevertheless I think it noteworthy that populist critics of the conglomerate and received microtheorists alike pay little heed to the resource-allocation consequences, in the form of capital market substitution effects, of internal organization. Finally, conglomerates come in a variety of forms and have a variety of purposes. Accordingly, any attack on conglomerates should be selective rather than broadside.

Responses to organizational innovations vary. The initial response of rival firms and financial analysts is typically to disregard such changes. Partly this is because 'reorganization' is a common reaction by firms that are experiencing adversity. Discerning whether the response is intended to eliminate accumulated bureaucratic dead wood or to buy time from the stockholders by giving the impression that corrective action has been taken, or whether (instead or in addition) it represents a really fundamental change in structure that warrants more widespread attention is initially quite difficult.[147] Expressed in transaction-cost terms, the problem is that opportunistic structural changes cannot easily be distinguished from fundamental ones on account of information impactedness and bounded rationality. Given the incapacity (or high cost) of communicating about, and abstractedly assessing, the importance of organizational changes, the tendency is to wait and see how organizational changes manifest themselves in performance consequences. In as much as performance is a function of many factors other than organizational structure alone, sorting out the effect of organizational changes is difficult. Therefore, a long recognition lag between fundamental innovation and widespread imitation is common.[148]

Public policy analysts of populist persuasions are prone to regard organizational innovations as having anti-competitive purposes. Rarely are such innovations thought to have possible efficiency consequences, mainly because efficiency is thought to reside in technological rather than transactional factors. Harlan Blake's widely admired assessment of the conglomerate and its policy implications is in this technological tradition.[149] Like Solo's, his treatment tends to be global rather than selective. References to 'mergers whose anti-competitive potential is so widespread that it might appropriately be described as having an effect upon the economic system as a whole—in every line of commerce in every section of the country'[150] is unguarded. An understanding of the conglomerate phenomenon will be better promoted by delimiting the attack.[151]

For one thing, organization form distinctions, of which Blake makes none, ought to be made. Size considerations aside, he treats all conglomerates as an undifferentiated group. But there are indications that even some courts may be more discriminating than this.[152] More generally, the point is this: just as the structure of markets influences the performance of markets, so likewise ought allowance to be made for the possibility that internal organization influences firm performance.[153]

Although Blake recognizes that the conglomerate may have had invigorating effects on the market for corporate control,[154] he does not regard its ability to reallocate assets internally from lower-yield to higher-yield uses as an affirmative factor. If anything, he seems to suggest that internal resource reallocations are undesirable as compared with reallocations in the capital market.[155] In an economy, however, where returning funds to, and reallocating funds by, the capital market incurs non-trivial transaction costs and/or where managers of specialized firms have an opportunistic preference to retain earnings, the internal realloca- tion of resources to uses returning a higher yield is what most commends the conglomerate as compared with similarly constituted specialized firms.[156] The conglomerate in these circumstances assumes miniature capital-market responsibilities of an energizing kind. That Blake is unimpressed with such consequences is explained by his assessment (which he shares with conventional microtheory)[157] that only economies having technological origins are deserving of consideration and his conviction that the supplanting of 'competitive market forces', however feeble these forces may be, by internal organization is anti-com- petitive.[158]

Blake also finds conglomerates objectionable because of 'hard evi- dence to support the no longer novel theory—and widely held belief in the business community—that large conglomerates facing each other in several markets tend to be less competitive in price than regional or smaller firms.'[159] There are two problems with the argument. First, I would scarcely characterize the evidence on which Blake relies as 'hard'. Part of the evidence cited by Blake is Scherer's discussion of the 'spheres of influence hypothesis'.[160] But Scherer is very careful to characterize the evidence quite differently, noting that even with respect to the pre-war international chemical industry, which aside from marine cartels is his only Western example, the evidence is fragmentary. With respect to other industrials he concludes that 'there is a dearth of evidence on spheres of influence accords'.[161]

Second, the definition of a conglomerate requires attention. Are all specialized firms (such as National Tea, to which Blake earlier refers)[162] that operate similar plants or stores in geographically-dispersed markets really to be regarded as conglomerates? Stretching the definition of a conglomerate to include geographically-dispersed, but otherwise special- ized enterprises, shrinks the number of non-conglomerate large firms to insignificance. If 'conglomerate' is defined in terms of product diversi- fication, Blake (and the Federal Trade Commission) ought to be ex- pected to generate examples of abuse of conglomerate structure from the universe of product-diversified firms. If instead all large multimarket firms, whatever their product specialization ratios, are the objectionable sub-set, the suspect firms ought to be expressly identified in this way rather than by designating them as 'conglomerates'.

Although I share Blake's suspicions with respect to the behaviour of *very large* product-diversified firms (which is the narrower definition of the conglomerate), the facts have yet to be assembled. As things stand now, the price-competitiveness of such firms cannot be adversely distinguished from that of other large multi-market organizations.

The data are somewhat better with respect to reciprocity. Blake conjectures in this connection that 'empirical research, if it could be carried out, would show that reciprocity is as inevitable a result of widespread conglomerate structure as price rigidity is a consequence of oligopoly structure'[163]—where apparently the latter (and hence the former) is believed to be extensive. Jesse Markham's study of conglomerates, which was unavailable to Blake, suggests otherwise: 'highly diversified companies are no more, and may be even less, given to reciprocity than large corporations generally.'[164]

Blake's principal policy proposal is that conglomerate acquisitions by firms above a specified size (the sub-set of firms that are to be restricted is not explicitly identified, but Blake makes several references to the top 200 firms)[165] be accompanied by a spin-off of comparable assets.[166] He further stipulates that no exception be permitted for acquiring a toehold in the new market. His argument against the toehold exception is that small independent firms are more apt to engage in price competition than large conglomerates—relying a second time on the purportedly 'hard' evidence referred to above—and contends that 'a size-based presumption would help restore the idea that internal growth is the normal, and usually the most socially efficient, means of industrial expansion, by making it the only means available to the largest corporations absent a special showing of pro-competitive effect or of efficiencies'.[167]

As already indicated, however, the evidence on which Blake relies is rather limited. Moreover, the basis for his refusal to admit a toehold exception is really unclear. By itself the acquisition of a very small firm scarcely contributes much to the growth of the large firm. Correspondingly, requiring the large firm to release assets in an equivalent amount whenever a toehold acquisition is made is scarcely more than a nuisance.[168] Furthermore, toehold acquisitions made for the purpose of securing a position that will subsequently be expanded *is* internal growth of the sort Blake favours. Either there is little point to Blake's toehold argument,[169] or he regards expansion by small firms as socially preferable to similar investments by large firms.

Assuming, *arguendo*, that the same investments will be made whether the small firm is acquired or not, it is easy to agree with Blake—though I repeat that the evidence on the competitive behaviour of small firms, as compared with product divisions in diversified large firms, is scarcely dispositive—but it is doubtful that the same investments will actually occur. This raises transfer process issues.

An examination of these matters suggests that small firms apparently enjoy a comparative advantage at early and developmental stages of the technical-innovation process.[170] Large established firms, by contrast, display comparative advantages at large-scale commercial production and distribution stages.[171] Not only may the management of the small firm lack the financial resources to move to the commercial stage in any but a gradualist manner because its credit standing does not permit it to raise significant blocks of capital except at adverse rates,[172] but the management of the small firm may be poorly suited to make the transition. Different management skills and knowledge are required to bring a project successfully to large-scale commercial development than may have been needed at earlier stages. If, because of management experience and team considerations similar to those described in section II above, the talents needed to facilitate internal expansion cannot be costlessly identified and assembled, transferring the project to an established firm that already possesses the requisite talents may be the more economical alternative. Again, it is transactions, not technology, which dictate this result. Put in these terms, it is unclear that the no toehold position survives.

I am nevertheless sympathetic with the proposition that the acquisition of already large firms by other large firms ought to be accompanied by a divestiture of equivalent assets. As Richard Hofstadter has observed, the support for antitrust enforcement rests less on a consensus among economists about its efficiency enhancing properties than it does on a political and moral judgement that power in the American economy should be diffused.[173] The widsom of such populist social and political attitudes is illustrated by the misadventures of the ITT Corporation in domestic and foreign affairs.[174] Much of Blake's disenchantment with conglomerates appears to be attributable to a concern that giant size and political abuse are positively correlated,[175] and I would urge that the case be made expressly in these terms. If giant firms rather than all conglomerates are what is objectionable, attention ought properly to be restricted to these firms.

A requirement that very large firms divest themselves of equivalent assets when larger-than-toehold acquisitions are made is also favoured by the prospect that this policy will help curb bureaucratic abuses associated with very large size. Although such divestitures sometimes occur voluntarily,[176] such efforts predictably encounter bureaucratic resistance. If, however, such divestiture commonly has beneficial effects of an organizational self-renewal sort, making divestiture mandatory is scarcely objectionable. It would merely strengthen the hand of those in the firm who are anxious to forestall bureaucratic stagnation. Absent such a rule, internal agreement on divestiture may be difficult to secure; parties with vested interests will make partisan (opportunistic) representations that will be difficult to reject. Given such a rule, however, the general office can simply plead that it has no choice but to divest (assuming that a large acquisition is to be made). The preferences of the general office, reflecting efficiency considerations for the entire conglomerate enterprise, are thus made to prevail more fully.

3. Policy Implications
A transactional intepretation of the conglomerate, which emphasizes the limitations of capital markets with respect to policing corporate management, reveals that conglomerate firms (of the appropriate kind) are not altogether lacking in social purpose. If maintaining the market for corporate control[177] is thought to be generally beneficial, if reallocating resources away from projects with lower returns to favour those with higher net private returns also generally yields social net benefits as well, and if the antitrust enforcement agencies are to maintain a tough policy with respect to horizontal and vertical mergers, a policy of moderation with respect to conglomerate mergers is in order. In particular, public policy with respect to conglomerate acquisitions should focus on (1) mergers where potential competition is meaningfully impaired, and (2) mergers by giant firms that are not accompanied by a spin-off (or other disposition) of comparable assets. Acquisitions of the second kind have been discussed above.[178] Consider therefore the potential competition issue.

As I have already indicated, Blake's views on potential competition are rather broad.[179] The law, however, appears to be moving in the direction of interpreting the potential competition issue more narrowly. Commissioner Dennison, speaking for a unanimous Commission in the recent FTC decision *Beatrice Foods Co.*, discussed the factual proof required to show that potential competition has been or probably will be reduced:

Complaint Counsel in essence attempt to rest their case on the existence of concentration ratios alone. The test for finding injury due to elimination of a potential competitor is not simple. Additional factors enter into any analysis of the loss of a potential competitor. Among these are: trends toward concentration in the market; extensive entry barriers; high probability that the lost potential competitor would have actually entered the market; whether the lost potential competitor was one of only a few such potential competitors and whether, if he had entered the market, his new competition would have had a significant impact on price and quality. Although the number of competing firms or trends toward concentration may be enough without more to condemn many horizontal mergers between existing rivals in a market, the *condition of entry by new firms as well as these other factors mentioned above must be considered when dealing with elimination of a potential competitor.*[180]

This reference to the condition of entry warrants additional development. As Turner has argued forcefully, potential competition is apt to be impaired if one of a few most likely potential entrants acquires a firm that exceeds toehold proportions.[181] If the industry in question is highly concentrated, so that, but for the threat of potential competition, competitive results will not reliably obtain, the quality of competition is degraded by the loss of one of a few 'most likely potential entrants'. I would like to urge that the appellation 'most likely potential entrant', has genuine economic significance, as contrasted with transitory business significance, *only* to the extent that non-trivial barriers to entry into the industry in question can be said to exist.

The antitrust distinction to be made is between firms which (for transitory reasons) may have demonstrated an acquisition interest in the industry and firms which, despite entry barriers (non-transitory considerations), are strategically situated to enter. Because the interest of firms of the first kind is unlikely to persist, being dependent on such factors as the current interests of the chief executive, temporary cash balances and immediate income statement considerations, prohibiting entry by acquisition to such firms is of little affirmative economic purpose. No long-term benefit to potential competition is thereby secured. Rather, the principal effect is to shrink the acquisition market, thereby impairing both the market for corporate control and the incentives for entrepreneurs to invest in new enterprises.

The situation is quite different, however, if the industry in question has non-trivial barriers to entry and the firm evidencing an acquisition interest is one of only a few firms for which *de novo* or toehold entry would be very easy. Consider in this connection the entry barrier conditions identified by Bain—namely, economies of scale that are large in relation to the size of the market, absolute cost advantages and product differentiation.[182] Although Bain describes these barriers without reference to specific firms, plainly the height of the barrier varies among possible entrants. Thus, though economies of scale may be large in relation to the size of the market, this impediment to entry is apt to be less severe for those few firms which have closely complementary production processes and sales organizations. Similarly, a few firms may be well situated with respect to absolute cost advantages. Although patents may constitute a severe impediment to entry, high-grade ore deposits may be in limited supply, or specialized labour skills may be required, a few firms are apt to stand out from all the rest by reason of a complementary technology, which facilitates inventing around the established patents, because they possess medium-grade ore deposits, or because their labour force has acquired, in a learning-by-doing fashion, the requisite specialized skills. Product differentiation advantages are likewise attenuated for those firms that market related types of consumer goods and themselves enjoy brand recognition. *Ceteris paribus*, those firms for which the barriers are least are the firms that are usefully designated most likely potential entrants.

In circumstances, however, where all such barriers to entry are negligible (economies of scale are not great; patents and specialized or otherwise scarce resources are unimportant; product differentiation is insubstantial), no small sub-set of firms can be said to enjoy a strategic advantage. In that case, it is fatuous to attempt to identify a group of most likely potential entrants the loss by acquisition of any of which would significantly impair the quality of potential completion.[183]

V. CONCLUDING REMARKS

Received microtheory provides the analyst with some very powerful tools, but it is also incomplete. Among other things, as Diamond has noted, standard 'economic models . . . [treat] individuals as playing a game with fixed rules which they obey. They do not buy more than they know they can pay for, they do not embezzle funds, they do not rob banks.'[184] Expressed in terms of the language introduced in section I, individuals are not opportunists. Standard models also, as Simon has repeatedly emphasized, impute considerable power of computation and analysis to economic actors[185]—which is to say that bounded rationality is rarely thought to pose a problem. The transaction cost approach relaxes both of these behavioural assumptions.

Although there is no necessary connection, those who rely exclusively on the received microtheory model of the firm are prone to express considerable confidence in the efficacy of competition. Problems of small-numbers supply and of adapting efficiently to uncertainty are apt to be dismissed or settled in a rather artificial fashion. The upshot is that many of the interesting problems of economic organization are either finessed or dealt with in a dogmatic way.

The transaction-cost approach is concerned with the costs of running the economic system, especially the costs of adapting efficiently to uncertainty. It expressly makes allowance for elementary attributes of human decision-makers—in particular, bounded rationality and opportunism—and permits the implications of these conditions to be explored in a way that received microtheory does not.

This does not require that received microtheory be rejected, however. Transaction-cost analysis is more a complement to than a substitute for received microtheory. It is appropriate for studying the frictions in the system which may prevent the implications of received microtheory from going through. This focus makes it especially well suited to help delimit the public policy issues with which the antitrust enforcement agencies are concerned. Moreover, transaction-cost analysis is comparatively value-free: it is biased neither for nor against the modes of organization associated with an unfettered market.

Perhaps the simplest application of the transaction-cost approach is to price discrimination. Not only does transaction-cost analysis call attention to the fact that price discrimination is costly to effectuate, which has been apparent to any student who has given serious consideration to the issue,[186] but it identifies the reasons for this and permits additional efficiency implications to be derived. The usual proposition that allocative efficiency is improved by fully discriminating monopoly, as compared with uniform price monopoly, is challenged. A private net gain but social net loss can plainly obtain when transaction costs are expressly introduced into the net benefit calculus.

With respect to vertical integration, the transaction-cost approach counsels caution. The more strident claims of those who proclaim vertical integration (and, more generally, vertical market restrictions of all kinds) to be altogether innocent of anti-competitive potential are shown to be exaggerated. Vertical integration can have entry-impeding consequences in highly concentrated industries if capital markets do not operate frictionlessly—which in this context means omnisciently. Where, however, the industry in question is not highly concentrated, this same anti-competitive potential is much less severe. Absent collusion, the presumption that vertical integration is innocent or beneficial is appropriate.

The transaction-cost approach also reveals that the oligopoly problem should not be uncritically equated with the dominant firm problem. It is much more difficult to negotiate a comprehensive collusive agreement, and there are many more problems to effecting a joint profit-maximizing outcome, than is commonly suggested. Accordingly, theories of 'shared monopoly' ought to be regarded with scepticism. An economically rational antitrust policy would presumably first address the industries with dominant firms and, where feasible, effect dissolution here before going on to attack oligopolies. Contrary to what is sometimes said, there *are* prospective benefits from converting a dominant firm industry into an oligopolistic one.

The broadside attack that some have levelled against conglomerates appears to be overdrawn. Again, frictions in the capital market turn out to be of fundamental importance. Absent capital market frictions impeding takeover or proclivities of incumbent managements to reinvest earnings (or otherwise behave in opportunistic ways), the conglomerate appears to lack compelling economic purpose of a socially redeeming kind. Since enthusiasts of received microtheory have been reluctant to concede that a corporate control problem has even existed, they have had little to offer in the way of a rationale for the conglomerate firm. Once such frictions are admitted, however, there is plainly a case for encouraging, or at least not impeding, organizational innovations which have the potential to attenuate internal organizational distortions of a managerial discretion kind. Subject to the qualifications about organization form, which I have repeatedly emphasized, the conglomerate has attractive properties both because it makes the market for corporate control more credible, thereby inducing self-policing among otherwise opportunistic managements, and because it promotes the reallocation of resources to high-yield uses. Except, therefore, among giant-sized firms, where the risk of offsetting political distortions is seriously posed, a more sympathetic posture on the part of the antitrust enforcement agencies towards conglomerates would seem warranted.

Dewey has described the role of economists in antitrust as follows:

The important issues in the control of monopoly are 'economic' in the sense that judges and administrators are compelled to make decisions in the light of what they think the business world is 'really' like, and it is the task of economists through research and reflection to provide them with an increasingly accurate picture.[187]

To the consternation of administrators and judges alike, the picture provided by received microtheory is sometimes vague and at other times simplistic. Transaction-cost analysis is intended to supplement received microtheory in such circumstances.

NOTES

1. To be sure, these models are sometimes tailored before applying them to particular antitrust problems. Examples of the application of received microtheory to antitrust issues are E. Singer, *Antitrust Economics* (1968); Baxter, 'Legal Restrictions on Exploitation, of the Patent-Monopoly:– An Economic Analysis', *Yale Law Journal*, **76** (267), (1966) Williamson, 'Wage Rates as a Barrier to Entry: The Pennington Case in Perspective', *Quarterly Journal of Economics*, **82** (85) (1968).

2. More generally, the issues posed involve an assessment of markets and hierarchies. For a discussion of these issues, see Williamson, 'Markets and Hierarchies: Some Elementary Considerations', *American Economic Review*, **63** May 1973, p.316; Williamson, 'Markets and Hierarchies: Analysis and Antitrust Implications' (August 1973) (unpublished paper held by author). This approach is similar to that advocated by J. Commons, *Institutional Economics* (1934), who took the position that the transaction

constituted the ultimate unit of investigation. Commons, however, had to fashion many of his transactional concepts himself, while I am able to draw, 40 years later, on much more extensive literature in both economics and organization theory. This is a considerable advantage.

3. For example the marketing practices of Arnold, Schwinn & Co. to which the Antitrust Division objected, can usefully be examined in transaction-cost terms. See *United States v. Arnold, Schwinn & Co.*, 388 US 365 (1967).

4. P. Areeda, *Antitrust Analysis*, **4** (1967).

5. In setting out what I think to be the main distinctions between the conventional and transactional approaches, I concede at the outset that my discussion of received microtheory is highly simplified. It is the theory of the firm as that appears in the conventional intermediate price theory textbook. In as much as I often find such a tactic to be a source of considerable irritation when reviewing the work of others who study the behaviour of the modern corporation, I resort to it with some reluctance. My defence is that the simplified presentation is an economical way to expose the issues.

6. This assumes that the firms in question behave in an independent (non-collusive) manner.

7. Among the leading types of models for these purposes are Cournot models and their variants, and entry-barrier models, which make allowance for potential competition. For an elegant review and extension of Cournot models, see L. Telser, *Competition, Collusion, and Game Theory* (1972). A classic example of entry-barrier models is Modigliani, 'New Developments on the Oligopoly Front', *Journal of Political Economy*, **66** (215) (1958).

8. For a discussion of partial equilibrium welfare economics, see Harberger, 'Three Basic Postulates for Applied Welfare Economics: An Interpretive Essay', *Journal of Economic Literature*, **9** (785) (1971).

9. See Williamson, 'Economies as an Antitrust Defense: The Welfare Tradeoff', *American Economic Review*, **58** March 1968, p.20.

10. The discussion in this section draws on Williamson, 'The Vertical Integration of Production: Market Failure Considerations', *American Economic Review*, **61** May 1971, p.112, and Williamson (1973).

11. See e.g., Arrow, 'The Organization of Economic Activity: Issues Pertinent to the Choice of Market Versus Nonmarket Allocation', in *The Analysis and Evaluation of Public Expenditures: The PPB System 47* (Subcomm. on Economy in Gov't of the Joint Economic Comm., 91st Cong., 1st Sess. (Comm. Print) 1969).

12. See e.g. J. Meade, *The Controlled Economy* (1971), pp.147-88.

13. See e.g. Hurwicz, 'On Informationally Decentralized Systems' in *Decision and Organization* (1972), p.297.

14. See e.g. H. Simon, *Administrative Behaviour* (1957). For a discussion of the limits of internal organization, see Williamson, 'Limits of Internal Organization with Special Reference to the Vertical Integration of Production' in *Industrial Management: East and West* (1973), p.199.

15. See e.g. E. Goffman, *Strategic Interaction* (1969).

16. This is merely a necessary but not sufficient condition for internal organization to supplant the market. Internal organization also experiences distortion. Shifting a transaction from the market to a firm requires that a net efficiency gain be shown.

17. H. Simon, *Models of Man* (1957), p.198; (emphasis in original).

18. The implications for contractual purposes of joining bounded rationality with

uncertainty are suggested by the following description of the decision process:

For even moderately complex problems . . . the entire decision tree cannot be generated. There are several reasons why this is so: one is the size of the tree. The number of alternative paths in complex decision problems is very large . . . . A second reason is that in most decision situations, unlike chess, neither the alternative paths nor a rule for generating them is available . . . . A third reason is the problem of estimating consequences . . . . For many problems, consequences of alternatives are difficult, if not impossible, to estimate. The comprehensive decision model is not feasible for most interesting decision problems.

Feldman and Kanter, 'Organizational Decision-Making', in *Handbook of Organization*, ed. J. March (1965), p.615. The infeasibility, or prohibitive cost, of describing the comprehensive decision tree and making *ex ante* optimal choices at every node means that collusive agreements must, except in implausibly simple circumstances, be highly incomplete documents.

A specific illustration of bounded rationality in the large corporation is afforded by the statement of R.H. Davies, President of Electric Autolite Company at the time of the Ford-Autolite merger. He testified on deposition as follows:

Electric Autolite was 'concerned' because, when Champion Spark Plug Company 'went public' in 1958, 'the figures that came out were very large—showing very large profits' and 'when Ford saw those figures and saw how much profit there was in it' Electric Autolite 'felt' that 'the very essence of that much profit going to a supplier would be enough to make Ford think in terms of integration.'

Trial Memorandum for Defendant Ford Motor Co., pp.14-15, *United States v. Ford Motor Co.*, 286 F. Supp. 407, 435 (E.D. Mich. 1968) (violation of Clayton Act found), 315 F.Supp. 372 (E.D. Mich. 1970) (divesture ordered), *aff'd*, 405 US 562 (1972). The example is interesting because it suggests that as large and successful a firm as the Ford Motor Company, with its staff of engineers, cost accountants and financial analysts, failed to discern the underlying profitability of spark plug manufacture until Champion went public (Champion was the first spark plug firm to go public). In a world of unbounded rationality, such disclosure would be unnecessary to stimulate Ford's interest.

19. In circumstances, however, where prices are sufficient statistics, see T. Koopmans, *Three Essays on the State of Economics* (1957), pp.41-54, reliance on the price system serves to economize on bounded rationality. See Hayek, 'The Use of Knowledge in Society', *American Economic Review*, 35 (519) (1945).
20. Williamson (1971).
21. This is over-simple. Internal organization also provides for contingencies by developing what are referred to as 'performance programmes', which are sometimes quite elaborate. Such programmes are more easily adapted to unforeseen contingencies than are inter-firm contracts, for the reasons given in the text. For a discussion of performance programmes, see J. March and H. Simon, *Organizations* (1958).

22. O. Williamson, *Corporate Control and Business Behaviour* (1970), pp.120-35. Internal organization affords two further benefits: it helps to overcome conditions where one party holds information not available to the other without some expense (information impactedness), because internal audits are more powerful than external, and is sometimes able to reduce uncertainty by promoting convergent expectations. Both of these are important but less basic to the present argument than the effects of internal organization on bounded rationality and opportunism.

23. See Williamson (1973).

24. See A. Chandler, *Strategy and Structure* (1962); Williamson (1970).

25. So-called 'second-best' issues are assumed away here and throughout the article.

26. So that a breakeven problem will not be posed if output is set at Q^*, I assume that scale economies are exhausted before this output is reached.

27. If the output of the industry in question is used as an intermediate rather than strictly as a final product, factor distortions at the other stages of production may be induced. See McKenzie, 'Ideal Output and the Interdependence of Firms', *Economic Journal*, **61** (785) (1951). For simplicity, let these be assumed away.

28. Generalizing the analysis by expressing the transaction costs of discerning true customer valuations and policing resale restrictions as a continuous function of output is relatively easy but yields little that the simplified assumptions do not. (One difference to be noted is that the price discriminating output will be less than the social optimum, Q^*.) The analysis can likewise be generalized to make the degree of precision of price discrimination a decision variable.

29. The discussion in the text assumes, implicitly, that the uniform pricing monopolist can price at P_m without inducing entry. If, however, the entry forestalling price ($\tilde{P}$) is les than P_m, the initial position to be evaluated is a larger output and lower price than that discussed above. For fixed T, the welfare gains of price discrimination are further reduced. (In all likelihood an entry threat will attenuate the private gains as well).

30. Williamson (1971).

31. Stigler, 'The Division of Labor is Limited by the Extent of the Market', *Journal of Political Economy*, **59** (185) (1951).

32. Stigler employs the separability assumption for convenience; relaxing it complicates but does not alter the general argument.

33. Stigler (1951), p.188.

34. For a discussion of learning by doing, see P. Doeringer and M. Piore, *Internal Labor Markets and Manpower Analysis* (1971).

35. Mergers would permit the firms involved to realize economies of scale with respect to the decreasing cost activity in question. Such mergers might also, however, result in market power. That such mergers are attractive in a private benefit sense is clear, but social net benefits need not obtain. See Williamson (1968).

36. Again, this is because the market for human capital is imperfect. Firm X cannot simply hire firm Y's experienced employees away without incurring very considerable transfer costs. The learning-by-doing knowledge is thus impacted in firm Y.

37. J. Bain, *Industrial Organization* (1968), p.381.

38. A. Smith, *The Wealth of Nations* (Cannan ed., 1937), pp.4-5.

39. The specialization of risk-bearing and strategic decision-making may also favour common ownership and the replacement of autonomous contracting by an employment relation.
40. Stigler, (1951), p.191.
41. Bork, 'Vertical Integration and Competitive Processes', in *Public Policy Toward Mergers*, (1969), pp.139, 148.
42. W. Bowman, *Patent and Antitrust Law: A Legal and Economic Appraisal* (1973), p.59. The discussion in this section follows Williamson, 'Book Review' *Yale Law Journal*, **83** (647) (1974).
43. Examples of information impactedness are given in this section and the sections that follow. For a specific illustration, see especially the text on implementation under uncertainty in section III below.
44. As H.B. Malmgren has noted, in a related context,

Some firms will see opportunities, but be unable to communicate their own information and expectations favourably to bankers, and thus be unable to acquire finance, or need to pay a higher charge for the capital borrowed. Bankers and investors of funds in turn will be attracted to those firms which have shown in the past an ability to perceive and exploit effectively new opportunities, as against new firms which can only give their word that what they think is good is in fact good.

Malmgren, 'Information, Expectations and the Theory of the Firm', *Quarterly Journal of Economics*, **75** (417) (1961).
45. See text accompanying notes 34 and 36.
46. If the knowledge advantage of the experienced firm is dispersed among a *team* of individuals, negotiations to hire away the team are likely to be prohibitively expensive.
47. This assumes that the cost of capital varies directly with the perceived risk of the incremental investment, *ceteris paribus*.
48. Malmgren (1961), pp.401, 405.
49. Provisionally, I define a very concentrated industry to be one where the four-firm concentration ratio exceeds 80 per cent.
50. Economies of scale at stage II can also serve as an impediment to entry if the monopolist has integrated into stage II. See Williamson (1974), p.656.
51. Coase, 'The Nature of the Firm' in *Readings in Price Theory* (1952), pp.338-9.
52. Stigler (1951), pp.190-1.
53. For a discussion of private carriage versus ICC regulated motor transport, see L. Schwartz, *Free Enterprise and Economic Organization* (4th edn. 1972), pp.359-62.
54. Dayan, 'Vertical Integration and Monopoly Regulation', December 1972 (unpublished PhD dissertation, Princeton University).
55. If, however, the condition of entry into the supply stage is easy, small numbers by itself will not occasion monopolistic prices. See Stigler (1951) p.188.
56. McKenzie (1951).
57. That a firm can expect to strike competitive bargains does not, of course, guarantee that it will earn 'normal' profits. This depends on supply and demand conditions. In a growing industry, however, the non-integrated but otherwise qualified entrant should be able to secure a niche for itself without

difficulty, although its profit rate may vary over a business cycle more than do the rates of integrated firms.

58. This assumes that stage II entry is not easy.
59. Vertical integration *within* a stage, I take it, poses no problems for anyone. The rationale here is that supplied above in the context of the pin-making example. Whether economies of vertical integration are realized *between* stages in what appears to be an unconcentrated industry is apt to turn on product differentiation considerations. Some of the components required by firms producing differentiated products may well be firm-specific, in which event a genuine large-numbers supply condition may not be feasible. Where, however, competitive supply terms (both presently and prospectively) can be anticipated, own supply has little to commend it. (On this, see Williamson (1973).)
60. E.g., J.K. Galbraith, *American Capitalism* (1952), p.58. The view that tight oligopoly and monopoly are equivalent is especially prevalent among non-industrial organization specialists.
61. Patinkin, 'Multiple-Plant Firms, Cartels, and Imperfect Competition', *Quarterly Journal of Economics*, **61** (184) (1947).
62. Two important treatments of the oligopoly problem to which I would call attention, but do not discuss here, are L. Telser (1972) and Shubik, 'Information, Duopoly, and Competitive Markets: A Sensitive Analysis', *Kyklos*, **26** (736) (1973). Both develop a useful modelling apparatus to help evaluate the issues.
63. Fellner, *Competition Among The Few* (1949), pp.9-11.
64. Ibid., p.16.
65. Ibid., pp.27-8.
66. Ibid., p.34.
67. Ibid.
68. Ibid., pp.34-5.
69. Ibid., pp.183-4.
70. Ibid., p.185.
71. Ibid., pp.188-9.
72. Ibid., p.129.
73. Ibid., p.135.
74. Ibid., pp.133, 196.
75. G. Stigler, 'A Theory of Oligopoly', *Journal of Political Economy*, **72** (44) (1964).
76. Ibid., p.45.
77. Ibid.
78. Stigler simply assumes 'that the collusion has been effected, and a price structure agreed upon', Ibid., p.46.
79. Profits here are expressed as expected, discounted values.
80. Stigler (1964), p.46.
81. Ibid.
82. Ibid., p.47.
83. Ibid., p.48.
84. Ibid.
85. Ibid.
86. Ibid., pp.48-56.
87. Turner, 'The Definition of Agreement Under the Sherman Act: Conscious Parallelism and Refusals to Deal', *Harvard Law Review*, **75** (655, 658)

(1962).
88. Ibid., p.663.
89. Ibid., pp.663-4.
90. If this interpretation is correct, Turner does not believe such a price to be collusive. Plainly, however, it is—at least in the sense that it is *not* the price that independently acting Cournot duopolists (or triopolists) would charge. Given linear demands and constant marginal costs, the Cournot equilibrium output (q), for each firm, where price interdependence is not taken into account (i.e. the conjectural variation term is zero), is

$$q = \left[\frac{1}{n+1}\right]\bar{Q},$$

where n is the number of firms in the industry and $\bar{Q}$ is the competitive output. The joint profit-maximizing output (q*) for each such firm, by contrast, is $q^* = \frac{1}{2n}\bar{Q}$. Plainly, $q^* < q$ for $n > 1$. (For $n = 1$, both formulae yield the monopoly output).
91. Turner, (1962), p.664.
92. Ibid. Note again, as pointed out in note 90, that independently operating Cournot duopolists do not charge competitive prices yet are not colluding in any usual sense either. Turner seems implicitly to hold that independent pricing will yield the competitive solution. Hence, any price that exceeds the competitive price is regarded as an indication of interdependence realized. Posner appears also to be of this view. See text accompanying notes 98-107.
93. Turner, (1962), p.666.
94. Ibid., pp.667-8.
95. Ibid., p.669.
96. Ibid., p.671.
97. Turner, 'The Scope of Antitrust and Other Economic Regulatory Policies', *Harvard Law Review*, **82** (1207) (1969). For a related discussion, see Williamson, 'Dominant Firms and the Monopoly Problem: Market Failure Considerations', *Harvard Law Review*, **85** (1512) (1972).
98. Posner, 'Oligopoly and the Antitrust Laws: A Suggested Approach'. *Stanford Law Review*, **21** (1562) (1969).
99. Ibid., p.1571.
100. Ibid., pp.1568, 1578.
101. Ibid., pp.1568-9.
102. Ibid., p.1575.
103. Ibid., p.1570.
104. Ibid., p.1578 (*emphasis added*).
105. 15 U.S.C. ss. 1 (1970).
106. Posner, (1969) pp.1578-93.
107. Ibid., p.1591. This conclusion appears, however, to be unwarranted because independently operating Cournot oligopolists do not produce competitive outputs. See note 90.
108. Telser (1972) does not make this last assumption. His analysis differs from mine partly for this reason.
109. I do not, however, mean to suggest that the antitrust statutes prohibiting collusion are without purpose. They certainly compound the typical oligopolist's problems.
110. See pp.214-19.
111. In the sense of Williamson (1970), pp.109-81.

112. For an operational treatment of the problem of joint profit-maximization in a multi-product firm where (1) product lines are *independent*, (2) only *heuristic* rather than full-blown optimization methods are attempted and (3) only the *financial* decision is considered. See Hamilton and Moses, 'An Optimization Model for Corporate Financial Planning', *Operations Research*, 21 (677) (1972). Their model contains approximately 1,000 variables and 750 constraints, ibid., p.686, and tests not one but various configurations of the strategic variables. Replicating such an arrangement by inter-firm agreement boggles the mind. Complicating the analysis further to include interdependent products (which, of course, is the case of oligopoly) and the full range of decision variables discussed in the text reveals the manifest impossibility of attempting comprehensively to maximize joint profits—even by heuristic simulation methods, much less by determinate written agreements.

113. Again, however, the view expressed in note 109 applies.

114. It is possible, of course, that oligopolists could reach agreement on some aspects of the market more easily than on others. Faced with diminishing marginal returns to their efforts to obtain an agreement (transaction costs), they would probably settle on an agreement of less than comprehensive scope. It is also possible, however, that the inability to agree on some matters would frustrate any agreement whatsoever, even on matters which might be settled if they could be considered in isolation.

115. See *Monitoring Execution* below.

116. Unlike the preceding and succeeding subsections, the argument here assumes that joint profit maximization is not attempted.

117. If the state of the world is described by a vector of n components, each of which can take on only one of two values, the number of possible states is 2^n. For $n=8$, which hardly constitutes a complex description of the state of the world, the number of possible states is 256, which is impressively large.

118. See *Joint Gains* above.

119. For discussions of defence contracting, see F. Scherer, *The Weapons Acquisition Process* (1964), and Williamson,, 'The Economics of Defense Contracting: Incentives and Performance', in *Issues in Defense Economics*, ed. R. McKean (1967), p.217.

120. Punitive market responses require firms to incur short-run profit sacrifices in the hope of discouraging future chisellers and returning the current chiseller to the fold.

121. Although the opportunistic behaviour described mainly reflects an aggressive effort to realize short-run individual gains, to the disadvantage of the group, firms may also engage in such behaviour for defensive reasons. Defensive opportunism reflects a lack of confidence in the trustworthiness of other members of the group and an unwillingness to risk being put to a strategic disadvantage.

While aggressive or assertive opportunism is to be expected whenever the viability of any particular firm is threatened, whatever the degree of 'maturity' of the firms in an industry, defensive opportunism will vary inversely with maturity. Because defensive opportunism, if widely practised, is mutually disadvantageous, and because this is self-evident to the parties, organizational learning is normally to be expected. Among other things, ways of announcing or signalling intentions in ways that will not be misinterpreted as aggressive, when no such intention exists, are apt to develop. Unless, therefore, the industry is one in which new entrants regularly appear, with obvious disruptive consequences for inter-firm learning and accommodation, occasions for defensive opportunism are likely to decline as an industry matures.

122. For a discussion of adaptive, sequential decisionmaking, see H. Chernoff and L. Moses, *Elementary Decision Theory* (1959), pp.166-94.
123. K. Arrow, *On the Limits of Organization* (1974).
124. See Williamson, (1972), pp.1528-30.
125. For some discussions and examples of cheating and the breakdown of oligopolistic collusion, see Patinkin, (1947), pp.200-4; Posner (1969), p.1570; R. Smith, *Corporations in Crisis* (1966), pp.113-66.
126. See Williamson, (1970), pp.54-73, 109-19.
127. Turner, (1962), p.669.
128. *United States v. United States Gypsum Co.*, Crim. No. 73-347 (W.D. Pa., filed 27 Dec 1973); *cf. United States v. United States Gypsum Co.*, Crim. No. 1042-73 (D.D.C., filed 27 Dec 1973).
129. *In re Kellog Co.*, No. 8883 (FTC, filed 24 Jan 1972).
130. See note 112.
131. C. Kaysen and D. Turner, *Antitrust Policy* (1959), pp.114-15.
132. Wasteful selling or product development expenditures among differentiated product oligopolists are sometimes observed, however. Specific steps might properly be taken to restrict this were a dominant firm to be split into independent, differentiated parts.
133. See sources cited in note 97. The reader may find a summary of the transactional approach and its antecedents useful at this point. The approaches often coincide, but there are many contrasts. The problem of oligopoly under the transaction-cost approach, as under Fellner's approach, is treated as a problem of interdependence recognized. Also, as with Fellner, the multidimensional nature of the interdependence issue is emphasized; price coordination is only a part of the problem, especially in industries with differentiated products. But whereas Fellner attributes the problems of interdependence to the complexities of discounting uncertain future values and in pooling risks, I put the issue in terms of 'contracting' about contingent claims. While these approaches are not unrelated, the latter highlights the issues of coming to an agreement and enforcing it which permits us to draw expressly on the transaction cost framework sketched out in section I. A more complete assessment of the problems of oligopolistic collusion is thereby afforded.

Stigler's analysis runs almost entirely in terms of prices. Moreover, he takes the collusive agreement itself as given, focusing attention instead on cheating and on statistical inference techniques for detecting cheaters. While this last is very useful, and calls attention in an interesting way to aspects of the oligopoly problem that others have rather neglected, it is also highly incomplete. The discussion in sub-section 3 reveals that monitoring is only one of a series of steps in the oligopolistic collusion, and not plainly the one that warrants greatest attention.

Both Turner and Posner also give primary attention to prices in their discussions of oligopoly. But their similarity to each other ends there. Whereas Turner emphasizes tacit collusion of the recognized interdependence sort and finds injunctive relief to be inefficacious, Posner regards interdependence theory as unsatisfactory, and discusses oligopoly instead of a cartel problem, concluding that injunctive relief is appropriate.

The spirit of my discussion is somewhat akin to Posner's cartel analysis, but the specifics plainly differ. I restate the problem in terms of what a *lawful* cartel could accomplish. Also, I am much more concerned than Posner with the details of and impediments to successful inter-firm agreements. Finally, I agree with Turner that injunctive relief in highly concentrated, homogeneous product, entry impeded, mature industries is unlikely to be effective. Structural relief is indicated here instead.

134. See text accompanying notes 41-42.
135. Peterson, 'Corporate Control and Capitalism', *Quarterly Journal of Economics*, **79** (1, 11) (1965).
136. Ibid., p.21; emphasis added.
137. Ibid.; emphasis added.
138. Ibid.
139. Smiley estimates that 'per share transaction costs are approximately 14% of the market value of the shares after a successful [tender] offer' and suggests that such a cost level warrants 'skepticism about the efficacy of the tender offer in constraining managers to act in the best interests of their shareholders'. R. Smiley, *The Economics of Tender Offers*, July 1973 (unpublished PhD dissertation, Stanford University), pp.124-5.
140. This assumes that the hierarchical structure and internal control processes of the conglomerate satisfy the requirements that I have stipulated elsewhere (Williamson, (1970), pp.120-53). Although there are certainly other types of conglomerates, those which lack for an underlying efficiency rationale (as contrasted with a temporary financial rationale) will presumably be sorted out in the long run. Those which pose financial problems are best dealt with by the SEC. My discussion sidesteps these and focuses on antitrust issues.
141. Depth of information problems can, however, appear as the specialized firm becomes very large. See Williamson, (1970), pp.14-40.
142. For a somewhat similar interpretation of the conglomerate, see Alchian and Demsetz, 'Production, Information Costs, and Economic Organization', *American Economic Review*, **62** December 1972, pp.777-95. For a study of the use of the computer to extend the firm's capacity to deal effectively with a wider set of investment alternatives, see Hamilton and Moses, (1972). For a cross-sectional study of conglomerates (which, however, does not make organization form distinctions), see Weston and Mansinghka, 'Tests of the Efficiency Performance of Conglomerate Firms', *Journal of Finance*, **26** (419) (1971).
143. R. Posner, *Economic Analysis of Law* (1972), p.204.
144. For a report that approaches this position, see *U.S. President's Task Force on Productivity and Competition*.
145. Some contend that reciprocity has attractive efficiency properties, in that it facilitates priceshading in otherwise rigid price circumstances. While I concede that reciprocity can be used in this way, I do not find it an especially compelling economic rationale for the conglomerate. Surely the entire conglomerate movement is not to be explained in these terms. Also, I think it useful to appreciate that reciprocity can have inefficiency consequences. Once begun, perhaps as a price-shading technique, it may be continued because it suits the bureaucratic preferences of the sales staff.
146. Solo, 'New Maths and Old Sterilites', *Saturday Review*, 22 Jan 1972, pp.47-8.

147. It is interesting in this connection to note that Gerneral Motors' executives went to considerable effort in the 1920s to apprise the business community at large of the character and importance of the multidivisional structure which they had devised, but to little avail.
148. See Chandler, (1962).
149. Blake, 'Conglomerate Mergers and the Antitrust Law', *Columbia Law Review*, **73** (555) (1973).
150. Ibid.
151. For an attempt to delimit the attack, see the discussion in section IV (3) below.
152. Thus the district court in the ITT-Hartford Insurance case was prepared to dismiss reciprocity arguments by the government because of organization form considerations. *United States v. International Tel. & Tel. Corp.*, 306 F.Supp. 766, 779, 782-83, 790, 795, (D.Conn. 1969) (hold separate order); *United States v. International Tel. & Tel. Corp.*, 324 F.Supp. 19, 45 (D.Conn. 1979) (judgement for defendant).
153. For an interpretation of the transformation of 'inside contracting' which was practised by New England manufacturing firms in the late 1900s, to vertical integration for transaction-cost reasons, see Williamson, (1973), pp.322-4.
154. Blake (1973), pp.562-3, 572-3.
155. Ibid., pp.571-2. Blake observes in this connection that '[O]ne objective of antitrust policy is to preserve a competitive system—a structure of the economy in which all economic units in the unregulated sector are subject to the continuing discipline of competitive market forces. The creation of vast conglomerate enclaves in which decisions with respect to resource use are insulated from these forces is inconsistent with the basic tenets of antitrust policy', (Ibid., p.574).
   I submit that, subject to the condition that the internal resource reallocations result in higher social as well as private yields—which is normally to be expected when investments are shifted from activities with lower to higher marginal profitability, one of the leading objectives of antitrust policy is being served.
156. For a discussion, see Williamson, (1970), pp.143-4. For a fascinating study of the internal resource-allocation process at work in one major corporation, see Hamilton and Moses, (1972). I concede that the system developed for and used by the International Utilities Corporation represents the leading edge of internal resource allocation capabilities in a conglomerate firm but it is not an isolated instance. Firms such as ITT have had a similar, albeit less formal, approach to the internal resource-allocation problem for years. See Address, 'Management Must Manage', by Harold Geneen, before the Investment Group of Hartford, Conn., 15 Feb 1968.
157. Blake, (1973), pp.566, 578.
158. Ibid., pp.574, 579. See note 155.
159. Ibid., p.570.
160. F. Scherer, *Industrial Market Structure and Economic Performance* (1970), pp.278-80.
161. Ibid., p.279.
162. Blake, (1973), pp.557, n.13.
163. Ibid., p.569.
164. J. Markham, *Conglomerate Enterprise and Public Policy* (1973), p.176.
165. Blake, (1973), pp.559-69.

166. Ibid., p.590.
167. Ibid., pp.590-1.
168. For the purpose of size control, a large firm that engages in a series of toe-hold acquisitions within a specified time interval might be required to spin off assets comparable to the aggregate of those acquired if some absolute value is exceeded. Even small percentage positions in some industries (e.g. petroleum) can represent quite large absolute asset values. Individual toehold acquisitions in these circumstances might exceed the absolute asset value threshold of, say $100 million. A spin-off might be indicated.
169. However, see the qualification in note 168.
170. See, Turner and Williamson, 'Market Structure in Relation to Technical and Organizational Innovation', in *Proceedings of the International Conference on Monopolies, Mergers and Restrictive Practices*, (J. Heath, ed. 1971), p.127.
171. Though it varies somewhat with organizational structure, projects for which only small-scale commercialization is anticipated are not ones for which large firms are typically well suited. For a novel organizational 'solution', see Sabin, 'At Nuclepore They Don't Work for G.E. Anymore', *Fortune*, **88** December 1973, p.145.
172. Moving from a prototype to a commercial stage commonly involves a substantial investment in organizational infrastructure, much of which has no value should the enterprise fail. Lacking a known performance record and tangible assets to secure the investment, lenders are apprehensive to invest except on a sequential basis. The risks of opportunism, given information impactedness, are perceived as too great.
173. Hofstadter, 'What Happened to the Antitrust Movement', in *The Business Establishment*, ed. E. Cheit (1964), p.113.
174. See A. Sampson, *The Sovereign State of ITT* (1973).
175. Blake (1973), pp.574, 576, 578, 579, 591. That giant size procures political favours does not imply that atomistic organization (e.g. farmers) is the favoured economic alternative. Often with the latter, however, the favours are more likely to be transparent.
176. See Coase, 'Industrial Organization: A Proposal for Research', in *Policy Issues and Research Opportunities in Industrial Organization*, ed. V. Fuchs (1972), pp.59, 67.
177. For a discussion of the market for corporate control, see Manne, 'Mergers and the Market for Corporate Control', *Journal of Political Economy*, **73** (110) (1965).
178. See notes 152-9 and accompanying text. Although I suspect that there is little real cost advantage that an already giant-sized firm can confer on an acquired firm that could not be as (or more) effectively conferred by a somewhat less gargantuan enterprise, it may be useful not to prohibit such acquisitions altogether so as to preserve the market for corporate control. If requiring the giant-sized firm to divest itself of comparable assets tends to forestall bureaucratic stagnation in the firm and has beneficial political consequences, a reasonable result would seem to have been reached.
179. See text accompanying notes 150-7.
180. Beatrice Foods Co., [1970-1973 Transfer Binder] Trade Reg. Rep. paras 20, 121, pp.22, 103, 22, 109, (F.T.C. 1972); (emphasis added).
181. Turner, 'Conglomerate Mergers and Section 7 of the Clayton Act' *Harvard*

Law Review, **78** (1313) (1965).

182. J. Bain, *Barriers to New Competition* (1956).
183. One might, however, wish to prevent entry by acquisition by 'dominant firms', the presence of which discourages rivalry (for deep-pocket reasons) and otherwise transforms the market in uncertain ways. The Proctor & Gamble acquisition of Clorox has been characterized by Justice Marshall in these terms. *United States v. Falstaff Bewing Corp.*, 410 U.S. 526, 558-59 (1973) (Marshall, J., concurring).
184. Diamond, 'Comment' in *Frontiers of Quantitative Economics*, ed. M. Intriligator (1971), pp.29, 31.
185. Simon (1957), pp.198-9.
186. E.g. A. Pigou, *The Economics of Welfare* (4th edn. 1952), pp.280-2.
187. D. Dewey, *Monopoly in Economics and Law* (1959), p.i.

12. On the Political Economy of Antitrust: Grounds for Cautious Optimism

SOME INDICATIONS OF PROGRESS

Although there is an ebb and flow to antitrust, and recent changes may be reversed, it is my judgment that antitrust has made remarkable progress during the past decade—and I would say that a decade is about the appropriate interval at which to take such observations. Some of the areas in which progress has occurred include greater respect for economies in assessing social effects, better understanding of vertical integration and vertical restrictions, a deeper understanding of predatory pricing, greater scepticism with unadorned market share analysis, and a delimitation on entry barrier arguments.

Treatment of Economies

The 1960s opened with the Federal Trade Commission taking the position that the 'necessary proof of violation of the statute consists of types of evidence showing that the acquiring firm possesses significant power in some markets *or* that its over-all organization gives it a decisive advantage in efficiency over its smaller rivals.'[1] In other words, efficiency and the prospect of extending efficiency were regarded unfavourably by the FTC in assessing whether a merger should be permitted. This perverse use of efficiency reasoning has mainly disappeared since, but vigilance is warranted. The Justice Department made similar arguments in resisting the acquisition of the Mead Corporation by Occidental Petroleum in 1978. The government's lead attorney advised the court that the acquisition was objectionable because it would permit Mead to construct a large greenfield plant, which was the 'most efficient and cost effective' investment, and that this would disadvantage Mead's rivals.[2]

I am prepared to believe, however, that this contorted view of antitrust economies is an aberration—a manifestation of 'creative lawyering' (see section on Market Share Analysis)—rather than a return to Foremost Dairy standards. For the most part, the past decade is one in which greater respect has been accorded to economies, both in the courts[3] and in the legislatures.[4]

Parametric analysis of economies versus market power effects has doubtlessly contributed to this result. Such analysis is useful in two respects. First, it shows the importance of being sensitive to economies if economic rather than emotive consequences are to be accorded serious weight. Secondly, and every bit as important, parametric analysis often permits difficult issues of quantitative net benefit assessment to be bypassed. Thus what difference does it make that demand elasticities are imperfectly known if, throughout the full range of relevant elasticities, the same net-benefit assessment obtains.

Put differently, thinking in net-benefit terms does not require that issues be addressed in fully quantitative terms. Conceptual benefits obtain by simply getting the issues straight, which would have avoided the mistakes made by the FTC in *Foremost Dairies* and by the Antitrust Division in resisting the Occidental Mead takeover attempt. If tradeoffs are involved, and if a net negative (or a net positive) assessment obtains over the relevant range of parameter values, a 'refined' net benefit assessment is unnecessary. That the matter of economies as an antitrust defence does not elicit the same hostility now that it did in the 1960s is presumably because an appreciation for these conceptual gains, including the power of parametric analysis, is now more widespread.

Vertical Market Relations

The antitrust atmosphere that prevailed in the area of vertical market restrictions in the 1960s was one of hostility. Donald Turner expressed it as follows, 'I approach territorial and customer restrictions not hospitably in the common law tradition, but inhospitably in the tradition of antitrust law.'[5] Such reasoning was responsible for the mistaken arguments in *Schwinn*.[6]

In an unusual reversal of precedent, the Supreme Court has recently overruled *Schwinn* in the *GTE-Sylvania* case.[7] Among the reasons for this surely has been the growing awareness that 'nonstandard' modes of organization usually arise in response to economizing opportunities. Accordingly, except as rather special structural preconditions are satisfied, vertical restraints should not be regarded with animosity.

This position has taken a long time to be recognized. Among the contributing factors was the stream of criticism provided by the Chicago School (Director, Bork, Posner, and others, like Baxter) increasing appreciation for transaction cost reasoning (Williamson, Phillips), and Turner's dramatic switch of position.[8] That reversals of bad precedent occur in the face of such criticism is surely a healthy indication of progress in antitrust.

Predatory Pricing

The leading predatory pricing case in the 1960s was *Utah Pie*.[9] Although the protectionist reasoning that the Court employed in this case has not been expressly reversed, the unsatisfactory quality of the opinion has been widely remarked[10] and considerable effort has been made to provide a more substantial economic basis for evaluating predatory pricing.

The standards that will eventually emerge are still unclear. As Paul Joskow has observed, the lower courts adopted the Areeda-Turner average-variable cost rule for evaluating predatory pricing with undue haste.[11]

First, this rule has not been accorded generally favourable reviews by economists; the rave reviews come from the courts. It does not represent a triumph of economic efficiency over political considerations. Rather, I believe that this rule has attracted so much judicial attention because it provided a way of disposing of cases that have arisen in an area where there are vague and conflicting rules proposed by political antitrusters, that often had to be applied to cases that seemed only to seek the preservation of particular competitors. I attribute the adoption of this particular rule to the desire of the judiciary to extract itself from the chaos of existing case law , not to their 'getting religion'. I attribute the elegant footnotes to their law clerks. I believe that we are seeing adopted what some of us view as an inappropriate rule from the perspective of economic efficiency because our friends the 'political antitrusters' were given too much rope. The courts were presented with vague notions about the value of small business, then were told that they shouldn't confuse individual competitors with competition, saw discussions of bigness *per se* confused with mergers of manufacturing of wooden spoons, heard the phrase competitive process a few times, and were left with nothing useful for coming to a decision. It was almost inevitable that a simpler *per se* rule would be eagerly adopted, whether it evolved from appropriate considerations of economic efficiency or not. If average variable cost is a bad rule I suggest that we have it because of the void that was left in this area by the political antitrusters, not because of triumph of economic efficiency considerations in the interpretation of antitrust statutes.

To be sure, the courts were in a difficult bind. Faced with the need to decide cases, the courts could not wait until the Areeda-Turner rule had been tested by academic commentary. Fortunately, however, such commentary has been quick to appear.[12] Much of this has emphasized inter-temporal efficiency. The likelihood that better tests for remunerative pricing will be adopted appears to be improving.[13]

Market Share Analysis

When confronted with a difficult case that appears to be beyond the reach of the antitrust statutes, there is a strong temptation to resort to what John Shenefield has referred to as 'creative lawyering'[14]—which is a euphemism for bringing a contrived case. Such a temptation is especially great in the merger area, where the language of the statute is very broad. If an adverse effect can be shown 'in any line of commerce, in any section of the country' all that a creative lawyer needs to do is define his lines of commerce and geographic markets with sufficient imagination.

Knee jerk reliance on market share analysis, however, has also come under increasing criticism. Partly this is a reaction to the arbitrary standards of the sixties and partly it reflects an appreciation that valued economizing purposes are frequently served by reconfigurating economic activity. The degree of disenchantment with a market-shares based approach to antitrust is illustrated by Richard Schmalensee's recent paper dealing with the *Rea–Lemon* case and Darius Gaskin's comments thereon.[15] The economizing purposes served by reconfiguring economic activity have already been remarked in connection with the discussion of vertical market relations. More generally, there is a growing awareness that transaction costs are central to an understanding of the organization of economic activity and that earlier antitrust traditions in which these considerations are ignored or suppressed miss much of what makes a high performance enterprise economy function.

Barriers to Entry

Barriers to entry analysis as a guide to antitrust policy peaked in the 1960s. The term carries an anticompetitive connotation and the more militant members of the barriers to entry tradition plainly believed that any action that had the effect of impeding entry by new rivals or disadvantaging extant firms should be regarded as anticompetitive and should be proscribed. Mergers that yield efficiencies were among the objectionable practices. Advertising economies were held to be particularly offensive. This view was pressed by the government and adopted by the Supreme Court in the 1967 decision regarding the illegality of Proctor & Gamble's acquisition of Clorox.[16]

Confusion on this matter continues to this day. Thus Leonard Weiss in contrasting Bain with Stigler on barriers to entry, insists that economies of scale be regarded as a barrier: 'To characterize such a situation as displaying "no barrier" is to give the term barrier to entry a meaning that is not very useful in evaluating market power.'[17] Why we should be preoccupied with market power to the exclusion of possible economies is not explained, but that is plainly the thrust of entry barrier analysis and its enthusiasts.

Fortunately, however, matters are changing. Bork, among others, has been instrumental in affecting the shift in emphasis, 'The question for antitrust is whether there exist artificial entry barriers. These must be barriers that are not forms of superior efficiency and which yet prevent the forces of the market . . . from operating to erode market positions not based on efficiency.'[18] Thus merit outcomes, not structure *per se*, are what matter. The distinction between remediable and irremediable impediments to entry is important in this regard. Little useful public purpose is served, and a considerable risk of public policy mischief results when conditions of an irremediable kind—that is, those for which no superior outcome can be realized—are brought under fire.

Remediable impediments, by contrast, are ones which, if removed, would lead to superior social outcomes judged in welfare (not market structure) terms. That this distinction is making headway is disclosed by the recent shift in position by Comanor and Wilson on advertising. Whereas previously they had emphasized the adverse entry effects of advertising,[19] now they adopt a more symmetrical position and counsel that the effects of advertising should be evaluated in welfare rather than market structure terms: 'to the extent that consumer information is increased in the same process that monopoly power is attained, we may be unwilling to adopt specific policy measures directed against the latter for fear of adversely affecting the former.'[20] Furthermore, whereas previously the indictment against advertising tended to be quite broad, it is now recognized that the concerns are 'concentrated in a small number of industries' where advertising-sales ratios are unusually high.[21] Even here, a presumption of net negative consequences is unwarranted.

What this amounts to is that, here as elsewhere, tradeoffs have to be recognized and that informed public policy will not mindlessly pursue 'desirable' market-structure outcomes at the expense of efficiency in its various forms. The view that economies must be recognized as a valid antitrust defence has thus gained ascendancy, despite great initial resistance and a few unreconstructed sceptics. This is a considerable shift from where antitrust enforcement stood in the 1960s. It is the principal basis for my claim that antitrust has witnessed great progress during the past decade.

CONCLUDING REMARKS

My review of antitrust developments of the past decade is a relatively encouraging one. Affirmative regard for economies is now widespread and the importance of an economies defence is broadly recognized. This was not the case a decade ago. Vertical market restrictions and other unfamiliar business practices were regarded with suspicion during the

1960s. By contrast, the possibility that nonstandard practices are driven by transaction-cost economies is widely conceded today. Abuses of market-share analysis and barriers to entry arguments are much less common today. When abuses appear, moreover, they are quickly challenged. Thus whereas much antitrust argument was uninformed by rudimentary price theory and economizing notions in the 1960s, the role of microeconomics is securely established and the importance of economizing on transaction costs is widely recognized today.

The credit for this transformation is diverse. The Chicago School's tough-minded insistence that individual organization issues be viewed 'through the lens of price theory' is certainly a major contributing factor.[22] Advances in transaction cost reasoning and application thereof to a variety of antitrust concerns have also been a factor.[23] The growing interest in industrial organization issues among the current generation of microtheorists has also contributed and, I conjecture, will play an even larger role as efforts are made to sort out what is at stake in the area of strategic behaviour—that is, efforts by established firms to take up advance positions and/or respond contingently to rivalry in ways that discipline actual, and discourage potential, competition. Whether such behaviour exists, what form it takes, how widespread each type is, and what antitrust ramifications attach thereto, are all open to dispute.

The reshaping of the structure-conduct-performance approach to make it more forward-looking and sensitive to tradeoffs has also contributed to the progress.[24] And the increase in the size and quality of the economics staffs in the Antitrust Division and at the Federal Trade Commission have helped assure that bad economic argument gets recognized quickly and that more sophisticated analysis is bought to bear.

The notion that 'ideas, not vested interests' drive outcomes[25] is understandably attractive to academics. Plainly, however, there are public-policy arenas where this is mainly wishful thinking. In particular, realpolitik is apt to crowd ideas where the vested interests are easily organized and the individual stakes are large. Neither, but especially the former, is often the case with antitrust. Accordingly, ideas matter more for antitrust than for many other public-policy issues.

The upshot is that, although good analysis may not have won, it is surely winning. As recent and future refinements are tested and operationalized, I am confident that these will have a useful impact on antitrust as well. To be sure, there will be lags. And the hazards of creative lawyering will be with us always. Occasional setbacks notwithstanding, I do not expect the accomplishments of the past decade to be reversed. Vigilance is nevertheless warranted. Discovering and exposing efficiency consequences will remain among the leading tasks of antitrust scholars.

NOTES

1. In *re* Foremost Dairies, Inc., 60 FTC 944, 1084 (1962), emphasis added.
2. The phrase was employed by the government's lead attorney, Barbara Reeves, in support of Count Four (Elimination of Actual and Potential Competition in Coated Free Sheet Paper), *U.S.* v. *Occidental Petroleum Corporation* (Civil Action No. C-3-78-288).
3. For a discussion, see Williamson, 'Economies as an Antitrust Defense Revisited', *University of Pennsylvania Law Review* 125 (April 1977): 728-9.
4. Ibid, pp.731-3. An economies defence was also incorporated in the recent no-fault monopoly proposal by the National Commission for the Review of Antitrust Laws and Procedures in its Report to the President and the Attorney General (Washington, D.C., 1979), ch.8
5. Turner expressed these views while he was Assistant Attorney General in charge of the Antitrust Division. The statement is attributed to him by Stanley Robinson, 1968 New York State Bar Association, *Antitrust Law Symposium*, p.29.
6. For a summary of the goverment's main arguments in *Schwinn* and a critique thereof, see Williamson 'Assessing Vertical Market Restrictions: Antitrust Ramifications of the Transaction Cost Approach', *University of Pennsylvania Law Review* 127 (April 1979): 975-85
7. *Continental T.V., Inc.* v. *G.T.E. Sylvania Inc.*, 433 U.S. 36 (1977).
8. Turner participated in the Amicus brief with attorneys for the Motor Vehicle Manufacturers Association asking that the *Schwinn* decision be upset. Motion for Leave to File Brief and Brief for Motor Vehicles Manufacturers Association as Amicus Curiae, *Continental T.V., Inc.* v. *G.T.E. Sylvania, Inc.*
9. *Utah Pie Co,* v. *Continental Baking Co.* 386 U.S. 685 (1967).
10. See Bork, *The Antitrust Paradox*, pp.386-389. Also see Posner, *Antitrust Law* pp. 193-194.
11. Paul L. Joskow, 'Comment on The Political Content of Antitrust', in Williamson, ed., *Antitrust Law and Economics,* 1980, p.168
12. Among the relevant papers are F.M. Scherer, 'Predatory Pricing and the Sherman Act: A Comment', *Harvard Law Review* 89 (March 1976): 869-890; Williamson, 'Predatory Pricing: A Strategic and Welfare Analysis', *Yale Law Journal* 87 (December 1977): 284-340; Richard Schmalensee, 'On the Use of Economic Models in Antitrust', *University of Pennsylvania Law Review* 127 (April 1979): 994-1050.
13. Recent court decisions have been more cautious about accepting the Areeda-Turner test than were earlier ones. The Ninth Circuit opinion in *California Computer Products, Inc.* v. *International Business Machines Corp.* reflects this. Memorandum Opinion in *O. Hommel Co* v. *Ferro Corp.* (Civil Action No.76-1299) by the U.S. District Judge William W. Knox likewise expresses scepticism with the Areeda-Turner test.
14. Hon. J.H. Shenefield, Testimony before the Subcommittee on Antitrust and Monopolies of the Committee on the Judiciary, United States Senate, July 18, 1978, p.65.
15. Schmalensee, pp.1004-16, and Gaskin, pp.154-8, in Williamson, ed., *Antitrust Law and Economics* (1980).
16. Bork, *The Antitrust Paradox*, p.310.

17. L.W. Weiss, 'The Structure-Conduct-Performance Paradigm and Antitrust', *University of Pennsylvania Law Review* 127 (April 1969); 1121.
18. Bork, *The Antitrust Paradox*, p.341.
19. W.S. Comanor and T.A. Wilson, 'Advertising, Market Structure, and Performance', *Review of Economics and Statistics* (November 1967) pp. 423-40.
20. W.S. Comanor and T.A. Wilson, 'Advertising and Competition: A Survey', *Journal of Economic Literature* 17 (June 1979): 472.
21. Ibid., p.470.
22. For a development of this theme, see Posner, *Antitrust Law*. Bork's recent book (*The Antitrust Paradox*) is an important contribution to this tradition. The main limitation of the Chicago School has been its reluctance to make allowance for transaction costs, especially as this relates to strategic behaviour. For a discussion, see my review of Bork's book in the Winter 1979 issue of the *University of Chicago Law Review* 46 (1979): 526-531.
23. For a discussion, see Williamson, 'The Economics of Antitrust: Transaction Cost Considerations', *University of Pennsylvania Law Review* 122 (June 1974): 1439-96, also see Williamson, *Antitrust Law and Economics*.
24. See R.E. Caves and M.E. Porter, 'From Entry Barriers to Mobility Barriers', *Quarterly Journal of Economics* 91 (May 1977): 241-62.
25. Keynes, *General Theory*, p.384.

13. Franchise Bidding for Natural Monopolies—in General and with Respect to CATV*

The orthodox attitude among economists toward regulation is one of 'disdain and contempt'. The general reputation is not undeserved, but it fails to discriminate among different economic activities and different types of regulation. An effort to distinguish between those circumstances in which regulation in some form is immanent from those in which market modes can be made to work relatively well is needed.

Discriminating assessments of regulated industries (extant and proposed) will be facilitated by examining transactions in much greater microanalytic detail than has been characteristic of prior studies of regulation and proposed alternatives thereto. My examination of franchise bidding for natural monopoly discloses that this mode suffers from much more severe contractual disabilities than have hitherto been acknowledged. Faced with both technological and market uncertainties, CATV, *c.* 1970, does not appear to be among the circumstances for which unassisted franchise bidding can be expected to work well.

I. INTRODUCTION

The limits of regulation are manifold and, in a general way at least, have been examined elsewhere by others. Merely to show that regulation is flawed, however, does not establish that regulation is an inferior mode of organizing economic activity. For one thing, the disabilities of regulation are apt to vary with both the type of activity regulated and the form of regulation attempted. Secondly, before regulation is supplanted there is an obligation to assess the properties of the proposed alternative—not

* Research on this paper was supported by a grant from the National Science Foundation (NSF SOC 72-05550 A02). The author acknowledges, without implicating, the helpful comments on an earlier version of the paper by Susan Ackerman, William Baxter, Victor Goldberg, Paul Joskow, Alvin Klevorick, Arthur Leff, Paul MacAvoy and Richard Nelson.

only in general, but also specifically with respect to the activity in question. If the proposed mode is flawed in similar or different respects the purported advantages of shifting out of regulation may be illusory.

The present paper is primarily concerned with the efficacy of franchise bidding schemes as an alternative to regulation in the provision of public utility services in circumstances in which there are non-trivial economies associated with monopoly supply. Granting that regulation is highly imperfect, assessed in terms of an abstract ideal, what are the conditions under which franchise bidding is a vastly superior solution to the supply of 'traditional' public utility services?[1] In particular, should public utility regulation be extended to cover community antenna television systems, or should franchise bidding be used instead (Posner, 1969, pp.642-3)?

My assessment of franchise bidding for the supply of CATV services, *c.* 1970, is that it differs mainly in degree rather than in kind from the regulation that such bidding is intended to supplant—though this does not deny that franchise auctions may sometimes have attractive properties for the supply of natural monopoly services (see section V). In circumstances, however, where franchise bidding predictably and actually converges toward regulation, the purported advantages of franchise bidding as compared with regulation are problematical.

I attempt here to examine franchise bidding issues in somewhat finer microanalytic detail than has been done previously. My emphasis on contractual detail is to be contrasted with that of Richard Posner, who argues that '[t]o expound the details of particular regulations and proposals . . . would only serve to obscure the basic issues' (1972, p.98). I submit, however, that the strategy employed elsewhere to study the employment relation (Williamson, Wachter and Harris, 1975) and vertical integration (Williamson, 1971) has general application. In both instances, it was necessary to examine the contracting process in greater detail than had been done previously to discern the types of difficulties which market-mediated exchange encounters and, relatedly, to establish in what respects and why internal (collective or hierarchical) organization offers an advantage.

It is of interest in this connection to observe that what Posner has referred to as the 'economic approach to law' (1975) is characteristically deficient in microanalytical respects. The economic approach which Posner favours traces its intellectual origins, in antitrust respects at least, to Aaron Director and his students (Posner, 1975, p.758, n.6). As I have observed elsewhere, this tradition relies heavily on the fiction of frictionlessness and/or invokes transaction cost considerations selectively (Williamson, 1974a, 1974b). However powerful and useful it is for classroom purposes and as a check against loose public policy prescriptions, it easily leads to extreme and untenable 'solutions'.[2] What Leff has referred to as a 'legal approach to economics' (1975), in which transaction costs are more prominently and systematically featured, is, I think, a necessary supplement to (and sometimes substitute for) the Director-Posner tradition.[3]

My assessment of the problems of supplying natural monopoly services suggests that there are no friction-free alternatives. Choice among alternative modes nevertheless has to be made. Among the relevant factors to be considered in evaluating alternative modes of organizing natural monopoly are the following: (1) the costs of ascertaining and aggregating consumer preferences through direct solicitation; (2) the efficacy of scalar bidding; (3) the degree to which technology is well developed; (4) demand uncertainty; (5) the degree to which incumbent suppliers acquire idiosyncratic skills; (6) the extent to which specialized, long-lived equipment is involved; and (7) the susceptibility of the political process to opportunistic representations and the differential proclivity, among modes, to make them. (Of special relevance in this last connection is the tendency for regulation, once put in place, to assert ancillary powers, thereby to expand its jurisdiction, often with dysfunctional consequences. Although it is beyond the scope of the paper to assess this issue here, creeping 'ancillariness' is one of the more severe disabilities to which regulation is subject.) The more confidence one has in contracting and in the efficacy of competition—both at the outset and at contract renewal intervals—the more one tends to favour market modes. Conformably, regulation, in some form, is relatively favoured when one is dubious that incomplete contracting will yield desired results and when competitive processes are prone to breakdown.

It should be noted in this connection that variants within both market and regulatory modes exist. Discriminating assessments within as well as between modes are accordingly indicated. Also, a once-for-all verdict with respect to the supply of a particular natural monopoly service is unwarranted. The better mode at an early stage of an industry's development may no longer be better later on when a lesser degree of uncertainty prevails. To the extent that difficult transition problems are apt to be posed in shifting from one mode to the other, this should be acknowledged and taken expressly into account at the outset.

More intensive study of the abstract properties of alternative modes at successive stages will be needed before a more confident matching of modes with activities can be accomplished. Considering the primitive state of comparative institutional analysis, however, more than abstract study is needed. Microanalytic examination of a number of *individual cases* will also be instructive. Among the cases that might be selected for examination, the 'study of extreme instances often provides important leads to the essentials of the situation' (Behavioural Sciences Subpanel,

1962, p.5). Subject to the conditions that only gross inferences are to be attempted and that the system is observed to respond to disturbances in a coherent way, such observations offer a relatively economical way by which to secure insights into the properties of a complex organization. The case study reported here is used only for gross inference purposes, appears to satisfy coherence requirements, and introduces a hitherto missing element of reality into the evaluation of franchise bidding for natural monopolies.

Franchise bidding under steady-state conditions is treated in section II. The more interesting issues relating to the efficacy of franchise bidding do not appear, however, until uncertainty is introduced. These are developed in section III. The Oakland, California, experience with franchise bidding for CATV is then described and evaluated in section IV. Concluding remarks follow in section V.

II. THE SIMPLE FRANCHISE BIDDING SCHEME

Partly out of a sense that the defects of regulation are so serious that patching it up is not worth the effort, and partly out of a conviction that market solutions have not been given a fair chance to deal with the problems for which regulation has been devised, numerous proposals have appeared recently suggesting that market modes be used more imaginatively. Many of these suggestions are traceable, directly or indirectly, to what has come to be known as the economics of property rights literature.[4] Ronald Coase's study of the Federal Communications Commission (1959) is an early and classic example. A more recent issue to come up for consideration is the organization of community antenna television (CATV) systems, of which Posner's study (1972) is an illustration.

Posner's evaluation of CATV franchising relies in part on Harold Demsetz's earlier treatment of the question 'Why regulate utilities?' (1968). Demsetz contends that even though efficiency considerations may dictate that there be one supplier in a natural monopoly industry, the unregulated market price need display no elements of monopoly.

The Basic Argument
Conventional analysis is flawed by a failure to distinguish between the number of *ex ante* bidders and the condition of *ex post* supply. Even though scale economies may dictate that there be a single *ex post* supplier, large numbers competition may nevertheless be feasible at the initial bidding stage. Where large numbers of qualified parties enter non-collusive bids to become the supplier of the decreasing cost activity, the

resulting price need not reflect monopoly power. The defect with conventional analysis is that it ignores this initial franchise bidding stage.

Franchise bids which involve lump-sum payments should be distinguished from those where the franchise is awarded to the bidder who offers to supply at the lowest per unit price. Awarding an exclusive franchise to the non-collusive bidder who will pay the largest lump-sum fee to secure the business effectively capitalizes the monopoly profits which thereafter accrue. But the product or service for which such a franchise is granted will be priced on monopolistic terms. To avoid this outcome, the franchise award criterion of lowest per unit price is favoured. Stigler, among others, evidently finds the argument persuasive (1968, pp. 18-19; 1974, p.360).

Demsetz illustrates the argument by examining a hypothetical example in which the state requires automobile owners to purchase automobile licence plates annually, where the plates in question are produced under decreasing cost conditions. To simplify the argument he strips away

irrelevant complications, such as durability of distribution systems, uncertainty, and irrational behaviour, all of which may or may not justify the use of regulatory commissions but none of which is relevant to the theory of natural monopoly; for this theory depends on one belief only—price and output will be at monopoly levels if, due to scale economies, only one firm succeeds in producing the product. (1968, p.57: emphasis added.)[5]

Provided that there are many qualified and non-collusive bidders for the annual contract and that the contract is awarded to the party that offers to supply at the lowest per unit price, 'the winning price will differ insignificantly from the per unit cost of producing license plates' (Demsetz, 1968, p.61).

Demsetz and others evidently believe, moreover, that the argument is not vitiated when the simple case is extended to include such complications as equipment durability and uncertainty. Equipment durability need not lead to wasteful duplication of facilities since, should a potential supplier offer superior terms, trunk line distributional facilities can be transferred from the original supplier to the successor firm (Demsetz, 1968, p.62). Whether regulation is warranted as a means by which to cope more effectively with uncertainty is met with the observation that '[l]ong-term contracts for the supply of [non-utility services] are concluded satisfactorily in the market place without the aid of regulation' (1968, p.64).

The dominant theme that emerges, occasional disclaimers to the contrary notwithstanding,[6] is that franchise bidding for natural monopolies has attractive properties. It is a market solution that avoids many of the disabilities of regulation. Demsetz's concluding remarks, in which he registers his 'belief that rivalry of the open market place disciplines more effectively than do the regulatory processes of the commission' (1968, p.65), are plainly in this spirit.

Some objections

Marginal cost pricing. Lester Telser takes issue with Demsetz's treatment of natural monopoly on the grounds that franchise bidding gives no assurance that output will be priced efficiently on marginal cost terms:

[Demsetz] leaves readers with the impression that he is content with a situation in which the firm is prevented from obtaining a monopoly return and he does not raise the question of efficiency. Hence he implies that direct regulation of an industry subject to decreasing average cost is unnecessary if it is prevented from obtaining a monopoly return. . . . This misses the point. The controversy concerns regulation to secure efficiency and to promote public welfare. It does not concern the rate of return (Telser, 1969, pp.938-9).

Another way of putting it is that Demsetz does not identify the relevant social welfare function or evaluate his results in welfare terms. Failure to do so, coupled with the prospect that franchise bidding will not lead to efficient marginal cost pricing, is, in Telser's view, a critical shortcoming of Demsetz's approach.

Demsetz has responded to these criticisms by observing that marginal cost pricing was of secondary importance to his paper (1971, p.356). Although a complete treatment of the natural monopoly problem would require that efficient pricing be addressed, his original article did not pretend to be complete (1971, p.356). He furthermore considers it doubtful that regulation leads to more efficient pricing than an appro-priately elaborated bidding scheme (1971, pp.360-1).

I suggest, for the purposes of this paper, that the marginal cost pricing issue be set aside and that the frictions associated with franchise bidding, which are glossed over in previous treatments, be examined instead. To the extent that filling the *lacunae* in Demsetz's 'vaguely described bidding process'—which Telser mentions (1971, p.364) but does not investigate— involves the progressive elaboration of an administrative machinery, the advantages of franchise bidding over regulation are uncertain. If, despite such machinery, the price-to-cost tracking properties of regulation are arguably superior to those of franchise bidding, the purported advantages of franchise bidding are further suspect.

Irrelevant complications. The irrelevant complications to which Demsetz refers—equipment durability and uncertainty—and dismisses in the context of his automobile licence plate example, are really the core issues. To be sure, steady-state analysis of the type he employs sometimes yields fruitful insights that have wide-reaching applications. I submit, however, that the interesting problems of *comparative institutional choice* are largely finessed when the issues are posed in steady-state terms. Knight's admonitions to this effect, although expressed in a different institutional context (1965, pp.267-8), have general application. The basic argument, which applies both to Knight's interest in whether internal organization matters and to Demsetz's concern with market modes of contracting, is this: rates of convergence aside, any of a large variety of organizing modes will achieve equally efficient results if steady-state conditions obtain.[7] In circumstances, however, in which the operating environment is characterized by a non-trivial degree of uncertainty, self-conscious attention to both the *initial* and *adaptability* attributes of alternative modes is warranted.

Demsetz's treatment of franchise bidding emphasizes the initial supply aspect and, as developed below, treats the matter of adaptability in a rather limited and sanguine way. As will be apparent, franchise bidding for public utility services under uncertainty encounters many of the same problems that the critics of regulation associate with regulation; as Victor Goldberg (1976) argues, the problems inhere in the circumstances.

III. FRANCHISE BIDDING UNDER UNCERTAINTY

It will be useful to examine franchise contracts of three types: once-for-all contracts, which appear to be the type of contract envisaged by Stigler; incomplete, long-term contracts, which are favoured by Demsetz; and recurrent short-term contracts, which Posner endorses.

Once-For-All Contracts

Stigler's views on franchise bidding are limited mainly to an endorsement of Demsetz's prior treatment of these matters. He observes simply that

> [n]atural monopolies are often regulated by the state. We note that customers can auction off the right to sell electricity, using the state as the instrument to conduct the auction, and thus economize on transaction costs. The auction . . . consists of a promise to sell cheaply. (1968, p.19)

Since he gives no indication to the contrary, Stigler apparently intends that such bidding be regarded as a serious alternative to regulation under actual market circumstances—which is to say, under conditions of market and technological uncertainty. Failure to refer to recurrent bidding also suggests that the bidding scheme proposed is of the once-for-all variety.[8]

Once-for-all contracts of two types can be distinguished: complete contingent claims contracts and incomplete contracts. The former require that each prospective franchisee specify the terms (prices) at which he is prepared to supply service now and, if price changes are to be made in response to uncertain future events, the conditional terms under which he will supply service in the future. It is generally appreciated that complete contracts of this kind are impossibly complex to write, negotiate and enforce (Radner, 1968). The underlying transactional difficulties have been set out elsewhere (Williamson, 1975, Ch.2; Williamson, Wachter and Harris, 1975).

Given the infeasibility of complete contingent claims contracts, incomplete once-for-all contracts might be considered. Contractual incompleteness, however, is not without cost. Although incomplete once-for-all contracts are feasible in the sense that bounded rationality constraints are satisfied, such contracts pose hazards by increasing the risk of opportunism. The problems here are substantially those discussed below in conjunction with incomplete long-term contracts.

Incomplete Long-Term Contracts

Demsetz evidently has in mind that franchise awards be of a long-term kind in which adaptations to unanticipated developments are accomplished by permitting renegotiation of terms subject to penalty clauses (1968, pp.64-5). Such renegotiation would be unnecessary, of course, if the parties to the contract could agree, at the outset, to deal with unanticipated events and to resolve conflicts by employing a joint profit-maximizing decision rule, thereafter to share the gains of the resulting adaptation. General agreements to this effect are not self-enforcing, however, unless the profit consequences are fully known to both of the parties and can be displayed at low cost to an impartial arbitrator. Absent this, each party will be inclined, when the unanticipated events occur, to manipulate the data in a way that favours its interests (Williamson, 1975, pp.31-3, 91-3).

To be sure, aggressive self-interest-seeking of a myopic kind is attenuated both by the existence of informal sanctions and by an appreciation between the parties that accommodation yields long-term benefits (Macaulay, 1963). But the hazards of opportunism scarcely vanish of these accounts. Among the problems to be anticipated when incomplete long-term contracts are negotiated under conditions of uncertainty are the following: (1) the initial award criterion is apt to be artificial or obscure; (2) execution problems in price-cost, in other performance, and in political respects are apt to develop; and (3) bidding parity between the incumbent and prospective rivals at the contract renewal interval is unlikely to be realized. Consider these several conditions *seriatim*.

(1) *Artificial or obscure initial award criterion.* The promise to 'supply

cheaply' is scarcely a well-defined commitment unless the quality of service is well specified and scalar-valued bids possess economic merit. Posner recognises the former, and proposes that subscriber preferences regarding quality be ascertained by a pre-award solicitation. The mechanics involve

an 'open season' in which all applicants were free to solicit the area's residents for a set period of time. This would not be a poll; the applicants would seek to gain actual commitments from potential subscribers. At the end of the solicitation period, the commitments received by the various applicants would be compared and the franchise awarded to the applicant whose guaranteed receipts, on the basis of subscriber commitments, were largest. In this fashion the vote of each subscriber would be weighted by his willingness to pay, and the winning applicant would be the one who, in free competition with the other applicants, was preferred by subscribers in the aggregate. To keep the solicitation process honest, each applicant would be required to contract in advance that, in the event he won, he would provide the level of service, at the rate represented, in his solicitation drive. (1972, p.115)

The comparability problems that would otherwise be posed if both price and quality were permitted to vary at the final competition stage are thus avoided. The pre-award solicitation not only prevents the quality level from being set by a political body, but also relieves the need to choose among disparate price-quality mixes, on grounds that are uncertain, at the final competition.

However imaginative this pre-award solicitation process of Posner, it is not obviously practicable. For one thing, it assumes that subscribers are able to assess quality–price packages abstractly and have the time and inclination to do so—which poses a bounded rationality issue.[9] For another, it aggregates preferences in a rather arbitrary way.[10] Finally, it assumes that subscribers will demand that winners provide the level of service at the rate represented or can otherwise obtain satisfaction of failure to perform. This poses execution issues and is discussed in (2) below.[11]

If, additionally, the prices at which service is supplied are to vary with periodic demands—a measure which often has efficient capacity rationing properties for public utility services—a complex variable load pricing schedule, rather than a single lowest bid price, must be solicited. Vector-valued bids clearly pose award difficulties.

The upshot of this is that, although franchise awards can be reduced to a lowest bid price criterion, this is apt to be artificial if the future is uncertain and the service in question is at all complex. Such awards are apt to be arbitrary and/or pose the hazard that 'adventurous' bids will be tendered by those who are best suited or most inclined to assume political risks. Again, this gives rise to execution issues, to which we now turn.

(2) *Execution problems.* Even if contract award issues of the kinds described above either were absent or could be dismissed as *de minimis*, we would still have to face problems of contract execution. It is at the execution stage and in conjunction with contract renewal that the convergence of franchise bidding to public utility regulation is especially evident.

I assume, for the purposes of this subsection, that there is a strong presumption that the winner of the bidding competition will be the supplier of the public utility service over the entire contract period. Only in the event of egregious and persistent malperformance would an effort be made to replace the winning franchisee.

The assumption is supported by the following considerations. First, the award of a long-term contract plainly contemplates that the winner will be the supplier over a considerable period. A leading reason to make the contract long-term is to provide the supplier with requisite incentives to instal long-lived assets.[12] If any slight failure to perform in accordance with the franchisor's expectations would occasion rescission of the franchise, the long-term contract would be a fiction and its investment purposes vitiated.

The prospect of litigation delays and expenses also discourages an effort to displace a franchisee. Moreover, even if such an effort were successful, non-trivial transition costs would be incurred. (These are discussed further in (3) below.) Finally, franchise award agencies, like other bureaucracies, are loath to concede or be accused of error. As Eckstein puts it, publicly accountable decision-makers 'acquire political and psychological stakes in their own decisions and develop a justificatory rather than a critical attitude towards them' (1956, p.223). Since displacement may be interpreted as a public admission of error, franchise award agencies predictably prefer, when faced with malperformance, to negotiate a 'compromise' solution instead.

Price-cost relations. In circumstances in which long-term contracts are executed under conditions of uncertainty, fixed price bids are apt to be rather unsatisfactory. If the environment is characterized by uncertainty with respect to technology, demand, local factor supply conditions, inflation, and the like, price cost divergencies and/or indeterminacies will develop.

To be sure, some of these divergencies can be reduced by introducing price flexibility by formula (Fuller and Braucher, 1964, pp.77-8; Goldberg, 1975, p.19). Adjustment for changes in the price in response to some index of prices is one possibility. This, however, is a relatively crude correction and unlikely to be satisfactory where there is rapid technical change or where local conditions deviate significantly from the index population. More precise tracking of prices to costs will be realized if, instead of fixed price contracts, cost-plus (or cost-sharing) contracts are negotiated. All of the difficulties associated with the execution of defence contracts of the cost-sharing kind then appear, however (Scherer, 1964; Williamson, 1967). Problems of auditing and of defective incentives are especially severe. (These, it will be noted, are disabilities associated with regulation. Franchise bidding is designed to overcome them.)

Other performance attributes. A lack of specificity in the contract with respect to the quality of service and a failure to stipulate monitoring and accounting procedures accords latitude to franchisees during contract execution. Despite *ex ante* assurances to the contrary, franchisees can rarely be made to fulfil the spirit of an agreement if net revenues are enhanced by adhering to the letter of the contract only (CTIC, 1972a, p.11). Moreover, technical standards, by themselves, are not self-enforcing; enforcement requires that a policing apparatus be devised (CTIC, 1973, p.7). Since individual consumers are unlikely to have the data or competence to evaluate the quality of service in a discriminating way (Goldberg, 1976) and since both set-up cost and specialization of labour economies will be realized by assigning the quality evaluation function to a specialized agency, centralization is indicated. But again, the convergence toward regulation should be noted.[13]

It may not be sufficient, moreover, merely to specify a common quality standard for all bidders. Thus, suppose that one bidder proposes to achieve the specified quality target by installing high performance, long-lived equipment, that a second proposes to have back-up equipment ready in the event of breakdown, and that a third claims that he will invest heavily in maintenance personnel. Although only one of these may fully satisfy requirements, both subscribers and the franchising agency may lack the *ex ante* capacity to discern which. Granting the franchise to the low bidder only to discover that he is unable to perform as described is plainly unsatisfactory. Although penalty clauses in contracts can help forestall such outcomes, it is often the case—as the history of defence contracting suggests—that successful bidders are able to have terms renegotiated to their advantage.

Accounting ambiguities coupled with the disinclination of franchising agencies to allow winning bidders to fail permit franchisees to use accounting data in a strategic way—to include the threat of bankruptcy—during renegotiations. The introduction of monitoring and accounting control techniques can prevent such outcomes, but this measure then joins the winning bidder and the franchising agency in a quasi-regulatory relationship.

Politics. In circumstances in which renegotiation is common and perhaps vital to the profitable operation of a franchise, political skills assume special importance. Prospective suppliers who possess superior skills in least-cost supply respects, but who are relatively inept in dealing with the franchising bureaucracy and in influencing the political process, are unlikely to submit winning bids.[14] To the extent that political skills override objective economic skills, the advantages of franchising over regulation are placed in question.

Indeed, if franchisees are subject to less stringent profit controls than regulated firms (where the latter are subject to rate of return constraints), it may well be that franchising encourages greater political participation. The argument here is that the incentive to invest private resources to influence political decision varies directly with the degree to which the resulting advantages can be privately appropriated—and that franchised firms have an appropriability advantage in this respect.[15]

(3) *Lack of bidding parity during contract renewal.* Lest meaningful competition at the contract renewal interval be upset, participation in contract execution should not place winners of the original competition at a substantial advantage over nonwinners. As discussed generally elsewhere (Peacock and Rowley, 1972, p.242; Williamson, 1975, pp.26-35), however, and as expressly developed in the context of CATV in the following subsection, there are reasons to believe that bidding parity at contract renewals intervals will not obtain.

Recurrent Short-Term Contracts
A leading advantage of recurrent short-term contracting over long-term contracting is that short-term contracts facilitate adaptive, sequential decision-making. The requirements that contingencies be comprehensively described and appropriate adaptations to each worked out in advance are thereby avoided. Rather, the future is permitted to unfold and adaptations are introduced, at contract renewal intervals, only to those events which actually materialize. Put differently, bridges are crossed one (or a few) at a time, as specific events occur. As compared with the contingent claims contracting requirement that the complete decision tree be generated, so that all possible bridges are crossed in advance, the adaptive, sequential decision-making procedure economizes greatly on bounded rationality.

Additionally, under the assumption that competition at the contract renewal interval is efficacious, the hazards of contractual incompleteness which beset incomplete long-term contracts are avoided. Failure to define contractual terms appropriately gives rise, at most, to malperformance during the duration of the current short-term contract. Indeed, recognizing that a bidding copetition will be held in the near future, winning bidders may be more inclined to cooperate with the franchising authority if specific contractual deficiencies are noted, rather than use such occasions to realize temporary bargaining advantages;[16] opportunism is thereby curbed as well.[17]

The efficacy of recurrent short-term contracting depends crucially, however, on the assumption that *parity among bidders at the contract renewal interval is realized.*[18] Posner faces and disposes of this issue.

[T]he fact that the cable company's plant normally will outlast the period of its franchise raises a question: Will not the cable company be able to outbid any new applicant, who would have to build a plant from scratch? And will not the bargaining method therefore be ineffective after the first round? Not necessarily: in bidding for the franchise on the basis of new equipment costs, new applicants need not be at a significant disadvantage in relation to the incumbent franchisee. For example, once a new applicant is franchised he could negotiate to purchase the system of the existing franchisee, who is faced with the loss of the unamortized portion of his investment if his successor builds a new system. Insofar as the economic life of a cable plant is considered a problem when the franchise term is short, it can be solved by including in the franchise a provision requiring the franchisee, at the successor's option, to sell his plant (including improvements) to the latter at its original cost, as depreciated. (1972, p.116)

I find these views overly sanguine. For one thing, equipment valuation problems are apt to be rather more complex than Posner's remarks suggest. Secondly, Posner focuses entirely on non-human capital; the possibility that human capital problems also exist is nowhere acknowledged. To be sure, human asset benefits which accrue during contract execution and which give incumbents an advantage over outsiders will, if anticipated, be reflected in the original bidding competition. But 'buying in' can be risky and the price-tracking properties of such strategies are easily inferior to average cost pricing in resource-allocation respects. The upshot is that recurrent bidding (at, say, four-year intervals) is riddled with contractual indeterminacies.

Concern over plant and equipment valuation is, of course, mitigated if investments in question are relatively unspecialized. I conjecture that this is the case for Demsetz's car licence plate example. If, with only minor modifications, general purpose equipment (for the cutting, stamping, painting, etc.) can produce licence plates efficiently, then a franchisee who fails to win the renewal contract can productively employ most of this same equipment for other purposes, while the new winner can, at slight cost, modify his own plant and equipment to produce the annual requirement efficiently.

Alternatively, concern over plant and equipment poses no problem if its useful life is exhausted during the contract execution interval. As Posner's remarks suggest, however, and as is generally conceded, it is inefficient to install utility plant and equipment of such short duration.

Unlike Demsetz's licence plate manufacturers, moreover, most utility services (gas, water, electricity, telephone) require that *specialized* plant and equipment be put in place. The same is true of CATV. Since the construction of parallel systems is wasteful and since to require this to be done would place outside bidders at a disadvantage at the contract renewal interval, some method of transferring assets from existing franchisees to successor firms plainly needs to be worked out.

Posner contends that this can be handled by stipulating that plant and equipment be sold to the successor firm, at its option, at the original cost less depreciation of the predecessor franchisee. Consistent with his emphasis on fundamental policy choices, Posner declines to supply the details. Unfortunately, however, the details are troublesome.

For one thing, original cost can be manipulated by the predecessor firm. For another, even if depreciation accounting procedures are specified under the original franchise terms, implementation may still be contested. Third, original cost less depreciation at best sets an upper bound—and perhaps not even this, since inflation issues are not faced— on the valuation of plant and equipment. The successor franchisee may well offer less, in which case costly haggling ensues. Finally, even if no disputes eventuate, Posner's procedures merely provide a legal rule for transferring assets. He does not address the economic properties of the procedures in investment incentive and utilization respects.

Whether the accounting records of original costs can be accepted as recorded depends in part on whether the equipment was bought on competitive terms. The original franchisee who is integrated backwards into equipment supply or who arranges a kickback from an equipment supplier can plainly rig the prices to the disadvantage of rival bidders at the contract renewal interval. Furthermore, and related, the original cost should also include the labour expense of installing plant and equipment. To the extent, however, that the allocation of labour expense between operating and capital categories is not unambiguous, the original winner can capitalize certain labour expenses to the disadvantage of would-be successors. Auditing can be employed to limit these distortions, but this has the appearance of regulation. Even if carefully done, moreover, the results are apt to be disputed. In as much as information on true valuation is asymmetrically distributed to the disadvantage of outside parties, the burden of showing excess capitalization falls heavily on the would-be new supplier.

Reaching agreement on depreciation charges, which are notoriously difficult to define (especially if obsolescence is a problem and mainten- ance expenditures can be manipulated in a strategic manner), poses similar problems. Therefore, costly arbitration, for both original equip-

ment valuation and depreciation reasons, is apt to ensue.[19] Rate base
valuations of a regulatory kind thereby obtain.

Indeed, the valuation of physical assets is predictably more severe
under franchise bidding than under regulation. For one thing, earnings in
the regulated firm are a product of the rate base and the realized rate of
return. Clearly, the regulated firm can be conciliatory about the rate base
if in exchange it receives allowable rate of return concessions. Additionally, the agency and regulated firm are prospectively joined in a long
series of negotiations. Errors made by either party on one round are less
critical if these can be remedied at the next rate review interval (or if, in a
crisis, interim relief can be anticipated). More is at stake with asset
valuation under franchise bidding, since degrees of freedom of both rate
of return and intertemporal kinds are missing. Accordingly, more
contentious bargaining leading to litigation is to be expected.

A related difficulty with Posner's physical asset valuation scheme is
that it merely sets an upper bound. In as much, however, as procurement
on these terms is left to the successor firm's option, there is little reason to
expect this figure to prevail. Without stipulating more, the successor firm
would presumably offer to buy the specialized plant and equipment at its
value in its best alternative (non-franchised) use. This will normally be a
small fraction of the depreciated original cost. Predecessor and successor
firms thus find themselves confronted with a wide bargaining range
within which to reach an exchange agreement. Since competitive forces
sufficient to drive the parties to a unique agreement are lacking,
additional haggling (which is a social cost) can be anticipated. Albeit
vexing, the details, which are neglected by Posner, nevertheless matter;
the frictionless transfer on which he appears to rely is simply not to be had
on the terms described.

Conceivably superior asset valuation and franchise bidding schemes
can be devised which mitigate these problems.[20] It is patently incumbent,
however, on those who believe that large numbers competition can be
made effective at the contract renewal interval to come forward with the
requisite operational details. Without such specificity, one must consider
dubious the contention that low-cost reassignment of physical assets can
be affected at the contract renewal interval for franchised services which
require specialized and long-lived plant and equipment to be installed.
Rather, non-trivial haggling and litigation expenses appear to infect
Posner's proposal.

Moreover, human asset problems, which Posner and Demsetz fail even
to mention, also need to be faced. Again, the matter of fungibility arises.
To the extent that the skills of operating the franchise are widely available
or, alternatively, that employees of the incumbent firm deal with rival
bidders and the incumbent's owners on identical terms, no problems of

this kind appear. If, however, non-trivial specialized skills and knowledge accrue to individuals and small groups as a result of on-the-job training and experience, the first of these conditions is violated. If, additionally, employees resist transfer of ownership in the bidding competition, rivals are put to a disadvantage.

The matter of non-fungibility of labour has been discussed elsewhere by Hayek (1945, pp.521-2) and Marschak (1968, p.14) and has been addressed in the context of task idiosyncracy by Doeringer and Piore (1971, pp.15-16) and by Williamson, Wachter and Harris (1975). The thrust of this literature is that significant differences sometimes develop between experienced and inexperienced workers in the following respects: (1) equipment idiosyncracies, due to highly specialized or incompletely standardized, albeit common, equipment, are 'revealed' only to experienced workers; (2) processing economies of an idiosyncratic kind are fashioned or 'adopted' by managers and workers in specific operating contexts; (3) informal team accommodations, attributable to mutual adaptation among parties engaged in recurrent contact, develop and are upset, to the possible detriment of group performance, when the membership is altered; and (4) communication idiosyncracies evolve (with respect, for example, to information channels and codes), but are of value only in an operating context where the parties are familiar with each other and share a common language.

As a consequence, it is often inefficient fully or extensively to displace the experienced labour and management group that is employed by the winner of the initial franchise award. Familiarizing another group with the idiosyncracies of the operation and developing the requisite team production and communication skills are costly. Accordingly, incumbent employees, who alone possess the idiosyncratic knowledge needed to realize least-cost supply, are powerfully situated to block a franchise reassignment effort.

The cost disadvantage referred to will obtain, however, only in so far as incumbent employees deal with the current ownership and outside bidders differently. The strategic advantage which they enjoy in relation to inexperienced but otherwise qualified employees is one which can be exercised against both the current owner and his bidding rivals alike. The issue thus comes down to whether current and prospective owners are treated differently at the contract renewal interval.[21] I conjecture that they will be. The main reason is that *informal* understandings (with respect to job security, promotional expectations, and other aspects of internal due process) are much easier to reach and enforce in familiar circumstances than in unfamiliar ones.[22]

This is not to say that employees cannot or will not strike bargains with outsiders, but rather that such bargains will be more costly to reach, because much more attention to explicit detail will be required, or that there is greater risk associated with an informal (incompletely specified) agreement with outsiders. Where additional detail is sought, outsiders will be at a disadvantage in relation to insiders, because the costs of reaching agreement are increased. If, instead, employees are asked to trust the outsider to behave 'responsibly' or, alternatively, the outsider agrees to accept the interpretation placed on incomplete agreements by the employees when unanticipated events not expressly covered by the employment contract develop, the implied risks are great and corresponding premia will find their way, directly or indirectly, into the bid price. As a consequence, idiosyncratic employment attributes coupled with the inability of outsiders to reach equivalent agreements at equal expense place original franchisees at an advantage at the contract renewal interval. Thus, human capital considerations compound the bidding difficulties which physical asset valuation problems pose. To contend that bidding parity can be expected at the contract renewal interval is accordingly suspect for this reason as well. Put differently, if original winners of the bidding competition realize non-trivial advantages in informational and informal organizational respects during contract execution, bidding parity at the contract renewal interval can no longer be presumed. Rather, what was once a large-numbers bidding situation, at the time the original franchise was awarded, *is converted into what is tantamount to a small-numbers bargaining situation* when the franchise comes up for renewal.

Contracting schemes which avoid these risks, which have superior price-tracking properties, and which do not experience offsetting disabilities are plainly to be preferred. Since both risk-bearing and price-tracking properties of regulation are arguably superior to those of franchise bidding, and if franchise bidding in practice is, in most other respects, difficult to distinguish from regulation, the net gain of franchise bidding over regulation is not transparent.[23]

It might be argued, of course, that the incumbency advantage will be anticipated at the outset, in which event discounted certainty equivalent profits will be bid down to zero by large numbers competition for the original award. This is not, however, an entirely satisfactory answer. For one thing, to come in at a price below cost for the initial award (perhaps even a negative price) and to set price at the level of alternative cost at contract renewal intervals easily result in resource utilization of an inferior kind. Additionally, buying-in strategies are risky. The alternative supply price can be influenced by the terms the franchisor sets on subsequent rounds, including terms that may obsolete the learning-by-doing advantages of incumbents.

A Summing Up

Once-for-all bidding schemes of the contingent claims contracting kind are infeasible and/or pose execution hazards. Incomplete long-term contracts of the type envisaged by Demsetz alleviate the first of these problems but aggravate the second. A whole series of difficulties long familiar to students of defence contracting and regulation appears. The upshot is that franchise bidding for incomplete long-term contracts is a much more dubious undertaking than Demsetz's discussion suggests.

Posner's proposal that franchise terms be kept short is designed to overcome the adaptability problems associated with incomplete long term contracts, but his discussion is insufficiently microanalytic and/or critical of the disabilities of short-term contracts to expose their shortcomings. The fundamental limitation of the argument is that, despite Posner's procedural stipulations (1972, p.116), bidding parity at the contract renewal interval between the original winner and rival successor firms cannot safely be presumed. To the contrary, there are reasons to doubt such parity, in which case the adaptability and price to cost properties that Posner associates with recurrent contracting[24] are not to be had on the frictionless (or low cost) terms he describes.

To be sure, some of the difficulties which infect the Posner proposal can be mitigated by introducing an extensive regulatory/arbitration apparatus. Assessing plant and equipment installations, auditing related accounting records, and arbitrating disputes between incumbent and rival firms over physical asset valuations are illustrative. But then franchise bidding and regulation differ only in degree.

It is perhaps unsurprising, in view of the foregoing, that Posner's recurrent bidding proposal has not been widely adopted. Rather, most CATV franchise awards are for 10–15 years, and contractual incompleteness has been handled by progressively elaborating a regulatory structure (CTIC, 1972c, pp.9-12)—a result which conceivably reflects a desire by CATV operators to insulate themselves from the rigours of competition. I submit, however, that the drift toward regulation is also explained by performance defects associated with CATV franchise awards which are caused in part by contractual incompleteness (CTIC, 1972c, p.9).

Still, the contractual incompleteness defects described above might conceivably be remedied by progressively refining CATV awards in the future. Stipulating appropriate penalties for unsatisfactory performance and setting out complex conditional responses to contingent events may serve to promote efficient adaptation and mitigate haggling expenses. Elaborating the contracts in these respects is not costless, however, and franchising agencies often lack the resolve to exact penalties as prescribed.[25] Although times have surely changed for the better, it is sobering to note that the limits of franchise contracts were described by Fisher over 75 years ago as follows:

Regulation does not end with the formulation and adoption of a satisfactory contract, in itself a considerable task. If this were all, a few wise and honest men might, once in a generation supervise the framing of a franchise in proper form, and nothing further would be necessary. It is a current fallacy and the common practice in American public life to assume that a constitution or a statute or a charter, once properly drawn up by intelligent citizens and adopted by an awakened public, is self-executing and that the duty of good citizens ends with the successful enactment of some well matured plan. But repeated experience has demonstrated—what should have been always apparent—the absolute futility of such a course, and the disastrous consequences of reliance upon a written document for the purposes of living administration. As with a constitution, a statute, or a charter, so with a franchise. It has been found that such an agreement is not self enforcing. . . . [Moreover, the] administration may ignore or fail to enforce compliance with those essential parts of a contract entrusted to its executive authority; and legal proceedings . . . are frequently unavoidable long before the time of the franchise has expired. (Fisher 1907, pp.39-40)

At the risk of oversimplification, regulation may be described contractually as a highly incomplete form of long-term contracting in which (1) the regulatee is assured an overall fair rate of return, in exchange for which (2) adaptations to changing circumstances are successively introduced without the costly haggling that attends such changes when parties to the contract enjoy greater autonomy. Whether net gains are thereby realized turns on the extent to which the disincentive effects of the former (which may be checked in some degree by performance audits and by mobilizing competition in the capital market forces (Williamson, 1972)), are more than offset by the gains from the latter. This is apt to vary with the degree to which the industry is subject to uncertainties of market and technological kinds.

IV. A CASE STUDY

Although the case study reported below cannot claim to be representative, it does reveal that many of the franchise concerns discussed in the previous section are not purely imaginary.[26] The study both indicates the importance of evaluating proposals to scrap regulation in favour of market alternatives in more microanalytic terms and discloses that, in practice, franchise bidding for CATV (and presumably other public utility services) has many of the qualities of regulation.

The Oakland CATV Experience
On 19 June 1969, the Council of the City of Oakland, California, passed a

city ordinance which provided for the granting of community antenna television franchises. The main features of the ordinance, for the purposes of this paper, were:[27]

(1) the franchise award was to be non-exclusive;
(2) the franchise duration was not to exceed 20 years;
(3) the city was authorized to terminate a franchise for non-compliance after 30 days' notice and a public hearing;
(4) the franchisee was directed to supply a complete financial statement to the city annually and the city was given the right to inspect the franchisee's records;
(5) the city had the right to acquire the CATV system at the cost of reproduction;
(6) the city manager was authorized to adjust, settle or compromise any controversy that might arise among the city, the franchisee or subscribers, although aggrieved parties could appeal to the city council;
(7) failure to comply with time requirements of the franchise were grounds for termination;
(8) in as much as failure to comply with time requirements would result in damages that would be costly to assess, an automatic fine of $750 per day would be imposed for each day beyond the three-year target completion date that the franchise took to install the system;
(9) any property of the franchisee that was abandoned in place would become the property of the city;
(10) a surety bond of $100,000 was to be obtained by the franchisee and renewed annually;
(11) property of the franchisee was to be subject to inspection by the city;
(12) the CATV system was to be installed and maintained in accordance with the 'highest and best accepted standards' of the industry.

Operationalizing the bidding process. The above constituted the basic legislative authority and ground rules. Rather, however, than solicit bids immediately, the Department of General Services engaged instead in a set of preliminary discussions with prospective franchisees.[28] Simultaneously, community groups were requested to advise the City on the types of services to be offered. The resulting dialogue was intended to elicit information regarding cost, demand characteristics, technical capabilities, etc., and would help define the 'basic service', which would then be stipulated in the contract. Comparability among bids for a standardized service would thereby be facilitated.

Ten months later, on 30th April 1970, the City of Oakland apprised five applicants that the city would receive their amended applications to construct, operate and maintain a non-exclusive CATV system franchise within the city. The main features, for the purposes of this paper, of the invitation to bid were:[29]

(1) Two systems were to be provided:
    (a) System A, which is the basic system, would permit the subscriber to receive the entire FM radio band plus 12 TV channels distributed as follows: 9 local off-the-air channels; one or more newly-created local origination channels; and one channel assigned to the city and school district. Payment of a monthly charge of 'X' plus connection charges (see items (5) and (6) below) would permit the subscriber to receive System A.
    (b) System B would provide special programming and other services. The mix of programming and other services were left unspecified, however. The charges for System B were to be determined later by the franchisee with the approval of the city council.

(2) All areas within the city limits of the City of Oakland were to be served.

(3) Franchise duration was set at 15 years.

(4) The franchisee was to make annual payments to the city of 8 per cent of gross receipts or $125,000, whichever was greater.[30]

(5) Connection charges for each of four customer classes[31] were stipulated, and thus common for all bidders. It was further stipulated that no additional fee be charged to the subscriber for switches or converters needed to receive System A.

(6) The basic bid consisted of designating the monthly fee 'X' which would be charged to each subscriber for the first TV and FM outlet connected to his living unit, with an additional monthly charge of $0.2 X$ to be paid for each additional outlet in his living unit. This would entitle the subscriber to receive System A.

(7) The franchisee was to provide the city and school district with certain free connections and services, including studio facilities for originating programming for up to 20 hours per week.

(8) The system to be installed was to be a dual cable system, and each of the cables was to be capable of carrying the equivalent of 32 video channels. A series of minimum technical specifications concerning signal quality, cable characteristics, installation methods, automatic controls, etc. were stipulated.

(9) Service requirements were described in general terms. The details were to be defined by the franchisee subject to council approval.

(10) The system was to be 25 per cent complete within 18 months of

franchise acceptance, with an additional 25 per cent being completed in each succeeding 6-month period, so that the system would be fully completed in three years.

(11) Proposals to raise rates to subscribers could be submitted annually. (No indexing or other criteria were offered in this connection.)

Bid acceptance. Bids were made on 1 July 1970, the lowest being the bid of Focus Cable of Oakland Inc., which stipulated an 'X' (see items (1) and (6) above) of $1.70 per month.[32] The next lowest bid was by Cablecom-General of Northern California, which set a rate of $3.48.[33] The TelePrompTer Corporation bid was $5.95 (Libman, 1974, p.34).

Focus Cable apprised the city at the time of its bid that TeleCommunications, Inc. of Denver, Colorado, whose participation had been vital to the qualification of Focus as an applicant, had elected to withdraw from the Focus Cable proposal.[34] Focus Cable reorganized the corporation under the laws of California and included a copy of the Articles of Incorporation, dated 1 July 1970, with its bid. In as much as Focus had entered the lowest bid (by a factor of two), was the only local bidder, and represented an ethnic minority,[35] the City was reluctant to reject their bid for lack of financial capability and technical qualifications. However, awarding the franchise to Focus plainly posed hazards.

It appeared that these were greatly mitigated when TelePrompTer Corporation proposed, on 16 July 1970, to enter into a joint venture with Focus Cable to construct and develop the Oakland franchise. As a part of the joint venture, TelePrompTer agreed to provide all needed financing for the project.[36] Why TelePrompTer was prepared to do this at a monthly charge less than 30 per cent of its own bid was not disclosed. Presumably, however, the prospect of earning substantial returns on System B was a contributing factor.[37] Focus Cable advised the City of Oakland, in a letter dated 21 July 1970, that 'the proposed financing of Focus by TelePrompTer can and will provide the ideal marriage of local investors, CATV expertise, and over-all financial strength to best develop the CATV franchise in Oakland.'[38] The Focus contribution to this ideal marriage was its local investor attributes.

The agreement between Focus and TelePrompTer provided that each should have equal ownership at the outset but that TelePrompTer would convert this to a majority interest immediately and could exercise options after the first year which gave it ownership of 80 per cent of the capital stock outstanding.[39] The joining of TelePrompTer with Focus was thought to warrant completing the negotiations. A report to the city council from the city manager and the city attorney, dated 28 September 1970, concluded as follows:[40]

Part of the concept of Systems A and B in the specification was, by competitive applications, to obtain a rate sufficiently low on System A which would encourage the early development of System B. It is staff opinion that the low rate submitted by Focus would motivate such a development. Also, the low rate will assure the widest utilization of System A by families of all economic means.

Focus is the applicant which has submitted the lowest basic monthly subscriber rate. The question has been raised as to whether Focus meets the specifications due to changes in its organization. From a legal standpoint, the organizational change does not disqualify Focus from further Council consideration. It is staff opinion that the proposed agreements between Focus and TelePrompTer, with the additional guarantees by TelePrompTer, will result in a useful combination of initial local representation with one of the largest and best qualified CATV firms in the United States.

Focus Cable and TelePrompTer Corporation entered into a subscription agreement on 21 September 1970, in anticipation of being awarded the franchise. Two hundred shares at $10 per share were to be paid for by the organizers of Focus.[41] Additionally, the Agreement provided:[42]

The Corporation shall purchase equipment and products from TPT [TelePrompTer] for use in its business in preference to other sources to the extent that the quality and workmanship of such equipment and products are comparable to such other sources. If TPT shall sell any such equipment or products to the Corporation, the price to be charged shall not exceed an amount which would be reasonably comparable to the charge for like equipment and products if obtained from an independent supplier dealing on an arm's length basis.

The subscription agreement also set out the TelePrompTer option to acquire an 80 per cent ownership position at an option price per share of $10.[43] The purchase of 800 shares at $10 per share would thus give TelePrompTer an 80 per cent ownership position for an outlay of $8000.

The council of the City of Oakland awarded the CATV franchise to Focus Cable on 10 November 1970.[44] Focus Cable accepted the franchise on 23 December 1970.[45]

Execution of the franchise. A rate for System B of $4.45 per month was requested by Focus Cable on 10 March 1971, and was approved on 11 March 1971.[46] The combined rate for System A and System B thus came to $6.15 per month.

Construction, which was due to be completed on 28 December 1973, did not go so quickly as the franchise specifications called for, fewer households subscribed to the service than anticipated, and costs escalated. Focus Cable appealed to the city to renegotiate the terms of the franchise. A reduction in the penalty period and the penalty fee was sought; a stretch-out of the construction period was requested; and a downgrading of the cable requirement was proposed. The staff of the Office of General Services summarized the requested changes as follows.[47]

Focus is requesting that: further construction be limited to a dual trunk/single feeder cable configuration; a two-year construction extension be granted; only 90% of the households be served at the end of the two years with the remaining 10% to be served only under specified conditions; activation of the dual cable system to be deferred until adequate demand develops; damage payments for construction delays be waived; rates of $1.70 for basic services and $6.15 for extended services continue but that additional set rates be increased; extended service subscribers be reduced from 38 to 30 channels; and that reductions be made in the city and school spectrum allocations.

The staff then considered four alternatives: (1) insist that the terms of the original franchise be met; (2) negotiate a revised agreement with Focus; and terminate the franchise, in which event (3) proposals from other commercial cable operators would be invited; or (4) shift the franchise to public ownership. The first was rejected because it would require great effort by the city 'to obtain a satisfactory result from a recalcitrant operator. Citizen complaints about service will proliferate and require enormous effort to resolve. Litigation may result.'[48] The third was rejected because other operators were thought unlikely to provide any more than the 'minimum requirements of the 1972 Cable Television Report and Order'—'28-channel capacity, some two-way capacity, three channels for local use, and "significant" local programming'—offerings which were characterized as 'significantly less than would be provided by Focus's recommended plant revision.'[49] Furthermore, public ownership was rejected for philosophical and financial reasons.[50] The second alternative, which the staff characterized as the compromise solution, was accordingly proposed.[51]

In the course of reviewing Focus Cable's problems, the staff reported that Focus claimed to have invested $12,600,000 to date and that Focus estimated that this would increase to $21,400,000 if the dual system were to be completed. The staff disputed these figures and offered its own estimate of $18,684,000 as the completed capital cost of the dual system. The original Focus estimate, by contrast, was $11,753,000. The staff attributed the increase over the initial estimate to 'possible mismanagement of construction activities; inflation, which was compounded by Focus's not meeting the original construction schedule; and an underestimate by Focus of the mileage and unit costs necessary to build the Oakland system.'[52]

Since 437 miles, or 55 per cent of the system, were already completed and furnished with dual cable, the staff recommended that the system be completed as a dual cable system. The second cable, however, would not be energized until a later date. Since only one cable was to be energized, a reduction of channel capacity on System B resulted, and a reduction of city and school spectrum allocations was proposed. The subscriber to the extended service (now designated A/B) would receive 12 channels on System A and 18 channels on System B.[53] Also, the staff was agreeable to the proposal that a construction extension of two years be granted and that only 90 per cent rather than 100 per cent coverage be attempted.[54] Additionally, the staff recommended that Focus pay the city $240,000 for lost revenues due to the delay during the period 1973 to 1976 and that any delays beyond December 1976 be assessed at the rate of $250 rather than $750 per day.[55] Finally, the staff recommended that the monthly rate for the initial System A connection remain at $1.70 and that the initial System B connection remain at $4.45 (so that System A/B remained at $6.15), but that the monthly rate on additional outlets for System A be increased from $0.34 to $1.70 and that the rate for additional System B outlets be set at $3.00.[56]

The 'compromise' that finally emerged and was approved by the city council had the following provisions:[57] (1) A shift from the dual to a single cable system was permitted with the understanding that additional transmission capacity would be put in place within one year after it was ascertained that the 'additional transmission capacity will attract sufficient revenues to provide a per annum rate of return on the gross investment required, over a 10-year period, equivalent to ten per cent.'[58] (2) The minimum franchise fee was increased by $25,000 in 1974 and each year thereafter. (3) Damages were assessed at the rate of $250 per day from 18 December 1973, until the first reading of the amended franchise—which resulted in a penalty of $36,000—rather than $750 per day for the entire period from 18 December 1973, until system completion—a penalty which would have been greater by a factor of 20 or more and which might have precipitated bankruptcy. (4) A deferred construction schedule was approved. Finally, (5) the monthly rate on additional connections was increased from $0.34 to $1.70 per month on System A and was set at $3.00 per month on System B.

The city passed an ordinance on 30 May 1974, to reflect most of these changes.[59] Attorneys for Focus forwarded Letters of Acceptance by Focus and TelePrompTer on 14 June 1974, and sent a cheque from TelePrompTer Corporation made payable to the City of Oakland in the amount of $36,000.

Focus Cable filed a progress report on 15 November 1974, which showed that 11,131 subscribers were connected. Of these, 770 took the basic service at $1.70 per month (of which 206 had additional outlets), and 10,361 had the extended service at $6.15 per month (of which 974 had additional outlets). This represented an overall penetration rate of 36 per cent.[60] The Office of General Services recommended that Cable Dynamics, Inc. of Burlingame, California, be retained as consultants to 'devise and perform tests to establish the degree of compliance' with technical requirements of the franchise.[61] Cable Dynamics estimated that the costs from Autumn 1974 to June 1976 would be approximately $10,750.[62] Focus agreed to reimburse the city for these costs up to an amount not to exceed $10,750.[63]

An evaluation

The franchising procedures employed by the City of Oakland, especially at the initial reward stage, are not without merit. As compared, for example, with those in New York City, which awarded non-competitive, 20-year contracts to Manhattan Cable TV and to TelePrompTer to supply CATV in Manhattan,[64] the Oakland exercise had the appearance of a genuine bidding competition. Franchise specifications were standardized and, with respect to System A at least, carefully described. Bidding competition in terms of a simple promise to sell cheaply (by designating the value 'X' at which System A services would be supplied) was thereby facilitated. However, numerous problems, many of which were anticipated in the discussion of incomplete long-term contracts, developed. Thus, consider each of the previously described disabilities which sometimes infect franchise awards: (1) the artificiality or obscurity of the initial award criterion, (2) the development of execution problems in price–cost, other performance, and political respects, and (3) the absence of bidding parity at the contract renewal interval.

(1) *Initial award.* Awarding the franchise on the basis of the lowest bid of 'X' to supply System A service simplified the award criterion, but the promise to supply cheaply proved to be specious. The lack of attention to System B (which was treated as a futuristic service and, except for capacity requirements, was left relatively undefined) in both quality and price respects may well have contributed to 'adventurous' bidding on the part of Focus. Trafficking in the franchise award quickly ensued.

To have regarded System A, which essentially supplies improved off-the-air signals, as the 'basic system' was misguided. Over 90 per cent of the subscribers took the combined A/B service, although the additional service thereby obtained was relatively mundane (mainly the import of distant signals). The rate of the combined service, however, was $3\frac{1}{2}$ times as great as the basic System A service. Surely a more careful effort to assess subscriber preferences at the outset would have revealed that System A lacked appeal. Indeed, in as much as most of the prospective franchises were experienced in supplying CATV services in other areas, it is difficult to understand that preoccupation with System A services during the extended pre-contract discussion between the franchisor and the prospective franchisees. The possibility that the staff was gullible and deliberately misled during these pre-contract discussions cannot be dismissed.[65]

Whatever the case—given the demand and technological uncertainties associated with CATV (CTIC, 1972c, pp.5, 12) and the complexity of the service, in quality and product mix respects—reducing the award criterion to the lowest bid price for System A resulted in a strained and perhaps bogus competition.

(2) *Execution difficulties. Price-cost relations.* Whether the Focus bid of $1.70 per month for System A can be regarded as close to 'per unit production cost' is doubtful in view of the following factors: (1) the disparity among bid prices raises a question as to whether an economically meaningful competition was conducted; (2) System B prices, which appear to be the more relevant dimension, were negotiated subsequent to the bidding competition; and (3) true cost levels are difficult to ascertain—partly because the vertically integrated supply relation obscures these, partly because inflation rates during the construction period have been abnormally high, and partly because the staff lacks an auditing capability. What is evident is that Focus and the staff of the Office of General Services are, together with the city council, involved in a long-term bargaining relationship over prices and costs in which political interests, bureaucratic interests and franchise viability all play a role.

Other performance attributes. The stipulation that the CATV system be installed and maintained in accordance with the 'highest and best accepted standards' of the industry coupled with technical specifications did not yield a well-defined quality outcome.[66] Sufficient customer complaints over quality have been registered with the staff of the Office of General Services[67] that the staff, unable itself to assess the quality of service, has arranged for a consultant to test the degree of compliance of service with technical requirements.

Politics. Whether the winning bid by Focus involved 'buying-in' is uncertain. An inference that buying-in did occur is supported by the following considerations. (1) The next lowest bid was double the Focus bid, while the TelePrompTer bid was more than triple the Focus bid. (2) The timing and nature of the Focus reorganization suggest a foot-in-the-door strategy—the object being that, once in, the franchising authority would be inclined to work with Focus and its affiliates in an accommodating manner. (3) Focus's local bidder status was affirmatively regarded by the franchising authority and evidently supported politicking.[68] Finally, (4) the extensive renegotiations undertaken by Focus, with evident success—the staff acceded to most of Focus's requests and the city council approved a 'compromise' in which energizing of the second cable was deferred (with a cut-back in System B services to 18 channels); the annual franchising fee was increased slightly; damages were reduced drastically; construction deadlines were extended; and rates on additional System A and B connections were increased—reinforce this judgement.

(3) *Frictionless takeover or transfer.* Although the enabling ordinance provided for buying up the plant and equipment of the franchisee, the city was plainly not prepared to upset the original award. The reasons appear to be that incumbents are strategically positioned to bargain—both in terms of service interruptions and the litigating and other expenses which franchise termination would entail—and, relatedly, because franchising agencies lack resolve. This lack of resolution appears be attributable to the reward structure in bureaux. Unable to appropriate the gains that reassignment of the franchise would prospectively yield and unwilling to concede error, the bureaux favour 'accommodation' whenever contract execution difficulties appear.

The interruptions and expenses which franchise termination would experience are presumably explained, in part at least, by physical and human asset problems of the kinds discussed in section III. Absent rules for valuing the CATV plant and equipment that are at once rational, unambiguous and inexpensive to employ, physical asset valuation problems predictably arise.[69] In as much as such rules had not been devised (and, realistically, perhaps could not have been devised) for the Oakland franchise, litigation expenses and delays would attend any effort to take over the physical plant in question.

The risk of service interruptions and related malfunctions would be compounded if the human assets associated with the franchise had acquired, in a learning-by-doing process, non-trivial task idiosyncracies. Given that the staff lacked qualifications in CATV area and was evidently unwilling to solicit bids from experienced CATV operators (possibly because the staff was unwilling to accept the risk of embarrassment should the new operator also prove to be deficient), the transfer of human assets would need to be worked out if city ownership were to be attempted. The incentive to displace the original franchisee would be attenuated to the extent that a frictionless transfer of such human assets could not be anticipated.

The upshot is that, good intentions to the contrary notwithstanding, *unassisted* franchise bidding for CATV conducted and executed under conditions of uncertainty has dubious properties. The franchising authority that assumes an accommodating posture is merely legitimating monopoly, while a concerted effort to exercise control requires the agency to adopt a regulatory posture. The purported dichotomy between 'regulatory controls' on the one hand and 'natural economic forces' on the other is accordingly strained. It confuses the issues to characterize market solutions as 'natural' where these are actually supported by an administrative apparatus of considerable complexity.[70]

V. CONCLUDING REMARKS

That franchise bidding for CATV, c.1970, has superior properties to regulation is not transparent. Microanalytic assessments of franchise bidding, both as an abstract exercise and in the context of a specific case study, suggest a mixed verdict. Not only is simple franchise bidding for CATV beset with numerous transactional difficulties, but the institutional infrastructure that predictably develops to check dysfunctional or monopoloid outcomes has many of the earmarks of regulation.

Surely no one would dispute that '[t]he correct way to view the problem is one of selecting the best type of contract' (Demsetz, 1968, p.68). But one also needs to be instructed on how to proceed. Although it may be possible to disallow some contracting modes on static allocative efficiency grounds,[71] the more interesting cases, I submit, involve an examination of the efficiency properties of alternative contracts executed under conditions of uncertainty. Contrary to normal practice, attention to transactional detail is needed if the real issues are to be exposed. Additionally, a check on the operational properties of abstract contracting modes is usefully made *by examining one or more actual cases* in which different modes are being employed.[72] As Bauer and Walters observe, 'the complexity, instability and local variation of many economic phenomena imply that the establishment or understanding of relationships requires that analysis be supplemented by extensive observation, and also that the inquiry must often extend beyond statistical information to direct observation and use of primary sources' (1975, p.12). The case study of CATV franchising in Oakland, California, as reported in section IV, is in this spirit. The complexity of this contracting problem exceeds that of Demsetz's car licence plate example by several orders of magnitude. That a different understanding of franchise bidding obtains is not, perhaps, surprising.

The 'appropriate' level of transactional detail is not well defined and may vary with the circumstances. The following proposal is advanced as a means by which to get at the transaction-cost issues; progressively refine the degree of detail until contractual problems are plainly exposed. Then ask the question, 'Do these issues have comparative institutional significance in the context of the specific problems at hand?'

The level of detail that I have found useful in studying related transaction phenomena is what might be called a semi-microanalytic level of detail. Given the infeasibility of complex contingent claims contracting for the services in question, the properties of incomplete long-term and sequential spot contracts need to be assessed. When unassisted market processes prospectively or actually founder—because the hazards of incomplete long-term contracts are severe and sequential spot contracting is beset with indeterminacies and/or distortions—alternatives to autonomous contracting, of which regulation is one, plainly warrant consideration.

It is relevant in this connection to note that there are striking regularities among the incentives to organize internal labour markets (Wiliamson, Wachter and Harris, 1975), the incentives for vertical integration (Williamson, 1971), and the incentives to regulate (or otherwise substitute an administrative apparatus for unassisted market exchange). The particulars differ, but the disabilities of recurrent market contracting which give rise to each of these non-market or market-assisted modes are substantially the same. To the extent that the organizational failures framework set out elsewhere has generality (Williamson, 1975) such commonalities are to be expected.

Lest the argument appear unsympathetic to the franchise bidding approach, I should point out that there are circumstances where I suspect that regulation or public ownership can be supplanted by franchise bidding with net gains. Local service airlines and, possibly, postal delivery are examples.[73] The technology for both is well developed, demand is likewise well defined, and idiosyncratic skills appear to be negligible. Furthermore, displacement can be made without posing serious asset valuation problems—since the base plant (terminals, post offices, warehouses, etc.) can be owned by the government and other assets (planes, trucks, etc.) will have an active secondhand market. It is not, therefore, that franchise bidding is totally lacking on merit,[74] but that those who have favoured this mode have been insufficiently discriminating in their endorsement of it.

An unbiased assessment of the abstract properties of alternative modes will be facilitated by examining the transactional attributes of each in microanalytic detail.[75] It will be useful for this purpose to regard rate of return regulation as a highly incomplete form of contracting in which the prospects for windfall gains and losses are strictly limited and, in principle and sometimes in fact, adaptations to changing circumstances are introduced in a low-cost, non-acrimonious way. The frequency and extent to which such adaptations are required and the differential ease with which these are effectuated by alternative modes are important in making an informed comparative institutional choice.

NOTES

1. By traditional natural monopoly services I mean electricity, gas, water and telephone. See Joskow (1975, p.18) and Jorden (1972, p.154)
2. Posner regards Coase's classic paper 'The Problem of Social Cost' (1960) as the entering wedge to the 'new law and economics field' (1975, p.760), It is noteworthy that this important and influential paper is in two parts: the first part features frictionlessness; the second qualifies the earlier discussion to make allowance for frictions. Much of the follow-on literature, including franchise bidding, is largely or wholly preoccupied with frictionlessness or deals with frictions in a limited or sanguine way.
3. For an important contribution to the contracting literature, of which I became aware only recently, see Macneil (1974). The 'relational' contracts described by Macneil are examined in a regulatory context by Goldberg (1976), whose treatment of the issues is independent of, but in a spirit that is consonant with, that developed here.
4. For a survey of this literature, see Furubotn and Pejovich (1972); for a selection of readings, see Furubotn and Pejovich (1974).
5. To the extent that Demsetz's treatment of natural monopoly is limited to a critique of elementary textbook discussion, the argument goes through. Plainly, however, Demsetz and others also contend that it has real world relevance. The 'irrelevant complications' referred to in the text are conspicuously present when this latter application is attempted. As will be apparent, the purported superiority of franchise bidding is a good deal more difficult to establish when these conditions are present.
6. Demsetz is somewhat more cautious about the merits of franchise bidding and highlights the qualifications to his argument in his reply to Telser's critique (Demsetz, 1971).
7. Consider in this connection whether, from an allocative efficiency point of view, it really matters if franchises are awarded on the basis of a lump-sum fee rather than a lowest-supply price criterion. I submit that the monopoly distortions commonly associated with the former mode of contracting will tend to vanish if steady-state conditions obtain. The reasoning here is that steady-state conditions facilitate low cost price discrimination, in which event the marginal customer is supplied on marginal cost terms, and/or that customers can more effectively organize their side of the market and bargain to an efficient result.
8. Possibly, however, Stigler intends that Demsetz's discussion of renegotiation and/or rebidding should apply. Demsetz's treatment of these matters appears below.
9. To observe that 'customers face and overcome [such problems] daily in choosing among products that differ in quality as well as price' (Posner, 1972, p,115) is scarcely dispositive. Issues peculiar to the supply of natural monopoly services are not even raised. For example, quality variability of electricity supply is apt to entail voltage variations or prospective supply interruptions, the implications of which are apt to be difficult to assess. Secondly, variable load pricing issues, with which most consumers have little familiarity may be posed. Third, collective choice issues which do not appear for most consumer good must be faced in deciding on electricity supply. Fourth, long-term interaction effects between electricity price and substitutes and complements are rather strong, albeit difficult to sort out in the context of

hypothetical solicitations.
10. Thus, if price–quality package A wins the competition, on Posner's criterion, over price–quality mixes B, C, D and E where A is a high-price, high-quality mode and B and E are all variants of a low price–quality mix, does it follow that package A is socially preferred?
11. Similar problems arise with respect to the matter of who in the community is to be supplied service and at what connection costs: Connect everybody who requests it at a flat charge? Only those who live where connected service exceeds some threshold? Anyone who bears his own incremental costs? Although a single standard can be stipulated by the contracting agency, is this optimal and ought such a connection standard to remain fixed for the duration of the contract?
12. The short-term contracting procedure favoured by Posner contemplates the transfer of long-lived assets from the winning franchisee to a successor firm. Appropriate investment incentives would thereby be realized. For the reasons developed in (3) below, I am sceptical of the properties of the asset transfer described by Posner.
13. The Cable Television Information Center expresses the issue as follows (1973, p.7):

[T]echnical standards do not enforce themselves. Enforcement requires testing the system, evaluation of the tests, and deciding upon corrective actions required. These activities add to the administrative burden of regulation. A franchising authority should not adopt standards unless it is willing to shoulder the burden of enforcement.

14. Note that a merger between parties who possess economic qualifications and those with political skills yields private and probably social gains in these circumstances. Such a merger actually occurred in the case study reported in Section IV.
15. This assumes that regulation is not a farce and that management-engrossing is strictly limited under regulation. Note also that the argument assumes that the *marginal* net gains of influencing the political process are greater under the franchise mode. For a discussion of politics and regulation, see Kahn (1971, pp.326-7).
16. This assumes that winning bidders are not fly-by-night operators, but instead are interested in remaining in the business on a continuing basis. Other things being equal, the franchising authority can be expected to continue with the current supplier or shift to a new supplier at the contract renewal interval depending on its experience with the current winner during the contract period.
17. Similar considerations have a bearing on the performance of the franchising agency. Posner puts the argument as follows:

[If] the duration of the franchise . . . is long, the parties may not have foreseen all of the circumstances that might require modification of its terms. Although this is a problem common to all contracts, the peculiarity here is that one of the contracting parties is not a true party in interest but a public body charged with overseeing the interest of the other parties (subscribers). Experience with regulatory agencies suggests that one cannot assume such a body will represent the consumer interest faithfully. When the cable company asks for a modification of the contract by virtue of an unforeseen change in circumstances, the public body may react ineffectually or perversely. (1972, pp.115-16).

With short duration contracts, 'no modification of . . . terms need to be entertained' (p.116), in which event the distortions referred to are avoided.

18. For prior discussions of bidding parity and its absence at contract renewal intervals, see Peacock and Rowley (1972, p.242) and Williamson (1975, pp.26-35).

19. The City of Los Angeles anticipated such difficulties in its ordinance on franchise award and execution (Ordinance no, 58,200). The ordinance stipulates that the City has a right to purchase the property of a franchise or find a purchaser therefore and further provides that

In the event said franchise shall expire by operation of law, said city shall have the right, at its option, declared not more than one (1) year before the expiration of the franchise term as herein fixed, which right an option is hereby reserved to said city shall so exercise its right under such option the said city shall pay to the said grantee the fair value of the property of such utility as herein provided.

(d) The term 'fair value' as used herein shall be construed to mean the reasonable value of the property of such utility having regard to its condition or repair and its adaptability and capacity for the use for which it shall have been originally intended. The price to be paid by the City for any utility shall be on the basis of actual cost to the utility for the property taken, less depreciation accrued, as of the date of purchase, with due allowance for obsolescence, if any, and the efficiency of its units to perform the duties imposed on them; no allowance shall be made for franchise value, good will, going concern, earning power, increased cost of reproduction or increased value of right of way or allowance for damages by reasons of severance.

(e) That the valuation of the property of such utility proposed to be purchased upon the termination of said franchise as herein provided, or otherwise, shall be determined by a board of three arbitrators of whom one shall be appointed by the city, one by the grantee, and the third by the two arbitrators so appointed. Said arbitrators shall be appointed within thirty days after the declaration by the city of its options to purchase said property of such utility, or to find a purchaser therefor. In case said arbitrators fail to make and file an award within the time hereinafter limited, a new board of three arbitrators shall be appointed as hereinbefore prescribed. The board of arbitrators shall immediately upon the appointment of its members enter upon the discharge of its duties. Any vacancy in the board of arbitrators shall be filled by the party who made the original appointment to the vacant place.

(f) In the event the grantee shall fail to appoint an arbitrator within thirty days after the declaration by the city of its option to purchase the property of such utility or to find a purchase therefor, or in the event of the death or resignation of such arbitrator so appointed and such grantee, its successors or assigns, shall fail to appoint an arbitrator to fill such vacancy within ten (10) days thereafter, or in the event that two arbitrators appointed by the city and grantee, as hereinbefore provided, shall fail to appoint a third arbitrator within sixty (60) days after the declaration of the city of its option to purchase the property of such utility, or to find a purchase therefore, then upon application made either by the city, or by said grantee after (5) days' notice in writing to the other party, such arbitrator shall be appointed by the presiding Judge of the Superior Court of the State of California, in and for the County of Los Angeles, and the arbitrators so appointed shall have the same powers and duties as though he had been appointed in the manner hereinabove prescribed.

(g) The award of the arbitrators must be made and filed with the City Clerk of said city within three (3) months after their appointment, and a majority of the arbitrators who agree thereto may make such award.

For a discussion of franchise valuations of a similar kind in connection with New York City's award of CATV franchises, see CTIC (1972a, pp.16-17).

20. One possibility is for each willing bidder, at the contract renewal interval, to indicate his asset valuation at the time he enters his bid on the quality and price of service. The problem here is that asset valuations and service bids are not independent. Franchisees will be prepared to pay dearly for assets if in the process they can charge a high price.

    Other schemes might be explored (see note 19) and possibly some can be shown to have attractive properties. It is plainly the case, however, that a good deal of hard thinking about the mechanics of the asset valuation process is needed before the rebidding scheme can be considered complete.

21. Relevant in this connection is the following issue: why have incumbent employees failed to exploit fully their idiosyncratic advantage over inexperienced employees during the contract execution period—in which event there is no unliquidated idiosyncratic gain to be differentially awarded at the contract renewal interval? A distinction between moving equilibrium and discrete bargaining behaviour is relevant in this connection. For one thing, there may be adjustment lags in the system which are tolerated during the operating period but for which correction is possible at the contract renewal interval. For another, collective action is necessary to appropriate the idiosyncratic gains. Enterprise owners may work out a *modus vivendi* with managers and labour representatives in which management and labour, in exchange for ownership support (including job security, emoluments, etc.), consciously decline to absorb the full idiosyncratic gain. Out of recognition that the 'leadership' is in this together, a reserve of unliquidated idiosyncratic gain has strategic advantages.

22. For a sociological discussion of some of the problems of succession, see Gouldner (1954). Macneil observes that 'the elements of trust demanded by participant views of relations make identity important, and simple transfer therefore unlikely' (1974, p.791).

23. A distinctive limitation of regulation, to which franchise bidding is presumably less subject, is the proclivity of regulators progressively to expand the reach of regulation to include 'ancillary' activities. More generally, the greater autonomy and degree of specialization associated with regulation, as compared with franchise bidding agencies, may have unfavourable long-run rigidity consequences. In particular, regulatory authorities are apt to resist vigorously anything which threatens their demise.

24. The basic argment is that '[e]ach bidder would submit a plan of service and schedule of rates. As long as there was more than one bidder and collusion among the bidders was prevented—conditions that ought not to be insuper-

ably difficult to secure—the process of bidding subscriber rates down and quality of service up would eliminate monopoly pricing and profits' (Posner, 1972, p.115).

25. Note, moreover, that not only are contract remedies 'among the weakest of those the legal system can deliver, [b]ut a host of doctrines and techniques lies in the way even of these remedies' (Macneil, 1974, p.730). Until franchisers and the legal system can be persuaded to behave otherwise, it is fatuous to contend that franchises can be induced to behave in ideal ways by the introduction of a complex set of penalty clauses.

26. It is also noteworthy that many of the franchising concerns reported by the Cable Television Information Center are consonant with those set out in section III. Among the concerns and recommendations of the CTIC are the following (CTIC, 1972a):

    (1) The renewal period has proven to be a period of great pressure on the city, with the cable operator often threatening to discontinue service immediately unless renewal is promised (p.16).

    (2) The franchising authority will . . . want to include buyback provisions as part of its effort to insure continuity of service. The provision should include . . . a method of evaluation or termination (s.4, p.6).

    (3) [The] right of transfer should be limited at the initial stages of the systems' development, and perhaps flatly forbidden before construction, to avoid trafficking in franchise awards (p.17).

    (4) Results of system performance and tests should be submitted periodically to ensure the system's quality (p.24).

    (5) [Day-to-day regulation involves] considering consumer complaints and passing on requests for rate increases (p.25).

    (6) Once a procedure has been developed for considering rate changes, the proposed changes are to be measured against the standard of what is fair to the system and to the subscribing public (p.30).

    (7) One of the most neglected areas of ordinances has been enforcement. Mechanisms such as arbitration, provision for leaseback, and the ability to seek court action will aid in achieving the type of Cable system the community wants (p.45).

27. City of Oakland, Ordinance no. 7989 C.M.S. 19 June 1969.

28. The dialogue period was described to me by Mark Leh, Assistant Manager of Electrical Services of the Department of General Services, Oakland.

29. City of Oakland, 'Invitation to Submit Amended Applications for a Community Antenna Television System Franchise', 30 April 1970.

30. The $125,000 figure was built up in successive $25,000 annual increments, starting with zero in 1970 and reaching $125,000 in 1975, thereafter to continue at this level.

31. The four customer classes were: non-commercial housed in buildings with less than four living units; non-commercial housed in multiple-unit apartments, motels, hotels; commercial; and special, including low-density users. The installation charge was $10 for non-commercial subscribers housed in buildings with less than four living units.

32. Amended Application for a Franchise to Construct, Operate and Maintain a Community Antenna Television System within a City of Oakland submitted by Focus Cable of Oakland, Inc., 1 July 1970.

33. Memorandum from the city manager to the city council, dated 28 September 1970, p.3.

34. See note 32.
35. Minority group involvement in cable—in ownership, employment and programming respects—is prominently featured in the CATV literature (CTIC, 1972c, p.13). The FCC requires cable operators to establish affirmative action plans (CTIC, 1972a, p.34).
36. Letter from Leonard Tow, Vice-President of TelePrompTer, Inc., to Harold Farrow of Focus Cable, dated 16 July 1970.
37. The rate of System B was not included in the original bid but was to be negotiated later. As things worked out, and probably ought to have been anticipated, most subscribers elected to receive System B—at a considerably higher rate than System A.
38. Letter from Focus Cable to the city manager of Oakland, dated 21 July 1970.
39. Stock transfer restriction and purchase agreement, dated 21 September 1970, Appendix A to Focus Cable of Oakland, Inc., subscription agreement.
40. See note 33.
41. See subscription agreement, note 39, p.2.
42. Ibid., p.12.
43. See note 39, p.6.
44. City of Oakland Ordinance, no. 8246 C.M.S. 10 November 1970.
45. Statement of Leonard Tow, Treasurer, Focus Cable of Oakland, to City of Oakland, dated 23 December, 1970.
46. Oakland City Council Resolution no.51477 C.M.S., dated 11 March, 1971.
47. Inter-office letter from Office of General Services to Office of the City Manager, dated 5 April 1974, p.1
48. Ibid., attachment, p.4
49. Ibid., attachment, p.5.
50. Ibid., attachment, p.5.
51. Ibid., attachment, p.8.
52. Ibid., attachment, p.8.
53. Ibid., attachment, pp.10-11.
54. Ibid., attachment, pp.8-9.
55. Ibid., attachment, p.11-12.
56. Ibid., attachment, p.12-13.
57. Memorandum from office of General Services to Office of City Manager summarizing actions taken by the city council at work sessions concerning Focus Cable, dated 22 April 1974.
58. Ibid., attachment 1.
59. City of Oakland, Ordinance no.9018 C.M.S., Amending Ordinance no.8246 C.M.S. and Ordinance no.7989 C.M.S. relating to the community antenna television system franchise, dated 30 May 1974. The only significant exceptions from the compromise described in the text are the following: the additional connection rate for System B was set at $1.30 per month and it was stipulated that System B should provide not less than 18 video channels.
60. Attachment to City of Oakland inter-office letter from Office of General Services to city manager, dated 20 November 1974.
61. Letter ibid., p.2.
62. Attachment to letter, ibid.
63. Letter, see note 60, p.2.
64. *New York Times*, 29 July 1970, p.1.
65. As Posner surmised, it is hazardous to permit a public agency by itself to declare subscriber preference for service.

66. Partly this may be because '[a]n initial high signal quality may, over time, slowly degrade to the point where the signal quality is not acceptable' (CTIC, 1973, p.9); partly it is that signal quality is multidimensional and varies with the capability of the system to receive off-air and microwave signal as well as headend and cable attributes (CTIC, 1973, pp.19-24).

67. The existence of customer complaints regarding quality of service was disclosed in an interview with Mark Leh (see note 28).

68. Libman (1974) reports that the award of the Oakland CATV franchise to the Focus group, despite its lack of expertise and adequate financing, and the subsequent implementation of the franchise appear to have been influenced by political considerations. A more spectacular and unambiguous case is afforded by the CATV competition in Johnstone, Pennsylvania, where Irving Kahn, the former chief executive and chairman of TelePrompTer, the nations's largest operator of cable TV, was tried and convicted of bribery and perjury. Kahn has also admitted bribing public officials in Trenton, New Jersey, to secure their votes. Politics appears also to have been a decisive factor in the award of CATV franchises in New York City. (See note 64.) Whether this holds for CATV awards in large cities more generally is uncertain. The incidence of corruption with respect to franchise awards for other types of services is also an open question.

69. Indeed they did arise. Witness that the completed system estimate by Focus exceeded the staff's estimate by almost $3 million. Note also that it is ill-advised to permit the franchisee to become affiliated with a firm that supplies equipment and products for the construction of the plant. The risk here is that the procurement costs of these items will be overstated, thereby to build up the rate base of the franchise and improve its bargaining position during rate negotiations. Despite claims that equipment will be procured on competitive terms, this is costly to check and violations are difficult to prove conclusively. The Oakland staff suspects unwarranted equipment cost escalation in the estimates by Focus of plant valuation, but admits that it has no definitive proof.

70. Posner employs this dichotomy in his 1969 discussion of natural monopoly, in which he urges that 'even in markets where efficiency dictates monopoly we might do better to allow natural economic forces to determine business conduct and performance subject only to the constraints of antitrust policy' (1969, p.549). He declines, however, to handle the CATV issue in this way but instead favours the market assisted bidding scheme described in section III, the administrative problems associated with which are formidable.

71. For example, awarding a franchise to the bidder who will pay the largest lump-sum amount will serve to capitalize the monopoly profits but, at least transitionally, will lead to a higher price and lower output than will an award of the franchise to the bidder who offers to supply at the lowest price.

72. To be sure, one swallow does not make a Spring, and a single case study does not settle the franchise bidding for CATV issue. It is thus to be hoped that more such studies will be performed. In the meantime, I submit, the Oakland experience gives occasion for pause.

73. A careful microanalytic assessment of both is needed, however, before the franchise bidding mode is introduced. Disabilities that are not apparent on the surface may be disclosed.

74. Not only might franchise bidding be usefully introduced in some cases where regulation is now employed, but it should continue in circumstances in which

it is plainly efficacious. The award of petrol station franchises on motorways is an example of the latter.

75. As Dewey has observed, '[T]he disdain and contempt for regulation [by economists] is nearly universal' (1974, p.10). Although much of regulation is indeed contemptible, I submit that *some* of the problems for which regulation has been devised are really intractable—in the sense that *all* of the feasible modes of organization are beset with difficulties. Arguments favouring market modes in which these difficulties are not squarely faced should accordingly be regarded with scepticism.

REFERENCES

Bauer, P.T. and Walters, A.A., 'The State of Economics' *Journal of Law and Economics* **18** April 1975, pp.1-24.

Behavioral Sciences Subpanel, President's Science Advisory Committee, *Strengthening the Behavioral Sciences*. Washington, DC: US Government Printing Office, 1962.

Coase, R.H., 'The Federal Communications Commission', *Journal of Law and Economics*, **2**, October 1959, 1-40

Coase, R.H., 'The Problem of Social Cost', *Journal of Law and Economics*, **3**, October 1960, pp.1-44

CTIC, *How to Plan an Ordinance,* Washington, DC: 1972(a).

CTIC, *A Suggested Procedure*, Washington, DC: 1972(b).

CTIC, *Cable: An Overview*. Washington, DC: 1972(c).

CTIC, *Technical Standards and Specifications.* Washington, DC: 1973.

Demsetz, H., 'Why Regulate Utilities?', *Journal of Law and Economics*, **11**, April 1968, pp. 55-66.

Demsetz, H., 'On the Regulation of Industry: A Reply' *Journal of Political Economy*, **79**, March/April 1971, pp. 356-63.

Dewey, D.J., 'An Introduction to the Issues', in H.J. Goldschmid, H.M. Mann and J.F. Weston (eds.), *Industrial Concentration: The New Learning,* Boston: 1974, pp.1-14.

Doeringer, P. and Piore, M., *Internal Labor Markets and Manpower Analysis*. Lexington, Mass.: D.C. Heath 1971.

Eckstein, H., 'Planning: The National Health Service', in R. Rose (ed.), *Policy-Making in Britain,* London: 1969, pp.221-37.

Fisher, W.L., 'The American Municipality', in Commission on Public Ownership and Operation, *Municipal and Private Operation of Public Utilities*, part I, vol. I, New York, 1907, pp.36-48.

Fuller, L. and Braucher, R., *Basic Contract Law*. St. Paul: West Publishing Co., 1964.

Furubotn, E. and Pejovich, S., 'Property Rights and Economic Theory: A Survey of Recent Literature', *Journal of Economic Literature*, **10**. December 1972, pp.1137-62.

Furubotn, E. and Pejovich, S., *The Economics of Property Rights*. Cambridge Mass.: Ballinger, 1974.

Goldberg, V.P., 'Regulation and Administered Contracts', *The Bell Journal of Economics,* **7** (2) Autumn 1976.

Gouldner, A.W., *Industrial Bureaucracy*. Glencoe, Ill., 1954.

Hayek, F., 'The Use of Knowledge in Society', *The American Economic Review*, **35** (4) September 1945, pp. 519-30.

Jordan, W.A., 'Producer Protection, Prior Market Structure, and the Effects of Government Regulation', *Journal of Law and Economics*, **15**, April 1972, pp.151-76.

Joskow, P.L., 'Regulatory Activities by Government Agencies', Working paper no.171, Department of Economics, MIT, December 1975.

Kahn, A.E., *The Economics of Regulation: Vol.2, Institutional Issues*. New York: Wiley, 1971.

Knight, F.H., *Risk, Uncertainty, and Profit*. New York: 1965.

Leff, A.A., 'Teams, Firms, and the Aesthetics of Antitrust', draft manuscript, February 1975.

Libman, J., 'In Oakland, a Cable-TV System Fails to Live up to Promises', *Wall Street Journal* 25 September 1974, p.34.

Macaulay, S., 'Non-Contractual Relations in Business', *American Sociological Review*, **28**, (1963), pp.55-70.

Macneil, I.R., 'The Many Futures of Contracts', *Southern California Law Review*, **47** May 1974, pp. 691-816.

Marshack, J., 'Economics of Inquiring, Communicating, Deciding', *The American Economic Review*, **58** (2) May 1968, pp. 1-18.

Peacock, A.T. and Rowley, C.K., 'Welfare Economics and the Public Regulation of Natural Monopolies', *Journal of Public Economics* **1** (1972), pp. 227-44.

Posner, R.A., 'Natural Monopoly and Its Regulation', *Stanford Law Review*, **21** February 1969, pp. 548-643.

Posner, R.A., 'Cable Television: The Problem of Local Monopoly', RAND Memorandum RM-6309-FF, May 1970, p.35.

Posner, R.A., 'The Appropriate Scope of Regulation in the Cable Television Industry', *The Bell Journal of Economics and Management Science*, **3**, (1) Spring 1972, pp. 98-129.

Posner, R.A., 'Theories of Economic Regulation', *The Bell Journal of Economics and Management Science* **5** (2) Autumn 1974, pp. 335-58.

Posner, R.A., 'The Economic Approach to Law', *Texas Law Review*, **53** (4), May 1975, pp. 757-82.

Scherer, F.M., *The Weapons Acquisition Process: Economic Incentives*. Boston. 1964.

Stigler, G.J., *The Organization of Industry*. Chicago: University of Chicago Press, 1968.

Stigler, G.J., 'Free-Riders and Collective Action: An Appendix to Theories of Economic Regulation', *The Bell Journal of Economics and Management Science*, **5** (2), Autumn 1974, pp. 359-65.

Telser, L.G., 'On the Regulation of Industry: A Note', *Journal of Political Economy*, **77**, November/December 1969, pp.937-52.

Telser, L.G., 'On the Regulation of Industry: Rejoinder', *Journal of Political Economy*, **79**, March/April 1971, pp. 364-5.

Williamson, O.E., 'The Economics of Defense Contracting; Incentives and Performance', in *Issues in Defense Economics*, New York: 1967, pp. 217-56.

Williamson, O.E., 'The Vertical Integration of Production: Market Failure Considerations', *The American Economic Review*, **61** (2) May 1971, pp.112-23.

Williamson, O.E., 'Administrative Controls and Regulatory Behaviour', in H.M. Trebing (ed.), *Essays on Public Utility Pricing and Regulation*, East

Lansing, Mich.: 1971b, pp.411-38.

Williamson, O.E., 'Patent and Antitrust Law: Book Review', *Yale Law Journal,* **83**, January 1974a, pp.647-61.

Williamson, O.E., 'The Economics of Antitrust: Transaction Cost Considerations', *University of Pennsylvania Law Review*, **122**, June 1974b, pp.1439-96.

Williamson, O.E., *Markets and Hierarchies: Analysis and Antirust Implications,* New York: Free Press, 1975.

Williamson, O.E., Wachter M. and Harris J., 'Understanding the Employment Relation: The Analysis of Idiosyncratic Exchange', *The Bell Journal of Economics*, **6**, (1), Spring 1975, pp.250-78.

Acknowledgements

Several of the articles have been published elsewhere. I am grateful for permission to include them here, and would like to express thanks to all concerned: 'Managerial Discretion and Business Behaviour', *American Economic Review*, December 1963, LIII (5), pp.1032-57; 'The Vertical Integration of Production: Market Failure Considerations', *American Economic Review*, May 1971, LXI (2), pp.112-23; 'The Modern Corporation: Origins, Evolution, Attributes', *Journal of Economic Literature*, December 1981, XIX (4), pp.1537-68 (American Economic Association); 'Assessing and Classifying the Internal Structure and Control Apparatus in the Modern Corporation', *Market Structure and Corporate Behaviour*, ed. K. Cowling, 1972 (Basil Blackwell); 'Franchise Bidding for Natural Monopolies – in General and with Respect to CATV', *The Bell Journal of Economics*, Spring 1976, 7 (1) (The Rand Corporation); 'Hierarchical Control and Optimum Firm Size', *Journal of Political Economy*, April 1967, 75 (2), pp.123-38 (University of Chicago Press); 'Transaction Cost Economics: The Governance of Contractual Relations', *Journal of Law and Economics*, October 1979, 22(2), pp.233-261; (University of Chicago Press); 'The Economics of Antitrust:Transaction Cost Considerations', *University of Pennsylvania Law Review*, June 1974, 122 (6), pp. 1439-96 (University of Pennsylvania Law Review and Fred B. Rothman & Company); material from *The Political Economy of Antitrust*, ed. Robert D. Tollinson (Lexington Books, 1979).

Index